Singing Our Way to Victory

MUSIC / CULTURE

A series from Wesleyan University Press

Edited by George Lipsitz, Susan McClary, and Robert Walser

Published titles

My Music by Susan D. Crafts,
Daniel Cavicchi, Charles Keil, and the
Music in Daily Life Project

*Running with the Devil: Power,
Gender, and Madness in Heavy Metal
Music* by Robert Walser

*Subcultural Sounds: Micromusics
of the West* by Mark Slobin

*Upside Your Head! Rhythm and Blues
on Central Avenue* by Johnny Otis

*Dissonant Identities: The Rock'n'Roll
Scene in Austin, Texas* by Barry Shank

*Black Noise: Rap Music and Black
Culture in Contemporary America*
by Tricia Rose

*Club Cultures: Music, Media and
Subcultural Capital*
by Sarah Thornton

Music, Society, Education
by Christopher Small

*Popular Music in Theory:
An Introduction*
by Keith Negus

*Listening to Salsa: Gender, Latin Popu-
lar Music, and Puerto Rican Cultures*
by Frances Aparicio

*Any Sound You Can Imagine: Making
Music/Consuming Technology*
by Paul Théberge

*Voices in Bali: Energies and Perceptions
in Vocal Music and Dance Theater*
by Edward Herbst

*A Thousand Honey Creeks Later: My
Life in Music from Basie to Motown—
and Beyond* by Preston Love

*Musicking: The Meanings of Perform-
ing and Listening*
by Christopher Small

*Music of the Common Tongue: Survival
and Celebration in African American
Music* by Christopher Small

*Singing Archaeology: Philip Glass's
Akhnaten* by John Richardson

*Metal, Rock, and Jazz: Perception and
the Phenomenology of Musical
Experience* by Harris M. Berger

Music and Cinema
edited by James Buhler, Caryl Flinn,
and David Neumeyer

*"You Better Work!" Underground
Dance Music in New York City*
by Kai Fikentscher

*Singing Our Way to Victory:
French Cultural Politics and Music
during the Great War*
by Regina M. Sweeney

REGINA M. SWEENEY

✌

Singing Our Way to Victory

FRENCH CULTURAL

POLITICS AND MUSIC DURING

THE GREAT WAR

✌

WESLEYAN UNIVERSITY PRESS

Middletown, Connecticut

Published by Wesleyan University Press, Middletown, CT 06459

"The Censorship of Singing, from Music Hall
to Trench" is reprinted with permission of the
University Press of Mississippi.

Library of Congress Cataloging-in-Publication Data

Sweeney, Regina M., 1958–
  Singing our way to victory : French cultural politics and music
during the Great War / Regina M. Sweeney.
     p. cm. — (Music/culture)
Includes bibliographical references (p.   ) and index.
   ISBN 0–8195–6454–0 (hardcover) — ISBN 0–8195–6473–7 (pbk.)
   1. Popular music—France—1911–1920—History and criticism.
   2. Political ballads and songs—France—History and criticism.
   3. World War, 1914–1918—France—Music and the war. I. Title.
II. Series.
   ML3489 .S94 2001
   782.42164'0944'0904—dc21   00–012914

Contents

❧

Illustrations

⤸

APPENDIX

Acknowledgments

Because I was raised by a professor, I learned great respect for the time and energy that good teachers give to their students. So I need to begin my acknowledgments with those who educated me. This project spent its formative years with Susanna Barrows, who showed me the wonderful potential of cultural history as a broad and inclusive field. She has helped me to be both a working historian and a teacher. Randy Starn offered his thoughtful, unwavering support and his critical thinking. My intellectual development also benefited from the teaching of Lynn Hunt and Stanley Brandes, and Jay Winter volunteered his years of experience and research on the Great War. I am also fortunate to have attended his World War I seminar at Berkeley, which he co-taught with Tom Laqueur. In addition, I wish to acknowledge the inspired teaching of Jane Bernstein, a musicologist at Tufts University, who encouraged my love for music and sent me confidently off to Berkeley (whence she had come) to study history instead of musicology.

It has been quite wonderful to be part of a field in French history that is so vital and provocative. I am proud to know such a remarkable cohort. This includes David Barnes, Marjorie Beale, Avi Chomsky, Joshua Cole, Sarah Farmer, Megan Koreman, Doug Mackaman, Sylvia Schafer, Matthew Truesdale, and Jeffrey Verhey, who all helped shape this project early on. We now seem to be taking varied paths, but we all recognize the love we each hold for our subjects. I would also like to thank Lou Roberts and Cathy Kudlick for reading portions of this work, and pushing me forward. My thinking profited from the comments of scholars and students at talks I gave at Pomona and at the American Historical Association, as well as from the astute remarks offered by students in my women's history seminars. I benefited at critical moments from two very important research assistants, Chuck Edwards and Ashley Waddell. My hope is for Ashley to find a research assistant as enthusiastic and patient with her as she has been with me.

Vanessa Schwartz, Sheryl Kroen, and Jeff Ravel have seen this project through every stage and never once hesitated to help when I called upon them. My thinking and questions were also enriched by contact with their work. I also want to thank fellow World War I scholars Nicky Gullace and Sue Grayzel, who read the whole manuscript and made very constructive suggestions. And I would like to acknowledge those colleagues at Middlebury who read portions of the manuscript at important moments, including Ellen Oxfeld, Paula Schwartz, Paul Monod, Jan Albers, and Cassandra Potts. My time in Paris was made easier by the friendship of Anne, Guy, and Beatrice Frot, and by the camaraderie of a study group that included Becky Rogers and Peggy Werth.

With a project that is so heavily dependent on archival materials, I am particularly grateful for the staff assistance at many archives, including the Bibliothèque de l'Arsenal, the Archives Nationales, the Bibliothèque Historique de la Ville de Paris, the Bibliothèque de Documentation Internationale Contemporaine, the Archives du Service Historique de l'Armée de Terre in Vincennes, and the Hoover Library at Stanford. The officials at the Parisian Police Archives were particularly patient, always willing to answer questions, while providing me with carton after carton of songs. At critical junctures, I received financial assistance from a Mabelle McLeod Lewis Dissertation Fellowship, the Heller Grant-in-Aid fund, and a Chancellor Dissertation Grant from the University of California at Berkeley. Middlebury College provided an Ada Howe Kent Research Grant and funds for illustration permissions. This book has also benefited from the professional and kind assistance of those at Wesleyan University Press, University Press of New England, and from my reader's comments.

Finally, I must thank my family—no small task. They have sustained me in so many ways all the way through, and this is a sustenance that is deep and wide. My parents gave me a love of music and of tackling difficult problems. Thankfully, my husband Gerry and daughter Anna are an immeasurable part of that wonderful collective. Gerry and I also need to thank Kim Smith and her family for taking such great care of us. Finally, this book is dedicated to my brother Jack. He did not live to see me finish it, but I know that, as a scholar and a brother, he would have appreciated it.

R.M.S.

Singing Our Way to Victory

Introduction

୬

Paul Cezano sat down after France's ignominious defeat by the Prussian forces in 1870 and wrote "Le Régiment de Sambre et Meuse," a song that celebrated the virtue of seeking immortality in a patriotic death. Cezano, like hundreds of other *chansonniers,* chose to compose rousing, assertive lyrics about French valor. His piece found favor in the burgeoning music halls and *cafés-concerts* of the Belle Époque and was taught to school children as part of the Third Republic's curriculum. It also punctuated Alfred Dreyfus's ceremony of degradation in 1895, a ritual meant to cleanse the military's honor. Twenty years later, in the midst of the devastating First World War, the French state chose this same song to accompany traitors to their deaths in front of firing squads. French soldiers and civilians had loudly intoned Cezano's words at train stations all over France in 1914—as the country prepared once again for war. But the mutineers of 1917 rejected it, turning instead to other rebellious tunes, including the socialist "Internationale," risking severe sentences for their musical decision.

"Le Régiment de Sambre et Meuse" provides a clear example of the vital role popular music played in a changing cultural and political landscape. A single song could convey the most fervent patriotism or the most cynical irony. Singing was a particularly important mode of communication at the turn of the century, since it existed as a popular practice of everyday life reinforced by the innovative, ever expanding musical entertainment industry. Songs and practices ranged across social and regional divides, an element of both urban and rural cultures. And when the Great War came, the French took up their well-honed skills of composition and performance. This book is about the many uses of singing in the period of World War I. It will show how songs not just reflected but also created the experience of the French in the Great War.

This is a particularly rewarding way to study the war, because singing provides a broad perspective on "total war." The question of what people sang takes us from government censors and prime ministers down to the frozen soldier in the abyss at Verdun. It takes us from formal, official propaganda, through energetic commercial institutions to everyday life, complicating the line between traditional and modern. Singing offers us expressions of ideas, but also, significantly, cultural practices. This book is not just about the war, but about a cultural transition that the war affected.

Historians have argued that World War I was the earliest "total" war, a war that required the complete mobilization and cooperation of the belligerents' multilayered societies.[1] The participants included not just soldiers, but women and men on the home front, as officials redirected their national economies to provide billions of artillery shells, timely transportation, and millions of articles of clothing for military personnel.[2] Public opinion or sentiment proved fundamental to the war's continuation, and mass communication helped to persuade all citizens to do their duty. Contemporaries came to accept the term "guerre totale"—especially in France, where the fighting occurred on native soil, and where eight million men had to be mobilized.[3]

"Total" war, however, has generally been defined in terms of economic restructuring or within a limited sphere of politics. Numerous monographs and collections have focused on the growth and power of state bureaucracies that were fighting a modern industrial war.[4] And scholars have carefully scrutinized the official administrative organs that created and disseminated propaganda. There has also been a more recent turn toward work about daily life, but much of this still focuses on material life.

This worldwide conflict, however, was waged within complex cultures and was shaped by the public's imagination. The total war was not restricted to military decisions, combat, or Parliamentary edicts; instead, it depended on rituals, artifacts, and ideas. Because people had lived through or "survived" the event, they all had their own experiences and narratives. In France, government police spies, Parisian shopkeepers, and music-hall vocalists created, imagined, and experienced their own Great War. Some citizens fought, while others built bombs, tilled fields, or sent sons to die. As one WWI scholar has cogently argued, "The war experience is an ultimate confirmation of the power of men to ascribe meaning and pattern to a world, even when that world seemed to resist all patterning. The war mobilized all the cultural resources of meaning available to Europeans in the first decades of the twentieth century."[5]

Unfortunately, much of the historiography on World War I France presumes that daily life became abbreviated, stunted, or telescoped; soldiers, especially, left behind their well-known surroundings and routines and entered a world of unexpected, unreasoned, or uncontrollable raw experience. Civilians, meanwhile, muddled through. Adhering to this idea, scholars of cultural forms or institutions have often interrupted their narrative at 1914 and continued in 1918, leaving a hiatus of four and a half years. As Elizabeth Kahn has pointed out, until recently, art history and World War I never met. Monographs either did not mention the war at all or spoke only of its outbreak.[6] This lapse has been as prevalent in studies of mass culture as in those on fine arts or literature. Volume after volume on French music halls omitted any mention of the war or relegated the tumultuous, ruinous period to a few sentences.[7]

New interest in cultural artifacts and processes grew out of the publication of Paul Fussell's wonderfully detailed work, *The Great War and Modern Memory*. He deliberately held up for analysis the "transection" or dialectic between art and experience, asking specifically how literature "confers" forms on life, and how, simultaneously, life "feeds" literature.[8] Trench life and the soldiers' literary attempts to represent and understand what they saw became interactive, as Fussell exposed readers to combatants' myths, rumors, and rituals. He carefully showed how soldiers reshaped prewar conventions and rhetoric during wartime. With this historiographic shift, "the novel, the poem, and the social response found in trench culture are conceived as far more than logical effects that merely mirror the wartime context; they are seen as complex translations that often transform, even disguise, the reality of the individual or group experience."[9]

Fussell and others, such as Samuel Hynes, have focused almost exclusively on elite responses to the war.[10] But "total" war depended intrinsically on popular participation that required the use of new mass cultural forms and technologies, as well as older, popular practices. World War I also came at a crucial moment in the early development of mass politics. In the years before, large populations had been drawn into politics through suffrage, newspaper reading, and street demonstrations. People were both participants and consumers. Once the war broke out, its meanings and forms were reconstructed through representations of the trenches, of the *poilus* (infantrymen) and their enemies, and of civilian sacrifices. Many of these representations took a musical form created by both professionals and amateurs. As in the case of "Sambre et Meuse," some representations resided in the memories of soldiers and civilians, having originated in the prewar era. A multitude of others were created each day during the war. Even representations of military technologies were culturally embedded. The French affinity for the bayonet, for example, was not simply or even primarily a military doctrine, but was instead part of a larger cultural value system that defined French nationalism and masculinity.

The power to represent became especially critical in wartime. As the stakes rose to encompass the survival of individuals and regimes, victory came to depend on public opinion and behavior. Groups such as soldiers or Parisians lived within different boundaries with regard to what they saw, read, or could sing—boundaries that were determined partly by censorship. These borders and their permeability changed over time. The fear that the war might last forever, for example, was unimaginable in 1914, but became a possible thought, or joke, by late 1916, predictably occurring first to the combatants consigned to the front. Although civilians could not "see" actual trench warfare, they constructed their understanding of it from the tableaux of musical revues as well as from film newsreels or firsthand reports from friends and relatives.

Certain individuals or institutions, however, had the power to fashion others' imaginings and to determine the dominant tropes. The state held much of this power, since the war occurred as large nation-states were accumulating more and more power. Each state sent citizens to death, controlled the allocation of massive resources of food and fuel, and determined the flow of ideas.[11] Propagandist songs, posters, and articles all tried to convince individuals that their every thought or act could be deemed either patriotic and thus helpful, or defeatist and thus treasonous. Furthermore, how the state portrayed the enemy was intricately enmeshed with the ability of governments to begin and to sustain the war. In the French case, when military leaders drew French troops back from their own borders as the Germans approached in 1914, the strategists understood the cultural dictate that the French be on the defensive. This maneuver served to highlight the Germans' aggression and tapped into French memories of invaders on their soil.

Too often in modern European history, we have chosen to look at politics and politicians at the top of liberal democracies as rational and logical, and the "masses" as separate and more impressionable.[12] But politicians also participated in the broader culture, and the government could not simply take culture and remake it. The process was far more complicated, especially since the French state had to learn how to conduct a total war in a cultural context that included such robust and obstreperous commercial institutions as the *cafés-concerts* and music halls. Individuals also retained a remarkable capacity to create or interpret meaning using their own cultural skills. All of this reshapes how we define propaganda.

The cultures of war were not singular or consistent; they were often contested and contradictory. Subversive tactics, for instance, grew out of prewar repertoires and cultural patterns of expression. Prowar sentiments frequently came from outside the government, which made the government reactive. Thus, this book also explores how a liberal democracy waged war in the early twentieth century. The relationship between war and cultural practices in World War I France was multifaceted; some forms flourished, some faltered, rules changed, and new ideas became imaginable. To begin to understand the relationship, we must consider what French culture was like in the decades before the war.

The late nineteenth and early twentieth centuries had witnessed a three-pronged revolution in the power and dissemination of print, visual, and aural culture. From the 1870s onward, Paris offered fertile soil for mass cultural innovations, such as photography, sheet music, advertising, film, and phonograph recordings. While the eighteenth century had seen the rise of the novel, with its ramifications for literacy and reading practices, the second half of the nineteenth century—a period called "the apogee of the French press" by the leading specialists—felt an explosion in the production and influence of mass newspapers.[13] "As for newspapers," one historian has declared, they were "as numerous and as diverse as any other time or any other country has known or will, perhaps, ever know."[14] The circulation of Parisian dailies went from only 235,000 in 1858 to 2 million in 1880 and on to 5 million by 1910.[15] This rapid expansion was based on an aggressive distribution network, heightened competition, and a wish to provide the world of news to the average reader.[16] By 1914, France had literacy rates close to 100 percent.[17] The ever expanding print culture depended on literacy, but it also encouraged new reading habits and new systems of analytic and abstract thought.

But the penetration of written culture and literacy was just one part of this sea change in France. Even as written or print culture spread out from Paris into the provinces, "the ability to make sense of images had become as important as verbal literacy as a means of creating community, for the public culture of the Belle Époque was profoundly visual."[18] Thousands upon thousands of caricatures crowded on to the pages of the burgeoning newspapers, competing with advertisements and wood-engraved illustrations. Officials and business entrepreneurs pasted posters across public spaces, and from the 1890s onward a deluge of four-color lithographs appeared, made famous by Jules Chéret and then Henri de Toulouse-Lautrec as they advertised Parisian modernity.[19] New technology also offered the picture postcard, dazzling millions of customers with thousands of choices and creating new epistolary habits.[20] Finally, cinema made its appearance in 1895, and by 1914 it comprised several genres, including newsreels, action films, and comedies with receipts in France up to sixteen million francs a year.[21]

Mass culture was not simply the power to reproduce a text or an image; it encompassed new technology and experimentation as well as a growing capacity for mass production. The process of experimentation led in turn to a desire for *nouveautés*.[22] For historians, the new attention paid to this period's world of spectacle has already complicated a once clear trajectory from a traditionally oral and visual popular culture to a literate mass society. Given the breadth and sophistication of French print culture and the graphic arts, a rich field of images, symbols, practices, and skills existed. 1914 represented the moment when war and mass culture merged, and the events are incomprehensible without examining this mixture. The new creative opportunities would not have been possible in an earlier war, since they were wholly dependent on the technological and mental transformations of the fin-de-siècle period.

Recent work on visual culture has unfortunately ignored the third prong, a lively and vibrant aural culture. An examination of singing offers a panoply of sounds through which to analyze the Belle Époque's developments. The number of *cafés-concerts,* music halls and cabarets where one could hear singing greatly expanded, which contributed to a booming music industry. Thousands of professional performers took to the stage and promoted both their repertoires and their fame, while the songsheet business took advantage of new print technology to produce colorfully decorated sheets for sale at low prices. As in film, new technology had developed at the turn of the century that would revolutionize the ability to capture voice and instruments on phonograph records.

While the period witnessed this rapid growth of commercialized, professional music, some singing practices remained within a purely oral (nonwritten) or popular realm.[23] Tunes echoed through provincial and Parisian streets at political protests and community rituals as an important part of everyday life.[24] Singing did not require special materials or even an ability to read to reach a wide variety of people. It drew upon oral methods of composition and performance. The most common recipe was to set new words to old, familiar tunes, a relatively old practice in French culture. The improvisation on a well-known song was then passed on and changed once more to suit a new situation. Thus, individuals carried with them in their heads catalogues of tunes, which varied according to region or social group. Songwriters of all sorts constructed songs with invariably consistent rhymes, short repeating refrains, and constant repetition of both words and tunes.[25] These oral processes relied heavily on a mental universe that encouraged a powerful memory and a well-honed ear.

Creativity was thus intrinsic not just to composition, but to performance, in which an important part of a song's message derived from the situation. Possible interpretations depended on an audience's knowledge of slang, jokes, comical signs, and a performer's interaction with the audience. This allowed both individual and collective renditions to be shaped in performance and overshadowed any sharply oppositional relationship between the performer and patrons.[26] Although the performer and patrons needed and expected some degree of repetition, for example with refrains, an ending's unexpected change also opened up opportunities for situational jokes or barbs. The creative potential of songs, the popular agency involved, and the ever changing performances and audiences were to be very important during World War I.

Most historical works have looked at either cultural "modernity" in the form of mass entertainment in the cities, or at traditional peasant practices. But even as mass audiences were evolving through national music-hall tours, the average size of an audience remained small and informal, and performers and their patrons constantly recreated the "texts." Amateurism still flourished, partly because of France's large rural population, and partly because of the richness of street and café life. Furthermore, with professionally written and printed sheet music more readily available in shops, at *cafés-concerts,* and on street corners, literacy was encouraged even as the form of songs remained open-ended. The inventory of songs vastly expanded over the course of the nineteenth century. A national body of tunes, verses, and refrains spread into the provinces through the efforts of both schoolteachers and *café-concert artistes.* Religious, revolutionary, patriotic, and folkloric songs intermingled.

Fin-de-siècle France highlights the problems with the rigid definitions of popular and mass culture. The neatest, most resolute categorizations have depicted popular culture as local, folkloric, and authentic to a people, whereas mass culture is mechanically reproduced, broadly disseminated, unauthentic, and banal (or degraded). Recent work has broken down this division, as "evidence grows that 'authentic' folk traditions often have metropolitan or elite roots and that mass culture often is 'authentically' incorporated into ordinary people's everyday lives."[27] With the blurring of the sharp distinction has come confusion. In an extremely insightful essay, Chandra Mukerji and Michael Schudson have offered a very broad definition: "that popular culture refers to the beliefs and practices, and the objects through which they are organized, that are widely shared among a population."[28] But their definition may be most applicable for "modern popular culture." In fact, for some twentieth-century historians, what is "popular culture" refers to what was most popular or well-liked, or what received the widest hearing.[29]

At the turn of the century, however, the same French national culture that excelled in the innovations of mass dissemination and investigated the forms of modernity with such decided fascination was also clearly divided by class and region. Older habits, rituals, and clusters of knowledge did not die or simply disappear, even after they entered the city or reached a certain social height. Instead, the late-nineteenth century brought the intermingling of written, visual, and oral cultural practices—not just a "residue of orality," to use Walter Ong's words, but a duality of mental worlds.[30] A series of subsets, with practices based on both oral and written modes of expression, existed. Contemporaries themselves were often confused, and the effort to define the boundaries between "elite" and "popular" was not merely academic; it was politically and socially contested.[31] One cannot simply paint the nineteenth century as traditional and popular, and describe postwar forms such as radio and film as mass culture. Instead, we need to historicize mass culture and see the late nineteenth and early twentieth centuries as comprising a blend of both popular culture and early mass culture.

In this work, I distinguish the concept of "popular culture" from mass culture. Popular culture was specific to a limited subgroup's identity, and its practices were more integrally part of people's daily lives than those of mass culture. It was also less commercially focused. I am arguing for the continuation of popular cultures based on definitions used in eighteenth- and nineteenth-century history. These cultures were not elite or necessarily legitimate, and were at times in opposition to a more general culture.[32] This definition sees both rural and workers' cultures as popular.

World War I has long engendered a debate over whether it was the last nineteenth-century war or the abrupt beginning of the twentieth century.[33] Despite the fact that the Franco-Prussian War of 1870 has been called the "first great war" *(la première grande guerre)*, a "guerre totale," and "modern," cultural forms and practices contrasted markedly to those that predominated during World War I.[34] Although the conflict had modern, industrial aspects—with its use of railroads and extensive artillery—it may be more appropriate to view it as a "dress rehearsal" for World War I, as Stéphane Audoin-Rouzeau has suggested.[35] In 1870, communications across the national territory still took days; the newspapers were concentrated in Paris and had low provincial circulations. Newspapers also could not yet use photographs. The government displayed posters of simple text without illustrations or graphics on city streets to keep the populace informed. Moreover, French literacy levels had reached only 73 percent for men and 60 percent for women.[36] Haussmann's overhaul of Paris was not yet finished, and boulevard life, with its repercussions for public culture, was just entering a new phase of animation. The Franco-Prussian War did ignite a Parisian craze for *cafés-concerts* and music halls, but it was a system that still needed to mature.

In some ways France was experiencing a transformation familiar to Great Britain or Germany, which also saw the increasing strength of the press and the entertainment industry, expanding public literacy, and greater cohesiveness of the public sphere. One could argue that the war would not have lasted as long as it did without these cultural structures in place. Four-color propaganda posters, for instance, exhorted civilians from Russia to the United States to beware the enemy and to contribute money to their governments' efforts, while German, French, and British soldiers found time to read and write in the trenches.[37] Moreover, music-hall repertoires were cherished and recreated in both French and British dugouts.[38] Despite shortages of materials, an unstable consumer base, and an unreliable work force, World War I actually stimulated many cultural businesses—in some cases, even forms that had been dying.

Upon closer scrutiny, however, each country's national cultures followed unique paths. In France, mass cultural structures were particularly widespread, well financed, and extremely adaptive. The newspaper distribution networks and the postcard entrepreneurs responded with alacrity from August 1, 1914, onward. Responding to the intense interest in *actualités* and the drama of the moment, newspapers published numerous daily editions, which flooded out from Paris.[39] Sales were spurred on by full-page spreads of photographs. With the war, the production of postcards also reached new levels, tripling over four years.[40]

The war also prolonged the life of the *cafés-concerts* and music halls and provided ample opportunities for impromptu choruses.[41] Over sixteen thousand songs, both old and new, were submitted to the police censors for use in the music spectacles of Paris, and newspapers such as *La Guerre sociale* and *La Vie Parisienne* made such songs readily available in Paris. In the meantime, itinerant singers hawked hundreds of different songsheets near the front.

But France also still had a huge rural population, in contrast to Great Britain, for example, and popular cultures came not just from the urban working classes, but also from the peasants. Within the French context, World War I not only encouraged larger cultural enterprises, it also led to a renewal of popular cultural practices and materials—especially in the trenches. There, songs, jokes, and rituals developed as local creations for local consumption.

Thus, myriad musical forms thrived in World War I France. Using a grid to visualize the variety of singing practices, the vertical axis could represent a gradient from individual to collective choruses, while the horizontal line would range from organized or scripted performances to impromptu music. From one extreme of solitary, unsupervised singing to the other of organized, collective singing, all the alternatives existed. French citizens sang, for example, while mobilizing for war, in order to express their participation in the nation's fight, to hide their concerns, and to expose their enemies. Song culture was interwoven with the experience of war, usually helping to sustain morale, but also, at times, acting as a medium for voicing individual or collective dissent. Songs proved a perfect form for this war, since they were portable, nondiscriminatory (not restricted to the active reader, for example), adaptable, and polyvalent. After the war, when mechanically reproduced music expanded through the enormous influence of radio and records, most singing moved toward professional performances, with a lessening of collective or extemporaneous singing.[42]

Was the calling forth of popular song culture a conservative grasping for tradition? The renewal was not necessarily conservative because it encouraged a popular culture that was still a part of everyday life for rural populations and workers. Though censored, songs were hard to control, since they were transmitted through impromptu performances and memorization. As the war progressed, a culture of resistance arose in which the medium's polyvalence grew in significance. Texts and performances took on new meanings and functions. Indeed, French culture proved most conservative when it was found at the very heart of modern politics, because of the war's emphasis on a nationalist culture, which in the French case came from political and cultural trends of the late nineteenth century.[43] This conservative power included the devaluing of the signs and symbols of the French left, or the "Internationale" and the "Carmagnole," in musical terms.

Far too much of the scholarship on the Great War has studied groups such as civilians and soldiers separately and exclusively. This has often led to the perception of an enormous chasm between the military front and the home front. While some contemporaries promoted this idea, others saw different divides or a more complicated landscape. A study of song in World War I affords us an opportunity to examine both civilians and soldiers — Paris and the trenches — and to reconsider this map. One finds that, as a medium, singing had special features that helped it move across boundaries or even redraw the borders. This book has three parts, each of which crosses a cultural boundary. Part I examines the transition from the divisive politics and pleasures of fin-de-siècle France to the apparently unified culture of wartime. Part II highlights the tension between repression and enthusiasm, and the contest over definitions of appropriate and inappropriate expressions. And part III outlines a cultural geography of war where specific practices, rules, and participants defined different zones.

The first part of this work takes us from the prewar period up through December 1914. Chapter 1 provides a tour of the energetic musical world of late nineteenth-century France, the durable traditions of regional rural musical practices studied by ethnographers of the period as well as the growth of the massive music industry with its stars and song sheets. Lyrics were not confined to a leisure sphere, as a look at political rallies and street riots illustrates. Participants used songs as weapons of insult and symbols of political struggle. Despite the political divisions, however, the French mobilized for war in August 1914 in a relatively orderly, if not enthusiastic, manner. Historians have tried to determine the level of fervor and to explain why all groups, but particularly workers, took up the national task. Chapter 2 investigates how the French actually performed a national ritual of mobilization based on historical example and a patriotic script found in song lyrics. The process reveals a national culture, built not just on mass culture, but also on older popular practices. The earliest months of war saw the formation of a musical *union sacrée* which contributed to a broader prowar ethos which embraced conservative, even ultra-conservative, values and symbols of nationalism, religion, and gender.

By the end of 1914, both sides had dug in on the Western Front, and a gap began to grow between the home front and the trenches. The distinction between front and rear should not, however, be taken as natural or impermeable.[44] Part II takes up the question of what representations or ideas could or could not cross boundaries. The government carefully positioned itself as the primary filter between the troops and Paris, controlling leaves and censoring information. Therefore, chapter 3 studies the censors who reviewed both songs lyrics and musical performances in order to shape the representational spheres in Paris and in the army zone. The examiners, songwriters, and performers all understood a song's potential malleability and power. In the Parisian arena, which set the pace for the rest of France, officials carefully tied morale to morality, whereas military commanders worried little about their soldiers' virtue.

Chapter 4 analyzes one of the most potent themes of wartime popular and mass culture: eroticism and images of sexuality combined with representations of the war and its weaponry. Normative roles for women were no longer limited to mothers and nurses, as offering sexual pleasure to soldiers became a patriotic act. Such representations colored the war as exciting and enticing. The soldiers in the trenches, meanwhile, played out both repressed fantasies and anxieties with homosocial songs created by Parisian songwriters and the combatants themselves. Songs played a particularly useful role in both cases, because of their common use of sexual double entendres. But one encounters the same themes echoed as well in other media such as postcards and posters.

Attempts by the authorities to control boundaries helped create the multiple cultures that offered different understandings of the war. Part III maps out three of the main cultural zones: the front trenches, the areas behind the lines in villages and camps (*cantonnements*), and Paris. Other areas clearly existed, such as the ten occupied departments and civilian areas away from Paris, but for the sake of time and space, I have chosen not to include them here.[45]

Chapter 5 investigates the capital in the early years of the war. The French experience in this war is especially interesting considering the nearness of the front to Paris—even closer than, in Fussell's words, London's "ridiculous proximity."[46] Occupying a sort of border space, the city sat in a precarious, unstable position involving shifts in population, rules, and outlook. We should not necessarily view Paris as the quintessential "home front," since it held its own unique position. But it was in Paris that a definition of "civilian" was created and negotiated. Musical entertainment, which had been a staple of Parisian life during the Belle Époque, raised the issue of proper and improper behaviors and the merit of patriotic demonstrations. Chapter 5 traces how, in the early years, the music industry became embroiled in the debate and conscious construction of a concept of *normalité*.

In chapters 6 and 7, the focus shifts away from Paris to the army zone. Chapter 6 explores the official musical rituals in which soldiers, led by their army officers, "performed" as part of their military training, in battle, and as an illustration of their patriotism. As eight million Frenchmen passed through the army during the four and a half years of war, the soldiers' marches and songs reinforced their own group. The military also encouraged musical entertainment to bolster morale, and found assistance from a new source—Parisian celebrities who performed for combatants behind the lines.

Soldiers also chose to sing as individuals or in groups in the trenches, often in open opposition to the organized entertainment behind the lines, and I treat this phenomenon in chapter 7. Opportunities in time and space for singing and performing proliferated with the long stationary war. Singing did not simply create or damage morale, but formed a part of combatants' attempts to understand and survive the war. Soldiers strove constantly to interpret events, calling upon trusted cultural icons, such as prewar conventions, traditional language, and symbols.[47] The combatants' experiences in the trenches may represent the most convincing evidence for the human need to impose meaning on experiences. Songs also played a role in the development of the soldiers' own subculture, through which they tried to define their own self-image and purpose in conjunction with a powerful critique of civilian representations and behavior.

Soldiers still had to contend with the home front's own constructions, despite all of their exclusionary tactics, as their ideas were appropriated and reshaped by a more powerful discourse in Paris. We return to Paris in chapter 8 to look at the soldiers' influence and to see the dominant culture in action in 1917–1918. The durable prowar ethos proved flexible enough to absorb dissent and to answer civilians' war weariness with solace and laughter. In the last year and a half of war, entertainment turned international again, led by a great thirst for things American which included the introduction of jazz, a new dance craze, and "international" stars. Signs of uneasiness in the face of this "invasion" appeared, set off by the intense nationalization of the war's early years. This anxiety fed the development of postwar nostalgia, which would be shared by both soldiers and civilians.

The nature of this subject brings its own unique research problems. Many cultural representations were lost in the trenches, partly because of the ephemeral nature of the popular culture. Many instances of improvised singing are irretrievable, especially since written accounts of the war came mostly from a limited, more literate stratum of society. But one can cull some occasions from memoirs, newspapers, and works on trench life. Even these essays, which concentrate on subjects such as the political changes in Paris or the course of battles, offer a multitude of references to music, including bands, drummers, and casual singing, revealing contemporaries' assumption that the music was *always* there. I have been forced to rely on these accounts and on the reactions of censors.

I have also had to use texts to learn about music and to imagine performances.[48] Many collections of published songs exist, particularly those by the more successful songwriters as well as lyrics in newspapers, on postcards, and on posters. A song text, however, is just that—a text that may only hint at the plasticity of words in performance and the importance of the music. Furthermore, I am *writing* about music, and have been forced at times to use vocabulary that reinforces the idea of textuality. We have a more limited vocabulary in cultural history for the effects of sound or the act of musical composition. I describe, for example, how songs "inscribed" patriotism, or I use the term "script," where the word libretto would not have the same connotations.

Historians of this war also walk a fine line in uncovering the truth, because they want to be respectful. Despite attention to entertainment in the Belle Époque, almost no work has been done on it during the war years.[49] The prevailing view has been that silence, darkness, and sadness reigned, in contrast to the abundant entertainment in fin-de-siècle France, perhaps because scholars have felt somewhat irreverent describing entertainment as having occurred in the middle of such a brutal war.[50] The French were in the process of losing 1.3 million men, but the true cost was felt only as time passed. Memoirs from after the war were shaped heavily by postwar awareness of the price of war and the struggle to go on. Even if at times songs disguised sadness or consoled audiences, there were also moments of silliness, humor, and even gaiety. The war may seem senseless as we view the whole picture (or as some soldiers viewed their piece of trench), but this was not necessarily so from each person's point of view. Although it is difficult to determine layered meanings and quickly changing purposes, we cannot refrain from the venture. If soldiers could have been convicted of treason because of the songs they performed, we must try to understand the threat perceived by the army, even if we cannot know the soldiers' exact intentions. The practices themselves need to be understood.

The distinct song culture of the French has also made this a complicated book to write. The French Revolution gave birth to the anthem "Le Chant du départ" which begins "La Victoire en chantant," roughly translated as "Singing our way to victory." This concept was celebrated from the end of the eighteenth century into the twentieth, and many took it to heart. Soldiers and civilians alike described World War I as a concert or performance, and the metaphor was a part of French military mythology. Propaganda from Paris had soldiers happily singing their way to their deaths—an image that came to anger soldiers, even as they wrote and performed musical revues. This reflects or embodies the tension that existed during the war between the dominant culture of Paris and that of soldiers in the trenches. My task is to tell the varying sides of the story, without fulfilling the soldiers' worst fears of being misrepresented.

PART I

❧

FROM A CONTESTED PEACE TO A POLITICALLY PEACEFUL WAR

❧

CHAPTER ONE

Musical Pleasures, Pedagogy, and Politics

Between February 21 and March 4, 1911, demonstrations and riots shook the center of Paris, as groups on the far right protested against a play at the Comédie-Française because it was written by a Jewish army deserter. The political shock troops massed in front of the theater and around the statue of Joan of Arc in the Place des Pyramides and taunted the police, yelling "A bas Bernstein" (the playwright), and singing "La Youpignole" (which was a variation of the much older revolutionary tune "Ça ira"). The police report recorded "the then-popular anti-semitic refrain":

A bas les juifs! A bas les juifs!	Down with Jews! Down with Jews!
Il faut les pendre, sans plus attendre.	We must hang them without further delay.
A bas les juifs! A bas les juifs!	Down with Jews! Down with Jews!
Il faut les pendre par le pif!	We must hang them by the nose!
Ah! ça ira, ça ira, ça ira!	Ah! It will be all right, all right, all right!
Tous les Youpins à la lanterne.	All the Jews to the lamppost.[1]

At this point on February 26 the commanding officer, apparently irritated by the song, ordered his subordinates to charge, which left demonstrators fleeing and a café in shambles.[2]

On the other end of the political spectrum, the socialist left distributed songsheets with the lyrics of the "Internationale" and "A bas la guerre" at massive antimilitarist rallies organized in 1911 and 1912. Newspaper reports described the crowds singing "Gloire au 17e" and the "Carmagnole," the first a labor song and the second another revolutionary hymn. In little towns of France, groups of socialists also used the "Internationale" to protest against their enemies, while Catholics fought for the right to hold religious processions and to sing hymns in public. These French musical conflicts continued right through July 1914, as Europe prepared for a much larger and deadlier confrontation. Why did all these people choose to sing out their sentiments, and what can these cases tell us about political practices?

In fin-de-siècle France, songs were integral to the expressivity of daily life; they were neither insignificant nor merely illustrative. Occasions for performing were abundant: workers sang at union meetings and strikes, peasants sang at work, and most people participated in old and new types of musical entertainment. Song texts were made readily available on the front page of newspapers and in periodicals, as well as on broadsheets and inexpensive sheet music, which flooded the routes from Paris out into the provinces. The public's willingness to sing relied on and further encouraged widespread musical literacy.

Tunes and lyrics took on a blatantly active political role in the song culture of the streets, linked to relatively new forms of mass politics. Across this recently literate society, citizens still called on songs to express their views and to take a public position on the most politically charged issues, such as loyalty to the Republic, the Church versus the State, the rapid expansion of socialism, and rising antisemitism. Songs initiated conflicts in public spaces, subverted authority, and helped shape political loyalties. More generally, people shared a well-known, common vocabulary of tunes, characters, and modes of humor, over which neither the left nor the right held a musical monopoly.

The Belle Époque also saw the growth of a massive music industry which coexisted alongside durable traditions of regional rural singing. As cafés-concerts spread in the early Third Republic, they offered a forum for musical commentary on political figures, scandals, or the latest fashions. The entertainment establishments and music publishing firms served as parts of an expanding commercial culture and a burgeoning urban modernity. They responded to both an expanding international mass culture and a growing nationalism.

Most historical studies of this period's music have chosen to examine either the enclosed "leisure" spectacles or the texts used in street politics. No one has looked at how these spheres may have overlapped or when and where songs moved from one arena to the other.[3] This separation has led some scholars to conclude that with the advent of mass culture, depoliticization or political pacification soon followed. Songs, however, were integrated in public and political life—in cafés-concerts, in the Third Republic's schools, and in the streets of the Belle Époque. An examination of all three arenas highlights the versatile musical skills and repertoires the French could call on in 1914.

The Adolescence of a Music Entertainment Industry

We must start at the center and work outward, since the rapid growth of commercialized music through the *cafés-concerts* and music halls drew its impetus from Paris and then permeated the countryside. The capital city presented a vivid medley of musical sounds. *Chanteurs ambulants* (street singers) set up shop on various corners to inform passersby of the latest scraps of gossip or political turn of events, hoping to sell a songsheet if the tune or lyrics caught someone's ear.[4] More formally, close to two hundred publishing enterprises offered low-priced songsheets with elaborate covers that could quickly be adapted to changing tastes.[5] (Some "firms," however, were tiny shops or cooperatives.) One needed only thirty-five centimes for sheets with a simple melody and the words, or one or two francs for a songsheet with a piano accompaniment. As the historian Charles Rearick has written, Paris in the 1890s "'consumed' twelve to fifteen thousand songs a year," and, following the turn of the century, the infant phonograph industry even brought recordings by the largest stars into bourgeois parlors.[6]

The fastest-growing arenas for songs in Paris, however, were the *cafés-concerts*, cabarets, and music halls spread throughout the city.[7] Though scholars commonly describe how the *cafés-concerts* took over from the *goguettes* (early-nineteenth-century singing and drinking clubs) only to be replaced by music halls, in actuality music halls and *cafés-concerts* existed side by side for well over sixty years.[8] Beginning in the 1870s, "In unprecedented numbers [the French] went to . . . hear songs sung one after another (*tours de chant*), practically without interruption all evening. In the last decades of the nineteenth century, these commercial places multiplied, their audiences grew dramatically."[9] The *cafés-concerts* thrived following the loosening of government restrictions on the use of costumes, accessories, and gestures in 1867, and were nourished by the explosive growth in the city's population. Although many places closed during the Franco-Prussian War and the Commune, the years just before and after saw new performance spaces abound.[10]

The world of the *cafés-concerts*, according to both contemporary bourgeois memoirs and recent historical works, had an ambiguous, somewhat seedy reputation compared to the larger, more formal theaters. Some historians have argued that the main clientele was the lower middle classes, but much of their evidence is embedded in middle- or upper-class perceptions of contemporaries.[11] The audiences actually comprised a wide range of classes, from the middle classes on down to workers who attended their neighborhood cafés. The uncomfortable housing conditions in Paris made local cafés attractive as warm, convivial venues for a variety of people, at a time when sociability relied less on private homes, and more on public places.[12] The police saw the cafés as a breeding ground for all sorts of vice. But Lenard Berlanstein's fascinating archival study of specific *quartiers* in and around Paris has highlighted how workers willingly spent hard-earned time and money for local entertainment for the entire family. In Saint-Denis, they patronized theaters and sporting events, but "preferred lively music-hall programs."[13] The worker Jeanne Bouvier recounted in her wonderfully detailed memoir how she loved to attend the Opéra-Comique and would remember "bits of songs which [she] hummed for weeks."[14] Workers could and did take advantage of the myriad choices offered by the new commercialized leisure activities. And performers regularly made tours of the smaller, less publicized places.

A typical evening at a *café-concert* included ten or more singers performing over three to four hours with variety acts mixed in. Just before World War I, the programs shifted from being mainly song turns toward a remarkable melange of songs, circus acts, ballet, and short films, as new forms of mass culture vied for attention and fed the audiences' love of novelty. Beginning in the 1890s, the musical revue with its string of anecdotal tableaux, opulent sets, and chorus lines also grew in popularity, although mainly on the larger stages.

The growth of commercialization was clearly changing entertainment with expanding numbers of business entrepreneurs, advertisers, and stockholders. Spectacles that used to be in the streets, markets, or fairs in front of ever-changing crowds were enclosed for a paying audience in fin-de-siècle France. Elements of modernity included the quick adaptation and reproduction of sheet music and an internationalism linked to growing tourism.[15] Yet we must not overestimate the transformation, at least not in the aural field. This was not the mass culture of radio or of mass-distributed records. Moreover, a vast range of room and audience sizes created varying relationships between spectators and performers, not simply passive, uninterested gatherings. A more direct look at singing practices will help us see the mixture of old and new.

Historians of the French song tradition have disagreed sharply over how well audiences knew lyrics. Some have argued that audiences could not hear the songs and did not pay attention. Others have claimed that the audiences knew all the words, since performers cultivated perfect diction in an era before microphones.[16] Neither position is easy to prove. But because scholars have concentrated far more on the mass cultural aspects of musical entertainment, they have ignored the more traditional characteristics of French oral culture and have failed to appreciate performative aspects—the small, communal audiences, the adaptive texts, the inventory of tunes, and the role of memory. In France, with its patchwork of forms and levels of literacy, many features of an oral tradition were still very much alive.

Musical literacy, a very complicated proposition, is hard to judge from our perspective. Individuals could have had an assortment of natural talents or learned skills, including an ability to recognize a melody, to mimic a tune, or to recreate a tune or a harmonic passage on an instrument such as the piano. Individuals may have also known how to sight-read music from musical notation. Too often, however, scholars have plotted a teleological path of decreasing or increasing skills. Musicologists have seen musical appreciation or facility becoming ever more sophisticated (at least among an elite), while students of mass culture have posited the reverse—a precipitous decline in skills as participation fell off. Instead, we need to think in terms of a variety of skills, coming and going.

One way to do this is to go directly to the songs themselves and to accounts of performances. The most common method of composition was to put new lyrics to an old melody. Composers constantly recycled melodies simply by indicating the name of the "air" above the text on "sheet music," or broadsheets. This process depended on a preexisting pool of tunes that would be known by the performer, listener, or sheet-music reader. The borrowing of tunes to write a new song was not particular to France, but it was an integral part of French popular culture from the early modern period onward.[17] A commonly used tune such as "Malbrough s'en va t'en guerre" was about 200 years old, while the popular "Marseillaise" was exactly 122 in 1914. But, by the end of the nineteenth century, the number of well-known tunes had increased dramatically, and the public's repertoires came from a wealth of mixed sources including folktunes, patriotic anthems, and newer commercial songs. These all went into very retentive memories.

We can see the importance of melodies based on the diatonic scale by looking at sheet music. It came in at least three styles. One form provided a melody and four-part harmony, almost always written for a piano accompaniment. This reflected the growing popularity of pianos. But this form was not the most common. One could also purchase sheet music with just the melody and words *(chant seul)* or with only the words and the name of the melody. Since the songs were not necessarily harmonized, they were in a sense simpler. But the actual melodies could be long and complicated, even if they relied on memory. It was the better known tunes that offered the most possibilities for adaptation, not necessarily the easiest. In the Parisian *cafés-concerts* as well as in the trenches, the ability to manipulate a complicated tune was quite prodigious.[18]

Programs comprised a mixture of old and new tunes, as certain melodies caught the public's attention and were then reused. In addition, the publication of songs in sheet music, in newspapers, and in the illustrated press fostered learning and competence with visual notation. This last was also taught as part of the school curriculum in the early Third Republic, as we shall see. With the prevalence of daily singing, listeners became diffusers as they learned songs at local cafés and bought the sheet music for a new catchy tune at the music halls or from performers on the streets. Thus, older practices and skills merged with more recent commercial developments, and literacy and the availability of texts spread.

Many *cafés-concerts* and cabarets had small rooms, which encouraged contact, friendly or otherwise, between the audience and singers. The lyrical structure of songs with their short lines and rhymes also enhanced the possibility of listeners quickly learning at least the refrain. Both songwriters and performers used the French language with remarkable aural facility, simply eliminating extra syllables with elisions to pack words into the tunes' rhythms.[19] In general, improvisation and copious gestures prevailed.[20] Humor came from the use of popular slang, an accumulation of incongruous situations, or a punchline at the end, which could be easily modified. Some sheet music explicitly encouraged improvisation by providing suggestive blanks or different endings with the words "Variante ad lib." Verses often told a slowly evolving story based on characters moving through changing circumstances. To take just one example, in the song "S'ils revenaient" (fig. 1), the performer hypothesized about the disappointment of various historical figures including Henry IV, Joan of Arc, Napoleon, and Molière as they returned to view the contemporary world.[21] Each verse had twelve lines, five of which were identical except for the new character's name. All of the lines rhymed either by twos or in alternating couplets. The melody was also built of short recurring phrases and rhythms ($ab^{1}ab^{2}ccd^{1}ccd^{2}ab^{3}$) within a small tonal range. Using this formula, old verses could easily have been eliminated and new celebrities introduced, with audience assistance, if the performer were so inclined. Commentary on current events was omnipresent, fostered by the adaptive nature of the texts and slang. A performer could hardly have been successful without the audience's comprehension and reaction.

Some historians have posited an absence of politics against a backdrop of the *embourgeoisement* of the Republic, a lack of revolutions, and the workers' "collapse" into World War I. The period 1866 to 1914, however, was anything but politically silent, and events such as the Franco-Prussian War, the Commune, Boulangism, and the Dreyfus Affair spawned all sorts of lyrics. *Actualités* fed mass cultural forms, and singing was an obvious way to reach newly politicized constituencies.

The French musical palette of that period encompassed a whole series of different genres, from *chansons idiotes* to well-known portrayals of social categories or stereotypes such as the "peasant." In the latter, a singer such as Sulbac claimed to have just arrived in the big city and used patois.[22] One very important genre, the *chanson réaliste*, also grew up in the cabarets of Montmartre during the 1880s, although its roots extended back past the *go-guettes*. It represented vital political expressions, helping to shape Paris's social identity. Many of the genre's pieces gave voice to the poor and marginal people of Paris, including prostitutes and thieves. Aristide Bruant worked assiduously to integrate common language and slang into each piece in order to heighten the realistic tone. Most historians of the *cafés-concerts* have stressed that this genre was a recreation of "reality," and that while Bruant's repertoire criticized the social problems of the time, it was not politically revolutionary. The songs did, however, allow the popular classes to appear as subjects and offered biting satire of current conditions.[23] The genre also gradually changed venues from the more limited world of the cabarets to a wider, working-class public.

Clearly, the constant incorporation of *actualités* in songs was not limited to casual subjects but contained commentary on the "political." For example, song texts shaped views of political figures, relations with police, and attitudes toward the army. More specifically, throughout the Belle Époque, the *cafés-concerts* provided a home for revanchist songs which pleaded for the recapture of Alsace-Lorraine—a politically volatile subject. As the authors of *100 ans de chanson française* have argued, "the war of 1914 was prepared for as much in the *cafés-concerts* as by the general staff."[24] In the flood of songs during the 1870s, the return of the lost provinces of Alsace and Lorraine held center stage.[25] Patriotic fever became intertwined with a new wave of fascination with songs. The well-known "Alsace et Lorraine," written in 1873, heralded the inevitable clash with the Germans:

Mais le grand jour où la France meurtrie	But the great day when deadly France
Reformera ses nombreux bataillons	Will re-form its numerous battalions
Au cri sauveur jeté par la Patrie	To the cry of deliverance thrown up by *la Patrie*
Hommes, enfants, femmes, nous répondrons.	Men, children, women, we will respond.[26]

Not surprisingly, the revanchist texts never mentioned the Commune, dwelling instead on the Franco-Prussian War and the need for revenge.[27]

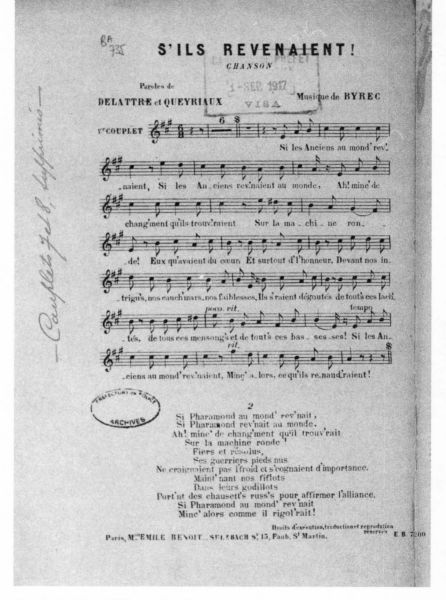

3

Si l'pèr' Noé au mond' rev'nait,
Si l'pèr' Noé rev'nait au monde,
Ah! minc'de chang'ment qu'il trouv'rait
Sur la machine ronde!
Ses fils étonnés
L'voyant s'piquer l'nez,
L'couvrir'nt d'un manteau pour effacer sa honte.
Si tous nos poivrots
Se couvraient d'manteaux
Jamais nos tailleurs n'auraient d'laissés pour compte.
Si l'pèr' Noé au mond' rev'nait,
Y a pas à dire, il en bav'rait!

4

Si Roger Bacon revenait,
Si c'fameux moin' rev'nait au monde,
Ah! minc'de chang'ment qu'il trouv'rait
Sur la machine ronde!
Il trouva, crénom!
La poudre à canon!
Mais ça sent mauvais, c'est pour ça qu'on l'chica-né.
Car son invention
C'est d'la dérision!
Un gaillard plus fort, c'est sûr'ment l'pétomane!
Si Roger Bacon revenait,
Il n'pourrait pas faire autant d'pet!

5

Si Henri quatre au mond' rev'nait,
Si Henri quatre rev'nait au monde,
Ah! minc'de chang'ment qu'il trouv'rait
Sur la machine ronde!
Il voulait, Henriot,
Mettr' la poule au pot
Croyant qu'ça s'trouvait à tous les coins des rues.
S'il v'nait aujourd'hui
Il s'rait bien marri
Car en fait d'poulett's il n'trouv'rait plus qu'des grues.
Si Henri quatre au mond' rev'nait,
Mince alors c'que ça l'épat'rait!

6

Si Béranger au mond' rev'nait,
Si Béranger rev'nait au monde,
Ah! min' de chang'ment qu'il trouv'rait
Sur la machine ronde!
Dans tous ces couplets
Tendres ou guillerets,
Il mettait d'l'esprit, d'la verve et d'la morale.
Maint'nant au concert
Tout c'que l'on nous sert
C'est idiot comm' tout quand ça n'est pas très-sa-le.
Si Béranger au mond' rev'nait,
Que d'cochonn'ries il entendrait!

7

Si Jeanne d'Arc au mond' rev'nait,
Si Jeanne d'Arc rev'nait au monde,
Ah! min' de chang'ment qu'il trouv'rait
Sur la machine ronde!
Maint'nant la vertu,
Ni vu ni connu...
Aucun' femm' n'en a, car ell's sont tout's trompe-ses.
Les rosièr's vraiment
Sont très-rar's sûr'ment,
S'il en rest' quèqu'uns, c'est parmi les chanteu-ses...
Si Jeanne d'Arc au mond' rev'nait,
N'y a qu'au concert qu'elle en trouv'rait!

8

Si Bonaparte au mond' rev'nait,
Si Bonaparte rev'nait au monde,
Ah! min' de chang'ment qu'il trouv'rait
Sur la machine ronde!
Quand un d'ses soldats
Mourait aux combats
Il versait un pleur sur la tomb' du vieux brave.
Maint'nant le journeaux,
Fortun' des cam'lots
Saliss'nt notre armée en la souillant d'leur ba-ve!
Si Bonaparte au mond' rev'nait
Tonnerr' de Dieu! quel coup d'balai!

9

Si l'grand Molière au mond' rev'nait,
Si l'grand Molière rev'nait au monde,
Ah! minc' de chang'ment qu'il trouv'rait
Sur la machine ronde!
Du Théâtr' Français
Y r'fus'rait l'accès,
A tous ces cabots, fomenteurs de cabale,
Et pourrait chaqu' jour,
Venir ici pour
Trouver des cornards! Moi, j'en vois plein la salle!
Si l'grand Molière au mond' rev'nait,
D'voir tant d'cocus il s'gondol'rait!

7200   Vielle Gr. 15 Fg St Martin   Imp. Crevel Frès 18 Fg St Denis

These songs presented militarism as the solution, glossing over the most recent catastrophe with historical references to the great French victories of Louis XIV and the French Revolution. Although all of them were pro-France, some of these songs opposed the Republic. With these revanchist performances, the country could restore its national self-image and reinstate the French masculine élan.

One of the best examples of the intersection between commercial popularity in the *cafés-concerts* and the political arena was the excitement the performer Paulus inspired when he modified the song "En r'venant de la r'vue" to fit the rise of Boulangism in 1886.[28] Here again, the themes of nationalism, anti-Germanism, and militarism recombined. Paulus sang Boulanger's praises for more than a year in Paris, while similar songs sprouted up, which slowly spread from Paris into the provinces. In his study of the army's role in politics throughout the Third Republic, the historian Alistair Horne attributed Boulanger's political appeal to lyrics, describing how: "On the streets, inflammatory songs were heard that seemed painfully evocative of the summer of 1870."[29] Mimicking song lyrics, people referred to Boulanger as the one who "would deliver Alsace and Lorraine." The songs struck a chord of popular sentiment and, in turn, heightened the enthusiasm of Boulanger's friends and the fears of his opponents.

Boulanger's prominence was obviously not due solely to the *café-concert* repertoire, but songs were especially important in spreading his popularity. Michael Burns, in his rich account of rural politics, described peddlers who "marched through the streets of Cahors (Lot) singing 'C'est Boulanger qu'il nous faut,' 'Il Reviendra,' and other popular Parisian tunes, and selling song sheets engraved with heroic portraits of the General. Local peasants bought most of the merchandise."[30] As Boulanger's popularity spread, "En r'venant de la r'vue" could be heard in Tunis, authorities seized copies of "La Revanche de Boulanger" in Mirande in southern France, and the Parisian "C'est Boulanger qu'il nous faut" incited a fist fight in the department of the Gers.[31] These musical artifacts represented an effective way to mobilize electoral support and became a part of local battles, since, in this unevenly literate society, songs were a part of daily communication.

In the years after the Boulanger crisis, myriad groups encouraged political activity outside of the restricted circles of parliamentary politics. A much broader spectrum of people were becoming politically aware on both the left and right. Cafés provided an excellent place for these sentiments to flourish, and songs could move from cafés to the streets and back again. But, was this appearance of politics in the *café-concert* simply a "conservative 'conformism,'" suggesting passivity, as Gérard Jacquemet has claimed?[32] And were the French *cafés-concerts* equivalent to the English music halls, analyzed by Gareth Stedman Jones, with their "comic stoi-cism," "political skepticism," and "culture of consolation"?[33] Whereas the *réaliste* genre was politically ambiguous and may not have directly engaged current social debates, there were performers whose songs did.

René de Buxeuil, Théodore Botrel, and Eugénie Buffet—all three na-tionalists and royalists—combined an obviously political message with suc-cessful *café-concert* careers. De Buxeuil wrote nationalist songs and was sympathetic to the Action Française, the avowedly monarchist and author-itarian political organization. Botrel had a twenty-year career in the *cafés-concerts,* where his strident nationalism intertwined with his renditions of songs about Brittany performed in the traditional clothing of the Bre-tons.[34] He represents an excellent example of the far right's integral nation-alism, where "True France" was composed "of many regional cultures but only one national one," as explained by Herman Lebovics.[35] Botrel also composed songs for the Ligue des Patriotes, published royalist material in his collection *Les Chansons de la fleur de lys* in 1899, and earned the nick-name "le petit sergent" from Paul Déroulède, one of the foremost leaders of the strident nationalist movement.[36] Botrel's song "La Terre nationale" directly challenged the socialist anthem the "Internationale," and in the *cafés-concerts* of the 1890s, Botrel got cheers for his "Coups de clairon" and "Pour la Patrie," benefiting from "the wave of rightist nationalism."[37]

These songs also challenged the anticlerical Republican ideology with references to Joan of Arc and Catholic saints. In "La Marche Lorraine," Jeanne d'Arc led the fight for France wearing sabots and fighting for the "sacred" soil. "Alsace et Lorraine" also began:

France à bientôt car la sainte espérance	France, goodbye for now, for pious faith
Emplit nos coeurs en te disant: Adieu!	Fills our hearts in telling you: Farewell!
En attendant l'heure de délivrance	While awaiting the hour of deliverance
Pour l'avenir, nous allons prier Dieu.	For the future, we will pray to God.[38]

In the meantime, other performers questioned the Republic from the left, raising the critical issues of class conflict and antimilitarism.[39] For ex-ample, "A bas la guerre" by Louis Bousquet and Henri Malfait had a grand-father describe war's carnage, horror, and futility to his grandson:

Chante la Paix, la vie est éphemère	Sing of Peace, life is fleeting
Refléchi bien et si tu me comprends	Having thought carefully and if you understand me
Tu haïras les armes et la guerre	You will hate arms and war
La douleur des petits fait la gloire des grands.	The grief of the young creates glory for the old.[40]

Politics also defined the career of Gaston Montéhus, probably the best-known songwriter of the social-political genre in the prewar period, who performed all over Paris and France, especially in specifically "popular" cafés. His works highlighted the great distance between rich and poor, but his ideas were drawn in broad strokes. Historians themselves have variously described Montéhus as a devout socialist, an antimilitarist, and an anarchist.[41] This imprecision may have actually contributed to his popularity. He wrote the beloved song "Gloire au 17e" as a tribute to the soldiers of the 17th Infantry, who had refused to march against workers during the strike at Béziers in 1907.[42] Here, Montéhus suggested nonviolent methods and a goal of peace, and the song ended on an optimistic note:

Esperons qu'un jour viendra en France	Let us hope that a day will come in France
Où la paix, la concord' règnera	When peace, harmony will reign
Ayons tous au coeur cette espérance	Let us all have this hope in our hearts
Que bientôt ce grand jour viendra.	That soon the great day will come.[43]

Crowds regularly sang this hymn at antimilitarist rallies, along with Montéhus's "Jeune Garde" and "Fusil, pourquoi es-tu." In the latter, he defended the worker's position against bourgeois owners, their government, and the army. The lyrics clearly displayed Montéhus's antimilitarism, with a gun describing its own terrible villainy:

Sans aucun remords j'fais souffrir	Without remorse I cause suffering
Les innocents je fais mourir,	The innocents I make die
. . . .	. . . .
J'suis heureux véritablement,	I am truly happy,
Quand je prends l'fils d'une vieill' maman	When I take the son of an old mother.[44]

Montéhus also swam against the current of revanchist tunes, arguing in a song such as "Voilà les Prussiens" that it was actually "the rich," "a fat cat," or "the nobility" of France who provided the means and motives to kill mothers' sons. These privileged figures were the true enemies of the Republic and the real "Prussians," since, as Montéhus starkly told workers, "It is in your blood that their glory bathes."

In the first decade of the twentieth century, Montéhus experienced widespread popularity in the music industry and beyond. As Lenard Berlanstein has argued, "performances [for workers] that included doses of 'realism' and specifically working-class commentary enjoyed considerable success—

enough to make profit-oriented theater owners cater to this interest. This meant that Montéhus headlined at the Casino in Saint-Denis repeatedly; in particular, it seems, at moments of 'heightened antagonism.'"[45] At these shows, he would often collect money for strikers or for those hurt in work-related accidents. Workers did not simply seek escapism with mass entertainment, but instead "were prepared to be moved, thrilled, and entertained in a number of ways, [including] poignant presentations of a world with which they were all too familiar."

Montéhus also tirelessly contributed a portion of his time to performing at political meetings, for groups such as La Ligue pour la Défense du Soldat, where disobedience and desertion by soldiers were openly discussed.[46] This circuit from private meetings, to commercial entertainment places, and into the streets, showed that these public spaces were overlapping subsets, not mutually exclusive spheres. In the social battles against the bourgeoisie, the army, and the police, leftist organizations recognized Montéhus's performances as taking place on the front lines. In its March 1, 1911, edition, the socialist newspaper *La Guerre sociale* denounced harassment aimed at Montéhus by the police. The paper ominously asserted that "every night in the popular theaters, whose proprietors have dared to resist police threats made to intimidate them into refusing the room to our friend, the cops are marshalled." The editorial exhorted all "revolutionary comrades" to go hear Montéhus sing.[47]

Unfortunately, we do not yet know if there were well-marked right and left cafés, nor if people attended to hear those with whom they sympathized, or to heckle those they disliked. But it should be clear that entertainers did not muffle their own political views. Songs certainly went from *cafés-concerts* to workers' meetings and street rallies, but one wonders how often, and whether they moved in only one direction.

If limited work has been done on Paris, historians have done even less on musical entertainment outside Paris. This is despite the fact that, as Eugen Weber has stated, "the most accessible entertainment for the lower and middle classes was to be found in music-halls and *cafés-concerts,* which could be enjoyed in the smallest towns, and where even working-class families or peasants who had made a profit on market day had access to the musical hits of a few years past for the price of a beer or a cup of coffee, that is, 10 cents."[48] This was a "veritable industry," which employed thousands of singers, comedians, and musicians across France.[49] Marseille already had ten music halls by 1863, and its Château des Fleurs, a summer music hall, held ten thousand customers. Thousands of sites allowed for the spread of the Parisian repertoire and cultural habits. The movement was not just from Paris to the provinces, however. Stars such as Félix Mayol and Eugénie Buffet grew up and trained in the provinces before they attempted their debuts in Paris. Others, meanwhile, remained provincial or single-town artists.

"Cet élement primordial d'éducation"

As we saw with the police surveillance of Montéhus, officials were well aware of songs' political and potentially subversive messages. But French administrators and politicians also promoted their own much more positive approach to singing.[50] The proper education of future republicans represented a cornerstone of the Third Republic's political program, and official pedagogy recognized songs as a particularly effective method. The government's campaign embraced singing's multifaceted nature, which could encourage memory and literacy while it instilled discipline and the correct ideology—if one used the right lyrics. Thus, in 1872, under the shadow of the Franco-Prussian debacle, the minister of public instruction, Jules Simon, initiated a national crusade to teach "proper" songs.[51] Songbooks were distributed and singing lessons incorporated into the elementary school curriculum. The effort gained momentum as the Republic consolidated its position in the late 1870s and early 1880s, accompanied by the publication of a slew of government reports and manuals.[52] Patterned on German and American models, the instruction was meant to "inculcate a sense of the fatherland, of civilization, and of moral ideals."[53] Students would learn republican patriotism and a noble sense of duty.

Officials appreciated that music, especially singing, offered an easy and accessible exercise. As one singing manual explained, this method did not require much time, since it was meant to be intermingled with a day's program. It followed older patterns of popular culture, rather than resembling the separate music classes of today. An instructor began on a Monday with the words and a tune displayed in front of the students and insisted upon memorization through repetition; then new verses were added each day. Teachers were encouraged to begin lessons at a very young age to take advantage of a child's impressionable nature, and to inspire learning. Experts realized that it was not necessary to read musical notation to sing, but they believed that learning to read the music would create "true musicians."[54] As a result, the children's oral skills improved alongside new visual training, and the printed text did not quickly erase oral tradition.

As Eugen Weber's work has underscored, the cultural integration of France proceeded slowly throughout the nineteenth century, and as late as

1893 one quarter of the French still lived in communes where no French was spoken.[55] But music helped. Singing lessons taught the French language and spread literacy, and patriotic hymns offered an exciting entrée into a broader, explicitly national culture. It became prestigious within individual communities to know the new and exotic language.[56] Teaching anthems in the schools shaped citizens from early on, while also making a nationalist repertoire available for broader community events.

Singing exercises were sometimes linked to physical development in order to improve both the body and soul. As one report proudly preached, singing combined the "culture of the mind, [and] culture of the body, because choral singing, practiced as often as possible in fresh air, represents a model exercise for respiration and physical education."[57] Musical training would also bind citizens together, emotionally and spiritually. In contrast to German songbooks, which as a rule taught four-part harmony, French publications generally offered a single melody and several verses, which developed the skill of unison singing.[58] This training also allowed the older method of improvising harmonies to continue. In 1911, the minister of public instruction proposed that "each of the establishments for boys and girls should have a choir creating a bond of solidarity . . . and giving one voice, one soul to the community."[59] The commitment to healthy collective activity remained strong into the twentieth century.

Not all singing was equally salutary, however, according to government officials and bourgeois commentators of fin-de-siècle France.[60] They showed great concern over the "contamination" of French music by the *cafés-concerts* and over the stubborn persistence of "popular" songs. If everyone was welcome to sing out, not all songs were embraced in school. In 1872, for instance, the minister of public education blamed some of the Paris Commune's "depravity" on "the orgy of songs produced during that epoch" in the *cafés-concerts*.[61] Another author called the *café-concert* a "disgraceful invention which is spreading across our country like leprosy."[62] Reformers wanted lyrics that created the correct political views, and that fostered cultural breeding and good taste. Therefore, they argued for song training at the youngest possible age in order to create musicians with an appreciation *(goût)* for good music.

Adolphe Borchard, in yet another early twentieth-century report, outlined a plan of action to encourage the taste for good music specifically through vocal exercises.[63] No coercion would be necessary, since everyone had a "natural" desire to sing—but, paradoxically, the "natural" had to be carefully reshaped. Borchard found two arenas in which to pursue his agenda: schools and military service. He wrote that, subtly, "the 'music' element would incorporate itself gradually into all age groups of society."[64]

In the end, he warned gravely, if time were not allocated for singing, "France would certainly be condemned to leave the exclusive privilege of this primordial element of education to a very limited elite."

It was to help inoculate small French girls and boys against "popular" mores that some leaders argued that the masses be initiated into "music." This assumed a separate elite category, which they variously described as "serious," "spiritual," or "pure" music.[65] The unfavorable term "popular" seems to have referred most often to the urban lower classes and their musical practices, rather than to peasants. Theorists proposed using the simple and pure "old popular songs" or "old rustic airs" which had sprung "spontaneously from the entrails of the people." But the peasants in the small schools across France still needed musical training—so in one way, authorities were proposing to teach the "popular" to the "popular."[66] Many proponents of musical education saw its benefits for democratic mass politics, but this meant raising up the lower classes, not having the upper classes participate in popular culture.

Officials faced some difficulties finding a sufficient repertoire for the schools to use. Along with condemning the *cafés-concerts*, they grumbled about the Catholic Church's musical inheritance, which, they felt, had not encouraged popular participation, nor was it particularly helpful for instilling republicanism. They turned instead to patriotic "hymns" and the revanchist texts of Paul Déroulède. The centerpiece of song education was the "Marseillaise," an extremely complicated icon which became the focus of republican ideology and was to be heard repeatedly during the Great War.[67] It became especially important as officials tried to make themselves the legitimate heirs to the French Revolution.[68] The "Marseillaise" had had a tortured past since its composition in 1792. Although gradually its association with French military glory began to overshadow its revolutionary roots, workers still sang it subversively in the 1870s. Then in 1879, the republican order again designated it the national anthem. It slowly gained acceptance on the right, as the left turned resolutely to the older "Carmagnole" and the brand new "Internationale." From the 1880s on, "it would be the schools that taught both the French words of the 'Marseillaise,' and the French sentiments—the French identity it stands for."[69] The song represented a powerful integrative tool to overcome disparate regional cultures. Typically, one school songbook began with the "Marseillaise" and gave instructions for school ceremonies to use: "the first [verse], then the verse for children, and finally the verse beginning 'Amour sacré, de la Patrie.'" The first couplet described a *levée en masse*, which was to frame the mobilization for war in 1914. The last verse was to be performed very slowly to affirm that "Under our flags, let Victory / Flow from your male voices / Let your dying enemies / See your triumph and our glory!"[70] Officials hoped young men would take the lyrics to heart.

The ever changing fortunes of the "Marseillaise" owed much to the shifting winds of the French political sphere. But its history also illustrates how individuals reshaped a text in order to appropriate its power for a different cause. Throughout the nineteenth century, when the words of the "Marseillaise" took on revolutionary connotations, it was because of those who sang them. The leaders of the Third Republic attempted to canonize and protect both the text and the circumstances of its performance. The marquis de Farges found himself sentenced to five days in jail and fined fifteen francs in 1883 for having denigrated the "Marseillaise" by calling it a "'filthy' song."[71] As late as 1911, the minister of public instruction was sending out a circular concerning the teaching of the "Marseillaise" in schools. He enclosed examples of both the words and music "according to the version" he wanted followed.[72]

In the twentieth century, the song's meaning and political use were to shift to the right. Even the far right came to accept the "Marseillaise" as its own. Maurice Barrès, a powerful leader of the nationalist right, enthusiastically proposed that "One sings 'La Marseillaise' for its words, of course, but one sings it especially for the mass of emotions that it stirs in our subconscious!"[73] Barrès was to be a visible, fervent supporter of the war effort after 1914.

At the turn of the century, the "Marseillaise" led the canon of patriotic anthems, which included the "Chant du départ" and "Le Régiment de Sambre et Meuse," where ideals such as patriotism, martyrdom for one's country, and liberty prevailed. But Mona Ozouf's study of this period's school textbooks has shown the fine line republican officials walked in trying to promote enthusiastic patriotism without committing to any real military acts of revanchism. They distinguished between ignoble wars and legitimate, defensive ones. An important intersection between the teaching manuals and revanchist songs was "admiration for the heroes of just wars."[74] This attitude was to play a critical role in 1914.

The French soldier's heroism was celebrated most effectively by Paul Déroulède, who became a staple of the school curriculum. Déroulède also shows the complexities officials faced in inculcating patriotism. He was a productive songwriter and poet whose works and reputation crossed social, geographic, and cultural lines; as well as being a controversial leader of the radical nationalist movement in the late-nineteenth century. He helped found the Ligue des Patriotes, which began as neo-Jacobin, republican clubs in the 1880s, but which gradually came to focus intensely on anti-German sentiment, combined with antisemitism.[75] Déroulède's efforts contributed to new methods of mass politics based initially on electoral organizations and then on street actions. These new tactics included two coup d'état attempts which he led against the Third Republic and for which he was exiled.

That such a prominent political figure as Déroulède could also write patriotic lyrics is illustrative of early Third Republic culture. In 1872, he published his *Chants du soldat,* followed by *Nouveaux chants du soldat* in 1875, *Marches et sonneries* in 1881, *Chants patriotiques* in 1882 and *Refrains militaires* in 1889. Déroulède's collections met with great success, especially his *Chants du soldat,* which went through 129 editions between 1872 and 1889.[76] His refrains served as a vital part of his political system of communication. At least one song, "Le Clairon," also gained a foothold in the *cafés-concerts.* His *Chants* became required material in schools following Jules Ferry's proposal in 1881, and school music experts wished other national figures would follow in Déroulède's footsteps.[77] Here, as the historian Raoul Girardet has explained, "All of the themes of nationalism and of Revanchism were found assembled, presented in simple terms, easily accessible to all, and illustrated with striking images: the heroism of the national resistance, the suffering of the lost provinces, the conqueror's ignominy, and the cult of the army."[78] In 1882 Déroulède wrote *De l'éducation militaire* to help transform, in his words, "'the youth of our schools into a legion of warriors.'"[79] He carefully and didactically cultivated the themes of French soldiers' valor and the glory of the French collectivity along highly gendered lines.

Déroulède's appeal was such that the archbishop Sébastien Herscher recalled hearing his words furtively presented by the schoolteacher in Alsace, at a time when singing them in the streets of Colmar courted danger from the German occupiers.[80] Weber has also pointed to Déroulède's widespread popularity, claiming that "by the mid-eighties, we hear the hills of backcountry Cantal echoing no longer with lewd ditties, but with the songs of Déroulède, yelled out by enthusiastic schoolboys."[81] In World War I, Déroulède would become a national hero, as his dream of revanchism became a reality.

The government itself was noticing significant improvements in the country's song culture by the 1890s; the inspector Félix Pécaut maintained that school songs had started to supplant "the bad songs that had been too current in France."[82] But officials still pursued the best possible musical curriculum. They held at least one song competition in the mid-1890s, which Maurice Bouchor won. His lyrics celebrated French rural life with songs about harvest, fishermen, and woods. But the anthology began, of course, with the "Marseillaise," followed by four other patriotic songs. In a purely revanchist spirit, which echoed the marching orders of the "Marseillaise," the "Chant des écoliers français" (the "Song of the French school children") fervently predicted:

Quelque jour,	Some day,
Pour elle emplis d'amour,	Filled with love for her,
Si la Patrie, enfants, nous crie:	If *la Patrie,* children, calls us:
Aux armes!	To arms!
Quelque jour,	Some day,
Pour elle emplis d'amour	Filled with love for her
Nous marcherons au rythme du	We will march to the beat of the drum.
tambour.	
Sonnez, clairons	Ring out, buglers
Et nous marcherons,	And we will march,
Pieux vengeurs de son sang et de ses	Pious avengers of her blood and her
larmes;	tears;
. . . .	. . . .
Nous marcherons pour elle, et nous	We will march for her, and we will
vaincrons!	triumph![83]

This potent mixture of a "joyous death" at a high price was to dominate in August 1914, as the French army mobilized an army of young men who had attended elementary school in the late 1890s and early 1900s. As he surveyed the sharp rise of anti-German jingoism bolstered by French righteousness in 1914, Michel Corday glumly recalled his primary school experiences: "At school they used to make us sing in chorus the song 'Queen of the world, O France, O my country . . .' So, clearly, we were brought up on the idea that France reigned over the world."[84]

The government was not oblivious to its successes. A 1911 report to the Parisian *Conseil municipal* happily touted its progress:

over the past twenty years, the musical movement has developed without respite. The campaigns, vigorously pursued in favor of pure music, . . . have prepared the public, not only to understand the magisterial works of the great classics, but have also nurtured in all social classes a happy emulation and production of often remarkable musical works.[85]

The Paris politicians were not content, however, with their success. After all, government officials were not the only ones aware of singing's political potential, and populist political groups knew they could turn singing practices to their own purposes.

Before the war, the school and *café-concert* repertoires had seeped into rural spaces, where urban song culture merged with deeply rooted regional traditions. Songs moved more easily and quickly than printed texts. In the late nineteenth century, peddlers and *musiciens ambulants* crisscrossed the provinces, carrying sheet music and broadsheets with *images d'Epinal* on which songs accompanied the drawings. Rural inhabitants maintained their own cultural practices, even as a national musical repertoire spread into many secluded corners of France by the 1890s. Older, noncommercial traditions did not simply fall away; for example, work songs were still used right up to the war. The practice of singing for dessert at family feasts continued in many regions in peasant and workers' families.[86] Moreover, peasants and villagers reinterpreted national lyrics and tunes within the context of local interests.

Mona Ozouf has also raised the intriguing case of her grandmother, who could not read French, had never attended school, who fought to keep her regional traditions, but who could sing the revanchist tune "Vous n'aurez pas l'Alsace et la Lorraine." Considering all of these obstacles, Ozouf asked "Who, therefore, told her that France was her country? From whom did she learn to sing 'Vous n'aurez pas l'Alsace et la Lorraine'? No public teacher, in any case, and no Jacobin official."[87] Songs, in particular, had a fluidity that helped them cross barriers such as illiteracy.

Small towns also had their own musical institutions, such as choral societies (*orphéons*) and bands. In the years leading up to World War I, these musical groups orchestrated the political map in the smallest communes.[88] They did not simply offer entertainment or a social activity for townspeople, they also participated in inharmonious political battles on the local terrain. Thus, in each village at least two choruses or bands existed—one for the left and the other for the right. To play in *la musique,* as they were often called, was an act of political allegiance.

Just prior to World War I, one particularly bitter debate brought the politics of the center down to the local level. As part of the separation of Church and State in 1905, a set of controversial laws had declared that religious ceremonies or processions could not be held on public property or even in public view, reflecting the powerful anticlerical focus of republicanism. Opponents of the law, in particular religious societies and conservatives, resented not being able to use church yards or village streets, especially while the Republic's leaders "tolerated revolutionary demonstrations where the Red flag was solemnly paraded accompanied by the singing of the 'Internationale' and the 'Carmagnole'—not just around a private monument, but in the streets of an entire village."[89] This controversy was continually played out in musical terms.[90]

Throughout 1913 and the first half of 1914, the Church, Catholic societies, and the political right sponsored processions across France to challenge the laws. The organizations characterized themselves as victims of "the basest violence by boorish anticlericalism."[91] At the rallies, according to the police and newspaper reports, even greater emphasis was placed on music and singing than on any speeches. In June 1913, for example, led by their band, "singing hymns and reclaiming the right to process," the Catholic societies Saint-Michel and Jeanne d'Arc marched through Cambrai toward the cathedral.[92] Not surprisingly, they clashed with police and finally had to disperse. Another religious procession, also in the North, was scheduled for September 1913, and was reported as usual to the minister of the interior. This time it inspired plans for a counter-demonstration entitled a "commemorative festival honoring the martyrs executed by the inquisitorial Church," arranged by the "department's groups for free thought." Both sides announced that their bands would participate and urged followers to prepare their repertoires. The bands, song selections, and participants represented two opposing factions that claimed the same public space both physically and politically. Their choice of music rallied the forces and helped define their position. Typically, ensembles of socialists favored the "Internationale," but France also had a deep reserve of anticlerical songs going back to the Revolution. The songs provoked opponents and the police equally well and encompassed a participatory mode of expression that helped generate publicity.

These processions and fights embodied the constant struggle over the appropriation of symbols. Republican leaders and members of the far right both claimed Joan of Arc, for instance, as their own source of inspiration.[93] But for the radical right, Joan of Arc was a religious icon and could not represent the Republic, and religious hymns had to take precedence over the "Godless" socialist anthems. Until the war, however, the State held the line, and public affairs progressed without religious help.

While the smaller towns experienced cacophonous public demonstrations, Paris partook in musical politics on an even larger scale. In the three or four years before World War I, a series of international diplomatic crises and a menacing arms race led to both a resurgence of revanchist nationalism and a vocal antimilitarist movement.[94] At the considerable antiwar rallies of 1911 and 1912, with which we began this chapter, tens of thousands of workers and other antimilitarists intoned Montéhus's "Gloire au 17e," the "Carmagnole," and the "Internationale." The working-class movement based its position on collective resistance, believing that soldiers should not fire on workers, that workers should not fight as soldiers, and that a general strike would cripple any government decision to go to war. In this case, a song such as Montéhus's "Gloire au 17e" had moved from the performer's repertoire to the audience's, and from the enclosed space of the *café-concert* to the streets.

Having developed during past revolutions and in the *goguettes,* the working-class musical repertoire emphasized the power of songs to educate and to subvert authority.[95] Certain songs had had remarkable longevity in France, such as the "Carmagnole" and "Ça ira." One Parisian testified to their continuing power in 1899, when he expressed his intense fear on encountering a disorderly parade of workers in the Place de la Nation, waving flags and singing "Ça ira":

Ça ira, ça ira, ça ira!	It's gonna be okay, be okay, be okay!
Les bourgeois à la lanterne,	To the lamp-post with the bourgeois,
Les bourgeois on les pendra!	The bourgeois, let's string 'em up!
Et si pendr'on ne peut pas,	And if we don't get to hang 'em,
On leur foutra la gueule en bas.	We'll flatten the bastards out.[96]

The original version had endorsed hanging members of the aristocracy. Now, the bourgeoisie had become the enemy, as these lyrics remained living, forceful expressions, with a frighteningly "sinister rhythm." The workers used their tactics self-consciously, according to Jeanne Bouvier's description of the same incident written from a laborer's point of view: "In the course of the march, all the unionists sang revolutionary tunes . . . We understood that the good bourgeoisie would not be very reassured before this column which hurled bloody songs, like during the Great Revolution."[97] Clearly, one should not take the workers' apparent acquiescence in August 1914 and read backward to diminish their sense of activism or the fear they engendered in the prewar period.

In addition, workers' singing groups continued the tradition of the *goguettes,* writing new material and passing around new tunes. The best-known cadre was the Muse Rouge, but there were others, such as the Chansonniers Révolutionnaires, which offered "hours of song among comrades."[98] As Pierre Aubéry recalled in his semi-autobiographical article "Poésies et chansons populaires de la Commune," "we sang in the workshop and at cooperative fetes, artisanal songs, satiric and political tunes and sentimental songs."[99] Labor newspapers also provided a song of the week written by a regular columnist for the front page. These songs normally relied upon the workers' library of tunes, using, for example Aristide

Bruant's "Belleville et Ménilmontant." Sometimes the melodies themselves could be particularly significant. Gaston Couté, for example, constructed a new song for *La Guerre sociale* in May 1911 using the tune from Déroulède's "Le Clairon." Not only did readers know the melody, but the new words played with the original lyrics to intensify the political message. Hence, Déroulède's "young soldier" no longer fought the Prussians, but had to defend "the property / of the rich proprietors," land which was soaked with his brothers' blood. And, instead of the wounded bugler sounding the military attack—a dramatic moment in the original song— the "brave young lad" (and the performer) stayed silent in protest.[100]

The main socialist anthem, however, was the "Internationale," written by Eugène Pottier in 1871 and set to music in 1888. In his lyrics, Pottier portrayed the State, business proprietors, and the law as the enemies, and he offered the suggestion that one should fire upon military commanders. "Peace between us, war to the tyrants! / Let us apply the strike to the armies."[101] Pottier had also, however, demonstrated the possible coexistence of a revolutionary critique and patriotism. Although he had been an antimilitarist during the Second Empire, he became very nationalistic in 1870, composing such songs as "Défends-toi Paris."[102]

Workers ritually concluded their meetings with the "Internationale" and delighted in pelting government officials with the lyrics at every opportunity.[103] Bouvier admitted that at her earliest meetings she could barely understand the socialist ideas but was thrilled to show her support by singing:

I didn't know exactly what everything meant, but in order to have the air of a true unionist, I applauded as strongly and with as much conviction as those around me. When the meeting ended all of those present intoned the "Internationale" and, like them, I sang at the top of my voice:

Debout les damnés de la terre!
Debout les forçats de la faim!

Then I returned home, humming the "Internationale."[104]

For Bouvier, the act of singing was part of her conscious and political identification of herself as working class.

Even after the socialists' unification in 1905, the leadership of the French left suffered from serious divisions.[105] It was a public rally replete with songs that brought them together, at least temporarily, in 1911. The September 24, 1911, antimilitarist manifestation represented a cooperative effort between the largest trade unions and the Socialist Party.[106] The labor leaders had originally planned to hold a massive march through the streets of Paris by bringing together all sorts of labor and radical groups. On

September 22, however, the prime minister issued an order banning any demonstrations on public thoroughfares, contradicting, at least in this instance, the far right's complaints about government permissiveness toward the left. But the organizers did not acquiesce. They simply shifted the rally to the Aéro-Park in the 19th *arrondissement* of Paris and declared that "the people still have the right to express and to demonstrate their opinion," which in this popular world included singing.[107]

Nonetheless, the delegates were forced to behave themselves while on city streets, since the police came very well prepared. As the protesters reached the park's entrance, the crowd began the "Internationale."[108] The chorus would stop, according to a newspaper report, whenever soldiers or guards approached, and they would then yell "Boo! Boo! Murderers! Murderers! 17th! 17th!"[109] "When the troops had passed, the 'Internationale' burst forth again more beautiful." Other songs abounded, most notably "La Carmagnole," "Gloire au 17e," and "Le Drapeau rouge." The organizers claimed success, and the press also believed that aside from the cooperation among the leaders, it was "the cohesion of the Paris popular classes" that gave hope, and here marching and singing were credited. The future simply required the populace to "resonate in unison."[110]

The government, of course, could not let the socialists' repertoire go unchallenged. In order to promote public support for the three-year military service law (which raised the required term from two to three years), the minister of war sent military ensembles through the Parisian streets playing patriotic anthems. As one foreign correspondent reminisced:

The best bands of the French Army went through the summer dusk playing stirring airs; with the first distant bourdon of the drum the streets filled with the dead-leaf patter made by all the little sons of all the concierges and the tradespeople running to the main road, and the more leisurely tread of their parents. When the band had passed, back they all came, and scraps of talk about "les trois ans" floated up to the open windows.[111]

This political entertainment stimulated discussion, if not conversion. The socialists, in turn, refused to relinquish their aural space and tried to stop the military's playing, but the police made arrests and, in this particular case, the revanchist "Sambre et Meuse" prevailed.

Finally, let us return to the demonstrations with which we began this chapter, since it was during this same turbulent year that Paris witnessed a different set of demonstrations, as groups on the far right fought to close Henri Bernstein's play at the Comédie-Française. Night after night for two weeks, the political troops used antisemitic refrains including "La Youpignole" to provoke police and to gain support.[112] On February 27, after being dispersed, the protesters regrouped at the statue of Joan of Arc, whom they called "the liberator" and acclaimed "frenetically." Each night their numbers grew, from one hundred activists to three thousand. The performances were finally stopped on March 4, after Bernstein had met with both the prefect of police and the prime minister.

The demonstrations had been organized this time by the Action Française, led by Léon Daudet, Maurice Pujo, and the Camelots du Roi, a monarchist youth group. Once again, these associations had an extensive musical repertoire, which served as weapons in their battles against the police and the political left. Their selections included the "Marseillaise anti-juive," which was sung as part of the Catholic antisemitic movement.[113] As political tactics, these songs took advantage of the musical literacy of various social groups. Many of the songs of the Camelots du Roi, such as "Quand on pendra la gueuse au Réverbère," also attacked the Republic, referring to "her" as a "whore." The lyrics proclaimed:

Vive la Patrie!	Long live *la Patrie*!
Meur' la Maçonnerie,	Death to the Freemasons,
La gueuse est malade et nous aurons sa peau!	The whore is sick and we will have her skin!
Nous te ferons de dignes funérailles	We will give you a worthy funeral
Fille sans entrailles	Gutless girl
Pour venger l'drapeau!	To avenge the flag!
Cam'lots du Roi, tous présents, tous debout!	Camelots du Roi, all present, all standing up![114]

Other Camelots lyrics portrayed the Jews controlling the police and army and starving the workers; only "our king" could lead the French out of their difficulties.[115] These particular protests took place both inside and outside the theater, but it was the street riots that drew the most publicity and frightened residents. Aristide Briand's government fell in the midst of this conflict on February 28 and barely received equal time in the press.

During the years leading up to the war and even in July 1914, the State was caught in the middle of many deeply divisive issues. It looked as though the French populace, increasingly politicized and splintered, would choose not to fight a war. Given the breadth of their musical education and singing practices, the French would have several repertoires from which to choose. Would they be willing to fight in August 1914, and to which repertoires would they turn at that moment?

CHAPTER TWO

A Chorus in Unison
The Ritual of National Mobilization

In the years leading up to World War I, France experienced a nationalist revival, the seeds of which had been planted by the Third Republic's educational projects. Its political culture, however, also suffered from deep chasms, for example between radical nationalists and antimilitarists, and between Catholics and socialists. Consequently, in envisaging a declaration of war, officials had serious concerns. Threatened by the antimilitarist movement, they predicted that 13 percent of the conscripts would desert during a general mobilization. The government prepared by drawing up the infamous Carnet B, a list of "subversive" figures who were to be arrested when mobilization was declared, including the socialist musical performer Gaston Montéhus.[1]

Why then did such a divided, contentious populace create a cultural and political *union sacrée* in August 1914? Citizens in big and small towns all over France entered the war through a national ritual that helped ensure success. This was a "collective or communal enactment" whose goals were to put a united country on a wartime footing and to propel soldiers to the front. The ritual expressed a nationalist ideology, while also actively propelling the mobilization along the right track.[2]

This ritual of mobilization rested on a nationalist cosmology, embedded in French national history and promoted in the *cafés-concerts* and schools of the early Third Republic.[3] This set of beliefs provided for the French people's response to an enemy invasion. It imagined war as fast, mobile, and offensive—a view shared by both the general public and military leaders. As Eric Leed has argued, "those who marched onto European battlefields in 1914 had a highly specific and concrete image of what war meant, an image that was anchored in the past and in their culture."[4] The French's expectations were built on memories and tales of previous French military mobilizations—in particular, the *levée en masse* of 1793 and the war of 1870. Citizens found a script for this ritual in nationalist and revanchist songs, most notably the "Chant du départ" and the "Marseillaise."

While based on historical examples and old texts, the ritual also adapted itself to early-twentieth-century political culture. France had to transcend specific divisions at this critical moment. War placed an intense demand on cultural values and forms, and as valences went into flux, images and meanings were reinterpreted. In the process, a wartime ethos formed in which symbols from the political right took center stage. Singing represented the most complicated instance of the war's reshaping of French culture, with individual and group participation at all levels. The "Marseillaise" was a good example. The national anthem had deep patriotic roots, but in the immediate prewar period it had been rejected by the left. With the mobilization for war, the "Marseillaise" was to ring out across the political and geographic map. Both civilians and soldiers went to war armed with their musical practices, so it is not surprising that singing occurred at all stages of the mobilization. Let us look first at the immediate transition from peace to war and the way in which this ritual worked.

The Mobilization for War

The authorities' worries in the summer of 1914 seemed justified. As July drew to a close, Paris experienced widespread discord, which swirled around the trial and acquittal of Madame Caillaux, reflecting the ongoing acrimony between the left and right.[5] But growing apprehension over the possibility of war and continuing hostility toward the army also flared up. On July 25, as they crossed a boulevard in the center of Paris, members of the 5th Infantry regiment found themselves serenaded by "thousands of people hanging out of windows and sitting at cafés" with the "Marseillaise"—just as groups of "revolutionaries" shouted "Long live Caillaux!" and "Down with the three-year [law]!" while fighting with members of the Action Française.[6] *Le Figaro* calmly remarked that "the sounds of war have naturally had their repercussions in the course of this small demonstration." Other "regrettable" incidents occurred in front of the German embassy, at the offices of the newspaper *Le Matin,* and in the Place de la Concorde at the statue of Strasbourg, where young men willfully blocked traffic and sang patriotic hymns. The far right chose to vocally support the military and the possible war with Germany.

Just two nights later, on July 27, as many as three thousand men reportedly from working-class districts (Belleville and the 18th, 19th and 20th *arrondissements*) poured into the Place de la République singing the

"Internationale" and crying "Long live peace!" "Long live Caillaux!" and, ironically, "Long live Jaurès."[7] In this instance, a riot ensued when the police charged, and "thousands of cries" of "Down with war" could be heard. The rightist opposition, of course, could not remain silent and aggressively countered with a song entitled "Conspuez, Jaurès, conspuez!" using "a well-known tune," as they battled the revolutionaries in several locations across the city.[8] As the diplomatic crisis deepened, the police took no chances and tightened their street patrols. Even so, other popular protests occurred across France right up to mobilization, despite the labor leadership's great hesitation to call for a general strike. *La Guerre sociale* also asked for calm and reminded the public of the workers' deep patriotism.[9] In spite of this appeal, the political constituencies remained sharply divided, and government worries grew.

On the fateful day of general mobilization, Saturday, August 1, 1914, however, crowds filled the boulevards and railroad stations of Paris singing the "Marseillaise" and shouting "To Berlin." At 4:15 P.M. the alarm (*tocsin*) sounded, and posters pasted on the walls of post offices and city halls declared, "By decree of the President of the Republic, the mobilization of the Army and Navy is ordered. . . . The first day of mobilization is Sunday, August 2, 1914."[10] People gathered together to receive the news and patriotic demonstrations followed. Orchestras in cafés worked unremittingly to satisfy customers' demands for the French and allies' national anthems, while throngs of people spilled out into the streets and joined in the choruses. One also heard the "Chant du départ," "Le Régiment de Sambre et Meuse," and "Alsace et Lorraine," in support of *la Patrie,* the army, and Joan of Arc battling the German Huns.[11] Moreover, ever ready for the latest eventualities, "street singers 'launch[ed]' a brand new patriotic song" which caught on with passersby who sang "the refrain in chorus."[12] Likewise, in a small town like Etretat the citizens experienced the announcement of mobilization together, as they gathered at the town hall to confirm the rumors. There they awaited the arrival of the government official who drove into town, reported to the mayor, and then posted the *affiche* on the outside of city hall. There was a momentary pause and then a man led the crowd in "Vive la France! Vive la République."[13] Across France, old tunes mixed with new, as the "sublime" and historic moment swept away dissent, at least in public spaces, and citizens chose to join the chorus in support of the government's actions. When the call-up of almost two million men requiring 4,278 trains actually began, it went far more smoothly than anyone had expected; the Carnet B was never used and few arrests had to be made. In the end, the actual level of deserters was a mere 1.5 percent.[14]

Why had this happened so easily, and where had the political divisions gone? The mobilization's success was due, in part, to the effectiveness of the national ritual that people *performed* in individual villages and urban centers. It was ordered by a sequence of events based on government orders and historical example—both officially explicit rules and a culturally implicit script. This is not simply because the moment of August 1914 caught the public's imagination and was reproduced in personal accounts, but also because the actual events followed these set steps.

The ritual's first stage was the posting of the solemn mobilization order followed by the sounding of the *berloque* (usually church bells, or sometimes a siren)—a symbol of the community at large and an intensifying tool.[15] Inhabitants then congregated in public sites to hear and react to the news. Memoirs, in a seemingly compulsory fashion, tell of the posting, or they note where different family members were when the bells rang out.[16] In describing the moment in Etretat, *Le Figaro* said tellingly, if somewhat condescendingly, "From instinct, without a word of orders, all the ordinary people moved slowly toward city hall."[17] As the ritual continued the would-be soldiers consulted their mobilization instruction books to see when and where to report and prepared to leave; career officers related having received yellow telegrams with instructions as simple as "Prenez mesures M" (Take measures M).[18]

This mobilization for war converged on urban public spaces such as town halls, public squares, or train stations, where impromptu performances of patriotic tunes unified the crowds and celebrated the French soldier.[19] Ritual requires public attention. In Paris, for example, on August 1, young men reportedly flooded into the Place de la République, surrounded the monument there, and covered it with French, Russian, and British flags. They then sang the "Marseillaise." Thus, a site that had been a bastion of workers' political culture was renationalized, and the newspaper report of the act carried its message to an even broader public.[20] Theaters and especially cafés also hosted patriotic demonstrations pulling bystanders into the process and then sending them forth to spread the word. The gathering and singing in public squares and train stations was not strictly a Parisian event, as much of the country agreed to commit itself to the war. In the town of Angers (Maine-et-Loire), the prefect described "a thousand people [who] poured through the streets singing 'la Marseillaise'" and shouting "Long live the Army."[21] Charles-Émile Nantois's daily journal entry for Sunday, August 2, besides noting his migraine, reported the following events surrounding the general mobilization:

We played a concert this evening at 6:00 in the center square. A civilian read the dispatch that he had just received. The crowd applauded, then the band played "la Marseillaise," "Sambre et Meuse" and "le Chant du départ"; we left playing the "Marche du 32e" [of the 32nd Regiment] amidst the crowd's enthusiasm. Major Maury proudly watched us pass.[22]

These public places included older sites, such as public squares and city halls, as well as the newer train stations of the Third Republic. They were the logical meeting places for the community, representing focal points of communal civic and national life.[23] The mobilization defined the national community as a whole. Individuals joined public gatherings as French citizens, brought together by the nation's crisis.

As the participants passed through the ritual, they began dividing into civilians and soldiers. This process continued throughout August with the departure ceremonies that sent combatants off. Corporal Emile Passinge recalled the mixture of soldiers and civilians singing together in the town square—in this instance, they sang "Le Salut au drapeau" and the ubiquitous "Marseillaise," as they proceeded from the town square to the train station.[24] Another musician described his experiences at Montpellier, where troops departed with an enormous crowd, the tricolor's presentation, the "Marseillaise," shouts of inspiration, and finally the farewell, this time to the sound of "Sambre et Meuse."[25] In the face of the German army on French soil, and with fervent hopes for a short war, the singing lent cohesion to the national body and encouraged enthusiasm. Civilians celebrated the soldiers, serenading them at their embarkation.[26]

Throughout all of these examples runs the thread of collective actions, and more specifically, participatory singing. In Paris, particular songs were "demanded"; people stood up for national anthems; and everyone sang the chorus of the "Marseillaise." Prefect reports sent to Paris from the departments described patriotic singing in big and little towns from many geographically distant areas, including the Hautes-Pyrénées, Basses-Alpes, Pas-de-Calais, and Aube.[27] *Le Figaro* also reported on a patriotic demonstration in Poitiers, for example, where the crowd not only sang the "Marseillaise" but also the Russian anthem, which was followed by cries of "Long live Russia" and "Long live England."[28]

The significance here is not just in the act of singing, but also in which songs were sung. Examining the choices gives us a clue as to what people thought they were doing, as well as revealing underlying beliefs.[29] The most popular song was obviously the "Marsellaise." In August 1914, it resembled a truly national anthem, cutting across regional, generational, and class barriers. The other song to have achieved anthem, or "hymn," status was the "Chant du départ." Both had come from the French Revolution, whereas songs such as "Le Régiment de Sambre et Meuse" and "Alsace et Lorraine" represented the revanchist repertoire. The scenario that all of these songs shared is of a national mobilization in the face of danger. Each song stressed the need to do one's duty for France, each asserted that a war could be justified, and each acclaimed the French soldier's impetuous power and effectiveness. The revanchist texts expressed French war aims in righteously reclaiming Alsace-Lorraine. Thus, lyrics helped transmit a national cosmology, which included a tradition of *levées en masse* as the proper national reaction to invasion.

This moment was immediately historicized, because it paralleled what ancestors had done before and had sung about doing again.[30] It invoked previous "great events" mythically and historically, back to the raising of the revolutionary armies in 1792–1793 and the beginning of the Franco-Prussian War in 1870. The historian Jean-Paul Bertaud has described ceremonies in both villages and in Paris in 1793 which included a proclamation, the community's assembly, the singing of the "Carmagnole," "Ça ira," and the "Marseillaise" (Fig. 2), and then the marshaling of draftees. At the soldiers' departure, officials had created "a civic festival, well organized to touch popular feeling and promote a collective psychology."[31]

Although by the early twentieth century the military's role in mobilizing troops was much more structured and better formulated, local events still kept a sense of popular spontaneity. A letter to the newspaper *L'Echo de Paris* put it quite plainly in describing the events of Sunday, August 2: "The calling of the battalion to arms. The commander bid farewell to the population of P . . . The raising of the flag. The presentation of colors and at 5:30, the batallion filed out. Embarkation at 6:30. Departure. We sang, we cried."[32]

The accounts of the 1914 scenes and songs were also strikingly reminiscent of the reports of July 1870. In the French nationalist ideology, 1870 had been about German, or more precisely Prussian, aggression led by a king named "Guillaume," against a defensive France. The events of 1914 called forth the same lyrics, cries and graffiti, and, as the historian Yves Pourcher has noted, no one thought to shout "A Vienne," even though the French were also at war in 1914 with the Austro-Hungarian empire.[33] Moreover, in examining morale in July 1870, the historian Stéphane Audoin-Rouzeau has uncovered instance after instance of the singing of the "Marseillaise," either as troops departed for the front or as they were greeted by civilians along the way. One blacksmith, for example, described his journey east to the Franco-Prussian War: "All the people called out to us: good luck my good friends. All along the way we sang 'the Marseillaise' at the top of our lungs . . . Finally we embarked at the train station of Laval on August 1 at noon. The village band led us there playing the 'Marseillaise.' . . ."[34] The geographic direction, choice of song, and even the date echoes.[35]

In 1914, many individuals still had strong memories of the last conflict with Germany.[36] Others, including the soldiers who marched east, had the

2.

Que veut cette horde d'esclaves
De traîtres, de rois conjurés?
Pour qui ces ignobles entraves,
Ces fers dès longtemps préparés? (Bis)
Français, pour nous, ah! quel outrage
Quels transports, il doit exciter!
C'est nous qu'on ose méditer
De rendre à l'antique esclavage!

Aux armes, &ᵃ

3.

Quoi! des cohortes étrangères
Feraient la loi dans nos foyers!
Quoi! des phalanges mercenaires
Terrasseraient nos fiers guerriers! (Bis)
Grand Dieu! par des mains enchaînées
Nos fronts sous le joug se ploiraient!
De vils despotes deviendraient
Les maîtres de nos destinées!

Aux armes, &ᵃ

4.

Tremblez, tyrans, et vous perfides.
L'opprobre de tous les partis:
Tremblez, vos projets parricides
Vont enfin recevoir leur prix? (Bis)
Tout est soldat pour vous combattre,
S'ils tombent, nos jeunes héros,
La terre en produit de nouveaux
Contre vous, tout prêts à se battre!

Aux armes, &ᵃ

5.

Français, en guerriers magnanimes
Portez ou retenez vos coups;
Epargnez ces tristes victimes
A regret s'armant contre nous. (Bis)
Mais ce despote sanguinaire
Mais les complices de Bouillé,
Tous ces tigres qui sans pitié,
Déchirent le sein de leur mère!

Aux armes, &ᵃ

6.

AMOUR SACRÉ de la Patrie,
Conduis, soutiens nos bras vengeurs
Liberté, liberté chérie,
Combats avec tes défenseurs: (Bis)
Sous nos drapeaux que la victoire
Accoure à tes mâles accents:
Que tes ennemis expirants
Voient ton triomphe et notre gloire!

Aux armes, &ᵃ

7

Nous entrerons dans la carrière
Quand nos aînés n'y seront plus
Nous y trouverons leur poussière
Et la trace de leurs vertus! (Bis)
Bien moins jaloux de leur survivre
Que de partager leur cercueil,
Nous aurons le sublime orgueil
De les venger, ou de les suivre!

Aux armes, &ᵃ

Figure 3. Songsheet, "Le Chant du départ." Courtesy of the Préfecture de Police.

‑çais doit vi‑‑vre pour el‑le, Pour elle, un Français doit mou‑rir!

‑çais doit vi‑‑vre pour el‑le, Pour elle, un Français doit mou‑rir!

‑çais doit vi‑‑vre pour el‑le, Pour elle, un Français doit mou‑rir!

UNE MÈRE DE FAMILLE

De nos yeux maternels, ne craignez pas les larmes,
Loin de nous, de lâches douleurs!
Nous devons triompher quand vous prenez les armes,
C'est aux rois à verser des pleurs,
Nous vous avons donné la vie,
Guerriers, elle n'est plus à vous;
Tous vos jours sont à la patrie;
Elle est votre mère avant nous.

Chœur des mères de famille: La République...

UNE ÉPOUSE

Partez vaillants époux, les combats sont vos fêtes;
Partez modèles des guerriers,
Nous cueillerons des fleurs et en ceindre vos têtes,
Nos mains tresseront vos lauriers,
Et si le temple de mémoire
S'ouvrait à vos mânes vainqueurs,
Nos voix chanteront votre gloire,
Nos flancs porteront vos vengeurs.

Chœur des épouses: La République...

DEUX VIEILLARDS

Que le fer paternel arme la main des braves,
Songez à nous au Champ de Mars;
Consacrez dans le sang des rois et des esclaves
Le fer béni par vos vieillards;
Et rapportant sous la chaumière
Des blessures et des vertus,
Venez fermer notre paupière
Quand les tyrans ne seront plus.

Chœur des vieillards: La République...

UNE JEUNE FILLE

Et nous, sœurs des héros, nous, qui de l'hymenée,
Ignorons les aimables nœuds,
Si, pour s'unir un jour à notre destinée,
Les citoyens forment des vœux,
Qu'ils reviennent dans nos murailles,
Beaux de gloire et de liberté,
Et que leur sang dans les batailles
Ait coulé pour l'égalité.

Chœur des jeunes filles: La République...

UN ENFANT

De Barra, de Viala le sort nous fait envie,
Ils sont morts mais ils ont vaincu,
Le lâche accablé d'ans n'a point connu la vie
Qui meurt pour le peuple a vécu,
Vous êtes vaillants, nous le sommes;
Guidez-nous contre les tyrans
Les Républicains sont des hommes,
Les esclaves sont des enfants.

Chœur des enfants: La République...

TROIS GUERRIERS

Sur le fer, devant Dieu, nous jurons à nos pères,
A nos épouses, à nos sœurs,
A nos représentants, à nos fils, à nos mères,
D'anéantir les oppresseurs,
En tous lieux dans la nuit profonde,
Plongeant l'infâme royauté,
Les Français donneront au monde
Et la paix et la liberté!

Chœur général: La République...

memory of 1870 transmitted within their families. One officer, the famous modernist playwright Jean Giraudoux, who led troops in Alsace during 1914, told of how the soldiers under his command traded advice on what to wear, carry, or save, gleaned from their fathers' experiences in 1870.[37] Others made the historical comparison explicit in their writing.[38] One also finds myths at work in the slippage between symbols and events. In 1914, some of the previous war's tales reappeared as contemporary news stories. This occurred, for instance, with the mythic story of a German soldier who supposedly bayoneted a small French boy because he was playing with a wooden gun. It was reported in newspapers, then was quickly made into songs, which spread the tale further afield.[39]

For most people, however, it was the songs that provided an historical script, songs learned in schools and cafés over the years. Structured, repetitive, and internally organized, a ritual has much in common with songs, and their form and content explains why songs would be the chosen vehicles of the mobilization ritual.[40] The "Marseillaise" (fig. 2), the "Chant du départ" (fig. 3), and the "Régiment de Sambre et Meuse" (app. fig. 1) all have an alternating verse and refrain, where the verses impart specific, complicated information, and the rousing refrains presume a chorus singing the main message. In addition, they are martial sounding, partly because they are in 4/4 time and rely heavily on triads mimicking military calls. The refrains return after only eight lines, which allowed people to join in in unison, even if this was the only part they knew. Moreover, these songs and others represented singing itself as contributing to success, as in the opening line of the "Chant du départ," "La victoire en chantant" (singing our way to victory).

Such songs often began with the people rising up or coming together, then they identified a vague, but ferocious enemy, and reinforced the French commitment, which included dying if necessary. As the first couplet of the "Chant du départ" fittingly announced: "from the Nord to the Midi, the warlike trumpeter / has sounded the hour of combat / Tremble enemies of France, . . . The sovereign people are advancing." Harmonically, they began in a major key, shifted to minor to represent the foe, and then moved back to the major key for the refrain. The classic chorus of the "Marseillaise" called citizens to arms to face the imminent danger of the "impure blood"—alternating between second person imperative and the inclusive first person plural.[41] It gave orders and encouraged action. The refrain for the "Chant du départ" also uses first person plural, beginning with "The Republic calls us / Let us conquer or let us die" (La République nous appelle / Sachons vaincre ou sachons périr). But it then shifts to a gendered message with "A Frenchman should live for her, / For her, a Frenchman should die!" (Un Français doit vivre pour elle, / Pour elle, un Français doit mourir!), which is then re-peated. Again, this is a six-line refrain with only four lines to remember.[42] In both the music and words, there is a tension between the French as an inclusive and genderless category, and the role of male soldiers.

The lyrics also prescribed generational and familial roles. For example, the famous "Alsace et Lorraine" ended with the lines: "To the cry of de-liverance thrown up by *la Patrie* / Men, children, women, we will re-spond."[43] In the "Chant du départ," headings designated that each verse be sung by a different singer or group: a deputy of the people, a mother, old men, a child, a wife, a sister, and three warriors *(trois guerriers)*. These verses delineated appropriate behavior for each group. The mothers, for in-stance, handed over their sons, and wives vowed to remember and honor husbands. All of these songs also celebrated "our proud warriors," a part of the national cosmology seen in the school curriculum and revanchist lyrics. Most verses invited a wide variety of participants within the national fam-ily, but without mentioning social categories such as peasants or workers. These were subsumed.

But what can all these incidents of collective singing tell us about the controversial question of how much enthusiasm the French demonstrated for the war? Eric Leed has argued adamantly that Europeans welcomed the war with alacrity as a release from boredom and as a solution to many polit-ical and social problems, and he has provided striking testimony of elation and euphoria. Robert Wohl's study of French intellectuals lends support to Leed's ideas.[44] Much of their evidence, however, deals specifically with the reactions of the upper class and intellectuals in urban settings. These sing-ing practices illustrate, however, that the manifestations of excitement were not limited to the realm of high culture. The "Chant du départ" and "Al-sace et Lorraine" were parts of a more general popular culture.

Nevertheless, the work of Jean-Jacques Becker, one of the foremost French World War I scholars, has cautioned us against exaggerating the ea-gerness in rural areas. He has concluded that the reaction to the war was less one of enthusiasm than of resolve.[45] Support for the war did increase over the first two weeks of August, but even then, Becker argues, the French ma-jority was not wildly impassioned. Many provincials could imagine the po-tential price—if only in the loss of crucial man and horsepower just before the start of harvest—but they also believed in their duty to fight against the Germans on French soil.[46] Becker has provided written observations by *in-tendants* and schoolteachers in the provinces who saw the singing as an at-tempt to cover feelings of fear and sadness. One teacher from Aubeterre in-sisted that "the songs of those who wished to 'show off' sounded false," and were only meant "to hide their emotions."[47] An *intendant* in Mansle also believed that the singing and joking of the new soldiers helped them avoid feelings such as fear, and that the "noisy gaiety" was, in fact, artificial.[48]

It is very difficult to interpret these and other accounts. But to argue that songs just disguised negative feelings is too limited a reading, as is drawing too sharp a separation between enthusiasm and earnest resolve. Much of what occurred in August 1914 might be viewed as having happened spontaneously. The demonstrations were not directed or orchestrated by officials, nor were they limited to certain groups. Official preparations had been made for the notification and military instructions, but overall the government found itself fully occupied with confronting the fast-approaching German army. Moreover, as it was August, most theaters and music halls were closed for the traditional summer break. A few, including the Petit Casino, did stay open and gave patriotic programs, but these were rare after August 3.[49]

If we take the process of mobilization seriously, then the question of spontaneity and public emotions becomes a much more complicated issue. As a "culturally constructed expressive act," a ritual differs from ordinary life, and brings expectations of certain responses. It "separates the private emotions of the actors from their commitment to a public morality."[50] The French understood the rules to be followed, and this included displaying certain emotions. In fact, some witnesses or participants described people as hiding their "true" feelings. Both passion and resolve were prescribed as appropriate behaviors for public spaces, a prescription reinforced by the media.

Some newspaper accounts and memoirs commented specifically on a unique blend of jingoism and calm. As the manager of the Opéra-Comique put it, "I have found Paris effervescent and grave at the same time."[51] He went on to explain that for the moment, any talk of the theater or of "la musique" (classical music) was "unseemly"; "only the 'Marseillaise' was recognized."[52] Likewise, *Le Figaro* commented on the August 1 crowd's "composure" and the need not to cry or laugh.[53] An American correspondent who arrived in Paris at the Gare du Montparnasse on that Sunday recorded his impressions in his diary: "Enthusiasm, confusion, and lamentation are the three words which best describe what I saw. But enthusiasm predominated."[54] The latter, he noted, was especially true at the train stations, in cafés, and along the boulevards—that is, in the most communal places.

People's participation in the national ritual, as both performers and listeners, brought the French cosmology of war to life.[55] The French were communicating with themselves. During the early days of August, for instance, the typical pattern in Paris was for the day to begin quietly, after which demonstrations would escalate and spread. Misgivings did not preclude someone's participation in a patriotic demonstration. And even if the optimism covered fears, it could still mobilize, especially when one considers the intense visceral effects of this collective singing.

Singing was an act that could transform doubts into confidence. Singing together, often in unison, served to intensify the experience, and both the bells (or alarms) and the songs activated "the extraordinary."[56] To give just one example, Fernand Darde described watching a battalion leave Cherbourg on August 5, 1914, with a rendition of the "Marseillaise" and no tears. Somewhat surprised, he remarked on the sense of complete unity ("pas un cri discordant"), describing how even he got carried away and found himself singing the "Marseillaise."[57] The singing brought cohesion based on a sense of belonging and purpose.

Some historians have also stressed the fact that newspapers may have been using isolated incidents of enthusiasm to portray a general feeling, leading scholars to overestimate the level of excitement. However, these reports, like the actual singing, not just reflected the mood but also created it. Interest in knowing public opinion was particularly high at that moment, and individuals read newspapers avidly, not just for news but for impressions of the national whole. Depictions of animation and unity spilled off the pages of the major Parisian daily papers in the first days of August, sending a positive message to the provinces. As *Le Figaro* proudly proclaimed in its August 2 edition, "Paris, throughout this decisive day, has been worthy of the country's admiration, and the admiration of all countries."[58] In the same edition, it noted how the ceremony of mobilization had been repeated all over France, giving a sense of how the ritual had reinscribed the national map.

In the end, how formalized was this ritual? It followed certain steps and timing, but it occurred in thousands of communes all over France with variations. It had developed within an historically established script with the French population having agreed on the rules. In 1914 it was the school's musical repertoire and historical memory that dominated, having been inculcated by the Republic and even supported by the left's patriotism.

The Musical Union Sacrée

In its breadth, this ritual was not just about the nameless crowds, however. It also helped to reshape the official political sphere and affected well-known professional musicians. On August 4, 1914, all of the political parties agreed to work together and unanimously approved the mobilization of troops. This created the political *union sacrée*. The implications of this process are actually far broader than the narrowly defined official *union sacrée*. The new harmony appeared before August 4 and went well beyond that moment's explicit political alliance. If not wholly enthusiastic, the French were remarkably responsive and united. The public reached for symbols and values with deep roots, selecting songs from the French national repertoire that crossed boundaries of age, political persuasion, and geography.

At the same time, a wartime ethos crystallized in which symbols and ideas recently associated with the far right prevailed. This ethos revalorized both national and conservative symbols, which did not include the working-class repertoire, heard in the Paris streets as recently as July. That the nationalists stepped forward is not surprising, but that ultranationalism commanded so much attention is more striking. Further, although the left had absorbed the Jacobin patriotism of the French Revolution, the Commune, and Jaurès, this ethos also meant abandoning positions such as antimilitarism and putting away practices like oppositional singing. The ethos's power derived in part from an extremely high sensitivity to words, symbols, and acts during the earliest stage of the war.

The rhetorical claims of the *union sacrée* connoted a bipartisan or depoliticized public sphere. Just as he had noted the inappropriateness of discussing the business of theater, Pierre Gheusi now also found "la politique" "quite 'disreputable.'"[59] The public's musical representations reveal, however, that despite the apolitical rhetoric, symbols promoted by the radical right dominated. The constellation of symbols and ideas included a powerful nationalism, the glorification of the army and the French *poilu*, a hope of revanchism, and a perception of unity across all boundaries—which made the rhetoric of class divisions no longer legitimate.

Within the world of Parisian musicians, we can chart the creation of the wartime ethos and the formation of a musical *union sacrée* in August 1914. Not surprisingly, the hardest-working wartime musician was to be the nationalist, royalist Théodore Botrel. He was a follower of Paul Déroulède and wrote in support of the army and the nation. Botrel quickly offered his services to the minister of war, Alexandre Millerand, himself a reformist socialist.[60] As one historian of the music industry reports, "with the greatest seriousness he delighted in his role as a singing morale booster."[61] He specialized in humorous, optimistic views of warfare and degrading images of the enemy. During the war, he wrote three sizable collections, totalling close to two hundred songs, many of which were reprinted by the army and in newspapers.[62] He also performed fifteen hundred concerts for troops, and his yeoman's service earned him three citations along with the name "le Chansonnier des armées."[63]

Beginning work on August 1, he quickly composed several songs that ridiculed the Germans and the kaiser, in particular. One song used the tune from a very old, humorous war song, "Malbrough s'en va t'en guerre," and described the kaiser "As a tiger enraged / Or as an aged jackal."[64] Lyrically, the kaiser provoked the French, and the French willingly and cheerfully gave up their lives, while singing. These lyrics would be distributed to the troops in the fall of 1914 in the official military newspaper. A song such as Botrel's "Hardi, les gâs!" in which the French went "as a single man" to fight the malicious Germans, also clearly advocated alacrity and optimism.

In Botrel's songs, France's overall perfection stood in contrast to Germany's malevolence. This polarity had roots in 1870, if not before, and was revitalized in 1914 with Germany's invasion. Songwriters like Botrel broadcast the material and physical inefficacy of the enemy.[65] The "boches" were ferocious, ugly, and cowardly. Whereas some songs about German atrocities were meant to provoke anger and aggression, other songs used ridicule to reduce the kaiser and German soldiers to a reasonable size.

Botrel's prowar stance seems logical, as does that of Léon Durocher, a fellow Breton and rightist. But some songwriters' support for the war was more startling. Gaston Montéhus, for instance, illustrates the power of the August 1914 consensus. As we saw in the previous chapter, Montéhus had taken a somewhat vague, but very persuasive, socialist/anarchist position, centered on antimilitarist support for workers against the bourgeoisie. With the advent of the war, Montéhus suddenly began to publish songs that encouraged everyone, including the working class, to support the war. His lyrics were as bellicose as Botrel's. In one of his first songs, he told workers to put away the "Internationale" until the war had been won, and he boldly set his new words to the socialist anthem's melody.[66] He shifted from a repertoire criticizing bourgeois owners, the army, and the government, to presenting images of soldiers offering their lives to a unified France. Designating it the "last war" during which socialism would triumph, Montéhus depicted the once antagonistic lines of soldiers and workers becoming unified regiments of proud soldiers of the Republic. This matched precisely what was actually happening. His "Pan Pan l'Arbi" also embraced unity wholeheartedly, explicitly including colonial soldiers who had often been badly maligned in prewar songs. In fact, Montéhus wrote the song in the first person, with the colonial soldier offering to give his life for liberty and fraternity.[67]

This configuration of nationalism in the musical *union sacrée* was a departure from prewar problems and divisions. Many earlier songs had displayed wide gaps between classes, had used derogatory stereotypes for "foreigners," colonials, and Jews, and had attacked the Republic. The government had had to fight both the left and the right. In sharp relief to these strident prewar lyrics, the songs of the war cheerfully proclaimed France's unity with positive images of colonial troops and no evidence of antisemitism.

Montéhus's material quickly came to resemble that of Botrel. He chose to write the song "Lettre d'un socialo" using the tune of Paul Déroulède's ultra-nationalist "Le Clairon." This choice signals how abrupt the turn to the right was, when one recalls Gaston Couté's parody of Déroulède's lyrics in 1911. Here, Montéhus expressed the need to fight:

C'est pour notre indépendance	It is for our independence
Que l'on marche sans défaillance	That we march without weakness
Comme si c'était le grand soir.	As if it were opening night.
Que l'on soit syndicaliste,	Whether one is syndicalist,
Anarcho ou socialist,	Anarchist or socialist,
Tout chacun fait son devoir	Each one does his duty
Certes cela est pénible	Certainly this is painful
Quand on a le coeur sensible	When one has a sensitive heart
De voir tomber les copains.	To see one's friends fall.
Mais quand on est sous les armes,	But when we are under arms,
On n'doit pas verser de larmes;	We should not shed tears;
On accepte le destin.[68]	We accept destiny.[68]

Regardless of any prewar political differences, a Frenchman was supposed to do his duty, by taking up "La Marseillaise" and his gun.

In a letter to *La Guerre sociale* published August 6, 1914, Montéhus claimed that he had written to the minister of war "to ask for my drumsticks in the 153rd," his former unit. "It will not be said," he continued, "that I will not be there to sound the charge!"[69] Montéhus's change of position held throughout the war, as he performed in the *cafés-concerts* of Paris. He even rewrote his famous "Gloire au 17e" in 1916, to celebrate workers as brave soldiers of the Republic "covered with glory," and his emphatic prewar references to the rich as the enemy never appeared in his songs composed during the war.[70]

Montéhus did not change allegiances alone. Other songwriters from the political left, such as Léon de Bercy and Charles d'Avray, wrote prowar songs in 1914. De Bercy, like Montéhus, contributed militarist songs to *La Guerre sociale*. A former anarchist, Charles d'Avray wrote his song "Au pays de la Marseillaise" expressly to echo the songs of the French Revolution, but he also encouraged workers to forget class loyalties in favor of citizenship and to take up arms. Jacobin patriotism flowed into the conservative ethos, with the "Marseillaise" as the recipe:

Au pays de la Marseillaise	To the land of the Marseillaise
Berceau de la fraternité	Cradle of fraternity
La Révolution française	The French Revolution
Nous a donné la Liberté	Has given us Liberty
Pour défendre cette relique	In order to defend this relic
Riches ainsi que plébéiens,	Rich as well as poor,
Pour la France et la République	For France and the Republic
Prenons les armes Citoyens!	Let us take up arms Citizens![71]

There were a few writers who exercised self-censorship and chose to re-main silent—a notable act for a musician. Some found ways to publish dis-sident songs, in Holland or Switzerland, but their extremely small number testifies to the restrictive sphere of expression. To be sure, not everyone went off to war gleefully or assuredly. The socialist songwriter Maurice Doublier, for example, who was called up immediately, sent a simple post-card to the older, well-respected muse Clovys, which ended simply, "Vive l'Internationale toujours."[72]

Most significantly, many of the symbols and figures favored by the far right and opposed by the left prior to the war—such as Joan of Arc, Paul Déroulède, the army, and the "Marseillaise"—became central motifs in all sorts of cultural representations. Some of these elements had had a long, complex history and became renationalized in August 1914. Joan of Arc would now fight alongside Marianne. In the course of the war, Catholic of-ficials and religious symbols were incorporated into the civic calendar and appeared at official ceremonies in public spaces. Moreover, Montéhus had not chosen the melody from Déroulède's "Le Clairon" by chance. The ultranationalist, who had died in January 1914, now became a martyr, as the passage of time had obscured his acts of treason against the Republic and had preserved or even enriched his position as the defender of *la Patrie* and a proponent of revanchism.[73] Thus, one of the most important leaders of the radical right became a *national* hero. People sang his songs and recited his poems in the streets, in churches, and at patriotic rallies. The first pro-war rally at the Sorbonne in November 1914 placed Déroulède's pieces prominently between Victor Hugo's poems and the "Marseillaise." Déroulède had become the quintessential patriot; his military background was now legitimate, and his Christian beliefs buttressed his strength.[74]

Concurrently, many of the left's songs, symbols, and causes disappeared or were put away, most specifically those involving antimilitarism, anticlericalism, internationalism, and class divisions. In one instance, when citizens gathered in a bar intoned the "Internationale" and Montéhus's "Hymne au 17e," patriots expressed their indignation and threatened violence over the singing of the "seditious" songs.[75] This suppression was not initially a question of official repression. One prefectoral report on the general mobilization in Allier marked a transition from the "silence of patriotic duty" to the fervent singing of nationalist lyrics: "In several locales," he claimed, "the musical organizations, formerly of opposing parties . . . have devoted themselves to an evening of captivating processions. A large gathering of people followed them, singing the 'Marseillaise' as well as vibrant patriotic refrains."[76]

World War I brought national identity to the fore—regardless of how small a part of a person or community's consciousness it had previously been. The privileging of national identity gave lyrics such as Botrel's fertile ground. It became necessary to specify what was "truly" French. Language was only one key to defining the nation and the new unity. Appropriate modes of behavior were also important. Nationalism, which encompassed the purification of France, emboldened groups to find and destroy the "enemy." Parisians, for instance, sang the "Marseillaise," while they broke the windows of German- and Austrian-owned stores.[77] Civilians also used patriotic songs as weapons to shame German prisoners or, in one instance, the consul of Austria-Hungary, who was requested to appear in front of a crowd "with his head bare" to hear its performance of the national anthem.[78] Almost immediately, in very early August, shopkeepers began to display the French flag, official certificates of French origin, their *livret militaire* or allied passports as visual symbols to prove their loyalties and to avoid being vandalized or humiliated.

Meanwhile, *La Guerre sociale,* echoing Botrel, contributed to the mobilization script, calmly instructing its readers to "march as a single man to the frontier to give the nationalists an example of bravery and discipline."[79] For its August 6 edition, which also contained Montéhus's pronouncement, the newspaper provided songs "which our Armies will sing" including the "Marseillaise" and the "Chant du départ." The paper also printed the refrain of the "Internationale," whose lines, "This is the final struggle / Let us gather together, and tomorrow / the Internationale / will be the human kind," now referred to a far less utopian fight. Remarkably, the editor even included the song "Sambre et Meuse"—the quintessentially revanchist military piece.[80]

With the Germans on French soil, those on the left were forced to choose between different loyalties and teachings. When the historian Mona Ozouf compared the Third Republic's school texts and the speech that

Léon Jouhaux, the secretary general of the General Confederation of Labor (CGT), delivered on August 4, 1914, to affirm the *union sacrée*, she found striking similarities. She concluded that "in 1914 the working class . . . did not break with the education it had received in the public schools. It did not have to. In fact, it had to break with the syndicalist education."[81] At least temporarily, that meant having to "put away 'l'Internationale.'"

Frenchmen into Soldiers

The mobilization ritual signaled the passage of France into wartime, and committed millions of citizens to becoming soldiers. In a multilayered rite of passage, as soldiers physically moved to the east, the nation also went to war. Ceremonies of separation at sacred sites such as town squares and train stations occurred over and over, marking civilians and soldiers. André Maurois even expressed his disappointment at not having been able to march out with his regiment; he thought "it was beautiful," accompanied by the singing "of women, old men, [and] children" (the categories of the "Chant du départ").[82] As soldiers moved away from their families and homes, they fashioned themselves according to their culture's images of soldiers.

The public's view of the French military changed dramatically once war was declared, as part of the wartime ethos. According to the military historian Alistair Horne, the army went "from being unpopular, underprivileged and at the total whim of government, as it had been from 1900 onwards," to "all-popular and all-powerful. The roles were completely reversed."[83] A positive image of the army had flourished in some French songs, however, celebrating the country's martial past and envisioning any future war as quick, decisive, and led aggressively by eager soldiers. Because certain songs fit the public's hopes for the new war, they were particularly effective. [84]

Patriotic cultural symbols and tropes also played a part in the new soldiers' self-fashioning. As they changed from civilian clothes to their bright red and blue uniforms, they carried their prewar song culture to war. They performed the "Marseillaise" from trains, as they moved through France toward the northeast and became inheritors of a military past. In addition to the patriotic anthems, soldiers also sang about the regions they were leaving behind. On its way to the front, Corporal Albert Cottereau's unit, made up of soldiers from Normandy and Paris, optimistically intoned, "I will see My Normandy again / It's the country that gave me life."[85] Songs literally moved across the French landscape, as soldiers brought together regional repertoires.

Once in the east, troops marched into towns with their musicians at their head and were welcomed by citizens. Jacques Heugel, an army musician who kept a detailed journal, described congenial receptions in August in villages near the Belgian border, where the soldiers received flowers and the regimental musicians performed.[86] Jean Giraudoux also recorded numerous instances of soldiers writing and using songs with martial rhythms. In one description, he recalled:

> Departure. The men begin to sing. Workmen and peasants, with little understanding of such excited emotions, they believe themselves to be joyous. Choruses are formed; our mess kits, too, resound against the steel of our guns. . . . My company sings the "Chant du départ," modifying, however, the name Viala with that of Vialard, our corporal.[87]

The men chose this old patriotic song for its marching beat, its cheerfulness, and its part in a longstanding national litany. Following common practice, they modified the song to fit their group, taking advantage of the humorous potential in the word "lard." Interestingly, Giraudoux's text itself demonstrated the shift from the separate groups of "workmen" and "peasants" using the third person, to the inclusive "our kits" and "our guns" of wartime comradery.

Giraudoux also remarked on the troops' learning how to march triumphantly into towns. Even in December 1914, after the war had settled into the trenches, Robert Fournier described his daily training, accompanied by exuberant singing: "We traversed paths, forests, pastures while singing and talking. We dreamt of combat, conquests, heroism. . . . [And] we seethed with impatience fearing that the war would finish without us."[88] With the conscripts dreaming of their own victorious entries, it is easy to imagine the types of heroic songs used.

These men were not, however, automatically soldiers, a fact their own memoirs and letters noted. Becoming a soldier required learning how much to pack, how to march, and how to fight.[89] Whereas Giraudoux had commented earlier on the inexperience of the regimental musicians, soon after he described how they "invent[ed] a more warlike style, and our scattered drummers and buglers hurriedly reassembled in front of each battalion."[90] Some also admitted to trying to resist the army's rules, for example in censoring their own letters. Louis Mairet, whose letters were published after his death in 1917, wrote to his cousin early on and admitted he was not a soldier, but went on to say he would have to be one.[91]

One of the most important components of this self-fashioning was its emphasis on masculinity. Whereas in the French Revolution the *levée en masse* put the entire country on notice, and there was some debate about women arming themselves or accompanying troops, by 1914 it was clear men would be soldiers and women would stay home. Songs and other texts comprised three themes that defined how to be manly, all three of which had appeared in prewar schooling and army training as well as in the *cafés-concerts* and *orphéons*.[92] The first was the separation from civilians, which was to be accomplished with hurrahs from the crowd and kisses from women. In song after song, female figures sent soldiers off with farewells that imparted courage.

The second theme called for calm stalwartness, no tears, and being able to sing cheerfully under fire even in the face of death. This came from the Third Republic's school curriculum, which had used songbooks to teach a boy's duty to defend his country. A 1908 school textbook by Jules Payot described this "sang-froid [literally, cold bloodedness] under fire": "In war, courage and steadfastness are necessary every minute. To march in the cold or in the heat, often with sore feet, . . . to sleep on the wet ground, to suffer from thirst and hunger. One must bear it all *gaily*."[93] Paul Déroulède's well-known "Le Clairon" also honored the common soldier who sounded his trumpet even after being mortally wounded. This song promoted music and singing as central to inspired fighting. Before his heroic death, the trumpeter sent the troops forward:

Il est là, couché sur l'herbe,	He is there, crouched in the grass,
Dédaignant, blessé superbe,	Scorning, proud wounded one,
Tout espoir et tout secours;	All hope and all aid;
Et sur sa lèvre sanglante,	And on his bloody lips,
Gardant sa trompette ardente,	Keeping his ardent trumpet,
Il sonne, il sonne toujours.	He sounds, he sounds still.[94]

Déroulède's lyrics emphasized a man's potentially deadly but glorious duty.

Songs in the French Revolution had contained a recurrent theme, called by John Lynn "the patriotic death," where falling in battle was viewed as not just act of bravery but a responsibility.[95] Hundreds of revanchist songs carried this idea forward after the Franco-Prussian War. "Le Régiment de Sambre et Meuse," for example, proclaimed that:

Tous ces fiers enfants de la Gaulle	All the proud children of Gaul
Allaient sans trêve et sans repos;	Went without ceasing and without rest;
Avec leurs fusils sur l'épaule,	With their guns on their shoulders,
Courage au coeur, sac au dos.	Courage in their hearts, pack on their back.[96]

Like other revanchist songs, "Sambre et Meuse" expressed yearning for the return of the lost territories, but it also demanded a soldier's noble death for his country. These representations spoke directly to an individual's identity as a soldier.

"Sambre et Meuse" praises the possibility of glory in death. But fighting was not always so funereal. A third theme of military masculinity promoted potency, forward motion, and the eroticism of war. More specifically, the French soldier was to accomplish his duty in hand-to-hand combat using his bayonet as the perfect weapon. This "cult of the bayonet" had developed out of the success of shock offensives in the French revolutionary armies. Paradoxically, the mythology had expanded after the defeat to the Prussians in 1870.[97] In song after song, French combatants dominated their opponents: "It was a battle of giants, / Drunk with glory, inebriated from gunpowder."[98]

Military leaders developed their strategy for August 1914 from within this same cultural milieu and its vision of war. Once the Germans had attacked France, the military's planning called for offensive battles aimed at recapturing Alsace-Lorraine. Calling on the French soldiers' traditional qualities, this war of movement would use forward motion called *attaque à outrance* to break through clearly distinguishable enemy lines and to push the invader out.[99] The members of the high command, as part of French society, were also influenced by the memories and myths of the revolutionary armies and Napoleon's campaigns. French culture steered them away from other strategies or the lessons of the American Civil War; any possibilities of trench warfare were swiftly dismissed.[100] As the war ministry's handbook released in October 1913 optimistically emphasized, "The lessons of the past have borne their fruit; the French Army, returning to its traditions, admits henceforth no law in the conduct of operations other than that of the offensive."[101] Thus, although the French moral position and motivation depended on the idea of German aggression and French defense, the war was to be made up of offensive battles in which the traditional French soldier would prevail.

Patriotic songs readily fused with the war of movement during the first two months of battles. Music was interwoven with activities on the battlefield, continuing much older customs. Military commanders very purposefully used rhythm, musical narrative, and harmony to raise the level of aggression and fervor among the troops. According to a system developed during the nineteenth century, all regiments had their own clarion calls, refrains, and songs.[102] Bugle calls were used to communicate, signaling an attack or retreat and alerting soldiers to comrades' positions. A soldier's life could depend on his ear's ability to pick out his regiment's tune. Jean Galtier-Boissière's *La Fleur au fusil* described a battle in late August 1914 in which confusion prevailed until the clarion stepped forward and sounded a charge.[103]

Most clarion refrains had one long line of text or two short phrases, usually with references to drinking, women, and marching. The 6th Infantry's "Here's the regiment from Armagnac" and the 13th's "Joyful drum, the pack is heavy" were both short and to the point, whereas others simply varied the formula of soldiers marching forth toward glory at the sound of the drums, bugles, or cannons. For example, the 133rd used, "The powder has exploded; the charge has sounded, let us march without fear, behind the tricolor."[104] The melodies for the regimental refrains were also formulaic—built on a C major triad, and rarely using notes outside of the chord. Most began on G or high C, and ninety percent were in military time, 2/4, with the rest in 6/8. These represented the most fundamental keys in Western diatonic music with the triad (for example, C, E, G) acting as the backbone.

Popular songs from the prewar revanchist campaign and those written in 1914 were tailored to this military tradition. They celebrated the idea of singing while attacking, and they created refrains that played with the appropriate words and melodic and rhythmic form to signify the expected forward motion. Just as military commanders in the field repeatedly called out "En avant" (forward), "A la baionnette," and "Hardi les gars" (Go to it boys), these songs' refrains constantly used these terms, as well as *chargeons, tambours, clairons,* and *chantant en victoire.*[105] Botrel's "Hardi les gâs," reportedly written on August 1 and then printed on the cover of the *Bulletin des armées,* also incited the soldiers to march forth, gaily singing to his beat:

Raillons tous comme un seul homme   Let us all rally like a single man
     Hardi, les gâs   Go to it, boys

Bouclons le sac et la giberne   Buckle on the pack and cartridge pouch
     Hardi, les gâs   Go to it, boys

A te [la Patrie] donner, gaiement,   To gaily give to you [the motherland]
     leur vie   their life
     Hardi, les gâs!   Go to it, boys

Chantant pour mieux rythmer le pas,   Singing to help punctuate their steps,
Comme ils vont te venger, ma France!   As they go to avenge you, My France!
     Hardi, les gâs!   Go to it, boys![106]

The author of "Allez-y, les gars" used the same sharp phrases and repetition in composing his refrain: "Go forward, boys / Rush into battle / Without fearing the machine gun, / Courage, we will get them! / Forward! Forward! / Go forward boys"[107] (app. figs. 2–4).

In the end, the high command's strategy would prove to be patently wrong and very costly. As one officer described it, his soldiers arrived in Lorraine with "une musique humaine" only to be met by the "terrible concert" of bombs.[108] By the end of 1914, nine hundred thousand Frenchmen were dead, wounded, or prisoners. But the army did not give up all of its traditions or theory, and chapters 6 and 7 will investigate the military's musical strategies in more depth as well as the combatants' own musical responses to trench warfare.

The advent of trench warfare marked the soldiers' second serious step away from civilians and the first distancing from home-front representations of the war. August and September 1914 had been the point at which Paris and the trenches were closest together in cultural terms. Life in the trenches was not at all what the soldiers had expected, and the combatants turned to the sustenance and creative capacities of cultural practices, as there arose an intense need for rehumanization. Music was part and parcel of this life—a means of uniting with comrades to fight boredom, and a way of escaping reality with memories of home. As one regimental musician wrote, after November, life settled down into a pattern— "Music, some random bombs, dispersements, meals with friends, from then on all this was everyday life. The war had become a condition, an equilibrium."[109]

As France mobilized against Germany, the fabric of French culture changed, and the wartime ethos was invented. Old symbols took on new meanings and the divisive issues of the prewar period were set aside. As the historian Louis Chevalier has described the transformation in Montmartre: "The red Virgin abandoned herself to love. For everyone a dissolution, a conversion."[110] This ethos developed very quickly. Eugen Weber has noted in his work on the Action Française, that the far right was surprised by the shift and by their sudden surge in popularity.[111] Simultaneously, most members of the left either repudiated or simply put aside prewar ideas and symbols to accommodate the changes. From then until the middle years of the war, "the expression of anything but unqualified support for the war was exceptional."[112]

This conversion did not happen just by chance. The public's understanding was shaped by a national mobilization ritual which came from memories, or myths, of 1870, a ready song repertoire, and the need for unity in the face of an invasion. A patriotic repertoire was already widespread and powerful, and its use drew new people into the national community and created resolve. The cohesiveness and smoothness of the mobilization owed much to the existence of a national popular culture.

By late 1914, civilians in Paris were working toward a sense of proper daily life, while soldiers faced a more sinister stability of their own. The government, however, was not about to rest on the laurels of a smooth mobilization and apparent national unity. Using well-ensconced habits of surveillance and older laws of censorship, the authorities mobilized themselves to solidify the correct parameters of discourse and behavior for wartime France. Before we turn to the issue of censorship, however, it seems only fitting to end this chapter with a quote from Déroulède's piece "En avant," which was to be used during World War I. Its last verse rang out:

En avant! Tant pis pour qui tombe	Forward! Too bad for those who fall
La mort n'est rien. Vive la Tombe!	Death is nothing. Long live the Tomb!
Quand le pays en sort vivant.	When the country comes out alive.
En avant!	Forward![113]

PART II

❧

CONFLICTING AGENDAS

❧

CHAPTER THREE

The Censorship of Singing, from Music Hall to Trench

❧

In the spring of 1915, with the war not yet a year old, Henry Moreau sub-mitted his song "Réveil nocturne" to the censorship office of the Paris pre-fect. Much to the songwriter's dismay, the examiner banned the second of three verses because of its "lewd" character. (The lyrics told of a married couple who stayed in bed instead of going down to the shelter during a zeppelin warning.) Moreau did not hesitate to respond, insisting that the second verse's "suggestive allusion" was "skillfully hidden." Unsure, the primary censor turned to the Paris police prefect, who, instead of agreeing with Moreau's interpretation, decided that the entire song should be *non visée*—which meant it could no longer be performed anywhere in France, except in the army zone. When Moreau sent a second letter with a new ver-sion, he carefully explained that he feared losing the song's royalty income, and he threatened to get help from friends in the government. The prefect responded simply that the piece was "one continual innuendo" (*sous-entendu*) and maintained his ban. We have no indication that Moreau ever got his visa.[1]

Despite what one might expect, French authorities arguing over the merits of song lyrics, particularly lewd ones, in the midst of their enor-mous, bloody struggle to remove the Germans from northeast France, was business as usual. Other than the composer's unveiled threat, the case of "Réveil nocturne" followed the general course of the sixteen thousand or so songs submitted to Parisian officials between 1914 and 1918—a process that found hundreds of old and new songs unsuitable. But what was at stake in the negotiations and judgments? What did officials fear or hope to gain?

Nineteenth-century French officials had attributed both positive and negative power to songs. The police understood the vitality of performances and the improvisation that occurred on a nightly basis in *cafés-concerts,* where audiences' own contributions often targeted political figures or issues. With an adolescent commercial music industry and popular singing practices overflowing into the streets, authorities had long watched for any seeds of discontent or moral corruption to grow in these fertile spaces.

In August 1914, however, the national ritual of mobilization in the face of German aggression had made immediate severe repression unnecessary. Nor had officials needed to whip up excitement. The unifying power of songs had reverberated with even Gaston Montéhus, the militant, socialist *chansonnier,* joining the chorus. The government, however, did not rest, for officials could not ignore the echoes of the Franco-Prussian War, which they heard not just in the revanchist songs but which also resonated in the accounts of fervent patriotism. War, they feared, begat instability—social, emotional, and political. So they turned quickly to censorship and surveillance, processes in which the French state had great expertise. When the national assembly declared a state of siege in early August 1914, it set in motion a large, complicated system of censorship, which affected most public expression. New regulations multiplied as did new bureaucratic offices. The procedures embraced newspapers and books, songs and theater pieces. Song after song had to be rewritten or dropped from repertoires.

A prewar agenda intersected with wartime demands in the case of cultural censorship on the home front, where the war added urgency to earlier concerns and granted greater powers. At stake was the power to create or impose representations—representations that could affect the legitimacy of the government, the reputations of military leaders, or the treatment of soldiers. French censors, on the one hand, encouraged the prowar ethos (or the *union sacrée,* broadly defined), which meant lending total support without interfering in politics. Pursuing an older bourgeois ideology, on the other hand, officials worked to uplift or civilize the social tenor of the *cafés-concerts* and music halls. They sought to create upright, moral citizens by molding musical entertainment to their tastes and purposes. These were not, however, two separate agendas. They converged in a new link drawn between public morality and civilian morale. As the government minister Aristide Briand declared in front of Parliament in 1916, "the moral behavior of the country is at least as important as cannons and guns."[2]

Yet, World War I scholars have often used the word "morale" in reference to civilians unreflectively. An amorphous concept of civilian morale was actually constructed as the war progressed, in part by French authorities who judged that "total" war required total commitment from all citizens.[3] The overwhelming concern for morale translated into an official distrust of certain places, times, and practices, particularly public gatherings and performances.[4] Police informants constantly surveyed the crowds that congregated to read the latest communiqué in public squares or to confer and sing in cafés and theaters. Few aspects of daily life went unexamined as new rulings regulated such diverse activities as drinking habits, fundraising efforts, the participation of soldiers in ceremonies, and the correct dress at theaters.[5]

The government recognized that performance and cultural products such as songs involved a fluid environment. Songs were powerfully popular because of their polyvalence and represented one of the biggest challenges to the forces of repression. Varying gestures, costumes, and possible inflections made meanings particularly hard to fix. At the same moment, new propagandistic techniques pressed forward, necessitating sharp clarity and didactic messages. Because the French songs of the Belle Époque were anything but fixed, their ambiguities posed a threat. Moreover, *chansonniers'* double entendres did not suit wartime, when loyalty was supposed to be obvious and transparent.

The intersection of old and new agendas, however, was not a perfect fit, and censorship was not a monolithic or simple process. The most serious differences developed between the Parisian authorities' goals and those of military officials at the front. Paris became an even more vital source of news and entertainment for the rest of the information-starved country and was also the hub of government censorship. In this metropolis, prewar objectives helped direct a relatively stable system of song censorship, although there were times when the demands of mobilization did not fit the older moral values. The army, in the meantime, established its own criteria within a decentralized system. Military officials allowed far more politics, more complaining, and more bawdiness. Further, with such a huge front, tight control proved much harder to enforce, especially in the forward-most trenches.

Overall, censorship in either place was hardly an exact science, and it was difficult to make perfectly consistent decisions. A historian works from either faint pencil marks, which give clues about the "inappropriate" words or questionable meanings, or from emphatic blue lines, which may have crossed out a verse only to designate it "bon" (good) at a later date. We do not have detailed memos listing the censors' objectives, but their surgical approach allows us to piece together the system's skeleton.[6] What follows is an attempt to explore the imagination of the censors and their concerns over these artifacts, as well as to look at the process of negotiating with performers and writers.

In general, World War I scholars have focused mainly on narrow political censorship, ignoring broader cultural strategies.[7] Jean-Jacques Becker, who forged new ground with his attention to French censorship and the "'psychological direction' of mass attitudes," has asked if it was "inevitable that authorities should have been able to introduce, and very quickly at that, a system of thought-control intended to avoid the threat of defeatism and also the danger of patriotic over-exuberance?"[8] Becker's concentration on the press, however—which had not been censored for over thirty years—led him to emphasize French unpreparedness.[9] Yet, as we shall see, the authorities did not limit themselves to print documents, and they had no difficulty putting song censorship in place.

The Blue Pencil's Power

The French government was the only power to set up a centralized system for songs from the beginning, although the Germans pursued censorship of popular entertainment in a decentralized manner.[10] Song and theater censorship began promptly in August 1914 and continued on past the Armistice until October 1919. The state of siege declared by Parliament on August 5, 1914, activated laws dating back to 1849 that gave military officials broad responsibilities for all censorship.[11] More specifically, this referred to the ministry of war. This quick imposition in the midst of a vast mobilization left little space for debate, since the laws sanctioned all measures necessary to "insure public order"—a very broad concept. Over four and a half years, the war engendered a complicated, continually shifting relationship between military and civil officials, which included negotiating the regulation of all media.

In the case of Parisian song censorship, historical precedence and limited personnel supported the use of a centralized civilian structure. Thus, in August 1914, the military governor of Paris handed the responsibility for monitoring Parisian songs and theaters to the Parisian prefect of police, who directed the operation throughout the war with some limited interference from other ministries.[12] The minister of war and the military governor of Paris ordered seizures of newspapers, pamphlets, or songs, but Parisian civilian personnel and politicians decided on the proper content of songs for the rear, as had traditionally been the case.[13] Outside of Paris, prefects had the authority to ban any performance piece, but a song or theatrical revue banned in the capital could not be used in the rest of

France.[14] In the case of the military zone, once it had moved east of Paris, the military managed its own censorship—although Parisian officials supervised civilian performers entering the army's territory.[15]

The immediate and relatively smooth imposition of the government's machine reflected not only the wish to eliminate all subversive activity but also a collective memory of how the censoring mechanism had worked. The *cafés-concerts* and theaters had only shaken off censorship in 1906, just eight years before the war began.[16] In 1914, directors, performers, and especially writers once again took up the ritual of submitting pieces, appealing decisions, and negotiating for publication visas.[17] And throughout the war, the prefect relied on precedents, such as a 1903 circular that required a monthly inspection of theaters by a police official.[18]

For Paris and its suburbs, a list of all songs for *salles de spectacles,* fundraising benefits, and public concerts had to be submitted. This meant that officials reviewed approximately three hundred new songs each month, although directors, composers, and performers also constantly resubmitted songs in an attempt to change a censor's mind.[19] The criteria for songs appear to have been centrally controlled.[20] In over two hundred cases sent to the prefect on appeal, all except one came from one civil servant, a Monsieur Martin. The prefect himself dealt with questionable cases and met with disgruntled composers or directors.

As the song examiners sharpened their pencils, they worried about any song, poem, or text that was to be used in a performance.[21] Examiners also gave some attention to melodies. For example, they protected sacred tunes such as the "Marseillaise" and the Belgian national anthem "La Brabançonne" from ridicule or insults. The song "l'Aca . . . cadémicienne" failed to get a visa—despite its previous appearance in a newspaper—because of its tune. The prefect, Emile Laurent, was unhappy that the "Marseillaise" would be used with lyrics that sarcastically questioned the importance of writers and intellectuals in the war effort.[22] He claimed he would reconsider, if the words could be adapted to another tune.

With an acute sensitivity to public performance, officers also attended dress rehearsals to evaluate the costumes, sets, and gestures. Police agents would then visit shows periodically to insure compliance with the censors' rulings and could, if necessary, request new modifications or a ban.[23] In one case, in March 1915, a district officer withdrew a visa for the song "Le Beau Grenadier" after a random visit to a *café-concert* where it was being performed revealed the use of obscene gestures.[24] During another patrol, an agent discovered that a loud crash of cymbals at an opportune moment drowned out the last syllable of a verse, leading to licentious interpretations—the song was thenceforth prohibited.[25] Obviously, although the censors strove in their analyses of lyrics to divine subversive performances, hidden meanings, and possible audience reactions, the inspections were essential for evaluating a song's delivery and effect.

The scale and efficiency of this operation owed much to the fact that these procedures had been used throughout the early Third Republic. France had experienced repressive political and cultural censorship of printed materials and performance up to 1881.[26] Allan Mitchell's work on the forces of repression following the Commune of 1871 has underscored the preoccupation with "popular cabarets and *cafés-concerts,* which were regularly denounced as dens of 'dangerous or unhealthy excitements.'"[27] Already in December 1871 the prefects had been told to devise ways to "control" the "repertoires" of the *cafés-concerts* which threatened "public morality and principles of order."[28] In 1879, just before press censorship was to fall, the undersecretary of fine arts reminded all theater directors that any work including songs had to be reviewed by the police as did sets, costumes, and accessories.[29] When the Third Republic's liberalized regime established greater political liberties for the press in 1881, the surveillance system for cultural materials and performance remained firmly intact.[30] "For the last quarter of the nineteenth century," James Smith Allen has noted, "both preventive and repressive censorship remained a brutal fact for the French theater."[31]

By the early twentieth century, however, an increasing anxiety over French citizens' morality gradually outweighed the intense fear of subversive politics. The prewar years witnessed countless battles over pornography and definitions of obscenity, led by Senator René Bérenger's League against License in the Streets. As the government took increasing steps to regulate "erotic pleasure" and expand surveillance of suspicious spaces, it also "attacked the ribald and rabelaisian spirit long associated with the Gauls."[32] Thus, although calls for dismantling censorship had arisen, supporters had argued for the need to protect citizens, especially women and children, from the vile effects of immoral songs, dances, and jokes. This attack on what was viewed as "popular culture" was to go much further with the wartime powers.

Although no song censor's memoir has come to light—an unlikely prospect given their low numbers—one gets some sense of their role from a newspaper censor's account. In 1932 Marcel Berger and Paul Allard published *Les Secrets de la censure pendant la guerre,* in which they carefully described their cases.[33] They admitted that censors themselves found it hard to decide what to cut and began from the point of view that "everything" was suspect. With postwar sarcasm, one censor explained "Such words, such information that would seem inoffensive [harmless] were, in reality, loaded, it would appear, with a subtle venom. It was up to me to sniff out *[flairer]* this poison, to neutralize it before . . ."[34] Apparently, the inspectors took the possible dangers facing France very seriously.

The one significant exception to this system was in the army zone, where military officers controlled songs written or performed by soldiers.[35] Individual canteens, or rest camps, had an officer in charge of censoring troop shows, and only the most serious cases reached top officials.[36] The camp commanders watched for antiwar sentiments or serious attacks on the military hierarchy. The surveillance worked best in the zone behind the lines, where the higher-ranking officers were. Because the front was enormous, however, and solitary singing and performances were more informal than in most Parisian cases, soldiers could quickly create and recreate pieces without submitting them to any censor. This was particularly true in the forward-most trenches. Overall, authorities gave soldiers much more leeway to criticize and complain than they did Parisian civilians—at least until the mutinies of 1917 caused a severe crackdown. This reflected army and civilian officials' varying agendas and definitions of morale.

The "Politics" of War

Not surprisingly, French censors of all media reacted very sensitively to representations of the war: its aims, progress, and participants. In this respect, song censorship supported the broadest government goals. Authorities created support for the war by permitting positive views of soldiers and the high command, and by limiting criticism of government efforts. No longer were the acrimonious political and social debates of the prewar period appropriate subjects, and many songs approved by the pre-1906 regime now faced tougher times. Performers were expected to promote the war effort without political commentary.

Although songs were not likely to give away military information to the enemy—a common justification for newspaper censorship—songwriters still confronted prohibitions closely related to political events. Examiners carefully monitored the treatment of current events to prevent songs from interfering with government policy and from being too critical. As one of Monsieur Martin's memos explained, he feared one particular song because "it was a bit satirical for the Republic."[37] References to peace negotiations had to be crossed out as well as commentary on negotiations with possible allies because it dealt with a "burning question of the hour" *(brûlante actualité)*.[38] Apparently, officials preferred no help from the *chansonniers;* not even patriotically well-intentioned aspersions directed at Rolland Romain, or "those who for Switzerland have departed," could be assured of approval.[39]

The musical treatment of France's allies provides a useful example of the delicate line between just mentioning political topics and finding fault with official business. One could praise France's cohorts and the war effort, but could not make fun of or malign them. A visa was denied for "Opérations Russes" because it "appeared disrespectful of our allies," according to an examiner. The songwriter then tried to satisfy the censors by adding an "opening couplet [which] . . . toned down in advance these otherwise harmless *[anodines]* jokes." The prefect maintained, however, that "this song['s humor] could be interpreted as offensive."[40] He judged the performance or "interpretation" as most important, not the composer's good intentions. And funny jokes—which some called "harmless" specifically because they were silly—were recast as disrespectful and deleterious for morale. Over time, the rules adjusted to new diplomatic relations—thus, the censors protected the Russians' image at first and later simply wanted them ignored, and songs that had made fun of Americans as stupid tourists before the war failed to pass the review.[41]

Although military officials also kept watch for politically subversive materials, greater overall latitude led to much more political satire in trench songs and newspapers. Stéphane Audoin-Rouzeau has argued that "the attitude of the military authorities was extremely variable at all levels of the hierarchy" and was both "intermittent" and "pragmatic."[42] As a result, soldiers were permitted to create and hear things civilians could not. One anonymous piece, called simply "Chanson," appeared in the trench newspaper *La Fusée* in November 1916 with a trenchant attack against the Germans and the neutral powers. The lyrics berated the worst bystanders—the Swiss, the Dutch, the Greeks, and of course the Yankees. Such a political denunciation would surely not have reached a Parisian stage.[43]

In Paris, not all censored partisan commentary related directly to the war itself. Examiners also worked to protect the political infrastructure and authority figures and to divert the course of fin-de-siècle complaints. An old reproach about the absence of the naked truth in Parliament, while naked bodies prevailed on theater stages, became unacceptable.[44] Censors especially targeted such silliness laced with ridicule, since it showed bad taste. But they also eliminated serious, habitual criticisms. Anticipating trouble, the writer Plébus submitted his "Quel beau spectacle" in 1917 with the fourth verse already crossed out; he claimed that he never sang it anyway. The lyrics had offered the traditional grievance against deputies and senators "trafficking in their influence / And tampering with our finances."[45]

Song lyrics about selfish politicians had lined up with other antiparliamentary ideas before the war.

In addition, a ban on most proper names was supposed to keep *cafés-concerts* songs from directly reprimanding leaders, and when directors included older songs on their programs, a slew of deputies' names had to be removed. The ban turned out to be flexible at times, and performers tried to unearth the exact line, while resorting to well-worn ploys to make their points. Showering praise was one possible tactic. In an example from late in the war, Monsieur Martin questioned "Hommage à Monsieur Clemenceau" because of its "political allusions," but the prefect granted the visa; the lyrics gave only the most positive picture of the current prime minister, calling him a "good tiger," and proclaiming that from the right and the left, "We will follow you as comrades."[46] The satirist Jean Bastia chose another route when he submitted a piece about "le Tigre" who directed an asylum where patients were badly treated. Monsieur Martin was not fooled, explaining in a March 1918 memo to the prefect that "evidently, they wish to depict Monsieur Clemenceau in a humorous way with pointed allusions to the *Instructions en cours,* without, however, any name being pronounced." The prefect carefully suppressed the most obvious clues and the worst jabs, including a detailed section on how the patients were grilled and simmered.[47]

Judicial proceedings that condemned defeatist or treasonous behavior represented a particularly potent aspect of political affairs, which the police watched carefully. As the rate of highly visible, public treason trials accelerated in 1917 and 1918, some satire was allowed, if it gave the correct message. But songwriters were supposed to avoid commentary, for the most part. In January 1918, the composer of "L'Equitable justice" appealed to the prefect, claiming he had only "purely patriotic intentions" and had purposefully avoided specific names. The first verse had indeed strongly condemned the traitors:

Entendez, traversant l'espace	Listen, crossing space
Les cris des soldats affolés;	The cries of terrified soldiers;
Tous ces héros, mourant sur place,	All those heros, dying in place,
Vers la victoire étaient allés.	Toward victory had gone.
Mais des traîtres à la patrie,	But some traitors to the country,
A l'ennemi livrant nos plans,	Handing over our plans to the enemy,
Ont, dans une atroce tuerie	Have, into an atrocious slaughter
Jeté nos malheureux enfants.	Thrown our unfortunate children.[48]

But Martin objected to the "transparent allusions to current events," and the prefect said simply, "visa impossible."

Taken all together, the web of rules regarding current events and influential figures aimed to depoliticize public entertainment in the sense of lessening active participation, discussion, or divisions. Political events and ideas were still present; clearly the war was a topic of songs, and political leaders and the allies could be applauded. But the political spectrum was to be covered over, and criticism carefully contained. This campaign represented a significant undertaking considering the dominant historical role of songs in providing trenchant satire and assessments. The wartime rules became much tougher than in the years immediately before, fueled by a new sense of vulnerability. This control of the "political" was to carry into the postwar years; in February 1919, for example, the police chose to ban a song called "Le Suffrage universel," because of what they termed its "inopportune" and "political character."[49] It was the war period that combined these two adjectives, making partisan political views "inappropriate."

In addition, the censors hoped to prevent performers from delivering individual opinions in an impromptu manner. Satirical songs were not supposed to initiate debates. To that end, the police scrutinized certain places and persons more carefully. The works of radicals such as Gaston Montéhus (despite his patriotic conversion to the *union sacrée*), Jack Cazol, and Robert Lanoff (whose repertoires specialized in political and cultural satire), all faced special surveillance and tougher censorship. The attack on satire amounted to a campaign against the stock and trade of these and many other singers, since critical commentary on any topic was an essential part of their appeal. The performers did not give up, however. They continued to negotiate, especially those from the small cabarets that specialized in popular caricature.

Officials also did not want help on the other end of the spectrum. Thus, despite the seemingly obvious benefit, not all descriptions of German atrocities were approved. To begin with, in August 1914, atrocity stories proliferated in songs, newspapers, and by word of mouth, but the government soon recognized the damaging side effects. The prefect of Seine-et-Marne in his report of August 30 noted falling morale in his jurisdiction and blamed it on the morning newspapers. "No doubt the papers want to whip up feeling against the Germans, but in reality they spread fear and demoralize the population." As a result, the minister of war "asked all prefects to instruct editors 'in the future to avoid detailed descriptions of acts of cruelty committed by the Germans; repeated accounts of this type might have a deleterious effect on the morale of the population.'"[50] In Jean-Jacques Becker's terms, the press censors' objectives were to calm and "anesthetize" public opinion.[51] They did not want to "whip up" public emotions, but to get civilians to dig in for the long haul. The song censors followed suit and tried to rein in the prolific and popular music industry.

A police memo that reviewed the theater scene in November 1915 also hinted at why French officials would not encourage representations of violence in the middle of such a destructive war, especially in Paris. The commentator made the telltale comparison between the current situation and the siege of Paris during the Franco-Prussian War, which was followed by the radical Commune:

[The theater] has not played the role of inciter of enthusiasm that we know it played during the siege of Paris. Without a doubt this difference is attributable to profound causes, and the two wars do not resemble each other in any way: our enthusiasm has no need to be excited, and the war of 1870 . . . did not touch as intimately the heart of the whole nation.[52]

The writer was reassured for the moment that morale was steady and strong, but implicitly he indicated that patriotism was politically volatile. He also attributed the calm to specific steps the censors had taken. They had banned from stage, lyrics, and screen, "war scenes" and "views of the devastation . . . caused by the German troops," until "calm had returned in minds accustomed to these ideas." This strategy involved an ongoing experiment in controlling popular representations that could "produce" "a painful impression" which in turn "jeopardized" public order.[53] The government allowed harsher representations of war only as the public adjusted.

Because of these apprehensions, government authorities strove to encourage "moderate" levels of patriotism, while allowing no room for violent outbursts or "defeatism." This management became necessary since much of the ingenuity, inventiveness, and vitality for fighting the war on the home front came from private individuals and commercial interests, and because officials understood the excellent possibilities offered by singing and entertainment for improving the morale of civilians and soldiers. Management meant limiting the ways writers could talk about subjects such as combat or the government, by signaling which expressions were now out of bounds. "Good morale" was defined as continuing, controlled dedication, not rabid patriotism.

Censorship also helped maintain or even broaden the *union sacrée* in political terms. In other words, the wartime ethos, which had crystalized in August 1914 and promoted conservative, nationalist, and religious symbols, kept its strength with the censors' help. Not even a joke about how difficult it would be for brawling politicians to preserve the *union sacrée* after the war could get past the blue pencil.[54] Tellingly, given the fierce battles over its proper role in the Republic before the war, the subject of religion made the examiners uneasy. The censors did not block religious references altogether, but they would not approve religious jokes or rude or indecent remarks about nuns and clergymen—thereby eliminating some religious or ethnic stereotypes.[55] In the interests of unity and harmony, the censors also curbed most attacks on the pope and on priests, denunciations that would have been seen as healthy anticlericalism before the war.[56] Just as much of the religious elite supported the war with sermons and masses, the censors encouraged the rapprochement between the State and Catholics as well as the integration of Catholics into the republican cause.[57]

While the censors seemed most edgy about civil politicians' reputations, possibly because singers and comics had always enjoyed attacking Parisian figures, they also carefully screened the presentation of the new stars—the military leaders and the strategically vital *poilus. Chansonniers,* of course, could not resist singing about the generals who were gaining fame on a daily basis. Composers were welcome to praise or compliment officers' selfless and intelligent leadership, but they could not show a general's vanity or ambition—the honorable "bâton d'maréchal," for instance, was earned, not coveted.[58] Overall, the army received many musical hurrahs, including Amelet's rhyming refrain: "These are the heroes / Joffre! Castelneau! / Whose names will be engraved in our history / And General Pau / The honor of our flag *[drapeau]*."[59] Thus it was not just by chance or military accomplishments that General Joffre became such a strong, popular figure by early 1915, as hagiographic representations flooded the public sphere. This eulogistic discourse marked another sharp shift from fin-de-siècle France, when the army had been attacked as reactionary and unreliable in its defense of the Republic, while royalists' celebratory lyrics had defended the military against radical contamination. The lyrics did, however, have older, nineteenth-century roots in songs that had lauded first Napoleon and then Napoleon III and General Boulanger.

All of the praise of the military effaced criticism, which might have promoted change. In the spring of 1917, for example, officials allowed lyrical tributes for Mangin and Nivelle, two of the currently powerful French generals, in Bastia's "L'Oubli du passé."[60] The song gained approval just before these two commanders led the deadly spring debacle. The protection and applause continued throughout the war. An early version of the very popular tune "Ils ne passeront pas" (app. fig. 10) offered admiration for the generals Castelnau, Maunoury, and Joffre; by 1918 Clemenceau was happily sandwiched between Foch and Maréchal Joffre (who by then had been quietly removed from power), with Pétain now appearing as the one who had "freed Alsace and Lorraine."[61] This manipulation also had implications for the postwar period, when the French's admiration or reverence for military figures continued unabated.

It was now soldiers at the front who had greater leeway to criticize officers, Parisian officials, and civilians. They heartily condemned *embusqués* (shirkers) and mocked Parliamentary fact-finding missions to the "front." They performed for very limited audiences, however. Parisian authorities, on the other hand, had to cope with established political themes of criticism and the entertainment industry's popularity. In addition, because the roles of civilian and wartime politician remained new and ill-formed in a liberal democracy at war, civilian censors proved to be touchier and more dogmatic.

They also needed to monitor the presentation of the quintessential *poilu,* as the army took in millions of common soldiers, and the military establishment moved to the center of the public stage. In both the songs and newspapers of 1914, a rhetorical shift to the invincible *poilu* occurred quickly and somewhat spontaneously, based on the older representations of wartime's potential glories. In song lyrics as well as journalists' accounts, French soldiers proved fearless in the face of German weaponry and eager to find glory.[62] As censors sharpened their pencils and went to work, they moved to buttress the positive rhetoric and to quash the negative. Tunes that depicted soldiers retiring quietly from war with minor wounds or a friendly encounter between a *poilu* and the kaiser were not tolerated.[63] Censors also contributed to this martial renaissance by forcing significant changes in the popular prewar genre of the *comique-troupier,* in which French soldiers had been humorously portrayed as unceasingly naïve and even stupid. A song such as "Bon soldat" lost three verses, since it made fun of dying for glory.[64] Instead, authorities sought to reinforce proper, masculine martial behavior. The squeezing aside of the *comique-troupier* genre opened space for the revanchist texts of Paul Déroulède and Théodore Botrel with their stalwart and able-bodied soldiers. Parisian censors even tried to restrain satirical empathy with a *poilu*'s lot. For example, the song "Suivant le grade" ended with couplets that outlined what various ranks could expect at the end of the war—the captain, for instance, would receive a promotion to colonel. But the last two lines had been sung: "And who simply makes . . . [a pause] his hole? / the simple *pioupiou.*" (*Pioupiou* was an older term for *poilu.*) The hesitation made the examiner nervous, and he accepted the lyrics only when the two offending lines became "Who is covered everywhere with glory? / It's the simple *pioupiou!*"[65]

Glorifying soldiers and military leaders was both a war-related and political goal. The protection of leaders' reputations put authorities in a more secure position by discouraging questions and lessening popular interference. The overall effects of this attempt to depoliticize vital public spaces at this moment should not be underestimated. To understand the French experience during the war, one cannot just ask why there was so little defeatism or why the French did not give up. And we cannot simply point to national resolve. We must also consider the lack of criticism and the slow rate of change in political and military strategies. Censorship clearly contributed to both.

"La Pudique Anastasie"[66]

For the authorities, however, depoliticizing and ensuring a prowar stance were not enough. The war also gave them the opportunity to expand earlier efforts to mold the *cafés-concerts* to their tastes and values. World War I did not invent the elites' fears of popular entertainment nor their attempts to reform it. Although the French had had a very long history of Rabelasian language and humor, the culture also had a more recent record of righteousness or anxiety toward it. Once the war began, this ideological project involved cleaning up language, fostering a discriminating sense of humor, and teaching appropriate behavior. The promotion of "good taste" spread middle-class values and undermined a positive working-class culture, as part of what Pierre Bourdieu has called the "symbolic work of fabrication of groups."[67] This prewar strategy moved forward, now intricately tied to the war effort.

In the name of the *union sacrée,* the censors aimed to efface bitter class divisions by portraying an ideal world where the bourgeoisie and working class worked and lived happily together. In this nationalist crusade, all classes were unified and encouraged to fight, especially workers.[68] But how explicit was the class dimension in the attempt to impose representations? There are some obvious clues that lead one to characterize the overall project as bourgeois.[69] Specifically, the examiners barred most antibourgeois sentiments from songs, suppressing references to "nasty landlords" and "big shots," and a song title such as "Bourgeois Rapaciousness" *(Rapacité bourgeoise).*[70] They rooted out negative descriptions and calls for class action. Officials were confronted with powerful material, for example, in the song "Salut les riches," submitted for the small cabaret Le Caveau de la République—a place that often featured satirical lyrics and had a working-class audience. The singer wanted to describe his lot "in misery" compared to that of the fat rich. He admitted that some would ask why he martyred himself and would suggest action:

Tu veux donc qu'on t'exploit' tout l'temps?	Do you like that they exploit you all the time?
Allons prends moi c'fusil qui brille	Come on, take me, this gun which shines
Et comm' les "Costauds" d'autrefois	And like the Costauds [sturdy ones] of the past
Qui démolirent la Bastille	Who demolished the Bastille
Fais feu sur tous les sal's bourgeois!	Fire on all the dirty bourgeois![71]

These lyrics overflowed with anger toward endemic oppression and inequality in French society, evoking a violent revolutionary past. The prefect upheld the block after a requested review.

Officials faced a difficult challenge, however, refashioning perceptions of working-class identity. Throughout the nineteenth century, workers had rallied around lyrics describing the hardship of unemployment or strained relationships with the boss, and these songs represented an integral part of working-class culture.[72] The repertoire was too pervasive to be easily eliminated, but officials now had free rein to change the details. Censors still allowed some general descriptions of a harsh daily life, but they erased bitter sentiments or calls to attack a ruling class or factory owners.[73] One song originally reached a crescendo with a verse about workers who had loyally given their sweat for the boss only to die in a corner, and then warned the owners to "watch out"; the police eliminated the aggressive couplets.[74]

Songs had not only depicted the shabby treatment of the working class by factory owners, but had also painted police agents as nasty, corrupt, or buffoonish instruments of the elites. During the war, examiners modified or deleted all slights. The police who manned censorship's front lines obviously had a self-interest in purifying their own reputation, but this gloss also legitimated the wartime power structure. In one case, a performer was told not to sing a particularly "stupid" song in the costume of a police officer, and even easygoing jokes were deemed potentially harmful.[75] The ban also affected many prewar tunes that had intoned the injustices of the legal system and, in particular, the countless tragic wrongful arrests.[76] So widespread were these beliefs that when some lyrics expressed a wish to assist the "good officers," censors found these sentiments impossible to believe and refused visas.[77]

The darker side of this "popular," or realist, genre was now, of course, also unwelcome. It had traditionally depicted various social groups, including the poorest layer of the Parisian community, with argot and graphic characters. Marc Hély's "Quand la nuit," copyrighted in 1913, had painted a very depressing picture of urban life, but it suddenly faced heavy edits in December 1914.[78] The cutting of this piece, which belonged to the old genre pioneered by Aristide Bruant, was more remarkable, since this set had had such a rich and successful tenure.[79] Not surprisingly, censors also rejected a song where an American legislator got a tour of Paris from a stupidly nonchalant police agent who dismissed the crowds of poor women in the streets with their children, saying in a refrain: "Oh! it's nothing, mossieur [*sic*] American / It's some unfortunates who have a dozen small kids! / The landlord just gave them vacation . . . Oh! it's nothing."[80] The censor disliked both the agent's indifference and having serious Parisian problems paraded in front of an ally.

Later in the war, censors permitted criticism of profiteers and other civilian behavior, but the complaint had to target the action itself, which was represented as unpatriotic, rather than criticize a specific class. Within the context of the war, the most important collective was the nation, divided only into soldiers and civilians. The category of civilian absorbed all classes, with individuals choosing to do good or bad deeds. Interestingly, in the song "La Vie chère," the composer constructed a tough critique of the new "grands seigneurs" or profiteers, and the censors went along with it. But they rejected the one line that called for violent action against the guilty parties.[81]

All of this recasting of class identity depended on a rewriting of French history in which the censors favored some episodes and excised others. Predictably, they placed great significance on revanchism, the French dream of recapturing Alsace and Lorraine. These songs represented France's war aims. But examiners did not allow any of the older complaints that had implicated Republic institutions in the class struggle. A song that described the State's schools as prisons, along with the army's habit of acting as strike breaker, suffered cuts.[82] More to the point, song lyrics that worried about the army as a threat to the Republic would have had an extremely dissonant ring at a time when the nation was depending so heavily on its military.[83]

Representations of the French Revolution proved particularly problematic, especially because of the fear that war sparked revolution and popular insurrection. The best scenario from a censor's point of view praised the tough and stalwart Parisians, without recalling their role in storming the Bastille. Given the censors' strictures, history would simply be rewritten.[84] In A. Montagard's "La Baïonnette," singers feted the beloved weapon for its many achievements, but the censor would not permit the verse honoring the bayonet's assistance to the "bon peuple en sabots" in getting rid of the "ancien régime."[85] Likewise, Henri Maheu's original "Les Trois couleurs" had heralded the "people" rising up to fight on the barricades for bread and vain dreams of equality. With corrected lyrics, the din came from hateful invaders instead of the people, who now took up arms intoning the ultrapatriotic "Chant du départ." The popular objective of fighting for "égalité" had been changed to "la Patrie," neatly reflecting the primacy of nationalism.[86] This concern was not new; Josette Parrain, in her analysis of nineteenth-century theater censors' treatment of the Commune, has noted officials' discomfort with any portrayals of the "people" in the streets and on barricades, or, in other words, with the "réveil populaire."[87]

Moreover, the censors' efforts to bolster the bourgeois position were not limited to explicitly political topics of revolution and class conflict. A far more sensitive struggle focused on cultural mores *(moeurs),* or standards of behavior in the broadest sense. Taste was a site of class struggle as aesthetics were socially constructed, and certain language, gestures, and practices were defined as legitimate and others as vulgar or immoral.[88] Take, for example, how Monsieur Martin explained his objections to the song "Rapacité bourgeoise": "Even the title, which seems to encompass a whole category of citizens under the same uncivil label, appears too violent. The song is not itself obscene, but rude *(grossière)* in tone."[89] As in Henry Moreau's case, with which the chapter began, standards of behavior were at stake, and being immersed in a long, deadly struggle did not excuse uncivil civilian behavior.

But if one wished to raise cultural tastes, one needed to define higher standards. In a January 1915 memo concerning a program for the Théâtre Belge, Monsieur Martin worked to do just that. First, he noted the overall high "quality" of the schedule, then he summarized the instances of crude or stupid lyrics:

[T]his program has a literary and moral quality *somewhat superior* to the average. Out of 36 numbers, 15 are proposed without reservation for approval. These are patriotic songs, comic songs referring to the war or sentimental songs. Seven are suggested without reservation for refusal of the visa, as being coarse or indecent.[90]

He then asked the prefect for assistance in evaluating a third set, which included "sentimental songs with a hint of triviality or ribaldry, or humorous songs, which, although decent, disarm the most severe judge with their stupidity. One among them . . . has absolutely no intelligible meaning." The best examples, in Martin's opinion, exhibited a mix of morality, erudition, and patriotism, assuming recognizable norms for all three. The worst, while not obviously unpatriotic or defeatist, were to be condemned as indecent, or simply idiotic.

Reforming audiences' sensibilities required two interrelated tasks involving the aesthetics of songs: the suppression of "popular" language and the elimination of explicit sexual descriptions and lewd double entendres.[91] In the first case, "vulgar" language was purged. Terms that might otherwise be considered colorful, earthy vernacular, were deemed improper, unbecoming, stupid, or crude. Scatological humor, discussions of *faire pipi* (urinating), and descriptions of body parts such as *fesses* (buttocks), *miches* (breasts), or any use of *queue* (tail), were no longer acceptable. The censors disliked references to body parts in general, and erotic parts in particular. Lines like "the dazzling breasts where one could get tipsy" and "a mouth where kisses dozed" drew forth the blue pencil.[92] The examiners favored modest, chaste descriptions and few vulgar terms. Songwriters needed to get people, or more specifically women, covered up.

Much of what the censors objected to involved some sort of transgressive behavior. Audiences were not to have the opportunity to laugh at accidental substitutions of food with excrement or chamberpots with teacups.[93] Name calling also became "unseemly," eliminating such age-old, useful insults as *cochon* (pig, bastard), *salaud* (bastard, swine), *couillon* (cretin, idiot), and *charogne* (slut, bitch)—even when they referred to William II.[94] Censors were not just removing "colorful" language, they were also undermining a traditional political tactic from the world of popular culture.

Even more widespread and troubling was the ubiquitous sexual humor of the French *cafés-concerts,* which heavily taxed the censors' crusade to promote decency. The allusions to sexual situations presented a complex problem involving suggestive gaps, musical interference, and gestures. As newspaper censor Paul Allard remarked, officials fought a running battle against "allusions and innuendoes"; the censor "cut even the *intention* of having an ambiguous rhyme heard . . . in the well-known game of slippery rhymes."[95] Many cases obviously rested on the censors' understanding of the audience, or their fashioning of an audience's sexual *imaginaire.* At times, examiners believed that even if they themselves could not think of the obscene interpretation, the audiences would be able to. Nothing could be taken at face value. Georgius's song "Qu'est c'que vous m'dites la?" represented the classic "fill-in-the-blank" form since the third line of each seven-line verse ended with an article of speech (*le, la, les, un,* and so on.) followed by a pause. Only the subsequent lines showed that the missing word was innocent, while the listeners had had the opportunity in the meantime to provide their own suggestions. For instance, a handsome young man "who comes surely for the . . ." *(vient sur'ment pour la . . .)* at a woman's apartment, turned out to have come "to court her a while" *(Pour la courtiser un peu);* likewise, he caressed "her . . . ," which became "her chin" *(le menton).* Because the first two lines rhymed, the ending of the third had unrestricted possibilities, and the performer could offer an audience all the time it needed. In addition, because of the consistent pattern of pauses, the audiences would have caught on by the second verse. Martin and the prefect could imagine the "smutty" alternatives "which appeared clearly with the suspended rhymes of each verse," and they moved to ban the song entirely. Georgius meanwhile responded to their concerns and removed the offending gaps, leaving unambiguous, benign lines in their place.[96]

With great ingenuity, however, other composers devised a wide variety of sexual double entendres using everyday objects and activities, for example "his bird" and her "cage," musical instruments like accordions or castanets, or women cultivated like gardens. Writers also used a favorite trick of placing foreign words or nonsense syllables at crucial moments, and performers were often provided with lines which could incorporate obscene gestures.[97] The censors also imagined the possibilities and tried to preempt the gestures. Concerning the song "Mirabeau Mirabelle," the *artiste,* although backed by the Olympia, a well-established and sizable music hall, still had to agree that he would sing the song "with its modified text, and without any exaggeration of gestures."[98]

Examiners often found themselves fighting semiotic uncertainty and silliness at the same time, and they worked to eliminate ambiguities. To fight the multiple interpretations or indeterminateness, the censors tried to tie adjectives or verbs to one single metaphor or to a literal object. Overall, faced with the censors' objections, composers showed significant linguistic skills in maintaining rhyming scheme and finding commonplace words to replace more colorful expressions. But what had been considered simply silly or funny before the war was now judged to be damaging for morale. There was something disruptive or insidious in the transgressive songs' message.

Songwriters repeatedly put forth their good intentions as a defense, whereas the censors worried much more about the actual performances and the public's interpretation. Both, however, were interested in the "reading," which was the slippery process. In a letter to Monsieur le Censeur dated March 26, 1915, Jean Bastia insisted that his songs had always found favor with the censor, but he now needed approval for a newly written second verse for his "Zeppelinade," which, he conceded, might be misread as obscene. Bastia carefully explained that he had written the piece before the airships' arrivals and had been "carried away" by the subject's "violence":

I have notably a second verse that could, in a completely different work, appear pornographic, whereas the invectives it contains were inspired . . . by a totally patriotic anger.
   I hope, therefore, that you will wish to grant a visa for my new version and that you will be persuaded that the images which I have used have no immoral goal, that, on the contrary, they are useful for reinforcing the effect of my imprecations.[99]

Highlighting the kaiser's ineffective "zeppelin," the controversial second verse described an "obscene" "fat phallus raping the virginity of the clouds," and the zeppelin's "sterile seed" which "serves only to depopulate the world." Martin's memo to the prefect noted Bastia's intent, but the prefect ordered that the second couplet be "modified completely."

This was not the end of it, however. Ten days later, Jean Bastia wrote another letter to the prefect himself, and, taking the high road, suggested that the censor had simply misunderstood the meaning of the transgressive words. According to his assessment, the "word" (phallus, one presumes) had a poetic purpose and "could not scandalize those who know the meaning." Besides, he claimed, it was "accompanied in a rather noble fashion by the lines that followed." The prefect said only "no response possible," and Bastia lost his case.

The censors had one last important task: to get songs to teach proper deportment. After all, this was a time when one's appearance or behavior had political, as well as social, implications. In the case of Henry Moreau's song with which we began, the offending couple's defiance of the air-raid rules did not help Moreau's case. With its pencils, the government tried to draw a clear line between respectable or patriotic behavior and improper or treasonous conduct, and songs provided an especially helpful forum because lyrics constantly addressed everyday life. In just one example, examiners blocked a song that celebrated alcoholic beverages and complained about the banning of absinthe.[100] As censors began their war work, they moved to buttress the bourgeois marriage and endorse repopulation while quashing representations of prostitution, adultery, and other examples of gratuitous sex. A morally pure nation was a strong nation.

As should be clear by now, the examiners were rarely comfortable with explicit sexual scenes regardless of the moral content, but they were strictest on gratuitous sex. At times even married couples could get carried away with too much gusto.[101] But far worse were the promiscuous, irresponsible acts of either men or women. In the *cafés-concerts* of the early Third Republic, audiences had often enjoyed a song genre about sexual initiations. Now, one could no longer sing about virginity or most seductions.[102] Women were not supposed to be promiscuous, by taking a different "dance partner" home every night.[103] In addition, just as some heterosexual activities went too far, references to masturbation were considered antisocial. One song that made fun of rationing, for example, lamenting about the days without meat, sugar, and tobacco, also complained about the lack of women and suggested men found a "Ligu' des Doigts d'l'Homme"—playing off the name of the earnest political association the Ligue des Droits de l'Homme. But the censor was not amused.[104]

We have seen how the concept of the *union sacrée* was broader than the official political coalition. This hope for unity extended even into the private sphere, where censors called for a truce in the age-old battle of the sexes. Dutiful wives were not to pick on or betray their husbands, and hardworking, virile men were to respect women. Interestingly, a part of the campaign for a conservative family ideal and civilian morale was to protect the reputation of women, and many older lyrics that had expressed violence against women were eliminated.[105] "Faut supprimer les femmes" faced an uphill battle for its visa, since its refrain called women "cholera," and one verse claimed that without women things would improve. Women were simply tarts who had to be paid off with jewels and clothes.[106]

Giving equal time, the censors also guarded the sensitive subject of Frenchmen's virility. They suppressed any mention of men's sexual problems as well as all references to their enslavement by women.[107] Not surprisingly, then, a prewar song in which a French soldier had tried to learn the "song of love" and could not get higher than "do re mi" was *non visée*.[108] Moreover, since examiners did not like explicit descriptions of sex or sexual parts, allusions to the size or shape of male genitals were not allowed nor were hidden references to castration—a popular prewar subject for double entendres.[109] This editing also helped banish vulgarity.

The censors hoped to reinforce the sanctity of marriage by discouraging mention of the transgressive behavior of adultery. The words "cocu" and "cornard" (popular terms for cuckolds) were usually suppressed. A tone of humorous assertiveness toward committing adultery, which had been unexceptional in the *café-concert* repertoires, was now suspect.[110] Of course if cuckolding any man was serious, betraying a soldier was even worse, since it affected the army's morale.[111] Censors changed explicit descriptions, for example, by making the unfortunate soldier into a traveling salesman who was also frequently away from home.[112] Parisian song censors also did not allow many obvious references to prostitution, while the army was actually supporting brothels for soldiers.[113] Officials forced a songwriter to modify his song that jokingly mentioned that, although the government had been closing bistros and theaters early, they had left open "les maisons closes" (regulated brothels).[114]

This management of morality on stage was actually quite complicated, since, despite all their efforts, the censors were confronted with thousands of popular representations that associated women's sexual benevolence with raising soldiers' morale (a link that will be explored in chapter 4). These wartime songs played off of the pain of separation and the loneliness of trench life, and made sex a compensation for fighting. Here, the censors' prewar and wartime objectives diverged, and the savvy *café-concert* veterans knew how to adapt the many modes of eroticism in popular culture to gain approval of their songs. The most "virtuous" erotic scenario had soldiers on leave meeting and then marrying eligible women.[115] And examiners could support lyrics about prostitutes who were nice to soldiers, and were then rehabilitated and married a *poilu*. Overall, the censors found it easiest to veto song lyrics with questionable morality when the context had nothing to do with the war. But when these same situations reappeared in songs about the *poilus'* leaves, they were endorsed.[116]

The topic of repopulation also proved to be especially troublesome. Examiners found themselves caught between wanting to further the cause of nuptials or promoting procreative activities whatever the moral costs.[117] Moreover, the war had made the government efforts to advance the pronatalist campaign even more urgent.[118] In most instances, references to soldiers going home on leave to make the class of '35 or '36 posed no problems, since "On travaille pour la République" (One works for the Republic). And songwriters could make all sorts of jokes about being an "irrepressible" repopulator.[119] Thus, at least for the stage, the examiners reacted more favorably to patriotic encounters.[120]

The performer Mauricet's "Faut des gosses" is a good example of an approved song that zealously advised all women to have babies. But it eventually ran into trouble on a charge of immorality. The lyrics optimistically assured women that the pain of childbirth was worthwhile, and the singer even counseled a woman in the audience to get together with a *poilu* behind her. The song was very popular in 1916 and early 1917, when it received a visa for various establishments. Finally, however, in March 1917 an indignant voice sounded. The prefect received a letter from "a poilu" who had had "enough of people taking soldiers for puppets. . . . I am against some songs which an artist at the Folies-Bergères, *Rose Amy,* sings. 'Faut des gosses' . . . invites our wives to *cuckold* us with anybody while we are at the front. It is disgraceful what the *censor* allows."[121] The prefect calmly asked for modifications and additional surveillance. The most important change came in the first refrain. Originally the performer had sung: "If you have a well-made body / Madams, give it without cost"; the last two words were changed, and the lines became "If you have a well-made body / Madams, give it to your husband." We do not know if this satisfied the critic, but we can see that the censors were not alone in their campaign. The timing of this letter also reflects the fact that concern over women's behavior increased as the war dragged on.

The army did not suffer this contradiction, since military officials readily accepted obscene language and sexual ribaldry in marching songs, at troop concerts, and in trench newspapers, as a means of intensifying proper aggressive attitudes. As one memo from the military archives explained, although directors of rest camps were to supervise the content and performance of songs, they were not to be overzealous, since soldiers were not "little girls."[122] Older regimental refrains had often joked about soldiers, pretty women, and drinking, and military teachings had recommended a repertoire of bawdy songs and broad jokes (*gaudrioles*) for morale.[123] Soldiers themselves also quickly turned to creating their own erotic song texts and musical revues, as well as sexually explicit trench memorabilia. Thus, jokes about efforts at repopulation flourished along with lyrics describing the provocative possibilities of what *marraines* (the wartime pen pals) had to offer. Given the army's focus on soldiers' morale, it willingly promoted a discourse on virility to create vigorous combatants, but this discourse was also popular among civilians. This put greater pressure on Parisian officials with regard to prewar tunes and composers creating and sending material to soldiers.

Supporting the War, Supporting Themselves: The Composers' Response

In the end, how well did this system work, and how readily did composers and performers conform to it? Clearly, the industry recognized the government's agenda and cooperated—more or less. But negotiations formed an integral feature of the censorship system, caused in part by the recurring ambiguities and by performers' ability to circumvent the rules. These debates highlight the points of contention and the strength of the police's position. According to the files of the most serious cases that came to the prefect's personal attention, the number of appeals reached a peak in the late summer and fall of 1915 as directors and songwriters were designing a completely new season, and then fell gradually in 1916 and 1917. Since the police apparently did not lessen their surveillance or change their criteria greatly, one might conclude that the rules became clearer and, at least in Paris, more generally accepted. Despite the large number of songs submitted, the censors were consistent, in that once they banned or modified a song, all theaters and cafés or performers followed these orders.[124]

For cases that went to the prefect, appeals came from composers, performers, music-hall directors, and editors. Whereas important people or places received some personal attention, they did not necessarily receive a more tolerant decision. Most songwriters and performers, however, showed a great willingness to modify the texts, gestures, or costumes according to the censor's instructions.[125] In addition, in November 1914, the directors of Parisian theaters had reached an agreement with the prefect that recognized censorship as a necessary process.

At times, the economic realities of the industry led to insistent dickering over visas, especially because the public closely identified many performers with their repertoire. The performer Enthovey urgently appealed his case after two recent blocks had left him short for an upcoming program. He explained to the prefect that he had "an extremely demanding clientele."[126] The music editor Jean Péheu resubmitted the song "Sous les bananiers" several times, because the lyrics were to be used by a big star—in this case, Dranem. One must also remember that a song's popularity and performance affected the sale of sheet music. In the case of individual composers who often had to absorb the costs of printing their own sheet music, even a modification meant a loss of income if the song had circulated before the war.[127] Anxiety over one's livelihood could induce absolute compliance. As Georgius wrote concerning the song "Julie dis moi": "Since all of the song's success resides in the music, which is very popular, I am ready to make all of the modifications that you judge necessary. . . . I will sing whatever you wish to allow and I will inform the other artists of what has been approved."[128] Martin and Georgius did reach a compromise.

Composers also attached the adjective "patriotique" to their songs when soliciting leniency. Paul Weil, in his fight for "Ferdinand de Bulgarie," questioned the prefectoral decision by highlighting his own fundamental contribution to the war effort:

Our manner of fighting certainly does not have the value of that of the young men who have the good fortune, because of their age, to be at the front; but the benefit of our songs cannot be disputed as each day our brave wounded men applaud us in the hospitals of Paris where we do our duty. Even in the workshops, where we go to give a little distraction to the courageous wives and daughters of those mobilized, our singing has the honor of being appreciated.[129]

One could hardly find a clearer defense of the music industry's self-appointed role. The industry had come of age at the turn of the century, but still faced criticism. Once the war began, its members sought to achieve respectability through patriotic contributions.

Along with promoting their own potential role in the war effort, many songwriters appear to have understood the opposition made between patriotism and obscenity. In Jean Bastia's argument over his song "Zeppelinades," he found it "intolerable to think" that the censor had confused his patriotic work with other indecent materials. The composer lashed out at the examiner who had compared his work "to some empty production in a *café-concert* . . . with its base goal of pleasing the public by throwing out an obscene word" and who had thus done an "injustice" to Bastia's "artistic conscience."[130] Bastia, who ran the cabaret Le Perchoir and was a central figure in the Parisian musical entertainment world, applauded the censors' goals, claiming that he too had "the keenest desire to see the level of art and integrity raised" in the "entertainment halls" *(salles de spectacle)*.[131]

On the other hand, one songwriter, a Monsieur Pinel, justified his song by calling it "gauloise" and pointing to the French tradition of humor—a clever tactic in the prevailing atmosphere of cultural chauvinism. This term's use revealed the blurred line between obscenity and earthiness that had bedeviled government debates before the war, and writers, performers, and editors were all aware of the controversial grey area.[132] Just as Pinel tried to convince the prefect that his lyrics had not reached the level of "suggestiveness of many other authorized songs," Moreau, the composer of "Réveil nocturne," argued that the censor's ruling seemed to be more stringent than the pre-1906 regime.[133] Nevertheless, Pinel and Moreau both insisted on the relative purity of their "modest" songs.

As the war went on and on, Parisian authorities allowed for some complaints as well as gentle denunciations of civilian comforts. But when new, potentially divisive circumstances appeared, examiners made fresh cuts. For instance, they suppressed lines that ridiculed aviators for showing off medals and ribbons, since flyers had become a focus of jealousy. Meanwhile, the censors maintained prohibitions on any direct attacks on the government or religious leaders, as well as on songs about workers' discontent.[134]

The authorities' adaptability also signified a certain assurance, since throughout the war support was greater for cultural than for political censorship. An outcry against interference in newspaper reporting began almost immediately in late 1914, and the government struggled to defend its position. No such campaign against official prerogatives grew up around censorship of songs, musical revues, or postcards. Thus even as political censorship eased up in late 1917 with the arrival of Georges Clemenceau as prime minister and minister of war, the control of cultural products and performance continued.[135]

In contrast to the relative steadiness of the Parisian operation, the army, facing the severe unrest of the mutinies in May and June of 1917, tightened its rules of surveillance. In June, for example, General Pétain ordered the confiscation of all songsheets with "La Terre nationale" following the arrest of two peddlars near the front. In this case, the song had been printed in Paris and then cleverly hidden between "nationalist songs" "with a patriotic imprint." He directed that "an active surveillance be exercised by the Censor on songs and other printed materials being peddled, which under the cover or appearance of patriotic songs, constitute a mode of pacifist propaganda, if not the incitement to disobedience."[136] Another song seized during the same period was entitled "Révolution," and began with the ominous words "Revolt, pariahs of the factories."[137] Moreover, an itinerant singer was arrested in Montbéliard near the front with an inventory that included the song "Tragique ballade des tranchées," which depicted the soldiers' desperate feelings in the spring of 1917 and harshly criticized official propaganda.[138] From 1917 on, the army moved more in line with the home front's censorship practices and objectives. A united government went on the offensive, with Clemenceau and Pétain working together.

In contrast to the military, the Parisian censors had benefited from familiarity with the ritual of cultural censorship and a ready legal structure; their quick response was hardly a surprise, nor was it negligible. It is clear that police, songwriters, and performers all recognized the potential power and malleability of song lyrics in performance. One sees a responsiveness to the goals and a willingness on the part of the *artistes* to follow the guidelines, if only to keep their repertoires intact—all of which suggests severe self-censorship. Silence, however, is difficult, if not impossible, to measure.

As the system moved smoothly along at the end of 1915 and early 1916, one government report confidently claimed that "dramatic adaptations of our national hymns at the theaters, and patriotic songs or satires of our enemies at the music halls, have served to sustain the public"; "in each case, they [the police] have almost always succeeded in eliminating any licentiousness in the works and unwholesomeness in the performances."[139] The analyst highlighted the police's sense of achievement and conveyed the multifaceted nature of their project.[140] The same report, however, noted that as management changed hands, some directors did not feel bound to the earlier agreement (of November 1914) and had "systematically organized shows without elevation and without patriotism." This telling comment hinted at continual haggling with songwriters and performers still pushing at the boundaries of satire and the "appropriate."

Though entrepreneurs often tried the censors' patience, we should not lose sight of their prowar zeal. World War I scholars have failed to appreciate how widespread and compelling "unofficial" efforts were, having focused too narrowly on "official," or government-produced, propaganda. Much of the ingenuity and energy for promoting the war on the home front came from private individuals and commercial interests including entertainers. This should hardly be surprising if one understands the vitality in the Belle Époque. But if individuals outpaced the government in their enthusiastic expressions, one cannot discount the role French officials played in dictating the terms of discourse in the public and commercial sphere. Officials in World War I set the ground rules which defined the borders of appropriate language and sentiments for soldiers and civilians, and at times reined in unofficial ventures. Defining the war as "total" gave liberal, democratic states such as France greater powers to control the public sphere, powers that in this case also involved pursuing older social agendas. As taste was constructed socially and politically, "patriotism" acted as the yardstick. The operations of the social struggle became more explicit because of the extensive wartime powers and the sense of urgency.

Moreover, just as fin-de-siècle modernity fed the prowar cultural energy, older criticisms of culture came into play. German censors attacked mass entertainment as immoral, wasteful, and "unseemly frivolity," because they carried into the war a broad dislike and suspicion of it.[141] Given the prewar cultural matrix in France, officials combated the unseemly, but not necessarily the frivolous, since some offerings were judged good clean entertainment. A suitable patriotic song could create cohesion and hope, rallying people and sustaining their energy. The government made itself the arbiter in deciding how far such efforts went.

The process and goals of censorship produced essentially conservative effects and help to explain why the French "stayed the course," as well as how they experienced the war. Censorship dampened political discourse, and with songs tightly controlled, lyrics were rewritten to offer positive views of leaders, soldiers, and Paris as well as exciting images of an eroticized war. The system also served to isolate the soldiers' criticisms, since the cultural border patrolled by the police and army proved to be relatively impermeable. The lack of criticism and its effects helped prolong the war and changed French political culture. Equally as important, officials were "cleaning up" the popular culture of the lower classes, at the very moment that "French popular culture" was to become celebrated. With a critical edge removed, this contributed to the creation of a postwar nostalgia.

CHAPTER FOUR

The Eroticization of War
Representations of Sexuality and Violence

The power of fin-de-siècle songs lay in their polyvalence and their complicated double entendres, an aspect that bedeviled Parisian censors' attempts to inculcate bourgeois morality. While officials drew in the field of expression by trying to restrict topics, types of humor, and political expressions, entrepreneurs, audiences, and soldiers pushed out the boundaries, and especially the line between the licit and illicit. In this chapter, we will approach the blurred line between the acceptable and unacceptable, not from the censors' side, but from the producers' side.

Starting promptly in 1914, one particularly potent, propagandistic discourse developed that represented war as exciting, vital, and even sexy. One of its two threads offered sexualized images of women motivating or rewarding combatants, since soldiering deserved the war's "perks." The transaction was rarely conceived of as economic or commercial; instead, images of the wife, fiancée, "pen pal/godmother" *(marraine),* and prostitute overlapped along a continuum. In addition, the representational flowed over into the experiential with the proliferation of female performers entertaining the troops, actual *marraines,* and the army's sanction of prostitution. The second thread included complicated representations of eroticized weaponry, identified with sexual acts or rapes. Thus, the sexual became linked to violence and aggression within the context of war.

Both sets of representations fed off of the intense anxieties that the war engendered for both soldiers and civilians. These pressures were caused by the separations (which must have stimulated desires) and the brutal confrontation with modern warfare. In fact, this discourse addressed several fears simultaneously: that men would refuse to go fight, that a soldier would fail to give a "manly" performance at the front, that soldiers packed together at the front might turn to homosexuality, and that the nation's population crisis would hinder its capacity to survive. In the French *mentalité* shared by officials, soldiers, and civilians alike, male sexual potency translated into superior fighters who would bring victory and have more children. It also reassured one of vitality and life in the midst of death. An erotic celebration of the national masculine community rested on a heterosexual orientation and a promotion of competition. It became important for men massed at the front to have feminine objects of desire, however abstract, or the national self-image was threatened.

This discourse appeared not just in songs, but also in postcards and posters; it played well across different media. In France, the promotion and remarkable length of the war depended heavily on the powers of mass cultural forms and genres that were highly adaptable. They could be quickly modified to fit any subject matter.[1] As a current event, the war became a compelling topic, which sold products while it reshaped older material.[2] In 1914, the proliferation of martial themes was rapid and widespread and helps to explain the strength of the French mobilization.

This chapter focuses on how these cultural forms promoted war by combining sexuality and violence. In examining how a liberal democracy such as France waged modern war, we need to look for mobilizing actions and expressions wherever they may be found. To date, most attention given to mobilization, and especially to propaganda, has focused on the official efforts of the state. Given the government's inexperience with modern war, however, "unofficial" propaganda far outstripped official efforts.[3] The most common definition of propaganda for the two world wars refers to government-produced artifacts that promoted the state's objectives, with ideas or representations that were supposed to be unidirectional and unambiguous. The discourse analyzed in this chapter clearly resembled official propaganda in that it supported the war effort. Popular images provided extremely creative and broadly based modes of communicating a prowar message. Furthermore, these representations, whether aural or visual, told people how their behavior could benefit the cause.

It was not, however, propaganda in the traditional sense, since it was not produced by the government or centrally controlled. In some cases, the motivation paralleled the government's—many of the major songwriters, for instance, worked to support the war with persuasion and enthusiasm. But the Parisian musical *artistes* and postcard entrepreneurs walked a fine line between patriotism and self-interest. A prowar stance was necessary to avoid police censure, and some participated to avoid questions of disloyalty.

The narrow parameters of censorship and the cultural *union sacrée* undermined artists' ability to be critical. Fundamentally, though, entrepreneurs also needed to entertain and please their consumers. The idea of "selling" the war lined up quite nicely with government needs, in some instances. But playfulness and humor were very common tools, which often introduced an important element of ambiguity. And a clear prowar message could be played with. In addition, in responding to their audiences, performers echoed the spectators' anxieties as well as their patriotic fervor or personal hopes.

We are not just talking about Parisian business entrepreneurs or *chansonniers* as producers, however. Erotic representations of war were propagated all over, even by soldiers themselves. The combatants represented both consumers and producers, as sexual images and lyrics flourished as a result of the greater editorial freedom at the front. And examination of these themes reveals an exchange or cross-fertilization between the trenches and the home front.

This exchange between soldiers and civilians occurred because wartime compositions drew upon a tradition of sexual humor deeply rooted in French popular culture. Prewar *café-concert* lyrics had consistently represented common, everyday scenarios as erotic and had relied on audiences' versatile imaginations to decode sexual connotations. Moreover, this familiarity with sexual humor was a part of a larger fascination with the "sexual" in fin-de-siècle France, which extended to other media.[4] Ouriel Reshef, for example, has argued that the world of political caricature between the Franco-Prussian War and World War I was "swamped" by "comic drawings or sketches of everyday ways, half-frivolous, half-lighthearted, often indecent, always very suggestive, " surrounding the figure of woman.[5] And, as early as 1900, France had become "famous for its libidinous visual exports."[6] The French had also long cultivated what they termed an *esprit gaulois,* which included humorously combining war and sex. Entrepreneurs were willing to risk some disapproval by using erotic material, because it was such an integral part of the French popular culture and because it sold.[7]

When the war began, however, the flood of eroticized representations was not simply an overlay of current affairs onto older forms, although it was the easiest and quickest commercial tactic in 1914. With the start of hostilities, the "sexual" became melded with ideas of traditional warfare to form a new alloy, one that spread a versatility in sexual puns across cultural forms in support of the war. The most important new and essential component was that everything could be done in the name of "patriotism." The burgeoning discourse, in other words, combined wartime imperatives and prewar cultural motifs.

The Mobilization of Sexual Desire and Fantasy

Wartime France witnessed the separation of millions of men and women, as soldiers went off to the front. It placed stress on relationships, increasing both anxieties and desires. Deferred sexual feelings were transferred representationally to patriotic symbols and weapons, and new erotic possibilities abounded. The sexualized promotion of war embraced two particularly vital moments in the experience of war: first, the initial farewell to soldiers and, then, the temporary homecoming on leave *(la permission)*.

LE BAISER

A "kissing" genre of songs from the prewar *café-concert* repertoire lent itself quite easily to the new conditions. In the Belle-Époque tunes, kisses had been given in humorous love scenes or during heartfelt farewells, and audiences appreciated the fact that in colloquial terms *baiser* (to kiss) also meant to have intercourse. A new collection appeared with the war's onset in which women, and in some songs the female inhabitants of whole villages, sent soldiers off to combat, armed with a last kiss—thus the titles "Baiser au régiment," "Baiser de gloire," and "Baiser de l'Alsacienne."[8] The stock figures became *French* women, or, more specifically, *Alsatian* women, while the only deserving male wore a uniform. (The Alsatian character was extremely well-known in revanchist songs and visual images.) This "delicious moment" set hearts beating, as men went to prove they were worthy of their love's "young heart." In "Filles d'Alsace," the song's performer told of Margot, an Alsatian woman, who sent her fiancé Jean-Pierre off with a kiss for good luck and declared that such kisses went only to the "courageous soldiers of France." When a German officer appeared and declared: "I desire your kiss . . . I am your master," Margot was saved only by the reappearance of Jean-Pierre, which kept her "kisses" for the French soldier.[9] The performer's shift from narrator to German "hun" and then to Margot for the final declaration of French patriotism increased the exciting tension.

The musical genre of the *baiser* overlapped with postcards, for which entrepreneurs immediately reshot prewar scenarios to incorporate soldiers in red pants and blue jackets as a part of every couple, or simply retouched cards to add a military symbol (figs. 4–5).[10] (Hard helmets and full blue uniforms became the proper symbol of the *poilu* only after the army had adapted to trench warfare.) In most cases, postcards portrayed common soldiers, illustrating the French concept of the democratic *levée en masse*. The women appeared with lace, bows, and sashes; some wore light, short dresses and black stockings, and most were young.[11] The couple was signified as French by the soldier's uniform, or in songs by the mention of a specific region. The settings—with a backdrop of classicized nature or bourgeois parlors—remained relatively unspecific, but offered visions of French civility to contrast with German barbarity, a prominent topic from the start of the war.[12]

The giving of a kiss was no longer a private act but became instead a political act of patriotism. The deed, provoked by the men's "martial air," gave courage and good luck to both partners. Tito Saubidet's drawing, for example, emphasized the power of the man with his height and grip (fig. 6). In the French *cafés-concerts*, the British soldier Tommy also received a last token from his tearful fiancée—a kiss that "gave him power" (*donne la force*) and left him "better armed."[13] The first refrain of "Un Baiser qui passe" put it precisely:

Un p'tit baiser	A little kiss
C'est le doux gage	Is the sweet pledge
Qu'on veut donner	That one wishes to give
A ton courage	For your courage
Tu s'ras vainqueur.	You will be the victor.[14]

The *baiser* channeled the power of heightened desire toward aggression for the enemy and the achievement of valiant deeds, while the lyrics hinted at other sexual acts.[15] The figure of the fiancée also stood for anticipated sexual love, which was temporarily sublimated into heroic violence.[16]

In many French songs, it was *la Victoire, la Gloire,* or *la France* who led the way as a sexualized, anthropomorphic figure; these allegories of women represented perfectly the desired but unattainable sexual object.[17] Many visual representations also showed provocative bodies with bare or partially covered breasts. In one song, *la Victoire* appeared enticingly "in a glorious dream" to a sleeping soldier, and sang softly:

R'garde moi bien	Look at me carefully
J'suis la Victoire	I am Victory
Et, si je viens	And if I come
Chanter ta gloire	To sing your glory

C'est qu'mon baiser	It is because my kiss
Tu l'as gagné	You have won
Va!	Go!
C'baiser là	That kiss
Jamais un boch' ne l'aura!	A *boche* (German) shall never have![18]

Like the Alsatian Margot, *la Victoire* aroused sexual competition between men, with the ultimate contest against the Germans. Sexualized and strongly feminized women provoked men to virile actions.

The female personification of victory, glory, or even death was not new to World War I, and neither was the soldiers' sense of duty. Composers or graphic designers had much to draw upon from nineteenth-century culture. In the traditional refrain of the 58th Infantry regiment from Rouergue, for instance, a combatant turned down an offer to marry a woman for either of two apparitions: "la victoire" or "la mort" (victory or death).[19] Likewise, World War I lyrics told soldiers explicitly that they should temporarily give their love to *la Patrie* or *la Gloire* as a substitute for their real partners. The transference was established structurally in the lyrics. A common formula listed different types of love: a mother's affection, "ardent" love found in "conquering" women, and love for *la Patrie* which involved "ardeur" and a full heart.[20]

The kiss also symbolized, or sealed, the quid pro quo whereby women promised affection in return for men's heroic performances. One postcard from 1915, for example, showed a soldier (a Scotsman) with puckered lips leaning toward a very fashionably dressed woman, who swore, "You shall kiss me when you have beaten them at the front."[21] Women sent their men off in some lyrics, with the request that they return with a medal; they made the relationship contractual.[22] Repeatedly in the *baiser* genre, the kiss was promised or deferred, since it had to be earned under fire.[23]

Patriotic objects of desire could also trigger erotic reactions with a religious subtext which lent them a serious tone; the patriotic passion paralleled religious ecstasy. According to the song "Adieu au drapeau," nurses found themselves moved with "exhilaration" and "delirious ecstasy," when they heard the trumpeter's call and saw the *tricoleur*.[24] The flag, like a religious icon, also had sexual appeal. In "Le Baiser au régiment," a company asked a woman to give a kiss to "the most valiant" for good luck. She could not choose between the common soldiers and the officer and instead embraced the flag.[25] This intertwining of holy and civic fervors was extremely beneficial in a Republic that had just separated the Church from the State in 1905 and that needed the deepest loyalty of its citizens.

Even death (also a feminine noun in French) was eroticized. It repre-

Figure 4. Postcard, "The Kiss." Collection of the author.

Figure 5. Postcard, "Your kiss is sweeter still / Than the dear voice which beseeches it." Collection of the author.

Figure 6. Lithograph by Tito Saubidet, "Le train de 9 h 45 Gare du Nord." Courtesy of the Musée d'Histoire Contemporaine — BDIC.

sented the ultimate reward to satisfy both national demands and sexual desire. In one piece dating from the Franco-Prussian War and revived in December 1914, the "Beau Sergent" in Lorraine was promised a kiss when he returned from battle. When he did not reappear, the girl had to search for him and delivered her "sweet kiss" to his corpse.[26] When another fictitious soldier died, a woman gave the pledged kiss, this time to bloodied lips. "Thus, with a long kiss the faithful Alsatian [woman] / Shut his lightless eyes and then, straightening up / Quivering, her lips still red with blood: / 'Prussians, Remember as I will,' she cried." Enraged, she returned to the village fountain to greet other French regiments and to incite them to kill Germans.[27]

It is noteworthy that even though France had conscription that dictated the nation's mobilization—in contrast to Great Britain's voluntary recruitment, for example—the genres of "kisses" and "farewells" became widespread and popular. These objects of popular culture helped to define the moment's importance and to reaffirm an individual's designated role. Furthermore, this genre of *baiser* persisted throughout the war. Jean Daris's song "Un Baiser qui passe," for instance, was still being sung by female performers at the Gaîté-Parisienne in February 1917.[28] The send-off was also played out on stage when several female performers became well known for hugging and kissing *poilus* from the audience at the end of their songs.[29]

Soldiers created their own renditions, both serious and humorous, since they found themselves at the front with time for their imaginations to wander between assaults. The trench newspaper *Le Gafouilleur* published a poem set to music in July 1916 entitled "Aux morts au champ d'honneur." In these lyrics, dead soldiers dripping blood, their bayonets stained, received kisses from "La France."[30] Soldiers could also be less reverent with sacred symbols. In a completely different tone, the musical revue "Trois ans après" had "La Victoire" agreeing to be the *commère,* or musical hostess. In all likelihood played by a man, "she" warned the soldiers not to fall in love with "her," singing:

Si quelqu'un par aventure	If someone by chance
Tombait amoureux de moi,	Fell in love with me,
Comme je suis un' jeun' fille pure,	As I am a pure young girl,
Qu'il calme vite son émoi	Let him quickly calm his emotions
Je lui dirais sans mystère:	I would tell him without a fuss:
"Tant pis si je vous ai plu,	"Too bad if I appeal to you,
Mais je ne puis vous satisfaire,	But I couldn't satisfy you,
Puisque j'ai des . . . (sifflé)."	"Since I have . . . (whistling)."[31]

The use of the gap and its erotic suggestiveness was a vintage *café-concert* technique. Once the audience had enjoyed the ambiguity of the figure, the last verse confirmed their own masculinity, proclaiming: "If these heroes of history / have fought so bravely. / It's because like *la Victoire* / They all have . . . (whistling)." Remarkably, this revue was performed in mid-1917.[32]

As the long, brutal war neared the end of its first year, a new circumstance presented itself fraught with erotic potential—*la permission,* or leave. Some song lyrics, supporting historian Marie-Monique Huss's interesting work on postcards, encouraged sex while on leave for the sake of procreation (or the production of the military classes of 1936 and 1937).[33] The pervasive pronatalism answered widespread fears concerning France's depopulation, which the war was aggravating so severely.

Civilian songwriters and soldiers discovered that taking leave in Paris offered all sorts of erotic possibilities. Songs advised soldiers on how to take full advantage of their time off. Valentin Tarault's "Dix jours de permission" celebrated ten days in "Panam" (Paris), when a soldier could visit "les p'tit's fafemmes" (women) and "show them [his] . . . program."[34] In the popular "patriotic fantasy card" genre, which showed men gleefully arriving from the front, "the moralistic theme was absent: instead there was an endorsement of male sexual pleasure. Girls should do all they could to make the fighting man happy."[35]

Called "douce récompense" (fig. 7) or promised to the soldiers as "A little delicious fruit," the woman, sometimes miniaturized in these images, represented the prize or object of desire. One card (fig. 8) adapted the extremely well-known phrase "On les aura," which usually referred to the French getting the Germans, to the soldiers having "les p'tites femmes" (the little or young women). Here, women replaced the enemy temporarily as the soldiers' target of conquest. The main goal was to reinvigorate the combatants, and the result for men was not simply personal satisfaction, but a positive part of the national war effort. Theoretically, even a soldier suffering from *le cafard*—a mixture of boredom, depression, and despair endured by combatants—would return to the trenches ready for the next assault, "his energy . . . reawakened."[36] In this particular case, the censors helped craft the message, thus coordinating official and unofficial efforts. They disapproved of Georges Millandy's original version, in which the soldier deserted to see his wife, Margot, was arrested and brought to court. In the final approved version from May 1916, the combatant returned on his own, led the assault, and earned a commendation. His visit had produced the right results.

These representations and the censors' cooperation reflected a belief that sex, far from sapping a French soldier's energy, helped create it. This inverted the Anglo-Saxon model, which argued that the body contained a closed system and an equilibrium of fluids and organs, which through

Figure 7. Postcard, "Sweet Reward." Collection of the author.

overuse would become imbalanced or depleted. Thus, soldiers could not give away vital fluids just before facing the demands of battle.[37] French officials, pundits, and composers obviously did not adhere to claims that having sex too often caused enervation, and they spoke early and often of the *poilu*'s virility. Indeed, cultural artifacts fostered the idea that the more often a man had intercourse, the more virile he became. In the case of

Figure 8. Postcard, "We will have them . . . the young women!" Courtesy of the Musée d'Histoire Contemporaine — BDIC.

Joffre's commendation to the soldiers of Verdun, military officials spoke with "virile eloquence" *(éloquence virile)*, and civilians such as Henri Lavedan, a playwright and member of the French Academy, stood "transfixed with admiration . . . and with impotence" before the *poilus'* "virile and terrible energy."[38] The censors also did their part in opposing any disparagements of men's, and especially soldiers', virility.[39]

The army also supported prostitution for the troops, for, as one general put it, "the prostitute and call girl are a necessary distraction, while a wife, who represents the home, weakens a soldier's heart."[40] Prostitution continued to thrive near the front, where women could make a fortune, despite the dangers. In Paris, although prostitutes lost customers at the start of the war when Parisians fled before the advancing Germans, business improved particularly around train stations, hospitals, and certain theaters once the first leaves were granted. Soldiers could even write ahead to reserve a particular woman. Léon Bizard, who wrote on prostitution in wartime Paris, put it succinctly: "this is a time when the military authorities, justly concerned for the health of the men and the maintenance of the troops, believed it necessary to favor the spread of the *maisons publiques* [regulated brothels], with a visit every couple of days from the personnel."[41]

Notwithstanding the general's ranking of prostitutes above wives, representations in songs and postcards did not make such a strong distinction. In numerous card scenarios (figs. 5, 9–11), women waited dressed in lingerie and greeted their *poilus* in bedrooms, representing the soldier's reward for his suffering. The captions described exquisite "hours of ecstasy," and loving from morning to night. Although some scholars have contended that soldiers on leave were "temporarily demobilized," since they had certainly reentered the civilian world, their attractiveness and the treatment they were supposed to receive depended on their special status. Theoretically, they were never to be confused with a *reformé* (those excused from

Figure 9. Postcard, "Hours of homecoming / Hours of ecstasy!" Collection of the author.

Figure 10. Postcard, "Sweet moments: An exquisite hour, which I will remember always."
Collection of the author.

military service) or, much worse, with *embusqués* (shirkers).[42] Inevitably, in
these erotic scenes, obvious signs marked the men as soldiers worthy of the
attention—whether the symbols were front and center or off to the side,
framing the picture. Hats hung on bedposts, kits sat nearby, and helmets
even occupied the bed with the couple—emphasizing the prompt move to
the bedroom (and possibly hinting at a future pregnancy). The immediate
welcome in the boudoir also implied that women would be waiting there,
which could have been both reassuring and erotic for soldiers. In addition,
in the private space of the bedroom, men were cleaned up and made desirable for women.

None of the cards in this genre indicated clearly that the woman was a
wife or that the couple was married. There were also few traditional signs
of domesticity, although the official poster for the "Journée des poilus"
(fig. 12) showed a soldier lustily embracing his wife next to a sewing machine, while the dog—a sign of fidelity—looked on. Instead, women appeared in lingerie, black stockings with garters, or transparent tops (figs. 5
and 13), and the representations made it difficult to distinguish between fiancées, wives, or prostitutes.[43] Some pictures were obviously more risqué
than others, with varying degrees of suggestive clothing, bare skin, and
gestures, but the range or continuum was not made up of sharply distinct
types. Signs marking these types were blurred or missing, occluding any
rigid dichotomy of good versus bad women. The representations also did

not create an opposition between commercial sex and the bourgeois ideal. In songs, prostitutes could become wives or fiancées, and wives might give comfort to another in the name of the missing husband. Even prostitutes had a positive role. In song lyrics at least, they gave free services, and, as one "pretty seller of pleasure" explained, then an *embusqué* or shirker "would pay."[44] Yet, whether prostitute or wife, most of these representations still involved prescriptive roles: women were mobilizers and prizes; men were fighters.

These images may suggest a shift from a prewar polarity. According to Ouriel Reshef's analysis of French caricature for 1871–1914, attributes for women were divided between *la Mère-patrie* and *la Grisette-Marianne*. One represented duty and fidelity, the other debauchery and perfidy.[45] The art historian Anne Wagner has also claimed that, "the centurywide gap between woman's identities as Madonna or Magdalen" had started "ever so slowly, to close" at the turn of the century.[46] If we accept this dichotomy, then the war material marked a significant departure.

We should not overdraw this binary opposition, however. Beatrice Farwell has noted the power of erotic subjects in commercial lithography, and their subversive influence on the world of "high art."[47] Wagner's proposed "closing" may have been, in part, a mixing of "high" and popular techniques, subjects, and definitions. Furthermore, the French had had a

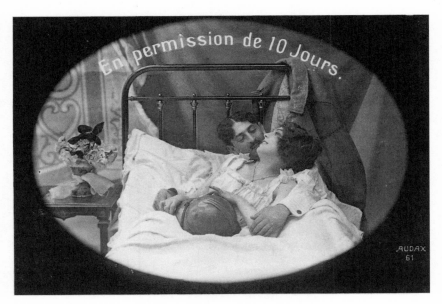

Figure 11. Postcard, "On leave for 10 days." Collection of the author.

Figure 12. Poster by Adolphe Willette, "Alone at last . . . !" for the "Journée du Poilu." Courtesy of the Musée d'Histoire Contemporaine—BDIC.

Figure 13. Postcard, "Tax on the Income/Incoming": "Since you have returned / Come pay the tax!" Courtesy of the Musée d'Histoire Contemporaine—BDIC.

powerful repertoire of sexy, patriotic women. Following the Franco-Prussian War, for instance, Guy de Maupassant's short story "Boule de suif" portrayed a prostitute with patriotic sentiments, and in his "Bed no. 29," a woman chose to sleep with Germans in order to give them syphilis and to steal German sperm. In the end, the character Irma Pavolin claimed to have killed more Prussians than an entire French regiment.[48] Moreover, the combination of the erotic and selling had developed in sophistication and range by 1914. In her work on the popular arenas of daily life in the late nineteenth century, Susanna Barrows has uncovered how drinking, for example, was sold with an eroticized campaign of young, "nubile" waitresses, and sexual clothing, decor, and advertisements.[49] If one could sell alcohol with sex, why not war?[50]

In much of the war material, women of all classes were enlisted, as the boundaries of bourgeois respectability were being pushed outward in the service of the nation. This may be because in feeding male fantasies and the national needs, the *poilus* held the privileged position, and it did not matter who a woman was as long as she was a woman. But representations emphasized sexualized femininity, which created a tension between the sought-after female, and the scarier, overly active female. There was both ambiguity and anxiety.

In examining the power of these propagandistic pieces, one must also consider the even more complicated question of their reception. Not only did individuals incorporate the illustrated side of postcards into

Figure 14. Postcard, "We are happy to see each other again / To love one another from morning to night . . ." Collection of the author.

their messages, but they deliberately rewrote the captions. One woman chose a 1914 card picturing a *poilu* and a woman kissing (fig. 4), and wrote on the back, "I send you my best kiss if I can do it like the card."[51] Another message wistfully asked, "When will your wonderful kisses arrive, Soon I hope," while others sent their own "fat kiss" *(gros bécots)* or "big smacker" *(grosse gnône)*. People also linked the front and back, not hesitating to cross out or add to the captions. On one printed phrase describing the couple in the picture—"We are happy to see each other again / To love one another from morning to night"—the writer changed the "are happy" to "will be happy" referring to her husband's anticipated leave (fig. 14). Clearly, some fantasies were applicable to daily life and were appropriated, which kept these themes strong throughout the war.

Interestingly, the writers of a study on wartime correspondence with southern France noted that combatants appear to have been less willing or able to choose the erotic fantasy cards than civilians, and that the illustrated postcards were often sent without comment. Gérard Baconnier and his co-authors conjectured that "They said it with the cards."[52] One soldier, however, did buy a complete set and wrote, "'My dearest fiancée. . . . I have purchased this series of cards today and I want to send it to you all at once; I think you will be pleased since you will see in these circumstances, the emotions I feel for you—X."[53] Another combatant had scribbled on his card, below a couple shown embracing, "When will we be like these two?"

LES MARRAINES

From early 1915 on, the public's erotic imagination was also sustained by another ambiguous female figure, the *marraine*—a new role, which cultivated patriotic behavior in women while feeding the fantasies and dreams of soldiers.[54] Charitable organizations first developed the concept of *marraines* or godmothers in early 1915 to assist those soldiers without families or whose families lived in the occupied territories. The system asked the *marraines* to send letters and gifts to the front to help maintain morale.[55] The idea was hailed as an important facet of the *union sacrée,* since the epistolary relationships would bring social classes and generations together. Their popularity was then fueled by widely circulated newspapers, which carried advertisements from soldiers and potential pen pals, and which led to all sorts of stories, illustrations, and jokes. Many of them were risqué, exploring the possibilities for all sorts of "charity" work. This enlistment, therefore, combined practice and the representational. One announcement, entitled "Demande de marraine," specified: "Artillery *Poilu* would be pleased to bombard a not too shy marraine with love letters."[56] Songs portrayed the *marraine* as medicine for a soldier's *cafard;* a letter from her and "the hardest miseries" were forgotten, and courage returned.[57] The fantasy was not limited to soldiers receiving alluring packages and letters in the trenches, but quickly became associated with soldiers' eager trips to Paris to meet a pen pal. In the lyrics, soldiers repeatedly made requests for young and beautiful *marraines,* strangers who were a part of the new undefined categories. Again, there were wholesome versions, which showed the soldier returning to the home front with a medal and eventually marrying his pen pal, but these still combined sex and patriotism.[58]

The flow of ideas surrounding the *marraine* represented one creative cultural link between Parisian wartime culture and inhabitants and the soldiers in the trenches. The soldiers themselves participated in the program, sending their requests to the Parisian dailies. In their trench newspapers, they wrote lists outlining the perfect pen pal, and the character frequently appeared in their musical revues (again, sometimes played by men). In a revue written for and about the 76th Infantry, a soldier sang of his *marraine:* "Her words are sweet like music / And when I dream of what she writes / I am transported into a magical world."[59] The depiction mixed reverence, fantasy, and homesickness, but could also have been sung with a tone that would have expressed the soldiers' incredulity.[60]

Stéphane Audoin-Rouzeau's study of trench journals has shown how much French soldiers wrote and joked about their sexual interests, and how much they protested the lack of women. The combatants' "prolonged abstinence," fettered desires, and "a traditional military licentiousness" explained the "vulgarity" in their newspapers.[61] One cover of *Rigolboche,* for example, had a drawing of a woman wearing a sheer negligee standing in front of a mirror fixing her hair. A small cherub hovered nearby having just delivered a telegram that read "4 Days Leave."[62] In another sketch, side-by-side scenarios entitled "Two Good Moments!" showed a French soldier driving his bayonet through the neck of a German soldier, on the left, while a soldier hugged a woman in lingerie, on the right. The caption said wistfully, "From day to day."[63] Song texts also fantasized. Lyrics prominently displayed on the front page of *Le Poilu du 6–9* described a soldier's amazement that a stranger would send him perfumed letters. She had promised, "My heart is yours / If you return a winner!" and the soldier requested her photograph so that if he fell "it would be with her."[64]

Furthermore, even when they tried to correct civilians' misconceptions derived from home-front propaganda, soldiers sometimes maintained an emphasis on their manliness. Lieutenant Bossuyt's song "Eh! dis donc, Poilu" offered a clarification of the true *poilu.* It had nothing to do with having a beard; instead, a real soldier could "eat boche," "had principles," and because he was "a man" he could produce the class of '36 while on leave.[65] In a steady cycle, the system of *marraines* was nourished by the soldiers' own sexual desires and need for diversions, which then led to the production of new jokes, songs, and erotic drawings. These then served to rekindle soldiers' imaginations.[66]

With the start of the Great War, new uniforms, weapons, and strategies made their way into mass cultural forms—all seeming to have an erotic capacity. A creative burst, both pervasive and invasive, militarized public speech, music, jokes, and images. Whether serious or humorous, the representations educated the public about the military world. Where postcards had previously compared women's breasts to apples or eggs, they now used grenades or helmets[67] (fig. 15). The sexual innuendos relied on the public's knowledge of military hardware to create the jokes about "the artillery of love": the famous 75 could "fire repeatedly," the 120 short "never failed," and the 400 had "explosive results" but was "dangerous to handle" (fig. 16). These particular jests rendered, or at least reinforced, an optimistic and exciting view of war.

Just as the phrase "On les aura" could be applied to either women or Germans, the rhetorical violence of the war proliferated on the home front with erotic/military double entendres. The most obvious puns equated sexual conquests with military campaigns, sexual advances with military assaults. In the forum of the *cafés-concerts* of the Belle Époque, everyday objects had always had provocative possibilities. Now soldiers could exercise their martial skills in successfully taking "the fort." Other songs reported

Figure 15. Postcard, "The Weapons of Love." Courtesy of the Musée d'Histoire Contemporaine—BDIC.

Figure 16. Postcard, "Artillery of Love." Courtesy of the Musée d'Histoire Contemporaine—BDIC.

on the triumphant *poilu* who returned home, received attention from his wife, and "gaily proved his love."[68] These feats emphasized male virility within a heterosexual context by stressing success or completion—not just interest or arousal at the first embrace, but the moments "après" (after). Therefore, sets of postcards also provided a narrative with before and after the "offensive en chambre." (For example, the couple in fig. 10 was reshot with the caption, "Doux moments, Après l'offensive le doux repos.")

One cartoon showed the precise stages to be pursued on the first day home on leave—modeled on an assault from the trenches: from preparations before the attack, to the first wave, and finally to strengthening the captured position. In this example, the female body was eroticized and depersonalized, with the curved parts seen through the transparent slip and her face hidden, until after the position "was taken." A paper such as *La Vie Parisienne,* which had pioneered the use of provocative graphics, quickly incorporated erotic pictures of women dressed in French or allied uniforms being sought after and "conquered" by men.[69] This war was to be an adventure—not something scary, abnormal, or ruinous.

The equation of military achievements with male potency had existed prior to the Great War; for instance, the song "La Petite Tonkinoise," which was written during the colonial wars of the late nineteenth century, equated the "conquering French" with a "conquering lover"—and the sexual act with violence.[70] The handsome, wolfish captain *(grenadier)* had also figured in short stories and musical revues. It was not new, and it was not forgotten by soldiers. Written in a timely fashion, just as the first wave of soldiers was getting leave in mid-1915, one combatant's piece described soldiers on leave "mounting an assault" and "grabbing the *teutons*" to make little *poilus*.[71]

Rosalie and Her Friends

Civilian lessons on the weapons of war had a risqué edge, both exciting and intimidating. But the purpose of the representations was not just to interest or entertain civilians. The government, or more specifically the army, had to produce killers out of civilized men, and individual soldiers worried about their performance. This mandate was recorded on a postcard that listed among "The Ten Commandments of the Soldier," "Thou shalt always kill."[72] To this end, an older, aggressive formulation of war, which promoted male potency by playing off of the male sex act and organ, spread representationally.[73] From the beginning, these songs and jokes aspired to motivate and entertain the soldiers and to bolster a male community based on the "other," or more precisely on representations of female objects. If the *baiser* and *perme* genres objectified women, helping create a community of men, characterizations of weaponry did so to an even greater degree. The French, like so many soldiers of later wars, chose to baptize their weapons with female names—the bayonet became Rosalie, the machine gun Mimi, and artillery guns Catherine and Nana. These objects were to be loved, protected, and cared for, while they offered pleasure and German deaths in return. But the same weapons in the hands of the enemy also brought fear.

Théodore Botrel, a well-known Belle-Époque singer, dedicated his song "Rosalie" (app. fig. 5) to the glory of "small French bayonettes," and it rose to prominence in the fall of 1914. In the first verses of his tune, the beautiful and elegant Rosalie appeared in a "tight-fitting dress," pursued by two to three million suitors.

Rosalie est élégante	Rosalie is elegant
Sa robe-fourreau collante,	Her sheath-dress tight-fitting,
Verse à boire!	Pour a drink!
La revêt jusqu'au quillon	Adorns her up to the neck.
Buvons donc!	Let us drink then![74]

The female personification, however, overlapped with a clearly phallic image when "she" rose up nude and danced excitedly "as a prelude to the cannon." She then pierced and punctured (*pique*) the enemy (*piquer* also means to excite or stimulate).

Mais elle est irresistible,	But she is irresistible,
Quand elle surgit, terrible,	When she surges, terrible,
Verse à boire!	Pour a drink!
Toute nue: baïonnette . . . on!	Completely naked: bayonet . . . !
Buvons donc!	Let us drink!

The imagery recreated a rape, whether of a woman or a man, and the sexual act was "consummated" with blood when the "bayonet" changed from "all white" to "vermillion" or bright red—hence the name Rosalie. Botrel's lyrical double entendre was not metonymical, since the correspondence between the bayonet as a woman or the bayonet as a penis was not set. Who were these suitors and what did they seek? Whose phallus was "she" as she apparently sodomized the Germans? The slippage left room for the audience's own interpretations, with fun and sporting lyrics overall. But there was also a subtext of anxiety toward women and their potential powers of seduction—Rosalie was "irresistible" and surged up terribly.

The sexualization also became closely intertwined with violence, and the combat was cast as exciting and participatory. The action combined dancing, fighting, and a sexual act with homoerotic or homosocial overtones. The fact that this was a drinking song also reinforced the idea of a male collectivity. As in other songs, the references to killing were not abstract; concrete words described the action. The multilayered imagery of a bayonet, a woman, and a penis, however, objectified the act of killing, with Rosalie performing the deed—removing it from the soldiers' own sphere of responsibility.

Eve Sedgwick's literary theory on homosociability might help us understand the workings of these representations. According to her study, male heterosexual desire for the objectified bodies of females could consolidate bonds between "authoritative men." The women are often present only as objects of desire to encourage "erotic rivalry" between men in a triangular arrangement. The competition forms as strong a bond among men as does the attraction for women, and could contain the "energies of compulsion, prohibition, and explosive violence."[75] In the specific case of World War I France, we have seen that female erotic objects abounded as did male competition. But how were these representations created and disseminated?

Botrel, who wrote his own songs, was one of the main performers who went into the army zone to give concerts. He gave thousands of performances with government assistance by the end of the war.[76] Other *artistes* included female performers who personified the figures seen on cards and in songs, some of whom clearly played up their sexuality. Eugénie Buffet described one woman in her troupe as someone who "adored masculine devotion, sought it out, provoked it."[77] Along with sanctioning these musical efforts, the department of war also distributed songsheets to the troops and "Rosalie" sat at the center of the November 1914 *Bulletin des armées* supplement.[78] In addition, military officials associated sexual jokes and obscene language with being manly and combative in contrast to "little girls."[79]

The song "Rosalie" differed from Botrel's prewar works, which contained nothing so sexually explicit or violent, but he had had over twenty years of experience with *café-concert* humor and patriotic tropes.[80] More important, Botrel was emulating a martial tradition that had identified the bayonet with the French soldier's "impetuous enthusiasm."[81] In his book *The Bayonets of the Republic,* John Lynn has examined what he termed "the cult of the bayonet"—a military doctrine and powerful philosophy, which viewed the bayonet as the perfect weapon for the French infantry's hand-to-hand combat with an enemy. The bayonet was germane to both the military game plan and the soldiers' self-image.[82] Having originated with the revolutionary troops, this cult spread in the popular imagery of the nineteenth century, focusing on the infantry's forceful, virile nature.[83] In this model of warfare—which commanded the public's attention in 1914—the fighting, although difficult, offered a sense of release and an actualization of self through taking risks. It also signified the expected forward motion, which had sexual connotations. This discourse remained strong, at least on the home front and among some top officers, throughout World War I. The link between soldiering and a language of masculinity with erotic overtones was not new, but its distribution had expanded through mass production.

With this well-entrenched picture of "traditional" war, "Rosalie" was destined not to be just one isolated and little-known song. Many Parisian songwriters composed their own tributes to the bayonet Rosalie, while others wrote in a style similar to Botrel's.[84] Rosalie was sometimes called "the best loved," or "our wife," with the gun designated as the child. To honor "the bayonet of our brave infantrymen," Alcide wrote the song "C'est Rosalie," which was then performed by Félix Mayol in both camps and hospitals for soldiers as well as in the *cafés-concerts*. Once more the *poilus* left behind their loves and took instead "the prettiest Rosalie," who was kept "close to their hearts"; though normally "pale," she "blushed" ("reddened") in battle.[85] With lyrics such as "a good Rosali' in the hide" or "Come! Go! My Rosalie / With love, with fury / You are the glory of the infantry!" she epitomized the admiration for forward motion.[86] At times it became even clearer that the bayonet had phallic connotations and served as proof of soldiers' masculinity. "Les Braves Poilus" by P. Alberty, for example, had a rather obvious double entendre:

Qu'est c'que les femm's aim'nt le plus? (bis)	What do women love the most? (twice)
Ce sont les braves poilus! (bis)	It is the brave poilus! (twice)
Quand ils pass'nt dans les villages	When they pass through villages
Les fillettes les plus sages	The most well-behaved girls
Donneraient bien un écu	Would happily give an écu [old coin]
Pour jouer avec leur baïonnette	To play with their bayonet
Donneraient bien un écu	Would happily give an écu
Et peut-être mêm' leur vertu!	And maybe even their virtue![87]

The figure of Rosalie also quickly caught the broader public's imagination and carried well into the war. Members of the French Academy confidently proclaimed that soldiers sang "Rosalie" along with the "Marseillaise" to keep their enthusiasm strong.[88] In addition, Rosalie was defined as a Frenchman's bayonet in the dictionaries of trench slang, and found her way into newspapers, postcards and onto commemorative plates[89] (fig. 17). The sheet music cover of "Rosalie-Mazurka" made the point quite clearly: "No one is unaware that 'Rosalie' is the name with which our good troops . . . have baptized the brave and terrible dear French bayonet."[90]

The soldiers themselves were caught between their own fascination and the way this discourse played into the home front's belief in proper soldierly enthusiasm. Some rejected the representation of "Rosalie" as strictly home-front fare.[91] But it was too good for others to pass up and too closely tied to shared cultural views of masculinity. In their very first edition of *81me poil . . . et plume,* in May 1916, the combatants offered the song "La Bochocrole," whose lyrics told of Guillaume (the kaiser) deciding to go after all the "petits Français." But he had not counted on "Cett' p'tite Française de Rosalie." He was tunefully told to come and get it.[92]

Other composers also mimicked Botrel's emphasis on motion and used erotic vocabulary such as "fervor," "excitement," or "penetration"; the war became a sexual pursuit, with success defined as a release or a breakthrough.[93] In the song lyrics, the individual soldier struck against another individual but always within a group, and the verbs of encouragement were almost all plural (for example, "rallions," "chargeons," "Hardi," or "lançons")—illustrating Sedgwick's concept of bonding. The common song form was particularly effective, since writers used short, direct lines and many exclamatory phrases. "Les Honneurs du front," for instance, blithely intoned:

Figure 17. Porcelain plate, "The Mask": "Rosalie goes to the masked ball." Courtesy of the Musée d'Histoire Contemporaine—BDIC.

Pan, pan! les gars,	Bang, bang! boys,
Tirons bien, tirons dans l'tas!	Let us shoot well, shoot into the crowd!
. . . .	. . . .
Allons-y fort, cré nom d'un nom!	Let us go firmly, hell!
Chargeons!. . . baïonnette au canon!	Let us charge! . . . bayonet to cannon!
Nous avons les honneurs du front!	We have the honors of the front![94]

These songs were meant to increase combativeness and to bolster male egos by dictating behavior, especially in the face of new and frightening technology.

Botrel himself had no trouble adapting his songs to the novel forms of warfare—new weapons called for new names, and these tunes were once again for both soldiers' and civilians' consumption. In his song "Ma Petite Mimi," which he wrote toward the end of 1915, he boasted of his feminine "machine gun," which he lubricated and polished autoerotically:

Plein d'adresse,	Full of dexterity,
Je la graisse,	I grease her,
Je l'astique et la polis	I rub and polish her
De sa culasse jolie	From her pretty breech
A sa p'tit' gueu-gueul' chérie;	To her little beloved mouth;
Puis, habile,	Then, skillfully,
J'la défile	I parade her
Et, tendrement, je lui dis:	And, tenderly, I tell her:
"Jusqu'au bout, restons unis	"Until the end, let us remain united
Pour le salut du Pays!"	For the welfare of the country!"[95]

The first verse had described a soldier's loneliness without a woman, until he was named a machine gunner and found a substitute—"What happiness." Again, Botrel's musical representation overlapped the fondling of a woman with masturbation or with sodomizing the Germans, but the emphasis remained on possessing the object. Moreover, enjoyment derived from violently "mowing" down the Germans.

The song "Le Rondeau du fusil," which appeared on an anonymous 1918 broadsheet, did not explicitly use the form of a woman, although the weapon was a "pretty gun." The composer did, however, use the metaphor of a phallus.[96] The lyrics were fraught with sexual implications as the soldier described taking the "quivering stick" or "barrel" *(canon)* in his hand. After being handled, the gun was ready to launch a "thundering shot" which "nothing could stop." Both the gun and the bayonet lent self-sufficiency to the soldiers with masturbation and fantasy (autoeroticism). There was even a rivalry between weapons—one "chansonnier-soldat" found Rosalie "charming" and "piquant," but liked his "pretty" machine gun more since she worked better and longer.[97]

Infantrymen themselves also wrote songs about their weapons with female personifications (fig. 18).[98] Georges Lafond, an officer with a machine-gun unit, detailed the company's first performance of its marching song, "Ma mitrailleuse"—a moment of "profound and vital emotion," linked to "the hours lived in the simple brotherhood of arms."[99] The use of the song may have helped make the technology familiar and therefore less frightening. Described as a "coquette" and the "queen of battles," the machine gun's "polished steel and the voluptuous curves of the brass invite[d] caresses"; her adornment demanded hundreds of men. The men "know their gun; love her; possess her," wrote Lafond. The soldiers' complicated relationship with their machine guns rested on a mixture of admiration and fear. In their lyrics, they vowed to await victory alongside her, impressed with her ability to "mow down *[faucher]* the Germans by the thousands."[100]

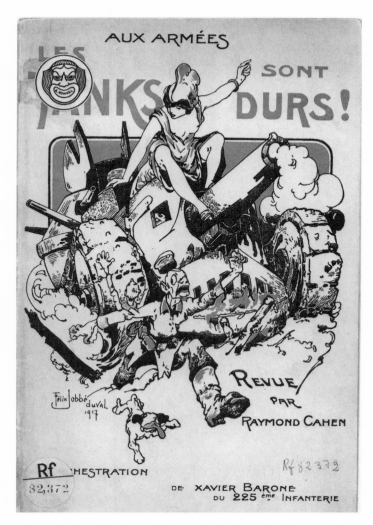

Figure 18. Cover for the musical revue *Les Tanks sont durs!* Courtesy of the Bibliothèque Nationale de France, Paris.

One might wonder whether singing and talking about sex became a substitute for sex or whether the representations encouraged masturbation or homosexual behavior. It would be very difficult to assess the actual prevalence of this at the front. But, whereas Fussell has argued that homoerotic literary expressions were part of "temporary homosexuality," homosociability does not necessarily include sexual relations.[101] The erotic can be imaginary, and not an indication of sexual acts. Moreover, Sedgwick has argued that homosocial bonds could be reinforced by attacks on homosexuality, and we find that the French ridiculed their opponent with innuendos of homosexuality or sexual deviancy.[102]

Anti-German propaganda frequently depicted the German troops and leaders as ineffective and effeminate, in stark opposition to the virile French soldiers. The portraits covered a wide range of negative characteristics from hostile cold-bloodedness to humorous ineptitude to sexual deviance.[103] Much of the ridicule that emphasized unmanly behavior centered on the crown prince, playing off of the idea of dynastic degeneracy. He was repeatedly shown as skinny, scared, stupid, and indecisive, as well as being a transvestite (fig. 19). In the song "Kronprinz va-t-en guerre," for example, he was found behind his troops "guarding their rears."[104] The issue of sexual impotence was not limited to the crown prince, however. The kaiser was quite unhappy that "his heavy artillery wouldn't fire" in the song "Adieux de Guillaume II à François-Joseph," although he did gloat about his success at shooting women and priests.[105]

Many images and songs belittled the Germans with constant blows to the buttocks. As the fourth verse of "C'est Rosalie" put it:

Il paraîtrait que les boches	It would appear that the boches
Trouv'nt son caractèr' pointu,	Find her character pointed [shrill],
Car, près d'eux, dès qu'ell' s'approche	For as soon as she comes near them
Vite, ils lui tournent le dos.	Quickly, they turn their backs.
Quand ell' leur fait la poursuite	When she pursues them
Les chassant avec entrain,	Chasing them with enthusiasm,
Qui donc pénètre à leur suite	Who then penetrates behind them
Facil'ment dans leur bas rein	Easily in their lower back
C'est Rosalie	It's Rosalie[106]

It became an easy joke to refer to Rosalie or French bayonets "giving it" to the Germans in retreat.[107]

The French soldiers expressed these anti-German sentiments in their trench journals and musical revues. Some had the kaiser and crown prince as characters who worried about their cowardice and made jokes about effeminacy.[108] And drawings on soldiers' tents in a military camp showed an ugly German soldier bending over and the French infantryman about to strike with a pointed 75 canister.[109]

Conflicting Discourses

As we have seen throughout this chapter, this discourse of eroticized warfare began in 1914 as part of the anxiety and excitement of the mobiliza-

Figure 19. Lithograph by G. Bigot, "Toys of the Crown Prince: The Booty," 1915. Courtesy of the Musée d'Histoire Contemporaine—BDIC.

tion and the initial war of movement. At that moment, the French had to cope with having had the nation invaded and with the real and imagined German atrocities, which included rapes. Thus on the figurative and literal level, French bodies had been violated. One response looked to older definitions of French fighters and found aggressiveness, virility, and élan. At that critical moment in 1914, there existed a striking overlap in language between newspaper accounts and song texts in describing French soldiers' easy successes in battles. Newspapers told of soldiers passionately kissing their bayonets and guns, and going gaily into battle as to a fête. More than one year into the deadly war, *Le Petit Journal* quoted "a lieutenant" who claimed: "They [the soldiers] looked forward to the offensive as to a holiday. They were so happy! They laughed! They joked!"[110] Accounts reiterated the soldiers' competitive nature as they rushed into battles. The nationalist Maurice Barrès talked about French soldiers shedding blood "cheerfully" and called the French 75s (cannons) "valiant and delightful comrades."[111]

Remarkably, these representations remained strong, as *cafés-concerts* and performers repeatedly submitted such songs for visas in late 1916 and throughout 1917. Recognizing that the discourse stayed popular amid the knowledge of pain and suffering is very important in understanding Parisians' lives up to November 1918. "C'est Rosalie," for example, was sung at the Folies-Parisienne in September 1916, when the battle of Verdun was eight months old, and even later at the Excelsior. The song "Ballade héro-ironique" which exalted "les p'tits soldats de France" and their bayonets was approved on November 29, 1917, less than one year before the end of the war.[112] "Le Rondeau du fusil" was published in 1918. In addition, the late years of the war saw the success of the song "Quand Madelon," with its young and sweet waitress serving soldiers. This community drinking song had a crowd of French males competing for the female, who was idealized to the point of obsession, putting the song clearly within the same genre of lyrics which reinforced the collectivity of men.[113] As with the popularity of "Madelon," which was much more marked in Paris, the discourse's continuing strength was especially true on the home front, away from the trenches. But the soldiers' fascination with *marraines* also continued; ads were still being placed in 1918, and stories on how to get a woman's attention, or providing a "Stratégie amoureuse," appeared in October 1918.[114]

But these representations were also, in several respects, a double-edged sword. Throughout the conflict, Parisian authorities tried to tie good morale to proper moral behavior, and some instances of what could be termed "sexual mobilization" were cut from song lyrics. Usually, it was the most obscene suggestions that were eliminated by censors.[115] But the censors found themselves having to interpret ambiguities, and were faced with decidedly patriotic presentations.[116] And there was, of course, constant wrangling with the censors.[117] Tellingly, however, despite their effort to purge popular vulgar terms and explicit references to sexual acts, the examiners did allow most of the military sexual double entendres, including Rosalie. After all, with the trenches just seventy miles away and no definite end in sight, this war needed to be sold. Alternative views with bawdy encounters and fanciful companions may have prevented the worst realities from sinking in.

The instability of the representations also raised the issue of who got pleasure and for what reason, as well as complications over what was supposed to be fantasy and what was actual behavior. Lynn Hunt has argued in her introduction to the collection *Eroticism and the Body Politic* that perhaps "eroticism itself remains ambiguous; it is at once the domain of women's mastery by men and . . . the domain of women's mastery over men."[118] In this case, the erotic thrived on the slippery double entendres and multiple meanings, which led to unpredictable interpretations. Moreover, since the authorship of songs could not be perfectly controlled, especially at the front, and audiences or individuals could act as composers, songs' popularity and the possibilities for further appropriation were enhanced.

The soldiers, meanwhile, were facing brutal trench warfare—which entailed an overwhelming repression of the traditional qualities of manly soldiering.[119] They suffered disillusionment and a sense of betrayal. As the war progressed, Botrel's performances became targets for derisive remarks, and song parodies of "Quand Madelon" appeared in which soldiers bemoaned the lack of "real" Madelons. In addition, although soldiers longed for leave, they sometimes reported ambivalence toward civilians and suffered feelings of sadness, apprehension, and dislocation once they arrived. French soldiers also feared what might be going on at home. The system of *marraines* and their representations may have fed soldiers' fantasies, but it also opened space for questionable behavior on the home front. Here, competition took a bad turn, between French men over real women. Louis Chevalier, in his examination of the entertainment and underworld of Montmartre, related tales of soldiers finding their wives with other men upon their arrival home; in one case, a crowd in Montmartre tried to prevent police officers from arresting a soldier "who had avenged his wife's infidelity."[120]

Mary Louise Roberts has provided excellent examples of French soldiers' reactions to the new opportunities (real or imagined) that women found.[121] A soldier's song entitled "Les Femmes de chez nous" praised the women waiting faithfully for soldiers, and sharply denounced prostitutes, referring to them as shrews and female monkeys.[122] During the war, however, these negative representations had to compete with the positive portrayals of women's work, forbearance, and patriotic "friendliness," which continued in songs and postcards. A divisive, hostile discourse had difficulty growing on the home front—partially because the Parisian censors would not approve obviously negative depictions. More common was the subtle critique of Paris, fashion, and women found in Jean Parigot's "Oui, Madame, c'est la mode." The songwriter made it clear with his lyrics that "the supreme elegance" was the wounded soldiers: "even if their face / or the rest is demolished / The splendor of their courage / will always make them attractive!"[123] At the same time, some materials carefully reassured soldiers that the women at home were being faithful and supportive. One "letter" from a woman to her love, written for a 1918 songsheet, began by fretting over his absence and the dangers of the war, but then explained that she felt compensated by her memories of feverish nights of never-ending kisses. She then reaffirmed the war's necessity, prodding her lover to fight for her love and their mutual devotion to *la Patrie*.

Aujourd'hui, chéri, c'est moi-même	Today, dear, it is I
Qui te dis: Marche de l'avant!	Who tells you: March forward!
Au revoir, va, puisque je t'aime,	Farewell, go, since I love you,
Tu reviendras certainement.	You will certainly return.
Sois vaillant, mais défends ta vie,	Be brave, but defend your life,
Et dis-toi bien, jusqu'au retour,	And tell yourself, until the return,
Qu'au-dessus de mon cher amour,	That above my dear love,
J'ai mis l'amour de la Patrie!	I have put my love of *la Patrie!*[124]

Here, in 1918, one found the continuing strength of the home front's optimistic inspiration and emphasis on patriotism.

With this alloy of sex and violence having appeared on all fronts, one wonders at its power and adaptability. This promotion of sex made soldiering and the war more exciting, while it also sold sex itself—a crucial strategy since repopulation remained important for future national strength. Selling sometimes requires piquing the public's imagination, and in this total war, the public had to be engaged and, even more difficult, kept engaged. Certainly, this discourse on male virility and wholeness remained stronger at the home front, where it helped counterbalance other portraits of the war. Not generated by state officials, these materials contributed to a larger "propaganda" effort in that they "sold" the war with positive, optimistic, and entertaining representations. It was enterprising individuals who often led the way.

Historians have long recognized that a serious divide grew between soldiers and civilians, but they continue to debate how severe it became. The "sexual" or more precisely the "erotic" was a meeting place or bridge between trench and Parisian culture. These ideas and images passed easily between home and front, and acted as a form of adhesive between the groups. The common ground derived from a shared prewar popular culture and from the appeal of the mass cultural forms that were so powerful during the war. As we saw with the popularity of *marraines* and the machine gun song, sexual themes that flourished in Paris were also very much a part of a soldier's universe, in his imagination, conversations, and cultural renditions. Soldiers shared the idea of masculinity based on heterosexual virility without being as blatantly prowar. They were most interested in their self-image and anxieties, and less in promoting the war. They also sought to escape their terrible surroundings through fantasy.

The representation of French vigorous soldiers performing their duty was not new. It extended back over at least a century. The prescription of sexy women caring for soldiers also had older roots, but it offered new innovations as the definition of a "civilian" took shape. Much of the recent historiography on World War I has drawn our attention to the figures of mothers and nurses, stressing the prescriptive, nurturing roles constructed for women during the war. And some historians have viewed these representations as a conservative step backward. According to the social historian Michelle Perrot, for example, "It seems that the moral effects of the war helped to consolidate traditional values and gender relationships. The destruction of feminism, the strengthening of the image of woman as mother, the glorification of feminine and masculine myths all seemed to go together."[125] Although images of caring nurses and respectable mothers did prosper in France—dictating roles within the framework of a domestic ideology—scholars' focus on the "image of woman as mother" has been too limited. Whereas songs and postcards certainly promoted motherhood and repopulation, one also found hundreds of portrayals of heterosexual couples luxuriating in sexual pleasures without any reference to marriage or procreation. To encourage women to offer sex for the cause may well have been prescriptive, but these presentations were not singularly traditional. These innovations in mass culture heralded later combinations of modern war.[126]

PART III

✦

THE CULTURAL GEOGRAPHY
OF WAR

✦

CHAPTER FIVE

Musical Entertainment in Wartime Paris

❧

On December 15, 1917, a police spy finished his daily rounds in the cafés and theaters of Paris and filed his report. It read, in part:

For some time now, life in Paris has taken a turn away from what one would have rightly expected, given the current events and especially following the calls for restrictions alluded to daily by the government.

Never have the performance halls, theaters, cinemas, or music halls been so crowded.

Never has one seen such a throng of clients in the grand establishments, restaurants, bars, and fashionable tea rooms, and yet the increases, already so visible, are gradually reaching often scandalous proportions.[1]

Clearly perturbed, this observer described a busy Parisian public life, in which restaurants overflowed and musical establishments played to appreciative audiences. It seemed sacrilegious to admit to such pleasures with France still mired in a contest that had worn on for over three years. Historians have also found it difficult to imagine such a scene. Many have portrayed World War I Paris as dark, silent, and virtuous. A literary work on the Parisian entertainment neighborhood of Montmartre, for example, written after the fact, devoted only three pages to Montmartre during the war, claiming, "It seemed almost as if the slopes of la Butte had been laid waste by shell-fire, for the death-like silence. . . . In its new guise, however, Montmartre amply justified itself, for joy was tempered by sorrow and it slept a sleep from which it was to awaken purified, regenerated."[2] All was not silent, however. The musical entertainment industry thrived, promoting and responding to a public thirst for patriotic, humorous, and satirical songs and musical revues.

The flourishing of activity in Paris was an aspect of modern war and a condition of French culture more specifically. With total war, civilians faced a novel situation. They were integral to the nation's success, but they were not actually occupied with fighting. Furthermore, they did not know how long the upheaval might continue, nor all that might be expected of them. As would be true at other times in the twentieth century, civilian society had to continue to function, despite hard times and new demands. People sought coping mechanisms, while the government looked for cooperative citizens. But unlike in more authoritarian regimes, where most decisions about public life were made without any public discussion, in World War I France a debate began in the fall of 1914 over what should or should not comprise "normalité."[3] The censors obviously struggled with the ambiguities surrounding the "proper" behavior for civilians, but here the debate broadened out.

With the war still not won by December 1914, Parisians themselves realized a need to reconstruct "la vie normale" or "normalité," as they chose to call it, and decided that it should include entertainment. In large part, this was because *spectacles,* as many forms of entertainment were called, had been central to daily life—commercially, socially, and politically—throughout the Belle Époque. They were a part of how Parisians defined their way of life. In the prewar period, the music industry had prospered, and as artists carried songs from hall to hall, they wove tunes and lyrics into the public consciousness, spreading information and helping create public opinion. The central role taken by musical entertainment in France during the war was not true in all belligerent countries. German officials in Munich found "culture and entertainment . . . more or less dispensable" during the war, while, more broadly, Germans viewed entertainment as "frivolous," "foolish," and even "sacrilegious."[4]

In wartime, the *spectacles* contributed to a cultural matrix through which civilians could "know" the war. Audiences learned about the trenches in the *cafés-concerts,* for example, with representations of prototypical soldiers, or *poilus,* on stage with Napoleon. The programs, ranging from the tiniest cafés to the grandest music halls, also offered a mirror in which Parisians assessed their self-image and level of confidence. From song lyrics and musical revue characters, Parisian audiences heard how they were doing—performers cheered soldiers on, admonished civilians for cowardice, or explained the dangers of gossip. The musical revue spread in popularity, based on a passion for music and songs and its comforting recreations of Paris life. With satiric wit, revues ridiculed the enemy and subtly contended with the problems on the home front.

Paris also represented an exceptional situation compared to London, as it sat as a sort of border town just seventy kilometers from the pitilessly brutal trenches where artillery barrages, mustard gas, rats, and soldiers coexisted. The city experienced instability with shifting populations of refugees pouring in from Belgium and northeast France, soldiers arriving on leave, and foreign infantrymen and dignitaries appearing in ever greater numbers. It also weathered economic dislocation and adaptations, which included new roles for women and foreign workers.

Ironically, because of the French capital's extreme proximity to the front, Parisians came to see themselves as the quintessential French civilians. The perilous border position made what these civilians did or did not do seem more important. Thus the Parisian identity overlapped with a construction of the national community, and mass culture's democratic impulse helped to welcome all. Whereas in World War II this national self-definition may have come from film and radio, in World War I it came from performers on stage and reports in newspapers.

With the front so close, "normalité" proved to be a tension-laden concept. Recreated in the midst of the abnormal circumstances of war, "normal" life engendered fears and suspicions. Thus the police spy was not alone in disapproving of Parisians' behavior. Despite its centrality, entertainment still carried some connotations of foolishness and escapism. Entertainment itself sat on a border between more serious occupations such as munitions work and more clearly defined defeatist acts of wastefulness. It thus provides a perfect nexus for examining the broader issue. Parisians first created a wartime "normalité" and then tried to live with it. But even with some doubts, French entertainers persisted, and officials never shut them down.

The Fall of 1914 and a Return to "Normalité"

When the French mobilized for war on August 1, many *cafés-concerts* and music halls were closed for vacation, and with the declaration of war, most others quickly shut. The *café-concert* Petit Casino did manage to put together matinees with patriotic songs, which were enthusiastically received, but this was one of the few exceptions.[5] The war disrupted businesses as some performers and directors were mobilized, and others headed for America. Maurice Chevalier, Gabriel Montoya, and André Perchicot, for example, went into the army, and older directors such as Jacques Charles of the Folies-Bergère, and Pierre Gheusi of the Opéra-Comique volunteered for military administrative positions. On September 1, the normal opening date for the new season, the halls remained dark, while Paris nervously prepared for the approaching Germans. In the first weeks of September, the Battle of the Marne raged within fifty miles of Paris, and with memories of the 1870 German siege in mind, as much as one third of the city's population fled south with the government. The theaters found themselves without performers or spectators.

The victory at the Marne represented a crucial moment—it turned the Germans away from Paris, reinforced the French soldier's heroic reputation, created confidence in the military command, and eventually brought the government back to Paris. But, at the same time, deep uncertainty remained over when the war would end and how to conduct life in the meantime. Pierre Gheusi, the director of the Opéra-Comique, claimed that by the end of September, while "a violent cannonade rumbled without cease [to the east], Paris, serene, almost carefree, imperiously demanded to live; families returned one by one, bringing back their schoolchildren."[6] Moreover, since mid-September, Gheusi had been getting many requests to reopen his State theater.[7]

As citizens slowly began returning to the capital, an influential concept of "normalité" (or "la vie normale") evolved—even before the military front had stabilized in the east or the national government had returned. Far too often historians discuss the shift from the war of movement to the static trench warfare in only military terms, but this shift had much larger implications, especially for the mood and behavior of the Parisian population.[8] The notion of *la vie normale* meant rebuilding daily routines within a precarious existence and emotional uncertainty. Parisians faced disarray caused by the mobilization and sharply rising unemployment, and they were already becoming aware of the high number of French casualties.[9] But life was not chaotic nor immediately threatened, and some commentators began to use the word "forgetting" to describe the Parisians' lack of attention to the front and the German threat.[10]

By November, inhabitants were debating or campaigning for normality. The idea needed to be justified, and key figures in the theater world led the way. There were those who argued that normality should not include entertainment, but should be limited to economics, especially considering the harsh German occupation of northeast France. As one police memo described this view: "the theaters did not appear to be really necessary for normal life, which included economic activity above all else. The theaters— while the enemy still occupied a portion of territory, and anguish and grief saddened so many families—did not match the attitude of reverence and gravity which appeared to suit the country."[11] For this group (unspecified in the memo), amusements did not fall within the boundaries of appropriate behavior. The French paralleled the German stance most closely at this point. And in October the prefect refused to let the theaters reopen, viewing it as premature.[12]

Other voices, however, supported a normality that relied on the power of entertainment to calm Parisians and to bolster their patriotism. That the French considered music such an important part of normal life strengthened this position. Although the public may not have conceived of the war lasting for four years, many had decided life should go on, and they began to seek out musical concerts. Eugénie Buffet, a well-known *café-concert* figure, described how the general public, craving music, began trying to sneak into her concerts for convalescing soldiers. Her troupe agreed to welcome only those who made contributions to help the soldiers, which made their attendance patriotic.[13] Within these negotiations, one finds the French working their way toward a definition of a good civilian. In his wartime diary, Michel Corday registered both sides of the argument in November: while a certain Monsieur Thomson was horrified at the proposal to reopen the theaters, since so many families were already in mourning, other people spoke of keeping cafés open later and "of encouraging recitals and concerts."[14]

By the middle of November, supporters were also stressing the economic needs of the entertainment industry. Police were lobbied in the interests of "the average worker in the theater world."[15] Unemployment in entertainment establishments paralleled the general economic disruptions in the fall of 1914. Whereas inhabitants of Montmartre had forced the closure of cafés in August, claiming that such places were inappropriate, in November a newspaper reported that twenty thousand out of seventy-five thousand people who had worked in the theaters were without resources and were being forced to get free meals at the Jardin de Paris and the Eldorado.[16] At least one observer claimed that this number allowed officials to view reopening the theaters as an issue of work rather than of pleasure.

One of the most persuasive voices was Pierre Gheusi, who had moved in August 1914 from managing the Opéra-Comique to assisting General Gallieni, the military governor of Paris. He combined the economic and emotional strands of the argument for normality, claiming that "from the first day of mobilization," he had had a "duty to insure bread for our three hundred families and to still preserve in Parisian life . . . the traditional refuge where they [French musicians] could be heard."[17] Gheusi took his mission to Albert Dalimier, the undersecretary of fine arts, in late September. "I announced to him my intentions to reopen the Opéra-Comique as quickly as possible. He looked at me in somewhat of a stupor, but I began to interest him."[18]

Gheusi's memoirs also explicitly linked his motives to what became a widespread slogan: "Pourvu que les civils tiennent" (So long as the civilians hold). According to this, the war could be won only if the civilians kept up their morale and contributed to the war effort—and entertainment would help. Gheusi and others maintained that reopening musical establishments would not contribute to "forgetting" the trenches, but would demonstrate the fortitude of the French in the face of the German threat. These arguments conflated Parisian decisions and acts with the national good and France's image. Paris was to set the highest standard for civilian behavior, which would be all the more impressive given its proximity to the front.

Finally, as individuals and the theater industry continued to push and prod, they succeeded in convincing Parisian officials of the positive effects of entertainment.[19] But the government, although intrigued, remained nervous. Believing that excessive jingoism during the Franco-Prussian War had contributed to the ruinous Paris Commune, they wanted to insure that entertainment would be *only* a distraction. After comprehensive negotiations between the police and the entertainment industry's directors, the prefect of police finally permitted the reopenings under an agreement of November 23, 1914. This approval came even before the national government had returned from Bordeaux. (Parliament did not reconvene until December 22, 1914.) The agreement stipulated that the closing time would be at 11 P.M., 5 percent of the receipts would go to charities, and the first openings could take place as early as November 28.[20] Most important, police would review all programs, which had to have "a high-minded and patriotic character." The agreement remained in effect throughout the war, although the police were complaining by the end of 1915 that, because of changes in directors, the industry was not holding up its end, especially with regard to moral and patriotic content.

With the normality of the fall of 1914, the directors took up a functionalist "public service" role, explicitly justifying their actions as patriotic. Given the uncertain reputations of *cafés-concerts* and their stars before the war, the industry walked a fine line, since they might easily have been suspect. But they had much to lose financially and much to gain in respectability.

Where music had led, other cultural forms quickly followed; after all, the music industry had a high profile both in the physical layout of Paris and in newspapers. Like many others, the newspaper *La Vie Parisienne* had suspended operations in August "for the duration of the war," but then began publishing again on December 5, 1914. By early 1915 the idea of normality had gained enough ground that the government approved French participation in art expositions to be held in San Francisco, London, and Spain, while the fashion houses announced they would present their new lines for foreign buyers in March, as usual.[21] Film studios also went back to work at the start of 1915.

Not everyone agreed with the decision to revive the entertainment industry, and the difficulty of defining "normality" remained. It was not always easy to draw a line between distractions for morale or solace and unseemly types of behavior or excessive consumption. Therefore, the police

and the press paid close attention to audience conduct. Following the December 6 reopening of the Comédie-Française, *Les Débats* reported on the
appropriately dressed and well-behaved crowd: "the room was filled. . . .
No display of furs at the end. A true public having its normal sensibility
[sensibilité normale]. Some emotion without a doubt, but positively no
nervousness."[22] This report obviously saw normal (and helpful) wartime
behavior as calm and respectable.

The Opéra-Comique also opened its doors on December 6 with a matinee "to profit victims of the war," and Gheusi described the struggle to reopen with a somewhat remarkable analogy. The project had "become, in
Paris, an event almost as sensational as a surprise attack—and as reckless—
before a trench reputed to be impregnable."[23] Gheusi, confirming
normality's heroic character, exclaimed:

We succeeded. In the deep shivers, in the signs of impatience and pride, I believe I
detect that Paris wants to live again, to affirm its vitality and faith before all. Its luminous existence, its lyrical spirit, its genius . . . one moment confined under the
threatening horde of Barbarians, all this reawakens, hour by hour. As quickly as
possible, the musicians of France in this sovereign City had to vouch for the immortal victory of French art over the insipid Kultur of the Boches.[24]

Paris sat on its own sort of battlefield, and French culture provided the civilian weapons. In this case, the triumph was immediate, as Gheusi had to
turn away fifteen hundred people a night in December 1914.[25]

Despite any negative voices, once the halls had the prefect's approval,
they worked expeditiously to reopen. Many actually raised their curtain at
the first opportunity on the night of November 28, 1914; the Moulin
Rouge premiered with its Tipperary girls, and the Nouveau Théâtre with
"patriotic tableaux of . . . bellicose songs or comic-warlike tunes."[26] According to the police count, at least 189 theaters, cinemas, and concert
halls were to open after December 1, 1914[27] (see appendix B). But what
would "normalité" look like, once they had decided to include entertainment? In this earliest stage, most programs provided dynamic patriotic
fare, including the "mandatory" "Marseillaise," as well as the other national hymns. These prowar lyrics came at the critical juncture when the
war settled into a stalemate, and illustrated that for the time being "normal" included the prowar ethos based on old rousing patriotic favorites
and a show of confidence.

One of the earliest musical revues, *Paris quand même,* opened December 23, 1914, at the Folies-Bergère. Revues had become a staple of the large
music halls before the war, with opulent sets, chorus lines, and an international audience and reputation. Much of this would change for the first half
of the war. In this case, *Paris quand même* had a relatively small number of

tableaux, and incorporated popular tunes with updated lyrics. The revue began with a prologue in which a performer came forward to thank the audience for coming. She explained that she understood the audience might expect a sumptuous display of riches as was normal, but, "As we say: 'A la Guerre comme à la guerre!'"—a message for all to take to heart.[28] She also pointed out that the audience's presence that evening at the theater happily contradicted stories that Parisians were downhearted; instead, Paris could obviously still smile.

Almost all of the revue's songs made references to the war. A sergeant sang optimistically about the new equality among the classes; no longer were there "big" or "little" individuals, since bankers, peasants, and lawyers had all become soldiers. And a musical tribute was given to "les p'tits gars" (the soldiers), followed by Miss Selby singing, "It's a long way to Tipperary" in English. Finally, in a song called "La Lettre de la tranchée," a soldier thanked his sweetheart for gifts and asked her to get her friends to send more; this idea anticipated the formal encouragement of *marraines* in 1915. According to this revue's prescription, Paris was to be cheerful, stalwart, supportive, while being entertained. Refashioned, the population was united and well directed.

The French did not "return to normal" just because they did not know what else to do. The move came from a series of decisions, as thousands of Parisians began to find their own individual sense of *la vie normale*. Paris could not have faced such an extended war without some concept having been formulated, nor would citizens have supported the entertainment industry's prosperity without it. Musical entertainment led the way back, based on its cultural power within the Paris public sphere, and because singing was so integrated into everyday life. Given its adaptive nature during the Belle Époque, Parisian mass culture could also re-form quickly. Still, whereas some supporters thought life should follow prewar patterns, this was precisely what other critics feared.

The 1914–1915 Season: Wartime Adaptability

The first wartime theater season, from December 1914 to June 1915, was an insecure period, but it also featured a wide array of enthusiastically patriotic material. Most prewar musical establishments reopened within the first year of war, and developed a certain momentum.[29] The industry adjusted as new directors oversaw the steady succession of premieres. The Little Palace had shows every night and three matinees per week by February 1915, and, of the top forty-four places listed by the police as open by November 1915, three quarters had opened by the end of

April.[30] By September at the start of a new fall season, "All places with the slightest importance were at least partially open."[31]

Though successful, entertainment's path during the war was not smooth or easy. A strong community of men and women, however, was able to continue as performers, songwriters, or managers in order to "contribute" to the war effort. The French musical entertainment industry had reached a particular level of maturity at just the right moment, which, to some extent, was a matter of age.[32] The most established figures had been born between 1863 and 1878, and had worked their way up the ladder (often from a young age). They were now at the height of their careers and too old to be conscripted.[33] One sizable group immediately began to perform for the troops in canteens, hospitals, and music halls. Another circle wrote music for performances in Paris, the provinces, and for the troops; these *chanson-niers*—Jean Bastia, Dominique Bonnaud, Paul Marinier, Gaston Monté-hus, and Vincent Hyspa—made up the backbone of the industry. They owned and ran cabarets and *cafés-concerts*, composed hundreds of songs, and published sheet music for worldwide distribution. Although changes in management came more swiftly than in the prewar period, new directors filled in for those missing. In the case of the Olympia, a very successful music hall before the war, the owner and director Jacques Charles was mobilized in August 1914, but the hall's orchestra conductor and another entrepreneur managed to reopen the hall in March 1915.[34] For many, the war provided a commercial and professional opportunity. New stars emerged, such as Claudine Boria, and Gaby Montbreuse was considered "launched" in 1914, when she happened to embrace a soldier at the end of her performance.[35]

With the 1914–1915 season, these performers and entrepreneurs created a "normality" that actually had many abnormal aspects. One early repercussion of the war's massive mobilization was that women enjoyed new opportunities on stage. At the *café-concert* Le Peletier in 1915, twelve out of fourteen singers were women, and a woman had written the vaudeville that closed the program.[36] At the same time, in one twenty-seven-scene revue at the Little Palace, all of the performers were women except three, and other places even used women for male roles, as at the Nouveau-Cirque where Mary Hett played Tommy. This set up a reverse image of the military zone and soldiers' own revues, and may have contributed to a representation of the home front as feminized. Interestingly, reviewers took the increase in numbers in stride, in part because it fit into the idea of everyone's just doing their share. The one major exception proved to be the small cabarets, which followed the Montmartre traditions and were mainly located on La Butte. Their main singers were all men from the prewar musical community.

Audiences were also comprised of unusually high numbers of women, older men, and small numbers of convalescing soldiers during this period of the industry's revival, since active soldiers did not receive regular leaves until July 1915.[37] More important, foreign tourists had disappeared as the Germans approached, and by early 1915 Paris was made up of a high percentage of tenacious Parisians, representing French courage. One American newspaper correspondent, who had chosen to stay, described the dramatic change: "Four months earlier Paris belonged to the Americans, North and South; her shops and her restaurants, her amusements and some of her society were for them alone, and American money was the dominating factor of external Parisian life. Without a word of warning she became French. . . . [S]uddenly she became as much French as any provincial town."[38]

The audience mirrored the content which became intensely nationalistic. This sharply reversed a prewar trend toward internationalization. The process of "re-Frenchification," which had marked the wartime ethos in August 1914, also appeared quite clearly in the classical music controversy of 1915. It began when the well-known and distinguished composer Camille Saint-Saëns began writing speeches and articles denouncing any performance of German composers, in an effort to purify the public musical arena. Saint-Saëns argued that France should come first, and musical or aesthetic considerations second—art subordinated to nationalism. Not surprisingly, Wagner was the focal point of the controversy, as the "musical symbol" of German despotism and imperialism. But the boycott extended even to the Italian Giacomo Puccini's *Tosca* and *Madame Butterfly,* until he demonstrated his anti-Germanism by donating his royalties in France to the Red Cross.[39]

Saint-Saëns's campaign for a German-music boycott did not go uncontested. In May 1915, in his column in *Mercure de France,* the music critic Jean Marnold challenged Saint-Saëns, arguing that music should be a universal language based on high musical standards and should represent neutrality in the midst of all of the polarity.[40] But neutrality had become impossible and musical standards changed. The war brought about a greater fluidity of borders between "classical" music and more "popular" songs. An emphasis on *French* music led to an eclectic mixing of pieces and performers as well as a more widespread approval of the *café-concert* during the war.[41] Performers came together to encourage the war effort at fundraisers, for example, reflecting an uneasiness with private financial or strictly aesthetic motives.

This controversy helped delay the reopening of the Opéra, since, with Wagner, Beethoven, and Mozart suspect, its repertoire was sharply reduced.[42] In the months before the opening, stars fought for lead roles by swearing their allegiance to France and producing their French birth certificates. Maurice Barrès, meanwhile, declared all defenders of Wagner to be traitors to France. This campaigning placed the classical music community in step with the war's rigid nationalism, while it contributed to the power and intensity of Germany's image as the enemy.

As nationalism swept across hierarchical cultural categories, in determining what *normalité* would be in 1914–1915, it also led to a resurgence of the *café-concert* form. With tourists gone, the international repertoires and stars disappeared, and programs that had been printed side by side in French, English, and Spanish at some halls were now printed only in French.[43] Instead, songs and simpler revues became the mainstay of programs cherished for their treatment of *actualités* (or current events), their humor, and wit. Entertainment establishments turned to celebrating "French popular culture" at the very moment when censorship was erasing or suppressing the political and class dimensions of nineteenth-century popular culture. It created something new, which looked old, and it was to feed the postwar nostalgia for the Belle Époque. The increased interest in songs stemmed from late-nineteenth-century developments in integral nationalism, in which local cultures, including songs, were absorbed or embraced as French. It also fit an older mythology of French stalwartness and gallic wit in the face of danger. The first line of the "Chant du départ" expressed it simply as "Victoire en chantant" (Singing our way to victory). Songs and revues also communicated information in a relatively easy and cheap fashion, and allowed people to join in.

That Paris rallied to singing is evident in the prevalence of songs on most entertainment programs at *cafés-concerts,* music halls, theaters, and cinemas. The Café Persan, a *café-concert* in the Marais, submitted its program for December 6, 1914, with seventy-seven songs headed by "La Marseillaise de 1914."[44] These lengthy programs had to have lasted several hours, so people were getting their money's worth. More often, seven or eight performers of varying stature took the stage to do "song turns" made up of four or five tunes each. The programs changed weekly, providing impressive opportunities for performers and lyrics to reach different audiences.

As the war continued, this urge for singing caught the attention of directors. The Renaissance Theater, for example, reopened in December 1914 with just four songs on its program, but by July 1915 it had shifted to forty-four numbers. Cinemas had always used songs for intermissions and music as accompaniment to the films during the Belle Époque, and this continued with the war.[45] But some cinemas incorporated even greater numbers. The Ciné-Olympic, for instance, went from seven to ten songs in December 1914 to programs of forty in mid-1916.[46]

In contrast, variety acts, such as jugglers or acrobats, which carried less nationalist meaning for that moment appeared far less often. Even the Olympia, whose format had set the pace in fin-de-siècle Paris by highlighting variety, saw "a progressive reappearance of the *tours de chant* [song turns]. The ballets, on the other hand, disappeared completely."[47] Larger theaters also used songs, although usually within remarkably long, complex programs. One evening at Le Peletier in 1915 comprised at least twenty-nine songs, a vaudeville, an operetta, and a one-act Fantaisie-Revue.[48]

In the beginning, artists relied on an old but rich nationalist repertoire. December programs overflowed with robust patriotic pieces like "La Marseillaise," "Le Chant du départ," Déroulède's "Le Clairon," and "Sambre et Meuse." The preponderance of martial themes overwhelms, especially when compared to prewar programs.[49] One program in March 1915 at the Gaîté-Parisienne comprised six out of ten rousing or earnest patriotic songs (in this case: "Marche glorieuse," "Lettre de la tranchée," "La Charge," "Le Rêve passe" (app. fig. 6), "Le Chant du départ," and "Le Canon"), and the rest all mentioned the war. As in this program, older songs such as "Le Chant du départ" or "Le Rhin allemand" were easily interwoven with newer pieces (see figs. 20 and 21).

Part of the incorporation of the war occurred because song culture had always incorporated *actualités,* and because war was a popular and profitable subject. Songs could be written, printed and distributed quickly and easily.[50] Much of the content was suffused with images of war, the enemy, and soldiers. An infamous atrocity such as the execution of Edith Cavell was quickly turned into a hit called "Le Martyre de Miss Cavell" using an extremely well-known tune, "La Paimpolaise."[51] The new "Le Chant de la Revanche!" reused the tune from "Le Chant du départ" and created an optimistic exhortation against the Germans. Just as significantly, civilians got to hear lyrics that described their own "war." German zeppelins that arrived in March caught the civilians' imagination, for example, despite the fact that they did not cause very much damage.[52] Songs lashed out at the enemies' sordid tactics and laughed about encounters in air raid shelters. This involved the regular process of incorporating *actualités,* but using the militarist topics also normalized the war. Singing or hearing a tribute was vital and comforting, at a moment when civilians could only wait and fear the worst.

Programs also illustrated the tension within the concept of *normalité.* If singing practices readily adapted the war as part of everyday news, there was also an older repertoire with which to avoid the war altogether. The war did not wipe clean the commercial or performative slate, and romantic and sentimental genres were still heard. Here, entertainment worked according to the government's wish—as a distraction, without causing too

Figure 20. Sheet music cover of "Le Jour de gloire est arrivé."

much excitement. Old standbys were perfect for recreating "normal life" despite the war, but rousing martial numbers worked best for supporting the effort explicitly.

The one other venue where Parisians could go for an evening of songs was a group of cabarets where the dominant style for both the song turns and the short revues was to satirize current events and fashions of Paris with trenchant humor.[53] These places combined what many considered quintessential Paris and the essence of "popular culture." They self-consciously saw themselves as descendants of the Montmartre traditions of the Chat Noir,

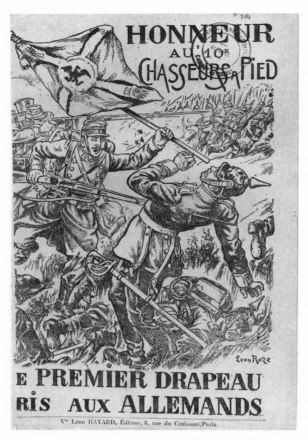

Figure 21. Sheet music cover of "Lettre d'un parigot du 10e chasseurs à pied à son frangin." Courtesy of the Préfecture de Police.

and they cultivated their popular French ancestry with programs that conformed perfectly to the wartime celebration of French culture.[54] One commentator warmly applauded their best aspects: "What creates the charm of Montmartre cabarets . . . is especially the intimate and cordial atmosphere. It seems as if one is with good, somewhat crude, people after dinner, and each comes up with his own modest song."[55] Most were small with makeshift stages that promoted audience participation. "They cultivate an acerbic wit," another newspaper columnist explained, "a rebellious spirit, pungency and irony, which were always the best qualities of a French *chansonnier,* before becoming almost exclusively the prerogative of the *chansonniers* of the Butte."[56]

But even as they adapted their content to the *actualités,* these cabarets were also popular because they seemed to freeze forms in time—a process that was reassuring in hard times, especially by implying that something worthwhile was being preserved. This genre of *café-concert* gained popularity as the war continued, and places continued to reopen. In 1916 a new cabaret opened, Le Perchoir, with its lobby adorned with a frieze celebrating the most famous refrains of French songs. Its program reassured its guests that songbirds needed a place "to perch," and that laughter was allowed.[57] The war gave these assurances a special context—a clearer reason to have to defend both singing and laughing.

THE WARTIME REVUE

Parisians' wartime taste for musical renderings of current events was also satisfied by one other very important form: musical revues. Peter Jelavich, in his work on postwar Berlin, has described the rise of the revue as a movement away from regular theater with plays, and as a shift toward less internal continuity of content and greater fragmentation; thus they reflected urban modernity.[58] The French case appears to have been different, at least in the prewar period and up through the middle of the war. In both countries, the genre was clearly an urban form, but the French revue's roots in older traditions of popular culture lent it familiarity. Whereas Jelavich posits Berliners' discomfort over the fragmentation, French critics found that the best Parisian revue offered a cohesive, amusing consideration of the city's mores.[59]

Pieces called "revues" had been around since at least as early as 1874, but these shows had gained most of their popularity between 1890 and 1910 at the large music halls. Immediately preceding the war, they had been moving toward a British model with variety acts mixed with skits, pantomimes, and ballets, along with opulent costumes, extensive scenery, and chorus lines.[60] The form was not a simple transplant, though, since French revues had much deeper roots in the *cafés-concerts*, in fairground entertainment, and, stretching further back, in street entertainment.

With the war, revues gained enormous popularity throughout Paris.[61] Although this genre had been popular before the war, during the war it became the single dominating form.[62] But as with songs, the affinity for musical revues engendered a shift toward the French formula (at least according to newspaper critics). International elements or attractions, sumptuous costumes, and exotic acts became less important. These modifications served to emphasize language and music, as *revuistes* celebrated a special association between French humor, Paris culture, and singing.[63] Critics identified this as a turn toward an older ideal.

In 1914–1915, audiences heard very recent hit tunes as well as much older tunes. In the 1915 revue *Alliés . . . tous à la sirène,* most of the melodies were prewar favorites, including "Très moutarde" and "Le Dernier tango." But the composer also used "Sur le pont d'Avignon," to which they sang:

Sur le front	At the front
Les canons	The cannons
Entr'nt en danse [bis]	Enter into a dance [twice]
Et des Boch's v'là qu'ils font	And of the Boches behold they make
Du joli p'tit saucisson.	Some nice small sausage.[64]

The stress on songs and dialogue was also linked to the audience's intense interest in *actualités,* which offset the lack of sumptuousness. The war offered a whole slew of new topics, and the most successful pieces interpreted the most recent events. As one commentator said, "it seems useless to present to spectators at this moment, a new vaudeville, an original piece that would not respond to their present preoccupations."[65] Now, older characters such as *la Parisienne* or *le Garçon* mixed with the unfamiliar characters of *le Poilu, Tommy, la Censure, l'Alsace,* and *la Journée du 75.*[66] Not surprisingly, the most common women's role became la Marraine, the "pen pal" for the *poilus.* This character promoted a civilian's proper role and contributed to the erotic representations.

An important part of the form's older roots was its satirical nature. "Aside from their musical simplicity," according to Robert Isherwood, "the popularity of vaudevilles can be attributed to their historical association with satire and ridicule."[67] In characterizing revues as French, commentators repeatedly pointed to their satirical nature, political criticism, and expressions of disgruntlement.[68] But with the censor's block on proper names, writers had to forego most political characters and some opportunities for political satire, while relying more on historic or literary figures. In one revue, Cyrano appeared as a French soldier and headed off to the front, proclaiming "Each day by fighting we bring about Victory *[la Victoire].*"[69] Social commentary still occurred with constant discussions over civilian habits, which included praise for patriotic behavior and blame for frivolous acts. In one revue, for example, Madame de Maintenon quarreled with Napoleon about the proper length for women's skirts.[70]

Much of the interest was in things Parisian, an important carryover from the earlier form.[71] Most of the scenes took place in the public spaces of Paris: the streets, markets, cafés, and theaters. Rarely, was a domestic setting used, and surroundings were not personalized. Writers used classic places such as la Rue de la Paix, the Bois de Boulogne, or the Gare St. La-zare, all of which carried specific connotations. Similarly, most of the characters represented stereotypic Parisians or Frenchmen—a waiter *(le Garçon)*, a husband *(le Mari)*, a spectator at a theater *(la Spectatrice)*, a peasant *(le Paysan)*, or a news hawker *(le Crieur de journaux)*—catego-rized by gender, occupation, class, or geography. Notably democratic, the characters were not just elites, although public officials as well as many his-torical and literary figures such as Voltaire, Napoleon, Descartes, Pierrot, and Cyrano appeared. Characters could also represent any facet of Parisian life, not just people; thus, fashions, intellectual ideas, events, and places were anthropomorphized and consulted or picked on.[72] These figures served to homogenize and spread Parisian and French culture, but they also highlighted its uniqueness compared to other national cultures.

The importance of defining a positive community to fight with in such a "total" war and Paris's unique position accentuated this attention to Pari-sian life during the war. These revues offered Parisians a way to construct a reasonable understanding of the war, and helped convince a Parisian com-munity to act appropriately. This entertainment did not run away from the "war"; revues contained myriad representations of it. But, whereas before the war, revues might have offered serious critiques, after 1914 the field of judgment narrowed, partly due to censorship, which lopped off the nega-tive part of the community's portrait.

Most critics of the period agreed that the essential element in revues and music programs' popularity was the intertwining of patriotic and comic themes. Humor was sought out and celebrated as a healthy civilian re-sponse. In late 1915, the administration gave its somewhat condescending opinion:

It is the revue such as it has been done over the last months, [which] without im-posing any sustained mental effort on the public, allows one to offer in the same show comic tableaux which relax its [the public's] spirit and patriotic tableaux which remind it of the present. The revue appears to respond to a double exigency and this may be the persistent cause of its success.[73]

This theory offered the compelling picture of spectators leaving daily cares behind and then returning to their duties with a suitably "patriotic" vision of current events. As described, the experience seems less cathartic than nourishing.

RIP'S *1915*

The biggest hit of the 1914–1915 season was the revue *1915* by Rip (Georges-Gabriel Thenon) which premiered at the Palais-Royal theater in April. Following a successful Paris run, it went on to the provinces, having created a model for revues for the first half of the war. The piece walked the fine line of both comforting and chiding Parisians. In its preface, Gustave Quinson argued that Rip had the necessary wit and good heart, but that he had also "pulled out his magnifying glass for warts." [74] Quinson credited Rip with knowing the "personnage collectif" of Paris.

Every scene in *1915* related to the war, or, to be more precise, each scene showed how the war affected Paris, which was designated "the true French city." As in prewar revues, stock characters and historical figures passed through the "streets" of Paris divulging their problems or escapades to the *commère* and *compère* (literally translated as "gossip," played by a woman, and "accomplice," played by a man). Using the older formula to express the new problems provided a normalizing process.

The revue began quite logically with Paris being cleansed of all things German, and a crowd-pleasing disparagement persisted throughout. Six "Expulsés" appeared, recognizable by their costumes, including *l'Opérette viennoise, le Style tartine, le Cubism, le Parsifal, le Tango,* and *l'Absinthe.* The agent's order read "The Expelled: Puppets, stooges, objectionables, and inconveniences which encumbered Paris this last year, and of which the war rids us. They are all hit with a ban on residency and directed to America."[75] All of these items had been very popular just before the war, and all, except absinthe, were viewed as foreign influences that had to be removed.[76] To the tune of the "Merry Widow," *l'Opérette viennoise* expressed her regret about leaving and then kept rudely trying to sing over the other characters' verses—reinforcing the stereotype of Germans as ill-mannered. While Camille Saint-Saëns made his speeches vilifying German composers, Rip took a funny, but still pointed, approach. Described as "anti-wagnérien," the agent repeatedly told her and Parsifal to be quiet. Meanwhile, *le Cubism* gaily sang about being "German." Kenneth Silver has noted the inaccurate attribution of cubism to the Germans as part of a conservative attack on the avant-garde at the start of the war.[77] Just as in the classical music debates, the war fed nationalist chauvinism, which had festered for years. Typically, revues addressed cultural issues from any stratum which was a part of their democratic appeal. Here the issue of eliminating the influence of cubism played to a broader audience. In the end, the agent was perfectly happy about all the departures except absinthe's, whose expulsion he found annoying.

Once all of the figures had had a chance to introduce themselves with different tunes, the Tango asked who the imports would be. At this point, an English officer appeared who was to double as the revue's *compère.* He immediately extolled the reliability of the British soldier, singing an ebullient, rhythmic refrain:

Quand les shrapnells	When the shrapnel
Traditionnels,	Traditional,
Pleuvent, nous disons: Well!"	Rains down, we say: "Well!"
. . . .	. . . .
Le sport! . . .	The sport! . . .
Qu'import! Ça vous donne du r'ssort,	What an import! It gives you resilience,
Le sport! . . .	The sport! . . .
Et l'on peut braver sans effort	And one can defy without effort
La mort! . . .	Death! . . .
Car c'est toujours du sport!	For it's always the sport![78]

This refrain saluted the British equation of war and sport, and paralleled other musical denials of death. Here, war was an amusement to be faced easily.

When the *commère,* called *la Parisienne,* made her appearance, she immediately calmed the *compère*'s and audience's fears that without the *expulsés* "There will be no more Paris." On the contrary, she explained, using a well-known prewar tune "Le Premier pas":

Paris redevient raisonnable.	Paris is becoming reasonable again.
Assez de plaisirs et de fêtes,	Enough of pleasures and fêtes,
De désirs jamais contentés,	Of desires never satisfied,
Avions-nous donc perdu la tête,	We had lost our head then.
. . . .	. . . .
Mais la guerre ne l'effraie pas . . .	But the war does not frighten . . .
Et pendant que dans la fournaise	And while in the furnace
Se battent nos fils, nos maris,	Our sons, our husbands fight,
Paris sait redev'nir Paris,	Paris knows how to become Paris again,
Paris, la vraie ville française!	Paris, the true French city![79]

According to these lyrics, the war was an antidote for fin-de-siècle decadence and would provide a context for renewal.[80] Reining in pleasures, amusements, and irresponsible conduct, the inhabitants of Paris were now to behave respectably. Seeking "normality" here corresponded to the censors' efforts to correct what had been wrong with the Belle Époque. Moreover, the lyrics drew a parallel between Paris and the front, reinforcing a positive self-image for the capital city. This was a remarkable position to take on a music-hall stage, but it provided an excellent defense.

Entertainment would keep spirits up and promote virtuous behavior. Meanwhile, curious to find out just how much had really changed, the *compère* and *commère* decided to stay around and meet the residents.

One of the most important features of the early wartime revues was the prescriptive humor directed at the Parisian community. Sometimes lyrics humorously derided "unpatriotic" behavior, while at other times the characters gave tips on what citizens could do for the cause. In some sense, the revue institutionalized the role of gossip, a common feature of some older forms of community. Women modeling English, French, or Russian uniforms while discussing various couturiers were judged frivolous by the *commère*. And the *compère* and *commère* expressed skepticism over "La Dame 'de Bordeaux's'" excuses for having fled to Bordeaux (remember this was just April 1915). Clearly, the Parisian community did not wish to sanction fear in the face of the German invasion. A large portion of the audience may well have been among the guilty ones, since one third of the Parisian population had evacuated. Consequently, many were presumably laughing at themselves.

The scene in the revue that drew the greatest response, and which launched the popular song "On les aura," contained one of the earliest appearances of the home front's "Poilu." The figure was formulated early in the war, before soldiers came home on leave, and it then stayed strong throughout the war. The characterization of military personnel on stage was not new in 1914; prewar revues had had *le Colonel, le Caporal,* or *le Adjutant.* The figure was also not new to *café-concert* audiences. As one police commentator said, it was "a legendary type in the café-concert." But with the arrival of World War I, the Parisian public seized upon a representation from its prewar culture and refashioned it to allow them to understand and cope with a difficult situation—that millions of Frenchmen had become soldiers. Officials painted the most positive view of the transformation, saying,

He [the Poilu] has kept the mischievous fellow from his origins which made him charming, but [he is] no longer at all ridiculous even when he evokes in a comic way the incidents of trench life; he persists like a sort of hero—at the same time, terrible and sweet, heroic and familiar, which incarnates in a very fortunate manner the soldier of the Great War.[81]

Officials themselves had, of course, had a heavy hand in the change, since censors were deleting the disparaging parts. But even the new Parisian representations which had more dignity did not satisfy combatants' definitions, and this particular image was to become a point of contention between the home front and the soldiers.

In the revue *1915, le Poilu* first appeared heading toward the train station (la Gare de l'Est) to go to the front. The *commère,* watching his departure, was overheard saying: "Again a soldier who leaves for the front! Poor guy!"—a line that was attributable to any civilian.[82] *Le Poilu* immediately took offense and compared his good fortune to that of the "poor civilians." At the front, life was very healthy, the cannons (75s) distracted them, and they lived like a family, playing dominos and singing. He then broke into the song "On les aura!" after inviting the audience to sing along at the refrain:

On les aura	We will get them
Quand on voudra	When we want to
Ah! sal' Boch', tu sortiras	Ah! dirty Boche, you will leave
De tes sacres trous de rat	From your damn rat holes
Vive le son	Long live the sound
De nos canons!	Of our cannons!
Qui vivra verra!	Those who live will see!
Les Boch's, on les aura!	The Boches, we will get them![83]

This character expressed the public's affection for soldiers, with his pride, cheeriness, and determination. The figure also embodied a Parisian view of life in the trenches, but used a soldier's "voice." That a Parisian *revuiste* was "speaking" for a soldier illustrated part of the power of Paris's dominant culture. Similar representations of the *poilus* surrounded the city's occupants in newspaper articles, published "combatants'" letters, and postcards.

One Parisian newspaper recorded the reappearance of the song "On les aura" at a benefit concert at the Trocadero held on May 1, 1915, for convalescing soldiers. The article claimed the song, sung by Vilbert who had originally played the character on stage, was the "hit" of the show. At this particular concert the refrain was taken up in a chorus by six thousand soldiers creating what was described as a moment of profound emotion: "all these brave men, who have faced enemy fire and shed their blood, cried out with fervent faith: 'On les aura, les Boches!'" The newspaper then reproduced the prologue, lyrics, and music, "in order that this refrain and this cry would be on all lips tomorrow."[84] One could not have asked for a better example for Parisians to follow.

Some memoirs of Paris also described the performance of patriotic songs in front of impassioned crowds. Michel Corday attended a concert by Yvette Guilbert and Pierre Loti in March of 1915 which included patriotic songs and religious poems. He remarked on the sharp contrast between this performance and Guilbert's shows in black gloves before the war.[85] The most violent songs could get an excited reception. Guy Breton's collection of anecdotes refers to one occasion when the song "Tricoter"—a song in which French soldiers drove their "needles" into Prussian stomachs—was welcomed by an "enthusiastic" audience in a *café-concert*. As the wave of patriotism would begin to fade in Paris, new songs would be written to revitalize it.[86]

"Normality," however, was still uncomfortable during the 1914–1915 season. Commenting on home life in January 1915, the correspondent Pearl Adam maintained that "entertaining was unheard of, and if any one played the piano, protests were certain to be made by passersby against such frivolity." Moreover, laughter in restaurants had to be discreet or one was frowned upon; "In early 1915 public manners were austere."[87] By May 1915, however, some were getting worried precisely because "normality" seemed too comfortable. The newspaper columnist Frédéric Masson, for example, did not approve of "her [Paris's] new activity" and wrote: "Give us back our grave, serious, magnificent, silent Paris of the autumn."[88] Corday also noted, "Paris is remote from the war. The restaurants are crammed. What a contrast with those tortured towns of eastern France. . . . That is one of the great tragedies of the time—the enormous gulf between Paris and the front."[89]

The Middle Years of War and the Growth of a Critique

The full flowering of normality, which so scandalized some critics, was not to be rejected, however. The 1915–1916 season had greater stability and high attendance.[90] After July 1915 audiences at entertainment establishments swelled with soldiers on leave or those recuperating. By the fall of 1915, theaters were setting aside seats for soldiers, while some places offered reduced prices or free tickets for soldiers on leave accompanied by their families.[91] In contrast, the kaiser chose to criticize Berlin's "unseemly nightlife," which he found "increasingly offensive to his soldiers."[92] During the summer of 1916 the management of the Gaîté-Rochechouart could even afford to restore its interior completely, and the theater reopened September 1, 1916, with "the brightest, gayest, most sumptuous setting one could possibly imagine."[93]

The songs during the middle of the war were often less overtly patriotic, except for programs at fundraising concerts. Performers still chose older numbers; for instance, one program at the Gaîté-Parisienne in February 1916 used "Alsace et Lorraine," "Le Régiment de Sambre-Meuse," "Ce que c'est qu'un drapeau," and "Maman Victoire." They also continued to promote other genres, especially caricatures of the Germans and the kaiser.[94] A police report from early 1916 concluded with satisfaction that "in the halls the patriotic songs or satirical lyrics toward our enemies have contributed to maintaining the public under these circumstances."[95]

Most notably, songs that presented soldiers charging into battle with nationalist lyrics falling from their lips remained popular. Adolphe Berard was said to have "triumphed" at the Eldorado singing "Le Père la Victoire, "Les Cuirassiers de Reichshoffen," and "Verdun, on ne passe pas," the first two songs from the prewar revanchist repertoire and the last written for the war. All three were adamantly prowar.[96] "Verdun, on ne passe pas" was probably the best known of the songs inspired by the enormous, devastating battle of Verdun, where hundreds of thousands of Frenchmen lost their lives. Its lyrics recall the 1914 songs with strong patriotism and a description of a running battle. The Germans advanced with rage, spreading death in their wake: "drunk from discord, carnage, and blood."[97] As the French responded, the wounded officer cried out "A la baïonnette," and the Germans were driven back, while the French sang the "Marseillaise."[98] One contemporary obviously enjoyed its rendition at the Gaîté-Rochechouart in June 1916, saying "we must note the remarkable conviction of Mademoiselle Armande Sogère, who sang 'On ne passe pas' resolutely and constitutes the most agreeable living citadel"[99] (app. figs. 7–10).

The most popular, and original, group of songs from this period, however, focused on the *poilus,* their life in the trenches, and their leave in Paris. Hundreds of songs appeared with titles like "Dans mon boyau" (In my trench), "La Boue" (Mud), "Journal de tranchée" (Trench newspaper), "Le Rêve d'un poilu" (A *poilu*'s dream), or "A quoi pensent nos soldats" (What our soldiers think about). Audiences seemed to want to keep track of the soldiers; they were not content with just prewar numbers or with ignoring the war. A song such as "Chantons ce refrain," which was written in 1916, actually taught an audience the soldiers' argot using the form of a sing-along and a very easy refrain.[100] Widely used songs also combined praise for the work of the *poilu* with the sexual humor discussed in chapter 4. In 1915 Vincent Scotto, a well-respected writer and editor, wrote his "Le Cri du poilu" (figs. 22 and 23) about the "petits soldats" who simply desired "A woman A woman!" ("Une femme Une femme!"). It was sung repeatedly late in 1915 and 1916 and gained enough reknown that its tune saw repeated use for other unrelated songs and for parodies.[101]

By late 1916, new places were exploiting the Parisian taste for timely songs and revues with wartime themes. Le Peletier and Senga opened in 1915 and Le Perchoir in 1916, all with long programs of songs. Other establishments that had been cinemas reopened as *cafés-concerts* or music halls.[102] This pointed to a particular interest in live entertainment.[103] In sharp contrast, Gary Stark has found that German officials refused to grant

Figure 22. Songsheet, "Le Cri du poilu." Courtesy of the Préfecture de Police. All rights reserved.

sal' gueul' des All'mands Ils aim'raient bien mieux certain'ment U _ ne fem_

_ me U _ ne fem _ me Cré bon sang qu'est-c'qu'ils n'donn'raient pas Pour t'nir un

moment dans leurs bras U _ ne fem_ me U _ ne fem_ me!

2

Quand en ribambelle
Ils bouff'nt la gamelle,
C'est vite avalé
En deux temps ça n'a pas traîné.
Ensuit' sur la paille
Allongés, ils baillent
Se f'sant, non de non,
Presque tous la même réflexion,
Et dans ce moment-là
A quoi pens'nt-ils tout bas?
Ne cherchez pas.

Refrain

A nos Poilus qui sont sur l'front
Qu'est-c' qu'il leur faut comm' distrac-
    -tion?
    Une femme *(bis)*
Quand ils ont bouffé leur rata
Qu'est-c'qu'ils demand'nt comm' second
    plat?
    Une femme *(bis)*
Sapristi pour calmer leurs nerfs
S'il leur arrivait comm' dessert
    Une femme *(bis)*
Quelle soit grande ou p'tit' ma foi
Ça ne fait rien pourvu qu'ce soit
    Une femme *(bis)*

3

Quand dans la tranchée
Ils pass' nt la journée
Par les p'tits créneaux
Ils envoient aux boch's des pruneaux.
Puis ils se reposent
Pens'nt à des tas d'choses
Qui leur font, cré non,
Passer dans tout l'corps des frissons
Avant de s'endormir
Ils ont, dans un soupir,
Le mêm' désir.

Refrain

A nos Poilus qui sont sur l'front
Qu'est-c' qu'il leur faut comm' distraction
    Une femme *(bis)*
Il y a tant d'amoureux là-bas
Qui pourraient faire plaisir à
    Une femme *(bis)*
A ce moment, c'est l'essentiel
Il faudrait qu'il leur tomb' du ciel
    Une femme *(bis)*
Et comme prière du soir
Ils dis'nt: "Bon Dieu! fais nous donc voir
    Une femme *(bis)*

JULIEN Gr.

Paris, CAYEL F??s, grav. imp, F§ St Denis, 18.

Figure 23. Postcard with the refrain from Vincent Scotto's "Le Cri du poilu." Collection of the author.

new theater licenses, since they were, according to the officials, "not in keeping with the seriousness of the present times."[104]

However, not everyone approved of the Parisian view of the war, nor of the crowds attending performances. As one observer remarked, "in truth, Paris offered an astonishing spectacle" as the theaters, cinemas, *cafés-concerts,* and restaurants overflowed with people.[105] The general secretary of the Comédie-Française even felt that that theater's attendance was surpassing that of peacetime. Beginning as early as November 1915, a critique of the entertainment business and its stars formed, partially propelled by returning soldiers. One line of argument criticized any pleasure and was directed at the entertainment industry from outside. Others, including performers, objected only to "excessive" delights. One other response used songs to question the behavior of Parisians more generally, pointing to the problem of escapism.

The issue of improper behavior and entertainment was sometimes aggravated by particularly "unseemly" displays thrown in the face of the purposefully classless *union sacrée.* At the reopening of the Opéra in December 1915, the display of wealth, with dresses reportedly worth 2,700 to 3,500 francs and "rivers of diamonds," caused such an uproar that Dalimier, the undersecretary of fine arts, was forced to recommend that less expensive clothing be worn. This corresponded to the promotion of austerity we saw in the revue *1915.* The edict was later extended to prohibiting evening dress in State theaters.[106] The change in the dress code and the high number of soldiers in audiences increased the mixing of classes in appearance and contact. But some complaints concerning huge crowds were directed at the "reckless" spending of the working classes, which had more disposable income as wages rose.[107]

Despite their confrontation with the war in the trenches, soldiers paid close attention to civilian actions and cultural constructs. And even with their growing dissatisfaction, they chose to come to Paris on leave. This shift was very difficult for many soldiers, since they were entering into a well-formulated, self-sustaining community. The tunes advertised exciting and satisfying leaves in the capital, but infantrymen had their own views of the Parisian crowds and singing. They often saw audiences' reactions as excessive, frenzied, or even as "orgies and debaucheries."[108] Part of this response was due to the stark difference between the trenches and Paris. But some combatants also feared that parts of the nation were adapting too well. Through their eyes, "normality" was quite abnormal. And this aberration could become permanent, since it lessened reasons for ending the war.

Many soldiers also saw the Parisian atmosphere as a very specific reaction to the war, not just as a continuation of prewar habits. Soldiers' writings repeatedly noted an impression of Parisian guilt and evasion. One soldier pointed out that "everywhere patriotic references are accorded frenzied applause. The audiences feel that they are thus making their sacrifice on the altar of war, discharging their debt to it."[109] This sentiment echoed other civilians' accounts of the almost perfunctory character of the singing of patriotic songs within every program.

Soldiers did, however, show some appreciation for the civilians' position, at least early on, and even sanctioned "unrealistic" entertainment. One article in the trench journal *Le Crapouillot,* for example, described a soldier's impression during a leave in Paris when he attended both a *café-concert* and a revue at a theater. At first he was taken aback and needed time to readjust to Parisian language and references—an expression of the distance and alienation that had grown up between the city and the front. But he did note how popular revues had become and how they dealt with Parisian life and complaints. Then he admitted that although he did not like the portrayals of the war, the audience was made up of soldiers and their families, and neither group needed to see the "real thing!"[110] Finally he made the interesting observation that an outsider looking at Paris might say that "Parisians do not appear to know about the war, life is completely normal." In his charitable opinion, however, "This was civilian courage! All the people who suffer, who hope or who cry in hiding, stoically continue their daily lives, without allowing their emotions to show; they have confidence, they brace themselves, they HOLD." This was relatively high praise, giving Parisians the benefit of the doubt.

Although the musical establishments represented a cornerstone for promoting and evaluating "normality," some of the soldiers' criticisms were taken up by those in the industry. This fed back into the discussion of proper civilian behavior. The song "Celle qui chante 'La Marseillaise'" made fun of the perpetual singing of the national anthem by Marthe Chenal who, a verse explained, had to have sung it at least forty-five hundred times.[111] In addition, Paul Weil, a well-known *café-concert* singer, also attacked performers for their abuse of the "Marseillaise" and other patriotic songs; particularly because many songwriters had not seen any fighting. Weil performed the song "Heroisme en chambre" to the tune of "Guillaume s'en va-t-en guerre," a reference to an earlier patriotic song by Théodore Botrel which had used the same tune. In these lyrics, Weil needled the average civilian:

M'sieur Pouf s'en va-t-en guerre	Monsieur Pouf has gone to war
Sans ôter de sa chais' son derrière,	Without lifting his derriere from his chair,

Ce héros exemplaire	This model hero
Veut aller de l'avant . . .	Wants to go to the front . . .
Dans son appartement,	In his apartment,
Il trouv' qu'on va lent'ment.	He finds that one goes slowly.
. . . .	. . . .
Ma chérie, pass'moi donc mes pantoufles,	So, my dear, pass me my slippers,
Je sens que je m'essouffle . . .	I feel out of breath . . .[112]

The harshest satires, however, could not get past the censors' pencils and thus the music industry's patriotic reputation did not get too badly tarnished.[113]

"Celle qui chante 'La Marseillaise'" was not alone, since several articles and songs voiced similar complaints during 1915 and 1916. The controversy over the song's purpose and meaning was a struggle over sacred property that could easily be profaned; a person's choice and manner of singing illustrated his or her allegiance. At least one composer, Jean Deyrmon, saw the constant singing of the "Marseillaise" as brainwashing. His song "Une Soirée au beuglant, ou le sabotage de la Marseillaise dans les Caf' Conc'," played on the images of various snakelike, rotund, and idiotic performers bellowing out the "Marseillaise," twenty times a night.[114]

The criticisms were not lost on officials, and in March 1916, two deputies introduced a bill to the assembly asking for a 100 percent tax on all entertainment, if the theaters could not be closed altogether. In their proposal, they bitterly outlined the problem, calling the droves of women, children, and men waiting at the doors of theaters or cabarets an "indecent spectacle."[115] Moreover, it was scandalous: "that such frenetic applause, such irrepressible laughter happens to accentuate the licentious jokes, the jeers, the misreadings of often outlandish repertoires, while in the trenches, in the line of fire, . . . soldiers . . . cry out in pain and are doubled over in the throes of death." These critics supported the censors' concerns that immoral lyrics could only damage morale, while mocking the soldiers' noblest accomplishments. Their plan absolved performances that entertained soldiers and that combined the idea of distraction with a higher sense of solidarity and sacrifice. But it condemned "the establishments making profits as in peacetime," where neither a sense of unity nor compassion could be found. Unfortunately, one could not always distinguish between the two types. With one last effort, the deputies proclaimed that ideally, "as long as cannons roared, and the machine guns rattled, Gugusse, Punchinello, and Harlequin should keep quiet." Despite this impassioned rhetoric, when the tax finally took effect in January 1917, it had been scaled down considerably. The final rate was only ten centimes for places costing under one franc; twenty-five centimes for seats between one and eight francs; and fifty centimes for those over eight francs. The majority of deputies had chosen to support the argument in favor of Parisian entertainment.

Together with the tax debate, in late 1916, as the war dragged on, the entertainment businesses were busy staving off other crises caused by war shortages and bad weather. To save electricity, the government issued an ordinance in November 1916 forcing the *spectacles* to close one night a week and to limit themselves to only two matinees.[116] At this point, most halls had been having evening and matinee performances every day in response to the high number of soldiers on leave. Then in February 1917, in the midst of a bitterly cold winter, the government took serious actions, eliminating transportation after 10 P.M. (except on weekends), closing museums, reducing days for pastry shops, and limiting theaters to five performances a week. There were those, however, who argued that inviting thousands of people to spend an evening together in a music hall was, in fact, a positive way to save coal.

But the government's steps did not satisfy the harshest critics. The crisis over the distribution of coal and the freezing weather highlighted the choices having to be made, for example, between munitions factories and theaters. Arguing that entertainment was frivolous and "distracting," the writer Jean-Bernard Passerieu pledged not to attend any performances as long as sons and friends were serving in the trenches.[117] Of course, like many others he approved of one exception—performances for soldiers, since they needed "true" distractions. Otherwise, Passerieu strongly believed that, "When the youngest go to die by the thousands, at that moment one should be silent." Enjoying oneself at a theater was both inappropriate and replaced more beneficial activities.[118] Passerieu also did not accept that the need to keep theater workers employed was a legitimate problem; he accused the managers of simply worrying about their subscribers, and suggested that one could send the employees to the front or at least to work on munitions. Much to his amazement, however, when he sought out others' opinions, some declared entertainment to be their right.

In March 1917 another newspaper columnist wrote, without any sign of disapproval, that "the Parisian public, despite or perhaps because of the circumstances, enjoys itself at the theater; it looks for a distraction there, the momentary forgetting of its miseries, of this we have no doubt."[119] But how could one know if all amusement, laughter, or fervor covered up grief or sorrow? What if people were actually enjoying themselves?

Despite the criticism, the bad weather, and the new tax, the theaters and *cafés-concerts* returned to a full schedule just six weeks later and saw still higher receipts.[120] The government never took the drastic step of closing the halls completely, as Munich officials did, for example, and the public made its choice to attend, in spite of the censure from members of Parliament. High attendance and visible crowds had set off the criticism, but the admonishments did not seem to dampen enthusiasm. According to police documents, the music industry experienced enormous receipts during the middle years of the war, far more than they had expected. And they even managed to avoid any unemployment during the summers of 1916 and 1917—a marked improvement over prewar patterns. Although the summer of 1916 had had some regular theater closings, places that stayed open had "a public eager for distractions," as the police spy had noted. In 1917 and 1918 new opportunities and troubles appeared as foreign troops increased audiences and the Germans once again threatened the capital. Chapter 8 will look at the later period, but first we need to hear from the soldiers themselves and examine how different the cultural rules and productions were outside the Parisian sphere.

CHAPTER SIX

The French Army's "Theater of War"

⤳

An Introduction to the Army Zone

In Paris, we encountered soldiers heralded in songs and portrayed on stage within carefully monitored representations. But how did this compare to the army zone and the soldiers themselves—the nearly eight million Frenchmen who entered the armed forces during the four and a half years?[1] What were army officials' reactions to the 1914 shift to defensive warfare? And how did the soldiers face the shockingly new form of warfare and compose their participation, or "performance," in what officials and journalists liked to call the "theater of war"?

The classic perspective on World War I has focused first and foremost on life in the trenches, where soldiers encountered horrendous physical abuse from the cold, rain, rats, and deafening artillery, accompanied by heavy labor, terrible food, and a lack of sleep. In addition, psychological hardships caused by the random danger and indescribable deaths became part of everyday life.[2] Until 1918 this war would not entail the "old-fashioned" battles and breakthroughs imagined in August 1914. Heavy artillery and the use of machine guns froze soldiers in their trenches, since the mortality rate rose quickly once soldiers ventured out. Instead, combatants faced periods of interminable boredom mingled with the repetitive work of building trenches or putting out barbed wire. Under these conditions, most acts of heroism involved quiescence or defensive moves rather than action.[3] Soldiers had to cope with depression, helplessness, and tedium, or, in French terms, *le cafard*.

Both veterans and historians have debated how combatants responded to these conditions. Did they cast off their civilian garb to be drastically altered forever? One veteran described front-line soldiers as having had "abridged personalities" with their boundaries set by war and death.[4] In other words, soldiers had little time, space, or inclination for cultural practices or forms.

Older works on French soldiers have tended to stress the distinctiveness of the soldiers' lives and the unfathomable separation from the civilians, although the sharpest presentation of the argument that trench warfare precluded normal cultural activities has come in Eric Leed's work. He has claimed that soldiers shed their prewar values and practices as they passed through a rite of passage and became integrated into army life at the front. His work highlights the extraordinary otherworldliness of trench landscape and rituals, which explained the soldiers' growing feeling that civilians could not possibly comprehend "their" world.[5]

Other scholars, however, have discovered that soldiers struggled hard to exploit cultural practices and forms in order to endure and understand what was transpiring as well as to construct their views of the war. But disagreements continue over how sharp a cultural separation emerged between the trenches and civilians. Did troops remain within the national collective because they maintained important links to the home front or because they brought their own national culture with them?[6] And how different were the cultural rules in the trenches compared to the home front?[7]

There is little doubt that French soldiers brought cultural practices with them. Soldiers turned to reading, letter writing, creating trench newspapers, and drawing to entertain and express themselves.[8] Singing, however, went further than other cultural forms, because it crossed the barrier of leisure and "work" time and overcame varying levels of literacy. It also involved both individual and group activities. Whereas time and space for reading and writing were restricted, soldiers could sing almost anytime and anywhere—on *repos* (rest time behind the lines), while moving up the line, recovering from the shock of assaults, or even in battle—especially since singing did not require any special materials. Songs spread through planned and impromptu performances and with texts that appeared everywhere—in newspapers, on large broadsheets or on postcards, all sold by itinerant singers and peddlers near the front. The soldiers' prewar experience had provided them with a vast inventory of tunes and the ability to manipulate lyrics. With the radio still in the future and the urban star system relatively new, almost anyone and everyone sang—especially in an army of peasants and workers.

Throughout the war, musical practices ranged from collective to individual, and from official to impromptu. From one extreme of solitary, unsupervised singing to the other of organized choruses, a variety of circumstances could be found. But the site of certain types of musical events was not random. Two main zones entailed differing musical practices. The trenches, which formed "the front," extended four hundred miles from the English Channel to the Swiss borders through northeastern France and

Belgium. This front was actually made up of at least three rows of trenches with only the most forward rows considered the true front by the troops. In this zone, one encountered most often the combination of individual, spontaneous singing, and creative, unofficial expressions. Here, the older practices of a popular culture flourished.

Soldiers, however, spent less than half their time in the lethal front lines. After a tour in the front line, a combatant moved back behind the lines or to camps for rest periods. A huge area existed in the official army zone, which included *cantonnements* (large and small camps), training centers, and administrative headquarters. In these spaces, one found a more hetero-geneous, hierarchical set of performers and audiences—soldiers, high-ranking officers and civilians, men and women—which affected the content and the interpretation of the songs. This area also had the most organized and closely supervised events, where civilian performers presented national culture to passive soldiers. Despite the cultural construct by contemporaries and many historians of two radically different and opposing fronts—the military and home fronts—this cultural geography actually complicated or broke down the dichotomy.

There was an important distinction, therefore, within the army zone, between the official army bureaucracy and the common soldiers' time and space. In keeping with this division, this chapter will investigate the army's use of music to encourage unity and discipline. The army pursued its nineteenth-century traditions, believing music, and particularly singing, could promote aggressive patriotism and help counter bad circumstances.

The army's cultural influence, however, could reach only so far, and chapter 7 will explore how soldiers found their own means to create their own musical culture. Once trench warfare began, the soldiers performed as a form of personal expression and as an integral part of their survival under gruesome conditions. While civilians found ways to contend with the war, soldiers also had to adapt. As the veteran André Ducasse reported, "in order to forget the worst, the soldiers kept themselves content with little": some sleep, food, tobacco, laughs, and songs. "Tunes quickly flourished: marching refrains or spicy womanizing ditties, taken up in chorus."9 And as time wore on, they expressed their dissatisfaction with the war not solely through the mutinies of 1917 but through more subtle, musical practices.

Music as a Military Force

The French army went to war armed with regimental bands and clarion calls, while soldiers brought regional and national repertoires. One might assume that trench warfare with its own volume and chaos would have overwhelmed these musical tactics. After all, this was the intensely modern warfare that was to give birth to the twentieth century. Nevertheless, the army's musical traditions, which had developed as part of an older form of warfare, continued, and were even adapted to the new conditions. Faced with the deadly, often bewildering, conditions of trench warfare, the army relied on codes of conduct to maintain respect for hierarchy and obedience to orders. In addition, rituals performed by soldiers sustained discipline and morale.[10]

But why should war and music have any relationship? Music connotes beauty, humanity, the sublime, whereas the trenches entailed disorder, ugliness, inhumanity, and death. But music was not incongruent. It has power, order, motion, even predictability—all things the army needed. In the conceptualization and prosecution of the war, soldiers could be refocused with rhythmic regularity, memorization, and volume. Officers could also promote directed aggression through singing with certain lyrics and melodies. We will look at how they did so, but we also need to appreciate that this army effort was part of a larger cultural structuring of the war, an effort revealed in the prevalence of musical or theatrical metaphors.

Indeed, French military leaders and other participants' texts employed the metaphor of a "theater of war" with astonishing parallels—battles were martial programs, spectacles, or performances; weapons were musical instruments; and artillery barrages were concerts. This was not a single, simple metaphor, however. Most broadly, the army zone was referred to as a "theater of operations" and combat as a *spectacle*. (In French, *spectacles* refer to a wide range of entertainment.) But the metaphor had both visual, and more often, aural versions. Having led his troops into one of his first battles, Emile-François Julia described how they had "attended a veritable theater of war; the Front was before us."[11] Julia and others commented on the curtain rising and the fireworks. Troops also repeatedly listened to "concerts" by rhythmic machine guns and told of being "serenaded" by bombs.[12] For others with experience in classical music, "a powerful symphony of shells" wound down as a decrescendo.[13] Such expressions may well have been an attempt to bring order to chaos, and to bring a familiar idea to bear on the unfamilar. It was certainly a common and seemingly comforting choice.

We find in other uses of the metaphor, however, that soldiers were not just audience members, watching or listening. Combatants became performers. One officer compared himself to an orchestra conductor, trying to get his soldiers coordinated to make the proper entrances.[14] Soldiers could also represent what combatants were supposed to do, based on the formula of "victoire en chantant" (singing our way to victory). The audience in these cases was the enemy or French civilians, through news reports, for example.

This metaphor appeared in *cafés-concerts* songs as well as in many soldiers' and officers' accounts, although the timbre of the metaphor's voice varied. It was sometimes used enthusiastically or solemnly in a straightforward manner. But it could also have an ironic inflection, where the metaphor was being set against the "reality." Cannons sang of death, for instance, or civilians were invited to experience the deadly side of the *spectacle*.[15]

One might ask, therefore: if war was a performance, then who was composing the score? These examples were not all just similes or colorful expressions. The army went to great lengths at times to write its libretto, to integrate performances into military instruction and strategy. Soldiers needed to perform, and military "revues" or spectacles were supposed to help.

Military Musical Rituals

Regimental units equipped with musicians and instruments acted as the backbone of the army's system of musical rituals for fighting and for ceremonies.[16] They were instruments of nationalization, most obviously with their constant performances of the French and allies' national anthems. Often referred to as simply *la musique,* these units were led by officers with military rank. The other musicians usually did double duty as *musicien-brancardiers* (stretcher-bearers) or as *soldat-musiciens*.[17] The original policy provided "musique régimentaire" for active regiments but not for reserve regiments. As the war continued, this distinction became imprecise, since the reserve regiments began creating their own music units, "when the corps commanders consider[ed] it indispensable . . . which was generally the case." And the ministry of war sought more funding from Parliament in 1918, arguing that "the regimental musicians are useful everywhere."[18] Although the army talked at times of reducing the musical sections to "simple fanfares" in order to gain men who could be officers, this does not appear ever to have happened.

The intermingling of musicians in the army's ranks differed from the treatment of army artists who remained in the separate *camoufleurs* unit. The art historian Elizabeth Kahn found that army officials and the artists themselves viewed art as above or outside of war.[19] In contrast, music fused with combat operations to strengthen the military's operations. A portion of the musical units were made up of trumpeters and drummers who continued as musicians into battles. Others, such as cymbal players or flutists, shifted into medical or support roles for attacks, and then moved back to performing under calmer conditions. The units had several responsibilities: performing for army rituals such as marching and revues, playing in battles, and giving regular concerts.

Fortunately, we have a journal by a *musicien-brancardier,* Jacques Heugel, which illustrates the daily routine of one musical unit. Heugel had grown up playing piano in a Parisian, bourgeois family, and had served his army time as a musician just prior to the war. In civilian life, he had moved within classical music circles, and this carried over into the war as he constantly ran across acquaintances from the Conservatory, Opéra, and Opéra-Comique. When the war broke out, the *chef de musique* of the 5th Infantry regiment recruited Heugel for his forty-man cadre. Heugel described how the war of movement fell into confusion in late August 1914, and how the possibilities for regular performances opened up once the front solidified. "From then on, except during difficult periods when they needed us as stretcher bearers, we devoted ourselves to the joys of harmony."[20] Heugel's journal portrays the remarkable mixture of music and trench life, as his account moves seamlessly from the task or joy of music making to tales of rat hunts and artillery shellings. The 5th Infantry served in some of the harshest sectors, including the Marne, Artois, Verdun, and Chemin des Dames, which earned Heugel the *médaille de Verdun, la croix du combattant,* and entry into the Legion of Honor. By the end of the war, 20 percent of the unit had been killed.[21]

Regimental musicians performed at two of the regular military ceremonies—citation awards and firing squads—where the State carefully constructed the circumstances and meanings marking the two possible extremes of citizens' civic actions. In both martial spectacles, trumpets and drums played an essential part in impressively inscribing the patriotic message for both soldiers and civilians. Georges Clemenceau declared that no more beautiful a spectacle existed than the citation ceremony he attended at the front (in Aisne) in 1917 with trumpets, drums, and a "splendid alignment . . . of soldiers with medals."[22] General Bon noted the ineffectiveness of a citation ceremony that lacked *la musique militaire.* "There were neither trumpets to open and close the proclamation, nor a band to play the 'Marseillaise.' The weather was grey; we left with heavy hearts."[23]

At the other extreme, the convicted traitor Bolo Pacha was escorted to the post at Vincennes with trumpets sounding the fanfare "aux champs." The music stopped as the firing squad prepared and fired. Then the troops left playing the "Sambre et Meuse."[24] Possibly the most famous precedent for this type of ceremony was Captain Alfred Dreyfus's ceremony of degradation in 1895. The fanfare had also marked the end of that ceremony and the military band had played "Sambre et Meuse." As the radical nationalist Maurice Barrès explained the process, "the military music spread honor and loyalty over the area and swept away the stench of treason."[25] The 1918 musical presentation at Vincennes helped structure the display and contributed to the air of formality and authority. The instrumentation broadcast a positive militarism, and the choice of song conveyed the French state's role in this staged version of death, punctuating the fact that the traitor had been punished and France purged. Although the public was barred from the 1918 "performance," the Parisian newspapers recreated the scene the following day for their readers.

Alphonse Marois also witnessed the execution ritual as a soldier in basic training in 1917. His regiment was awakened at 3 A.M. and marched to a spot close to Vincennes. What followed shocked the trainees, especially since the condemned man insisted on denouncing the ceremony as a comedy and continued to revile the government and President Poincaré in competition with the sound of the trumpets, thus disrupting the script. After the shooting, as the troops returned to their quarters, the officers encouraged the recruits to sing the facile song "Quand Madelon," but without success.[26] The soldiers had been baptised with an army ceremony to assure their understanding of potential punishment. In this case, they attended as members of an audience. In the future, participatory singing after violent attacks would be encouraged, and soldiers came to accept this method of diverting thoughts and effacing problematic issues.

Most infantrymen encountered musical ritualization more routinely in regular training sessions and in marching. If the army wanted to give some order or sense of control on the battlefield, what better way than by using "rehearsals"—the term used by some to describe military exercises before an attack. This practice was also a carryover from the prewar period, when troops gave military drills during military fêtes; these included cavalry or bayonet demonstrations, or, in the case of the 7th Regiment de Dragons in their 1897 fête, pieces entitled "La charge" and "Marche du 6e Lanciers."[27] The double entendre of a "revue"—military or musical—referred to a simple stand-to or inspection as well as to a fully staged battle. Movements were coordinated by the rhythms and melodies of regimental bands. Louis Mairet and his troops attended "battalion maneuvers" in December 1916 with French and Belgian troops, where a simulated battle was mounted with music, explosions, and a fake enemy barrage. First and second rows of trenches were taken, as the waves of men "marched, always in step, as if on parade."[28] In his novel La Percée, Jean Bernier also gave a striking account of the powerful effect of twelve thousand soldiers being transformed from men in a random, chaotic group ("sans cadence") into a tight military formation of geometric rows—their bodies, propelled by bursts of military music, passed proudly in front of their general. "The war marches past set to music."[29]

Troops were not immune from responding jokingly or cynically to these techniques, however, despite the army's best efforts. Some junior officers criticized the high command for monopolizing "rest" time with performances.[30] Musical revues included humorous "Pot-Pourris" of marching songs, and memoirs joked nervously about officers too eager to have their musicians lead their troops into battle.[31] One letter recounted how the music "resounded strangely on earth still soaked with blood."[32] Such jokes and criticisms did not bring a halt to the use of music, however, and soldiers' journals and letters from 1917 still mentioned being sent off on marches or into battle led by their musicians *(la musique en tête)*.

Moreover, the army's musical rites did not require the presence of bands or musical instruments. Officers at all levels were well aware of singing's power and their troops' proficiency. They encouraged harmonizing, especially while marching throughout the endless months of war. Marching represented one of the most closely supervised activities. Transitions from sector to sector took place behind the lines and often meant long twenty-five-to-thirty-kilometer marches at any hour. Singing helped set a pace, coordinated the collective motion, and occupied the soldiers' minds. It offered rhythm as well as ascending and descending scales. In what Maurice Genevoix called "a barbarous and familiar rite," troops also moved "up the line" which was especially painful, since it was done with a full pack (weighing up to eighty-five pounds) and often at night.[33] They could sing, for example in communication trenches, until they were quite close to the German lines.

One finds both army-directed and individual musical efforts to keep up spirits described in primary sources. Jean Giraudoux's troops chose to sing the "Chant du départ," as they learned how to march in 1914. Sometimes the inspiration came from one individual who happened to have a suitable repertoire. A Doctor-Major Hubert L. described to his wife how he constantly sang to keep spirits up. His most helpful songs included well-known pieces from Montmartre by Xavier Privas and Paul Delmet.[34]

Social class and military background determined who was most likely to lead the chorus. Career officers had been trained to sing and had a repertoire at hand. As one prewar officer's booklet instructed "Before departing on a campaign, it's good to have a small repertoire of songs."[35] Some officers took the idea of "victoire en chantant" to heart. They would often begin, followed by the enlisted men. Sergeant Georges Lafond noted how his lieutenant loved "a quick pace and a marching song." Occasionally, "at the top of his lungs, he would begin one of those bawdy songs full of expressions of shameless obscenities. . . . And the section leaders would take up the refrain in chorus." Quite typically, either he chose well-known songs or the troops were picking up the refrains with ease.[36] Regiments also had their own marching songs such as "Les Poilus du 20ème" written for the 20th Infantry or "Les Grospères" written by the 113th Territorial to the tune of "Tipperary." The latter's refrain adapted easily:

It's a long way to Tipperary	It's a long way to Tipperary
De Marseille à Calais	From Marseille to Calais
On n'voit qu'poilus et tommys	We see only *poilus* and tommys
Travailler pour le succès . . .	Working for success . . .[37]

These regimental songs served a physical and ideological use. Some carried on a military army tradition by reinforcing or inventing a regiment's history and by fostering pride with such musical instructions as "marziale et bien chanté" (martially and well sung) or a refrain to be done "fièrement" (proudly).

Newer officers who came from educated, middle, or upper-class backgrounds, however, appear to have been less comfortable leading the singing, and often yielded to others. The educated classes had moved away from the practices of popular culture, whereas peasants or workers were far more likely to sing on their own or to entertain others spontaneously. Some officers extolled the French for having a true popular culture among spirited peasants, compared to the Germans who disdained their lower classes.[38] Louis Mairet complimented one of his subordinates who once "joked and sang" for over twenty kilometers, and "whose laughter and songs broke out beautifully refreshing during discouraging periods."[39] But many were taken aback by the popular or "stupid" songs "bellowed" out repeatedly.[40] In the end, however, neither officers nor soldiers could remain passive listeners; they often became performers themselves.

Some superior officers even wrote pieces themselves. Colonel Pallu drafted words for a war song and had them put to music by the assistant musical commander of the 119th regiment. His couplet exhorted plainly:

Douzième brigade,	12th brigade,
En garde!	On guard!
Régiments,	Regiments,
En avant!	Forward!
Cinquième,	5th,
Cent dix-neuvième,	119th,
Quand même!	No matter what![41]

This structure matched the traditional clarion calls' abrupt, short phrasing and used words such as "forward" taken from an older fighting style. The new regimental songs also fit into the gendered militarist discourse with their attention to male bonding, forward motion, and soldiers' potency. The "Marching Song" for the 13th company of the 246th regiment, written in July 1916, fantasized about the unit's soldiers spending a year away from the war with a village of women. The break produced a hundred babies and a promotion.[42]

These songs helped prevent boredom or depressing thoughts on marches, particularly when the men did not know where they were going. Georges Lafond's memoir provides an excellent example of how songs got composed and used repeatedly. Lafond's second lieutenant Delpos, who had served in Senegal and Morocco before the war, wrote "Ma mitrailleuse" (My machine gun), which the troops described as "completely new . . . composed for us, by one of us, and premiered by us."[43] Lafond explained that the song used a readily available "military march," in which, "like a clarion call, the alternating refrain 'Ma mitrailleuse,' sung in chorus, sounds."[44] The sixth verse addressed the greedy machine gun:

Avec tes tac tac réguliers	With your regular rat-a-tat
Fauche les Boches par milliers,	Mow down the Boches by the thousands,
Sans t'arrêter, noire et fumeuse,	Without stopping, black and smoky,
Ma mitrailleuse.	My machine gun.

The eight verses were constructed to aid memorization with rhymes every two lines and "Ma mitrailleuse" every fourth line. After the second lieutenant had written the lyrics, the whole unit learned and performed the song for their commanding officer. The performance, reportedly accompanied by hugs and tears, reinforced the unit's cohesion. The officers subsequently deployed the anthem over and over for entering or leaving the trenches and while anticipating battles. Delpos ordered the soldiers to sing it after one particularly painful battle, and Lafond reported on its apparent success. "The company filed by, singing the heroic, joyous song, and their hopes rose with their voices, which resonated with all their triumphs."[45]

That soldiers sang while marching is evident in memoirs and the song artifacts themselves, but whether infantrymen also sang in battles is a much more complicated question. We do have many accounts in memoirs, letters, and newspapers. Some recorded impromptu renditions, while others followed the script of the military revues.[46] But it is difficult to interpret the evidence because of the propagandistic power of the musical metaphor. Were these tales all invented for home-front consumption? Were they embellished upon in postwar nostalgia? This was, after all, a national culture that prided itself on singing in the face of danger. We have at least four layers of use and meaning to work through: the actual music in the trenches, the retelling of stories of musical rituals by soldiers at the front, the recounting for civilians, and the incorporation of stories as part of post-war memory. Some of these accounts may represent modified memories that glorified the fighting, but the examples are numerous and not limited to the earliest, most patriotic works (although one does find more there). They appeared in soldiers' letters and memoirs written during and after the war, as well as in newspapers. There is also a variety of types reported from the tactical or programmatic to the impromptu.

Spontaneous occasions may have occurred because the musicians were readily available. In one case from February 1915, a battle incorporated the musicians in the 46th Infantry regiment. When the preliminary artillery barrage stopped, an officer shouted "46th Forward!" and the regimental musicians moved at the same time.

Immediately, the music conductor Claude Latiz raised his white baton and on his command the roar of the "Marseillaise" swelled into the air. While the orchestra did its part in the assault, the baritone Magny got a bullet through the arm and the bass Tilloche fell gravely wounded. The circle drew closer and the musicians continued to play without a false note.[47]

Georges Lafond also provided an example in which a German attack was advancing steadily on a burned-out village, until a musician pounded out the "Marseillaise" on a church organ and revitalized the troops.[48] Interestingly, most of these stories cited well-known pieces such as "Auprès de ma blonde," which points to a shared culture. Most often, however, the accounts mentioned the "Marseillaise" in very specific, concrete stories. This reflected its central position in the prowar ethos and how well known it was. In addition, the "Marseillaise" was a particularly powerful piece with its martial rhythm and aggressive, nationalist message.

Clearly, these stories could have been helpful propaganda, but this does not necessarily make them apocryphal. Soldiers' accounts actually noted this ambiguity, while expressing their own skepticism. The officer Emile-François Julia related in his 1917 memoir how soldiers told a story, "repeated hundreds of times," about the playing of the "Marseillaise" in the trenches by regimental musicians (la musique) brought together to celebrate a successful allied assault.[49] He did not deny the possibility despite his reservations, and seemed intrigued by the power of the narrative.

Moreover, some soldiers described the musical effects critically, but showed an understanding of the army's purpose. One combatant on leave talked about the military bands, and "the trumpet calling for a bayonet charge." He said he realized these were "mechanical aids," but that "even on ordinary maneuvers they [the soldiers] were all seized with the fighting lust."[50] One other soldier admitted, "in the French army, the sound of the charge has always been a kind of stimulus of indescribable enthusiasm. For myself, I welcomed it with a sort of relief, because this advance in the face of machine guns became demoralizing in the end."[51] In Pierre Chaine's novel *Les Mémoires d'un rat,* the main character, who is going up the line to Verdun, also commented on the use of "fanfares, choruses, theatrical performances" to "divert" the soldiers' attention.[52]

In fact, it is precisely the soldiers' awareness that brings us back to the army officials and their view of music. That the concept of revitalization through patriotic music even became a trope in the war literature reflected a belief in its power, a belief that originated with the army. As seen in the use of regimental refrains, the army purposely employed music to encourage aggression, even in the face of new weaponry. They did not repudiate older tactics. Section leaders shouted the old standbys repeatedly: "En avant," "A la baïonnette," and "Hardi les gars!" as the clarion sounded. The confusion of the battles mixed with the trumpet calls of individual units. The melodies drove the soldiers forward quite literally, since as the charge continued to sound it signaled that the French artillery barrage would soon move forward directly behind the advancing troops. Stopping meant getting caught under French fire.

Although some instances of singing were impromptu occurrences, others were performances composed by officers. The coauthors of *Vie et mort des français,* all veterans, remarked on the prearranged presentation of the "Marseillaise" at a battle on September 25, 1915, a performance the infantry received with some skepticism, though they were impressed by the massive planning involved.[53] The army's complete "orchestration" included an artillery barrage, pre-battle alcohol, officers' orders to charge, and the "Marseillaise." The ritual created military aggression through a specific musical piece.[54]

With its discordant clash against the oppressive conditions in the trenches, the use of such songs did not always obtain positive results. Many of the front-line soldiers saw the material as absurd and reacted against it with parodies and sardonic humor. Paul Vaillant-Couturier, who was to become a pioneering member of the Communist Party, recorded an astonishing incident in his wartime diary *La Guerre des soldats* during his command in the trenches. His narrative offers a strikingly different voice from Lafond's description of the organ's rendition of the "Marseillaise."[55] In the spring of 1915, when the Italians announced their entry into the war, Vaillant-Couturier received orders from his superior officer to celebrate the announcement with an attack on the Germans. The commander outlined the program *(un programme des réjouissances):* a "Salvo by the artillery, . . . The trench-mortars will all fire, a fire of hell . . . We must make them all understand. Some [soldiers] will cry 'Vive l'Italie!' and some should sing the 'Marseillaise.'"[56] The "performance" began at noon, without regard for a French shortage of ammunition or the inevitable German retaliation. Vaillant-Couturier set the lines of the "Marseillaise" (fig. 2) contrapuntally to the events of the battle scene, accenting the irony of the situation.[57] The weak cries for Italy and the dogged singing of the "Marseillaise" intertwined with the sound of the shelling:

"le jour de gloire est arrivé [the day of glory has arrived] . . ." Each soldier sang the "Marseillaise" in a different tone. It was sinisterly ridiculous, cacophonous, and meager in the thunder of the firing. "L'étendard sanglant est levé" [The bloody standard is raised] . . ."

In the meantime, the Germans began to return fire, and he heard his sentry get hit and scream while the song continued: "Mugir ces feroces soldats [These savage soldiers bellow] . . ."[58] Vaillant-Couturier's "reading" countered the usually positive musical metaphor. This concert was not harmonious, nor did it have a coordinated, powerful sound.

The audiences, in this case, were the Germans and the French civilians. Vaillant-Couturier's last thought was that Paris would be happy to hear the next day that the "Marseillaise" had been sung in the trenches of Champagne.[59] He understood that Parisians would read the news through their own eyes. The "program," however, had cost the lives of seventeen Frenchmen.

The scene is frightening because of the actual deaths, but also because of the general staff's lack of insight, the soldiers' obedience, and the manipulation of the song. Vaillant-Couturier never considered stopping the battle or challenging the orders; he kept his men going, and used what he was ordered to use. Many other soldiers' accounts stress this type of inertia or a sense of being caught within a "text" or script, or should we say musical score, which dictated behavior. So where does this leave a historian? As we shall see, the home front did constantly re-represent soldiers' deeds, but the meaning changed. In the next section we will find Parisians bringing their own representations to the soldiers.

Entertainment in the Army

Citing a need to "fortify morale," the high command promoted music—both instrumental and vocal—not just for military operations but for entertainment.[60] They hoped it would encourage an *esprit de corps*, relieve boredom, and compensate for a lack of leave. Most of what we will discuss here took place behind the lines (in zone B), usually while soldiers were on *repos* in camps, but also in hospitals, training centers, or at army headquarters. This zone covered an enormous territory, in which the army exercised its tightest control over content at its largest facilities. The encouragement reflected army traditions, but also found new support from the modern music industry in Paris. Performances were meant to bring national culture to the soldiers. The programs integrated elite culture of classical music and short plays with *café-concert* fare, a combination similar to what we encountered in wartime Paris. Smaller, more informal events also continued, and although zone B was an ideological space, it was not nearly as constricted as Paris in terms of censorship.

As with the regimental bands and clarion calls, the army brought theatrical customs into this war with what had been called the *théâtres du camp*. The best known historical examples came from the military theater of the eighteenth century and from the Crimean War. The persistent retelling of the story of Charles-Simon Favart's theatrical performances for the Maréchal de Saxe's army in 1745 actually tells us much about twentieth-century hopes. The story, which appeared in newspapers and journals throughout the war, consistently praised French ingenuity and the power of theater to prepare troops for battle.[61] One early 1917 article explained, "It's a tradition of ours [the French] to unite a taste for arms with a taste for the arts, and to listen to a poem or song between battles."[62] There are also records of *théâtres du camp* from the 1860s, and the 1880s and 1890s brought varied programs of regimental fanfares, military demonstrations, singers, short comedies, and operettas at different garrisons. The 106th regiment inaugurated its annual fête on July 6, 1888, with a seventeen-hour program, marking the anniversary of Wagram. Generally, such events resembled the evolving mass culture of music halls particularly in their eclecticism, but they also accentuated a militarist culture.[63]

In the years preceding World War I, there was a renewed emphasis on soldiers' education and amusements. A flurry of government orders between 1904 and 1907, newspaper articles, and works such as René Thorel's *Un Cercle pour le soldat* (published in 1909) expressed a growing interest in regimental solidarity.[64] Thorel's 496-page book outlined the importance of "distractions" for the "moral education" of soldiers, arguing that extending the system of recreations halls at regimental camps benefited the soldiers and citizens of the Republic. Reflecting nineteenth-century social thought, his work argued soldiers needed healthy alternatives to "sites of debauchery and cabarets."[65] These worries paralleled officials' concerns about schools and *cafés-concerts,* and singing was again viewed as building strong bodies and minds. This moved the theories of republicans and military advocates closer together than they themselves may have admitted.

To accomplish these improvements, Thorel promoted a critical role for the *officier éducateur,* as well as for civilian charity organizations. Officers were to be both organizers and monitors.[66] In addition, he wanted to correct the impression that "soldiers take pleasure only in simple and often crude distractions."[67] The right inspiration gave them cheap and "wholesome" entertainment, and as a result, they remained in camp and avoided less desirable sites. Much of Thorel's thinking anticipated developments between 1914 and 1918, when the army helped build theaters for soldiers while overseeing a flood of civilian efforts. Thorel himself could take some credit for this, since he had reached out to persuade prominent people, both civilian and military, of the importance of his work.

Once the war broke out, the French army put this philosophy to work. At the simplest level, World War I officials provided songbooks, songsheets, and musicians to foster singing, taking advantage of private initiative. One civilian composer, for instance, sent twenty-five thousand copies of his song "C'est en chantant," which had been used at the Sorbonne ceremonies, for distribution among the troops.[68] What was good for Paris was good for the troops. In addition, the *Bulletin des armées,* the official army newspaper, gave the trench song culture a significant boost by printing Parisian tunes that encouraged soldiers to submit their own. Throughout the fall of 1914 and into 1915, the biggest names from the music industry appeared, including Dominique Bonnaud, Jean Bastia, and Paul Marinier, as well as the lyrics of Paul Déroulède. The songs of Théodore Botrel, the *armée chansonnier,* covered the front page of the November 1, 1914, supplementary edition. As early as February 1915, soldiers began sending in their own songs and revues, and, at one point in 1916, the *Bulletin* published a full set of soldiers' compositions.[69] Because combatants were aware of the distinction between zone A and zone B, they saw the *Bulletin* as representing zone B under the home front's strong influence. And they frequently belittled this journal for being out of touch with the front-line infantry. But many soldiers still viewed the paper as their muse and saw publication in it as an honor.

The *Bulletin* also acted as a site of transfer between the home front and the combatants — an official checkpoint. Civilians offered patriotic songs to "their" soldiers in order to support the realization of revanchism. The soldiers also asked that songs be printed for certain civilians. One sub-lieutenant explained that he wanted his unit's song printed, because the "example of courage and good morale [would] perhaps shame those rare individuals who are still shirking and show them that the place of all Frenchmen worthy of this name . . . should be at the front." With a sense of cultural distance, soldiers also attempted to expose the *Bulletin* to the

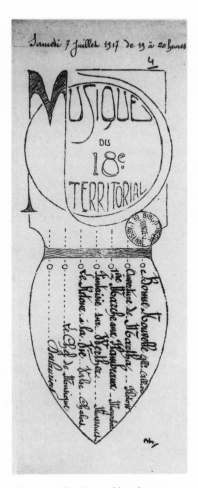

Figure 24. Regimental band program
from 18th Territorial. Courtesy of the
Bibliothèque Nationale de France, Paris.

"real" trench culture. A certain Boussart sent in a song about *pinard* (wine)
as a particularly interesting example of a "chanson du front."[70]

The most important structure for implementing the prewar philosophy
in wartime was the regimental bands. Once the trenches were built, they
gave concerts, sometimes on a daily basis, for large and small units, as well
as playing at religious services.[71] They designed blank program forms
which could be quickly filled in with a list of seven or eight pieces (fig. 24).
Scattered evidence suggests these programs usually included classical
music and patriotic standards, but were not limited to these (fig. 25). By

Figure 25. Program for the 95th Infantry regiment, directed by the Chef de Musique. Courtesy of the Bibliothèque Nationale de France, Paris.

1916 and 1917, for instance, Jacques Heugel's unit was composing musical revues made up of tableaux with colorful characters and songs. These revues entailed makeshift sets, rehearsals, and several performances for all sorts of units during *repos*. The composers entitled one revue *Navarre sans peur*, based on the motto of the regimental ancestor of the 5th regiment. Heugel's participation is particularly striking given his serious lifelong commitment to classical music, but regimental musicians found themselves responding to a heterogeneous population and varied musical tastes.

Whereas the most famous and well-established army band was, of course, the Garde Républicaine, founded in 1848, other units became valorized because they performed under severe conditions. Concerts and rehearsals, for instance, often went on despite constant heavy bombings and injuries. After the musical regiments of the Third corps had played courageously for beleaguered troops at Verdun, they moved to the Trocadero in Paris, and then attended a musical festival in Turin, Italy, in July 1917. Furthermore, one of their conductors, who had been wounded at Verdun, went on to write a "very impressive" piece which "produced . . . considerable emotion." Thus performances at the front could be translated to the home front to great effect, but the primary purpose of these units remained focused on the front and the combatants.[72]

In the realm of military musical entertainment, however, the regimental concerts were only the tip of the iceberg. Hundreds of other concerts and *spectacles,* both scheduled and impromptu, occurred at or near the front. Ranging from divisional down to company concerts, performances became less official, less controlled, and much less likely to involve civilians, and especially women. The line between official and unofficial is somewhat hard to draw, because the documentation very rarely indicates clearly who planned or controlled performances. This difficulty also reflects a continuum from official to unofficial based on a variety of factors, including who directed, who attended, where performances were held, and how tight the surveillance was. In the most obvious cases, officers organized or ordered troops to arrange concerts. In the case of Lafond's lieutenant, for instance, not only did he believe in singing while marching, but he insisted that soldiers organize concerts.[73] But the degree of support was sometimes based on individual officers' taste for music or their wish to have their own troops well entertained. General Mangin, for instance, reportedly arranged concerts because of his own love of music.[74] Junior officers sat in an ambiguous position, sometimes encouraging singing, sometimes watching bemused, and sometimes turning a deaf ear. They moved with their troops from the area behind the line into the trenches, so they heard the full range of official and unofficial performances.

Overall, though, official concerts tended to take place in the larger camps and stations. One observer, in his book on the psychology of soldiers, called *cantonnements* an essential stage for soldiers in adhering to French society, a type of halfway house.[75] It was here that "Paris," representing the nation, came to the soldiers. But the army also viewed rest time as a time of great danger, since the incidences of disobedience or desertion rose. Thus, more than one approach was necessary. By the middle of the war, civilians and the army had each come up with their own solution.

PARIS COMES TO THE TROOPS

If having theater at camps was not new, the development of a system like the American USO, in which Parisian performers went to the Army zone to entertain the troops, was. Private individuals, including Parisian theater entrepreneurs, began the process and kept it going, while government officials positioned themselves between the troops and Paris. Authorities chose the locations, censored the programs, and restricted all information by prohibiting interviews by the entertainers. The performances represented sites where the powerful culture of Paris spread to the soldiers. Quite literally, famous stars carried their repertoires to the troops by distributing sheet music at their performances. All of this reflected the power of mass cultural institutions and the star system as well as the role of newspapers in promoting the cause. It also nourished the new calling of the "civilian."

Private initiative was most obvious in the early stages of the war. All sorts of performers gave concerts, including prominent stars, such as Dominique Bonnaud, Damia, and Lucien Boyer. We have already heard about Rose Amy and Gaby Montbreuse hugging *poilus,* and Polin and Bach appeared with their well-known renditions of the *comique-troupier.* The repertoires ranged from comic and bawdy songs to patriotic pieces, with concerts usually ending with the "Marseillaise." The songs did not include descriptions of day-to-day life in the trenches nor did they mention any soldiers' complaints. The lyrics on weapons also ignored the deadly effects of artillery and machine guns, opting instead for the erotic, playful portraits.

Two of the best examples were the Parisian performers Eugénie Buffet and Théodore Botrel, both of whom had extensive and well-publicized wartime careers, aimed at encouraging the soldiers. They began performing for troops on their own initiative early on, and then attracted official support; Botrel alone claims to have given at least fifteen hundred performances.[76] They followed differently gendered paths, however, which gave them contrasting styles and repertoires, despite the fact that they both had conservative political backgrounds.

Before the war Buffet, like Botrel, was a radical nationalist and a member of La Ligue des Patriotes. She began a typical wartime career for women by volunteering as a nurse in August; she then progressed from nursing to singing for the wounded. She soon received support from the French Red Cross and many other government officials, both civilian and military.[77] By October, she had formed her own troupe, which traveled behind the front visiting hospitals. They performed patriotic songs, drinking tunes, and "gay and consoling refrains." According to one commentator, Buffet knew "how to speak to the hearts of these brave young men with simple souls, who prefer without hesitation the refrains of the *faubourg* to the most beautiful opera arias."[78] All of her concerts included printed song sheets and sing-alongs—a continuation of prewar patterns, but also a means of government control. The troupe used older Parisian tunes and also had new patriotic pieces written for them by composers such as René de Buxeuil[79] (app. fig. 4). Buffet's memoirs described the troupe's success, her occasional disgust at seeing certain injuries, and the reactions of the wounded—their "wild joy, the enthusiasm."[80] Projecting a female role of sending the soldiers forth, at the end of concerts she would say, "we have cared for you well here, and you can soon prove it out there, at the front. Good luck, boys!"[81]

Botrel had also been a fundamental constituent of the musical *union sacrée* in August 1914 and had tried to enlist to perform for troops. No one accepted his offer to begin with, so he went off toward Belgium on his own. Botrel explained, in an article published after the war, that he had acted so quickly, because he believed that those who had already gone "toward glory and martyrdom would not understand how those who had soothed them with the proud songs of Revanchism could remain far away, when the hour of danger had come."[82] By the end of August, the minister of war had given him an official mission to perform for soldiers in canteens.[83]

Botrel represents an excellent example of what Elizabeth Kahn has called a "cultural warrior," someone who fought the war by mobilizing his cultural talents to serve the nation.[84] Articles about Botrel highlighted his willingness to continue his performances under artillery shelling; he was wounded at one point and required a month-long recovery. Where Buffet nurtured and inspired wounded soldiers, Botrel worked to energize the active combatants. Botrel's repertoire was marked by its ridicule of Germany, its optimistic views of the war, and its celebration of French soldiers' virility. Remarkably, there is very little indication of change in his lyrics, despite what he must have seen.

Botrel and Buffet were both showered with praise. Buffet earned the nickname "la caporale des Poilus," and entered the Legion of Honor in 1933. Many of the tributes to Botrel's work came from the high command and from Parisian commentators such as Maurice Barrès.[85] He garnered accolades throughout the war and finally received the *croix de guerre* and the *médaille militaire,* along with the names *le chansonnier des armées* and *le Pinard moral.*[86] There is also some evidence of soldiers' approval. One corporal and his companions of the 62nd Infantry sent a letter "from the trenches" to the *Bulletin* to wish Botrel, their "adored chansonnier," a happy birthday, especially since they too came from Brittany.[87]

On the other hand, his nickname of *le barde aux armées* was modified to *la barbe aux armées* (the beard—or bore—of the army) by some troops, and one song called "Histoire d'un poilu" had a soldier singing about how he could not escape Botrel's ubiquitous performances.[88] Combatants also sometimes called their attendance at such performances "concert duty" *(la corvée de concert)*.[89] As will be seen in the next chapter, these quips illustrate how soldiers turned to parody and satire ever more insistently as the war progressed, in particular to respond to representations created by officials or civilians. Botrel, meanwhile, carried on serving his country with his musical "Rosalie."

LE THÉÂTRE AUX ARMÉES

The idea of stars performing for troops had become commonplace by the end of 1915, but such performances still occurred on a random basis, which made some in the high command nervous. In early 1916, the acting director of the Comédie-Française, Emile Fabre, founded the Théâtre aux Armées under the auspices of the undersecretary of fine arts, Albert Dalimier. It also had the approval of both the minister of war and the army high command. Fabre claimed that he got the idea in late 1915 from officers who were worried about the approaching winter nights, when soldiers would have "melancholy" hours to pass. He set out to get the free assistance of the "*artistes* of Paris . . . the most famous and best loved."[90] They had to be willing to work under the crudest conditions in front of one thousand to fifteen hundred soldiers at a time. As he explained it, "the sole desire [was] to provide a bit of relaxation and pleasure to our magnificent soldiers." Well aware of French history, the troupe wanted to follow in Charles-Simon Favart's footsteps.

In early 1916, Dalimier and Fabre agreed to certain rules: the "troupe" could not exceed six performers, a tour would last no more than two to three days, and all performances would take place "within the army zone in areas located behind the line of fire in *cantonnements de rafraichissement*"—in other words, in zone B.[91] Front-line soldiers never failed to note that the Parisian-based Théâtre aux Armées performed at camps well away from danger. The volunteers took their jobs seriously, however, and their accounts offered a different perspective, stressing their proximity to the Germans and the danger of bombardment.[92] Beatrix Dussane, an actress who volunteered her time, described the camaraderie of the troupe and its sense of making a contribution: "we felt great solidarity and most of us worked with heartfelt humility; happy to give joy, anxious not to spoil our work with either snobbishness or publicity."[93] Sarah Bernhardt contributed her services to the Théâtre aux Armées with performances in barns, hospitals, and mess tents in front of crowds of two thousand men. This followed her surgery in February 1915, when she had had a leg amputated; she was thus able to joke with the soldiers about surviving mutilation, while the newspapers designated her "la glorieuse blessée." In a letter to a friend she described her impressions of her visit, using the rhetoric of the home front: "I have been to the front to give our dear soldiers a little idealism; those who are the creators of beauty have had the pleasure to hear beautiful verses; . . . I went to Bois le Prêtre and to Pont à Mousson. It was admirable, stirring, grandiose!"[94] She also explained how, when led to within five hundred meters of the German trenches by the generals, she was not afraid of the Germans: "What can they do to me? They can only put a glorious end to my career. But that would be too wonderful, and I dare not dream of it."[95] This dream was rather far from those of many front-line soldiers.

In entering zone B, the troupes were under military jurisdiction. Dalimier wanted groups to stay together, and forbade interviews and the publication of pictures in general, although some were approved.[96] Max Maurey, the director, was charged with insuring that the programs contained "nothing which could offend anyone's political or religious convictions." All performers had to submit their full programs to the administration, and no changes were allowed. The military continually reminded its officers that all performances by "non-military performers" had to come through the Comité du Théâtre aux Armées.[97] Once the organization began work in February 1916, its performances increased in frequency. By March 1917 the organization was doing as many as eighteen performances a month, having set up more than one troupe, and by the end of November 1918, the organization had delivered one thousand performances for close to two million soldiers.

This operation was run by a civilian elite looking for the military elite's approval. Its managing committee represented elite cultural institutions such as the Music Conservatory and the Academy, for example.[98] In newspaper articles, the *poilus* were always represented as an undifferentiated group, while the attendance of specific colonels or generals was emphasized by naming each one. Much was made, for example, of the presence of Philippe Pétain at the special five hundredth performance, also presided over by Albert Dalimier.[99] These events also represented the most obvious example of the common soldiers' passivity as listeners. The performers courted the anonymous "little guy" quite blatantly, describing his "youthful enthusiasm" and ready emotions.[100] Documents continually emphasized how these performers were the "most famous" or "a pleiad of *artistes*," and many came from the state-subsidized theaters including the Comédie-Française and the Opéra.[101] But the elite, in this case, was not limited to the traditional high

Figure 26. Program cover for the Théâtre aux Armées. Courtesy of the Bibliothèque Nationale de France, Paris.

culture; it also included celebrities of mass culture who shared professional status and considerable reputations. Volunteers came from theaters such as the Capucines and the Gymnase, and from the biggest music halls—the Eldorado, the Folies-Bergère, and the Olympia. This broke down older divisions, and further legitimized top entertainers. Thus, Jean Bastia of the cabaret La Pie qui Chante found himself in excellent company. The military even warned individual army units to exercise "a discrete inspection" with each troupe, confirming performers' credentials in order that "no amateur (male or female) be allowed to join the professionals."[102] This was in sharp opposition to the soldiers' own popular culture, which celebrated amateur status in the name of the common soldier.

Despite the rules, most trips included eleven to twelve individuals, split almost evenly between men and women. The participation of so many (well over seventy-five) women helped define zone B, and reinforced the sense that these troupes could offer something exceptionally precious. Women played an important role in opening and closing programs, usually involving the "Marseillaise." The documents do not explain why women sang the anthem most of the time, but this practice did create a living metaphor of "la France."[103] In several cases, women expressed a regret that they could not serve, or equated their performances to military service.[104] But for soldiers' ears, regret was a civilian or home-front response.

The common denominator in performance content was that it was French; otherwise, it was an eclectic mix of mass and high culture. Soldiers heard Charles Gounod, Jules Massenet, and Georges Bizet, mixed with *chansons de route,* Montmartre tunes, an *imitateur* "in his transformations," and a comic juggler. French "masterpieces" still predominated, but professionals from the elite theaters also sang tunes that had "little in common with the austerity of the house of Molière [or the Comédie-Française]."[105] The government official Dalimier also asked Miguel Zamacoïs, a well-known playwright and columnist, to create a prologue in "hommage to our heroes," to be used for each performance. It was delivered for the first time on July 14, 1916, at "two great performances, on the Champagne front."[106] In Zamacoïs's "Salut des comédiens," the performer, always a woman, likened the troupe's coming before the formidable audience of *poilus* to "going under fire"—wouldn't "one hesitate a bit / at the edge of the trench." "Yet," said the following couplet, "We must obey our buglers!" A rather explicit example of how a "theater of war" brought the metaphor to life.

LES THÉÂTRES DU FRONT

Just as the home-front efforts had gotten organized, 1916 also saw the creation of the Théâtres du Front, championed from within the army itself. Although sometimes confused with the Théâtre aux Armées by contemporaries, the Théâtres du Front were a part of the military, designed to be by and for the soldiers. The idea came from two separate impulses. In November 1915, the *peintre militaire* Georges Scott, who had faced frustrations in organizing early tours of "Parisian artists in the villages at the front," drew up the blueprints for a mobile theater, and submitted the idea to the minister of war, Joseph Gallieni, in early 1916.[107] Meanwhile, Gallieni had expressed his own worries in a January 1916 memo about the soldiers' time away from the trenches. He supported the civilian "clubs" as "healthy distractions," but noted that they existed only outside the camps. He argued instead for entertainment within the canteens two or three times per week with songs, revues, films, and gramophones. When Scott arrived with his plan, Gallieni happily took it to the general staff and got quick approval.[108]

The timing coincided with the development of the Théâtre aux Armées, and their goals overlapped. Both wanted to provide "clean" and "healthy" entertainment for soldiers, and both got support from civilian fundraising.[109] But there was also tension over the military's prerogatives. Military officials believed that, although Parisian stars improved morale, women and other civilians had to stay too far away from the "line"; having mobile theaters that relied on the soldiers' own talents meant serving a much larger part of zone B (or getting as close to zone A as possible). Further, a detailed postwar memo claimed that it was the military command's "need to entertain the soldiers between tours in the trenches" that led to the support. They sought to "chase away *cafard*" (or "black thoughts"), while also providing soldiers with a memory they could mull over for weeks after. This would include giving them new tunes. As a result, the army would nourish zone A with sanctioned cultural rations. Moreover, with a touch of utopian social engineering, officials hoped to integrate the roles of "performer, soldier and Frenchman," creating "a military confraternity" of all social classes and all ranks."[110]

Indeed, when the supervisor for the Théâtre aux Armées, the assistant secretary of the fine arts, questioned the need for the Théâtres du Front's existence, headquarters responded that while the Théâtre aux Armées gave performances of a "high artistic and literary value," the troupes only played to big rooms in the big *cantonnements*.[111] In contrast, the "'Théâtre au Front' [*sic*] [was] an institution simply and principally destined to improve, in an artistic sense, the smallest performances given by the men for themselves using their own resources." Unfortunately, in the eyes of officials, these often included "makeshift scenery of dubious artistic quality, improvised programs, etc." Amateurism was identified as objectionable or problematic. The army was not completely happy about developments on either side of its cultural purview. It worried about the soldiers' own efforts, especially those closer to the trenches. And it saw Parisian civilians as outsiders, or, as one memo put it, "elements foreign to the Army." Commanders decided both the Théâtre aux Armées and Théâtres du Front were necessary, but they were to have no "point of contact."

To begin with, however, even the Théâtres du Front looked Parisian. The first mobile theater was displayed in the center of Paris at the Invalides in July 1916, and heralded in the main newspapers. Its first performance, at Châlons-sur-Marne, was arranged by the Comédie-Française using well-known professional performers. According to an interview in *La Rampe* dated July 20, 1916, Georges Scott, who was to direct the organization from Paris, believed "they should offer the *poilus* gay performances of light plays without ill-considered irreverence along with judiciously chosen song sets."[112] The article concluded that soldiers could now attend performances as "brilliant" as those in Paris. As with the Théâtre aux Armées, the soldiers were to be the audience, not the performers.

After this start, however, the guidelines did encourage the use of local military talent. The theaters were designed to be mobile, "self-sufficient," and operable under adverse conditions; they contained a stage, scenery, curtain, acetylene lamps, and fifty folding benches.[113] Each theater's director organized volunteers from among the troops stationed at the camps, and had to ensure that all lyrics and texts won the approval of the camp commander. The organization was to take advantage of local talent, but under carefully controlled circumstances. Even possible encores had to have prior permission, and absolutely no improvisation was allowed.[114]

The content of performances for the Théâtres du Front, although hard to categorize, differed somewhat from the Théâtre aux Armées. This is partly because the cast of characters included both Parisian professionals and local talent. The Théâtres du Front had a more eclectic mix or looked more like a *café-concert* version of the Théâtre aux Armées.[115] For one program in mid-1917, for example, the orchestra played "Hitchy-Kôo," a Mademoiselle Voirin sang an aria from *La Bohème*, four soldiers did a Schubert string quartet, and one performer did songs from the *comique-troupier* repertoire.[116] At another, "organized by the Artistes of the Théâtre du Front for the 127 Division" (fig. 27), they included the "Marche américaine" by John Philip Sousa, and had performers from "the Eldorado," "the Concert Mayol," "la Cigale," "le Ba-Ta-Clan," the "Concerts Lamoureux," and the "Folies-Bergères"—a remarkable line-up.[117]

One sees the Parisian cultural influence also in the opening and closing numbers: "Ce que c'est qu'un drapeau" and the "Marseillaise." The former had a rousing refrain about the flag representing France as a symbol of hope. Its tune used sets of triads, imitating a clarion call. Written in 1914, it had also been performed in Paris, at least from 1914 to 1916.[118] Performers also received assistance from the regimental musicians in the local units, who brought along the army repertoire. Whereas Parisian columnists insisted that most troop performances finished with the national anthem, this

Figure 27. Program cover for the Théâtres du Front. Courtesy of the Bibliothèque Nationale de France, Paris.

was true mainly with these two government-sponsored organizations— Théâtre aux Armées and Théâtres du Front. These concerts sometimes also featured the latest Parisian hits, for example, "Quand Madelon" or "Elle le suivait."[119] The song "Ballade hygiénique," an erotic song about a soldier and "Suzon" rumpling clothes out on the fortifications, had been modified by censors for Paris, but appears to have been performed unchanged for the troops. In addition, songs and revues examined "life in the trenches" more directly, with jokes about leave and attacks on *embusqués*. In the end, however, even though the army was trying to influence *all* troop performances, much of this was specific to zone B.

The theaters met with great success, at least in the eyes of the high command, and like so much else in the wartime bureaucracy, its personnel and structure kept growing. In November 1916, Pétain and Nivelle ordered thirty more theaters, which were up and running by March 1917; forty more theaters were ordered in January 1918.[120]

It is not clear, however, whether or not these performances should be considered indigenous to the army or how much they came from the common soldier. Guidelines asked for local talent, and the soldiers permanently attached to the theaters came from the lower ranks; of thirty-eight personnel identified in a March 1918 memo, half were common soldiers, and only three came from ranks higher than sergeant. But these singers, violinists, or comedians moved with the theaters and had centralized direction. They also faced steady censorship. Furthermore, 1918 saw further centralization of recreational ventures in music, film, and sports. With the upheaval caused by the German attacks in the spring of 1918, it became more difficult for local soldiers to prepare new performances, and the system moved toward permanent troupes of five to six men who gave more homogeneous, well-controlled programs. Still, by the end of October 1918, the mobile theaters had helped deliver 5,896 performances to approximately four million officers and soldiers; in the month of May 1917 alone they gave 125 performances to 188,000 spectators, at the very moment of the soldiers' mutinies.[121] The system left such a positive legacy that officials turned to it again in 1939–1940.

Although memos from 1918 continually heralded the efforts of the Théâtres du Front and Théâtre aux Armées as having been "very appreciated by the troops," evidence related to audience response or, more specifically, soldiers' reactions is difficult to uncover.[122] Articles from Paris, as well as interviews with performers, spoke of the soldiers' great enthusiasm, of men jumping up and applauding. But we must take some of this with a grain of salt.[123] Two particular accounts of Théâtre aux Armées performances illustrate the way response to the shows depended on one's viewpoint. The first response appeared in a long article by Henry Bordeaux in *La Revue hebdomadaire* dated June 3, 1916.[124] Bordeaux had been a writer and theater columnist for the *Revue* before the war, and was a mid-level officer in 1916, when he attended what he called the Comédie-Française, at the "Poilus-Park." The Poilus-Park was "an immense hangar" which had been converted into a theater where up to three thousand men could come. It was normally a soldiers' theater, and Bordeaux noted that it was exceptional for Parisians to be appearing in such permanent troop space. Bordeaux himself was most interested in what sort of an audience "they" (the infantrymen or *poilus*) would be; his use of the third person plural made visible the military and cultural hierarchy. This division was reinforced by the seating arrangement, where, in Bordeaux's words, "our small group of officers" sat separately from the common soldiers. The "sea" of blue uniforms struck him as particularly odd compared to prewar theater attire, as did the fact that many of these soldiers had never seen such a performance.

With an eye to a Parisian reader, Bordeaux interwove details of "military life," including the sharp contrast between the front trenches and the rest camps. On *repos,* one found peace "where heroes, who the day before had been holding out under a storm of fire at Mort-Homme or in the ravine at Vaux, [now] play like children." He described the soldiers as patient, "if somewhat indifferent," obedient, unworldly, and hard to impress. Because the audience was made up of peasants, Bordeaux predicted that Parisian performers, even a Sarah Bernhardt, would have a hard time. The officers were also not a particularly well-educated or well-cultured group, according to Bordeaux, who seemed to be realizing just how small a portion of France was made up of sophisticated Parisians.

He noted that the content had been adjusted somewhat—"in fact, this is a rather motley Comédie-Française which goes from the songwriter Fursy to Mme Bréval," with only one "representative of the house, Mlle Dussane." He then described Dussane "in a short beige skirt": "She brings in her songs, in her clear, sweet voice, in her face, in her whole person, a youthful joy that is virtually prohibited at the front *[la zone de l'avant].* On stage, she is a luminous apparition. She was adopted immediately by two thousand godsons as their *marraine."* Interestingly, Bordeaux attributed her attractiveness, which so impressed him, to her youth, without mentioning her possible sexual appeal. He seems to have been uncomfortable on some level with the differences in class and background that related to issues of taste. Despite his insistence on a considerable divide between himself or his fellow officers and the *poilus,* he noted that when Dussane took up old, beloved *chansons de route,* the crowd joined in, indicating some shared culture. But as Sarah Bernhardt approached the stage, he worried over whether they would applaud with the same enthusiasm "an old saw from the *café-concert,"* especially after Dussane's reception. After all, Bernhardt lacked the usual publicity, and the *poilus* would not understand what was going on because of the lack of scenery. Once again, making a sharp distinction between "le monde" and the others, Bordeaux said "For us, she is everything. . . . But for these men here?"

When Bernhardt did finally perform, however, she carried the day. Bordeaux described an expert performance, and in the end, "Her charm worked with the magic of her golden voice. And the room filled with triumphal applause." Bordeaux described the soldiers as an intimidating audience, who in the end responded well. Their response preserved Bordeaux's faith in the national whole, and civilians could also take heart from his report.

The soldiers, however, often had a much more cynical reaction to the performances of Parisian stars at the "front." In his journal, a certain J. Villevielle discussed the anticipated visit of Bernhardt, Dussane, and Henri Fursy, who were scheduled to perform nearby at the Château de Boucq. "Far from the noise and lots of other things," he carefully noted. He knowingly explained, with a sense of alienation and distance, that the performance was actually meant to "distract" "the officers corps of the army," and that the infantrymen would be there so that "they" could "photograph the soldiers for the newspapers." Even so, Villevielle groused about his bad luck, since, despite getting picked by the lottery system, he had to miss the concert because his unit had six remaining days up the line. And despite his harsh cynicism, he then admitted that he would have liked to have seen "Sarah up close, although she is ghastly for her age, with her wooden leg. . . . I have only seen her from afar, at her theater, and I was in the gallery." But Villevielle, while intrigued by her fame, was far from impressed by the proposed program: "Some of the idiocies that they will deliver, I don't give a damn about. . . . Patriotism, as expected . . . This would have caused me to see my sergeant's mug forever."[125]

Although soldiers may have had more ideological freedom at the front than civilians did in Paris, this was not because of army structures but *despite* the army's concerted efforts. The tight control of information in communiqués and letters helped to isolate the individual within his own sector and circumstances, and the government moved to suppress subversive actions located in such signs as incorrect clothing, salutes, or songs. At the local level, the army enforced censorship of songs and performances from the beginning, watching most closely for passages viewed as *antipatriotiques* or pacifist. In spite of the surveillance, soldiers did have more room for free expression as members of an enormous army, especially during their movement up and down the lines from trenches to rest areas and on leave. They were also aware of the standards set by the Théâtre aux Armées and other Parisian performers and made their own efforts to go their own way. Soldiers developed all sorts of tricks for eluding officials, if only temporarily.

Official military entertainment was in many ways closely aligned with the culture of the home front. One finds this, for example, in the design and typeface of the *Bulletin* from 1914 to 1917. The army also relied on its

own, nineteenth-century rituals and traditions in World War I. As it became more and more aware of the cultural geography of trench warfare, it
attempted to break down these divisions with its performances in battle,
with its encouragement of the Théâtres du Front, and with the revamping
of the *Bulletin*. The military redoubled its efforts after the mutinies of 1917,
as we shall see.

CHAPTER SEVEN

Entertainment at the Front
The Soldiers Go It Alone

Jean Renoir's classic film *Grande Illusion* begins in a small café where a phonograph grinds out a French music-hall number. From this opening scene to the climactic singing of the "Marseillaise" in the middle of the prisoners' musical revue, music is woven into the everyday life of the camp. Using song lyrics, the prisoners warn newcomers to hide money; they entertain themselves individually and together with different tunes, and they synchronize their escape using a flute.[1] Memoirs of the war corroborate Renoir's portrayal of the ease with which French soldiers turned to songs as a means of communication, as well as a way to keep away *le cafard*. For French soldiers, the war created additional exigencies, space, and time for singing. And, despite Théodore Botrel's track record, most musical performances, or musical practices, were not prearranged, packaged, or controlled by the government.

French combatants developed their own culture, marked overall by a remarkable resurgence of an older popular culture. As the famous historian Marc Bloch wrote of his own experiences, trench warfare saw "a prodigious renewal of oral tradition, the ancient mother of myths and legends." He described this "oral tradition" as a "mental state of olden times before journals, before news sheets, before books," where rumors were born of a cast of characters from the ancien régime: "peddlars, jugglers, pilgrims, beggars."[2] This culture grew up from within face-to-face communities, where singing occurred as a spontaneous part of daily interactions and impromptu concerts—feeding the culture's orality. For everyday "performances," audiences coalesced and re-formed quickly, and songs were unrehearsed. Each gathering represented an opportunity for new versions or adaptations according to local idioms, which were then transmitted orally, along with stories and jokes, within the soldiers' community. This process relied heavily on memory and singing skills. The trench culture emerged for subgroups and was participatory, noncommercial, and responsive to its audience.

This particular form of popular culture developed because of the prewar skills soldiers brought with them, and because of the material and mental conditions they encountered. In the French army, a broad range of soldiers had an oral or musical literacy that involved patterns of rhyming and refrains. Because of the sociological makeup of the army, a wide variety of people could create songs, and these were then transmitted across social, cultural, and geographic barriers.

In spite of Bloch's description, this "mental state" did not wholly emulate a preliterate world, since it also contained elements of modern cultural practices. Soldiers, for instance, also produced printed songs, theater revues, and trench newspapers, but these, in turn, fed the oral culture. In showing that 45 percent of the trench newspapers were published for small units, Stéphane Audoin-Rouzeau has explained, "The front-line press thus acquired its truest significance only when it was published by and for small groups of men who knew each other well, who had shared in the same ordeals and lived together constantly."[3] The soldiers' popular culture flourished best in zone A; the military had a tougher time influencing soldiers as they moved away from the big camps or *cantonnements* toward the trenches. The army and soldiers themselves recognized the varied geography. The army sought to move their performances closer to the trenches, while the combatants disparaged Botrel and the Théâtre aux Armées for performing only in protected areas. The front lines contained common soldiers and junior officers; there were few higher-ranking officers, no civilians, and no women. Performing at the front also meant facing constant dangers and hardships.

This popular culture was not necessarily conservative or stabilizing. It came from an eclectic pooling of resources and *mentalités* and lent itself to democratic use. Circumstances encouraged earthy, ribald language, and soldiers' complaints turned to satire, which was potentially subversive. Gradually, this subculture also took on a sense of being on the outside. It struggled against a dominant culture identified as Parisian, or at times as the broader "home front." But should we use the term "dominant" to describe the Parisian representations and practices? As we saw, the cultural and political sphere in Paris was protected by censorship, and it self-consciously spread and promoted itself. Further, civilians were aware of and studied elements of the subculture. Most significantly, the soldiers often saw themselves in conflict with home-front culture—at stake was the power to create representations, whether of the war, of soldiers, or of patriotism, and then to determine their meaning. Parisian performers and writers often represented their expressions as quintessentially *French,* but soldiers had their own ideas on defining the nation. Their subculture allowed them to express both their patriotism and their dissent. Combatants, however, felt some tension between seeking to be separate and wanting to belong to a bigger military or national community. Thus, even as they worked toward a separate culture, they tried to communicate with and influence civilians.

While lyrics, like trench newspapers, enable us to glimpse the soldiers' *mentalité* and shifts in their attitudes, the singing itself involved actual practices and a more immediate purpose. In the face of a static, dehumanizing war, the agency of singing was central to its popularity. Creativity in performances was rich on a collective or individual level. Therefore, let us begin with an exploration of the soldiers' musical practices — who sang or made music, when, and where. This examination will offer us a context within which to put their musical observations, and having looked at both practices and content, we will better understand the turn to dissent.

Amateurs Welcome

COMPOSITIONAL PRACTICES

Amid all of its horrors, World War I was a boon for musical amateurs. As soldiers searched for ways to express themselves, fill time, and avoid thinking about terrible subjects, informal composing and singing burgeoned. These practices were easy, versatile, and required no special equipment. They also fed an egalitarian side of trench culture. Most often, soldiers who had no professional musical or theatrical background began their efforts individually, only to end up participating in a collaborative project. One does not consistently find the anonymity of folk cultures, in which time blurs songs' authorship and origins, but versions came and went, and some anonymity protected composers of subversive songs.[4] Geographically, fluid texts and performances flourished the most in the front trenches, while zone B had more formal performances.

Soldiers' songs and scribbled notes to the army's official *Bulletin des armées* offer us glimpses into the soldiers' own song culture. Judging from these letters, most lyricists were amateurs, who came from the lower ranks, as three quarters of the letters and songs were written by those with a rank of sergeant or lower. One letter frankly admitted, "this is my debut and . . . the patriot has been more inspired than the poet," while another adjudant confessed: "Neither poet nor songwriter, I have done my best."[5] A telephonist from sector 24 also allowed that, despite the fact that in civilian life he was a "sales representative" and not a lyricist, he still sometimes wrote "songs in the Montmartre style but taking no account of the rules of verse."[6] Although singing had remained a commonplace activity for the French in the early twentieth century, the circumstances at the front—including time and encouragement—meant even greater numbers became producers. That they wrote "without pretensions," "without any ambitions," or as "only an apprentice" reflected their own sense of being amateurs in a world where the music sphere was often professionalized. Soldiers also explained that they had sent songs into the *Bulletin* only at the behest of their "comrades."[7]

Soldiers wrote for themselves and especially for others. Some, following a much older tradition, kept song journals, sometimes with the help of more literate officers. Henri Meynard, for instance, carefully handwrote a catalogue of twenty-three songs between September 1914 and March 1916 and called it quite appropriately *L'Anti-Cafard*.[8] His songs attacked the kaiser, eulogized soldiers, and described the pains of army life. Soldiers also had an unofficial forum in the hundreds of trench newspapers scattered throughout the trenches. The *81 me poil . . . et plume*'s first edition dedicated one third of its front page to the song "La Bochocrole," which taunted Kaiser Wilhelm. The number of songs appears to have increased in the more informal, handwritten front-line papers compared to the more formal, well-established ones (some of which were actually printed in Paris), reflecting the geography of the army zone.[9] These makeshift operations allowed all sorts of soldiers to try their hand, as written examples encouraged oral expressions.

The collection of letters to the *Bulletin* also shows us that combatants composed songs at all hours—under shellings, immediately after battles, and during precious leisure moments with compatriots. The actual composing and singing may have encouraged soldiers to think in terms of the musical metaphor, as the practices served as a contrapuntal to the war. Soldiers literally wrote songs with bombings as accompaniment. One October 1916 letter calmly explained: "I am sending you one [song] which was created by a comrade and myself after the attack on Verdun, at the moment when we were making our way to rest."[10] "To chase away the tedium of trench life," a common soldier in the 52nd Infantry regiment sometimes scribbled "simple rhymes, somewhat unrefined *[paysan]* it is true."[11] Even revues that were to be performed behind the lines were put together at odd hours in the trenches. The infantrymen from the 211th described taking turns writing:

[The revue] was begun in the woods of "Chevaliers" Tuesday, December 14, 1915, and continued each day. . . . Each sheet was copied over as we went along by the performers between guard duty—even on Thursday the 16th and Friday the 17th, days of intense bombardments, as noted in the official communiqué. . . . The revue was finished December 23 when the 211th came down from the bois des Chevaliers.[12]

In most cases, soldiers proudly emphasized their creativity, their toughness, and their cooperation.

Collaborative efforts were quite common. Composers were listed as "groups of *poilus*" and a revue such as *Bouche Ah! Veine* had one author, three lyricists, and one *chef de musique*.[13] Moreover, correspondents often assured the editors that they had tried the song out with their inner circle of compatriots or at company concerts and had benefited from suggested changes. They now wanted to share it with a larger audience of soldiers. This was a world of concentric circles in which immediate surroundings and compatriots were the most important. But soldiers were also trying to be part of a larger "front," peopled by soldiers or *poilus*. One writer, a Henri Jouin, claimed to have done his best "to distract . . . compatriots" in the "Orient," but now wanted to help "*all* the brothers in arms who are fighting under the flag."[14] Others wanted to foster a song's fame or, as one officer put it, to "popularize [*vulgariser*] on the front" a patriotic tune which had had "a great success" in one region.[15]

But what sorts of skills did these amateurs have to call upon? In the French case, almost half of the army, and well over half of the foot soldiers, were peasants who brought with them rich networks of regional songs as well as some national songs.[16] Most had experienced the Third Republic's musical pedagogy, but they also had parents and grandparents with partial or little literacy who had exposed them to oral cultures, including in some cases patois. Workers had also experienced widespread singing practices in cafés and political meetings. With this background, many had acquired a huge catalogue of tunes and an ability to adapt new words to old tunes. As one scholar has said, "More widely spread still [than writing] seems to have been a love of song, a sort of popular and extra-academic culture. . . . The war revived the habit, tied to the fact that recent generations knew how to write in song journals. . . . For certain soldiers . . . the song was the only explicit cultural reference."[17]

Most songs sent into the *Bulletin* came with the lyrics handwritten or scrawled on any sort of paper. The authors simply gave the title of the tune, for example "La Paimpolaise" by Botrel or "Le Pendu" by Maurice Mac-Nab, assuming that fellow performers knew the melody. This allowed songs to be composed and dispersed much more quickly. Some reassured the editor of the *Bulletin* that the music was "easy and well known," whereas others knew musical notation and provided handwritten melodies, "borrowed" from a "well-known song."[18] In a rare instance, one provided four-part harmony, but he happened to be both a *musicien-brancardier* and a professional musician in civilian life. Interestingly, he also noted, that "in a pinch," the tune "Quand les lilas refleuriront" could be used. In typical fashion, Henri Meynard carefully indicated the "airs" in his journal's table of contents including the much older "Auprès de ma blonde" and "Malborough," Montmartre tunes such as "Le Pendu," as well as recent hits by Paulus and by Félix Mayol.[19] He also created a complicated "pot-pourris," a form used in *cafés-concerts* and musical revues. In Meynard's example, the "song" moved through fragments of nineteen different tunes with as few as two lines from any one melody, or as many as eight.[20]

It is striking how complicated this process could be and how good some of the soldiers were at it. They did not just use short, repetitive tunes, they chose music-hall tunes with six-line verses and ten-line refrains.[21] They then wrote words to fit, and fully expected others to be able to remember the tunes and to learn the adaptation. To assist learners, most used refrains, rhyming, and open-ended structures that invited additions—all traditional techniques in oral cultures. Soldiers even joked about the process, and their "obligation" to perform. One musical revue explained:

Text perpetrated by two sergeants pressed into service—Music plagiarized from the best authors and sung by the police squad—Piano duty by a detained foot soldier—Instrument out-of-tune, military requisition—. . . Final refrain sung by the whole battalion on alert, under pain of disciplinary sanctions.[22]

All of this evidence indicates that amateur musicians with very different levels of formal education had a facility for creating new renditions and did not hesitate to modify each others' performances.

Yet professional songwriters and musicians had also been conscripted as regular soldiers, carrying their own musical traditions and skills with them.[23] Fame in civilian life did not translate into military rank, however, which contributed to a democratizing effect in cultural terms. Reports of professionals' musical talents spread quickly, and fellow soldiers requested their assistance for ceremonies and concerts. One such soldier, suitably nicknamed "Father Music," sometimes "accompanied a military mass [in the morning], while in the evening he gave improvised concerts on a fortuitous piano, . . . accompanying brazen *[grivois]* lyrics sung by amateurs, as well as playing the Allies' national anthems, and astonishing himself with the patriotic choruses." In this case, a man who had known only classical music found himself "singing at the top of his lungs the refrains of 'Viens Poupoule,' lowly *[beuglant]* marches, and the ballads of the *faubourg*."[24] The professionals offered a great variety of skills within specific repertoires, but usually found themselves moving far beyond their training into a more mixed realm of mass culture.[25]

Other professionals followed their own initiative. Paul Clérouc, formerly of the Paris *café-concert* Noctambules, wrote numerous songs and at least nine revues during his time at the front, and then signed up his old colleagues from Paris to perform for troops.[26] There was some tension between their prewar and military identities, however.[27] One soldier-journalist, Marcel Mirtil, placed Paul Clérouc and his troupe La Tournée Chanteclair within the same proud national lineage of Charles-Simon Favart, cited so often in Paris. But he also underscored differences between soldiers and civilians:

It is not so much the theater brought to the army *[aux armées]* that we must praise today, but the army putting on the theater *[sur le théâtre]*. These are not actors from back there *[là-bas]* who come to entertain our comrades, but actors of our own. . . . Born from the heart of our army corps, members first, then observers of its [the army's] suffering, its work, and its glory.[28]

Mirtil also claimed the troupe "deliver[ed] none of the commonplace pieces of the rear, instead [it voiced] the grievances or the war songs born from the *poilus'* current life." Notably, these performers were the most likely to have simply transmitted Parisian works, but chose not to.

Paul Clérouc himself described the fine line he walked, feeling a need to distinguish himself from someone like Botrel. If all that was needed to win was to sing, he argued, the *poilus* would be "howling the latest lyrics by Théodore Botrel." But Clérouc also recognized that singing had certain powers, in particular to relieve boredom, and the most deserving audience was the average soldier. According to Clérouc, "Monsieur Poilu" disliked "banality from some *café-concert*" and "patriotism in bad taste." Having good taste defined the French soldier, setting him apart from those who admired the cultural products of Paris. And only a *poilu* (like Clérouc) could understand a *poilu*.

In contrast to their earlier life, professionals like Clérouc participated in a noncommercial trench culture. Their cultural practices and products helped define and reinforce a community for reasons other than economics—for entertainment, morale, and solidarity. In several letters to the *Bulletin,* soldiers rejected the idea that they sought payment, asking instead for copies of the edition, if the song was printed.[29] Songs were extremely cheap to produce, especially since they were often transmitted orally.[30] Soldiers took pride in their amateur status, and sometimes belittled more formal "bourgeois" forms "of tasteful musical entertainments given by veritable virtuoso performers" in the "calm" towns of zone B.[31]

PERFORMANCES IN ZONE A

One should not talk about composition, however, especially in the trenches, without also considering performance. If songwriters incorporated suggestions from fellow soldiers, songs also took on lives of their own as they were passed along. Singing occurred informally and was well integrated into daily expressiveness. Compared to other forms of cultural production such as writing literature, diaries, or poetry, singing followed a much more collective process. Much of the time, song lyrics reflected this in using the first person plural, instead of the first person singular. Singing was also more prevalent than any other cultural practice because it was less elite, although not everyone sang in equal amounts or the same repertoire. One commonly identified type was the Parisian, who knew the music-hall repertoire better than most. In Georges Lafond's unit, it was a corporal from Paris who sang more than he talked, especially with songs that reportedly "made one blush."[32] Paul Vaillant-Couturier entitled one of his memoir's sections "Un qui faisait des chansons," which was about a Parisian baker who "made songs" that helped soldiers "drown out" the sounds of barrages.[33] Parisians spread the lyrics and melodies of the latest songs from the immediate prewar period. Having had twenty to twenty-five years to spread, older *café-concert* hits had become part of a national culture.

On the other hand, there were those from the upper classes who did not break out into song as easily, and were struck by the fact that others did so. In encounters between classical, mass, and popular musical cultures, one sees some of the strain between prewar identities and soldiering. Some soldiers, for example, found spontaneous singing a novelty or as something foreign and somehow distasteful. Some felt self-conscious entering the oral culture. These differences were thrown into high relief in the army because of both the heterogeneity of the population and the heightened importance of culture and community. Unlike writing poetry or studying mathematics, where individual soldiers did or did not have the habit and choice of doing it, singing could draw anyone in at times, either as a listener or as a more active participant. And soldiers were sometimes ordered to join in.

A very important part of everyday culture, singing offered a means for mental and emotional survival, and a way to react to the army and civilian representations. André Pézard's diary recounted all sorts of everyday musical expressions, from humming before reveille to informal music sessions. He even annotated specific melodies.[34] Georges Lafond's memoir of his artillery unit also described fellow soldiers wandering by singing, day after day. One soldier passed by with "a Neapolitan song"; others vocalized while they did laundry; and the quartermaster, Burette, replied to everything in the repertoire of the famous Parisian *café-concert*, the Eldorado.[35] At one point as Lafond happened to be leaving, Burette simply sang out "in his amazing voice":

Moi! je m'en fous,	Me! I don't give a damn,
Je reste tranquil'ment	I stay quietly
Dans mon trou! . . .	In my hole! . . .[36]

Confronted by an upcoming battle, yet another soldier found himself humming the latest song, "Ferme tes jolis yeux."

One music-hall professional turned machine gunner, named Grizard, showed how soldiers did not give up their prewar repertoires or civilian identities, but instead adapted older habits to their new duties. Grizard had performed in suburban theaters of Paris before the war and was obviously well schooled in theatricality. Ordered to shoot down a German plane that threatened a convoy, he transposed the mission into a show for his fellow soldiers. "Ah! Attention, ladies and gentlemen," he began, "You will see what you will see. On with the music." The audience then heard the "music" of the machine gun with its "rhythmic tac-tacs, spaced like the prelude to a slow waltz."[37] Grizard "searche[d] for the tempo," while the spectators waited silently. Having fashioned his accompaniment, Grizard began humming, "as if he had found himself before his public at Belleville or at the Gaîté-Montparnasse" (both Parisian spots):

| Rêve de valse, rêve d'un jour, | Dream of a waltz, dream of a day, |
| Valse de rêve, valse d'amour. | Waltz of dreams, waltz of love.[38] |

Finally, after hitting the plane, Grizard bowed to the audience and said, "'The quarter of an hour is past, Messieurs. I release you.'"[39] Grizard had recreated his customary performance in the face of danger, calming himself with humor and bravado. He had also transfixed his colleagues who had suddenly become a convenient audience.

As soldiers faced long periods of boredom, they entertained themselves to ease feelings of extreme dislocation and loneliness, remembering home and its traditions and distancing themselves from the physical realities of the war.[40] A certain Michel D. explained the process in brief, "We began the modest song and during this time, *le cafard* passed."[41] This explanation attributed great power to singing, since *le cafard* often referred to a deep, foreboding depression. Even government misuse did not turn soldiers against singing.

Fighting on French soil, troops benefited from the cafés, theaters, churches, schools, and other civic buildings scattered in the towns and villages throughout the front. Compared to the Germans or even the British, the French had a somewhat easier time scavenging or negotiating the use of pianos, organs, or theater space—a fact that made their time at the front less "foreign."[42] Soldiers often passed through towns as they changed sectors or had short stints outside the trenches. Combatants had much less supervision here than at any other time except on leave. The officer Jean Giraudoux's diary described several different cafés where soldiers gathered on their short time away from the trenches to listen to phonographs, write poetry, play musical instruments, and sing.[43] One regimental musician admitted, "As often as possible, we gathered around the piano. Many soldiers of all ranks—even one or two officers."[44] Louis Mairet recorded having attended a concert near a destroyed farm with "vocals, regimental instruments, a flute, [and] reed pipes." This led to more music making; as he put it, "My men made music furiously [avec rage]."[45] Lighter instruments, such as harmonicas, pocket-bugles, and violins appeared in the frontmost trenches.[46] One article even described a makeshift orchestra, for which members built their instruments in the trenches, and some learned how to read music.[47]

Overall, though, in much of the army zone, and especially in zone A, soldiers relied more on singing, which brought in many more participants. In conjunction with his argument that individuals survived because of "informal social relationships among combatants," Tony Ashworth has argued that musical experiences helped build a "shared consciousness," which came from the collective learning process and the subsequent creativity as new verses or lyric changes were improvised.[48] The solidarity among combatants may have helped soldiers fight together more effectively, but, in the French case, it led also to collective dissent. This process did not just sustain a nationalism or national identity that soldiers had brought with them. It was about building a national identity that could supercede or conflict with other definitions.

The bonding sometimes occurred with the traditional practice of singing as "dessert" following a meal, a common practice among peasants and the working class throughout the nineteenth century. During the war, these occasions involved exchanging repertoires and griping. After one particular dinner, a soldier named Timbal, a *chanteur ambulant* and songwriter before the war, performed, accompanying himself on a guitar.[49] First, he sang about missing his home in the Midi, then he parodied the war and sang about the prejudice he had encountered, in particular, from a previous commanding officer. As Timbal continued, the other men in the room began to join in: "[T]hese men who were going to die, looked at each other and took up in chorus the refrain with the beautiful sounds from the voices of the South, and while the cannon thundered in the night, they overwhelmed the sound with the peaceful melody."[50] The officer Vaillant-Couturier, who had attended, remarked that even those men who could not understand the southern dialect reacted to the melody. The music overcame differences and countered the physical and emotional effects of the war.[51]

André Bridoux also remembered evenings when he and his cohorts would have their soup and then would "yield the floor to the performers in the troop: storytellers, singers, or wrestlers; . . . the audience was indulgent and disposed to laugh at everything."[52] Markedly amateur and resembling traditional popular culture, this community reinforced itself with its tolerance. Bridoux himself had come from a "restricted social circle" and described meeting workers and peasants for the very first time. As he began the war as a corporal, he talked of having his intellectual or learned self fall away. In the end, he claimed, he and his fellow soldiers formed "a small civil society."[53]

This cohesion sometimes extended across No Man's Land to include the Germans.[54] The bonding took place where the "popular" aspects of the culture—the most informal, oral, spontaneous, and obviously unofficial forms and practices—were the strongest. Despite the apparent invisibility of the enemy, the proximity of the two sides and the similarities of trench life for them both led to informal truces, involving exchanges of cigarettes, newspapers, and conversations.[55] Some accounts of such exchanges show that music or singing often led the way, as with the well-publicized Christmas truces, when both sides sang carols to each other.[56] With musical instruments in the trenches and some trenches quite close together, opponents could hear each other's evening concerts.[57] In one particular example recounted by a German soldier, the episode began when he sang a tune, despite getting advice to keep quiet, and the French joined in the refrain.[58] Shortly after, a French infantryman began the German anthem, "Deutschland, Deutschland über alles" which elicited first astonishment and applause from the instigators, and then a German rendition of the "Marseillaise." This eventually led to a truce and photographs.[59] In this description, the songs lessened the level of aggression and reinforced the "live-and-let-live" strategy of individual units. Soldiers found themselves united against the nationalist aims of their leaders and the civilians. An international repertoire of Christmas carols contributed as well as classical music (there are mentions of Schumann and even Wagner), but soldiers also used each other's best-known national pieces.[60] A notably high level of musical skills was the important link.

Among the French themselves, this trench culture helped break down class boundaries, partly by mixing high, mass, and popular repertoires and practices. Informal performances drew upon available repertoires and talents. One program given by "a group of *poilus*" for the 12th Infantry Division intermingled the *café-concert* songs "Je suis malade" and "Faite des écono-

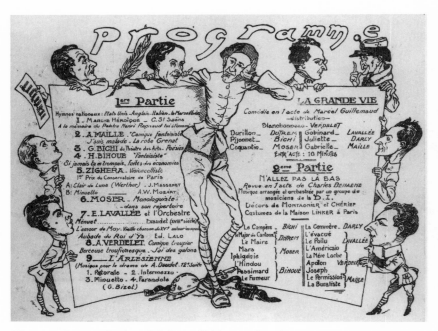

Figure 28. Program for the 12th Infantry division, no date given. Courtesy of the Bibliothèque Nationale de France, Paris.

mies," with a minuet by Mozart and the "Marche Héroïque" by Saint-Saëns (fig. 28). Soldiers were exposed to classical music often by professionals at odd moments and in odd places, but there was also a revalorization of amateurs and their skills. While the general public had heard "serious" music in a growing number of places before the war, as a part of the government's cultural campaign, classical music and *café-concert* repertoires had not been placed on such an equal footing.[61]

PERFORMANCES BEHIND THE LINES

This confused diversity carried over into zone B, where troops undertook more elaborate presentations while on *repos* in canteens or stationed in villages. Soldiers availed themselves of every possible locale for concerts and musical revues: barns, churches, hospitals, and village theaters. They could be quite enterprising; one soldier's letter described the conversion of an airplane hanger, with tent canvas made into a curtain and acetylene projectors for lighting. Volunteers came forward to design the sets and play in the orchestra, and instruments and props were brought in on food trucks. The troupe had planned for an audience of eight hundred people, but they welcomed twelve hundred, offering officers the good seats.[62]

Although this chapter is entitled "Going it Alone," behind the lines the soldiers were not quite alone. This space was much more heterogeneous than the front lines, as we saw with the arrival of the Parisian performers. Some shows took place in local towns for civilians, in hospitals, or in training camps quite a ways back.[63] The Poilu's Music Hall in the town of Commercy (Meuse), for example, held a Gala Matinee on Sunday, July 9, 1916, to which they invited local families. The program incorporated regimental musicians and other professionals as well as cinema—all signs of performances held toward the rear with more formality.[64] In this case, they charged for seats and had regular box-office hours. For a three-and-a-half-hour concert in May 1916 at the Théâtre du Parc in Vitry-le-François (near Bar-le-Duc), the "Chansonnier Edmond Teulet" was brought "specially from Paris," the program proclaimed. Teulet, a well-respected songwriter and performer of Montmartre, delivered "his latest works of war."[65] But this was also a theater whose 1917 programs were entitled "Campaign 1914–1917 / For the Poilus / By the Poilus"—a phrase soldiers commonly used to mark off their own cultural productions. In looking at the program (fig. 29), however, one would not guess that this performance was near the front; it resembled a prewar *café-concert* with older and more recent songs,

Figure 29. Program for the Théâtre du Parc de Vitry-le-François, September 9, 1917. Courtesy of the Bibliothèque Nationale de France, Paris.

including Alcide's "C'est Rosalie," mixed together with cinema. It also included a "Salut au 85e" (for the 85th regiment, one presumes) and ended with the "Marseillaise."[66]

One soldier also recounted how convalescing patients commandeered a nearby theater in order to put on concerts. At a typical concert, "Songs, monologues, morsels of music succeeded each other, performed either by the hospital's personnel, or by amateurs from town, or sometimes by professional artists receiving treatment."[67] Many of these events were still not very far from the front or out of danger—and this was sometimes noted by soldiers. In the letter explaining their "Revue de détails" to the readers of *Fantasio,* the authors indicated that it was performed only "six kilometers from the front," and rehearsals and performances faced the possibility of bombings.[68]

In addition, soldiers wrote revues outside the official army zone. *Charrie pas trop,* for example, took place in Vendôme near Orleans at a training center for artillery officers, where they could even have a woman for a *commère* (the revue's hostess). In other words, this "army" revue was not written at or for the "front," but was still very much within the military. In fact, the characters made sure to define themselves in opposition to civilian criticism that saw musical revues as inappropriate for officers.[69] In tableau fourteen, *le Civil* (the civilian) showed up and exclaimed, "Really . . . officers . . . It's shameful . . . One ought not to allow it," those who "have the honor to wear a uniform like yours . . . to make fun of such serious aspects of the military profession in public." In their defense, the *commère* argued, "Do they not have the right, those who have risked their lives, to defend our land, to pass some days gaily to distract themselves as well to work. It's true you can't understand . . . if you had like them . . ." She then made her point with a song, telling *le Civil* to get his hat and "leave us alone," and ended with "Let us sing / And amuse ourselves."[70]

The creation of troop revues came from all branches and most ranks, including many infantry regiments (both regular and territorial), and subgroups such as stretcher bearers, the engineering corps, aviators, cavalry, Moroccan, and Senegalese units (fig. 30). The earliest World War I revue, according to archival listings, dates from when the front stabilized in November 1914, and productions continued throughout the war.[71] In a Paris column written in mid-1916, Guillot de Saix listed seventy-nine different revues that had already been performed by troops.[72] It is difficult to determine which ranks were most likely to write or direct revues, since only 25 percent of the names mentioned in the archives were identified by rank.[73] Again, one finds collaborative efforts by both amateurs and professionals with amateurs prevailing. One soldier writing to the

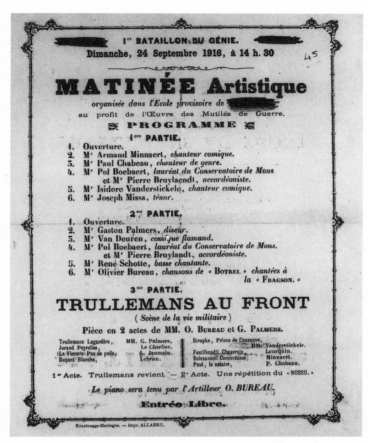

Figure 30. Program for a Matinée Artistique by the 1st Battalion of Engineers, September 24, 1916. Courtesy of the Bibliothèque Nationale de France, Paris.

Bulletin referred to his having scribbled down lyrics, which were then given the "sumptuous name of 'Revue.'"[74] Carefully rehearsed or spontaneous, these performances often played to very large assemblies. Accounts repeatedly refer to twelve or fifteen hundred soldiers packed into barns or airplane hangers. One offering of the First Moroccan Division reportedly drew four thousand.[75]

There were also more substantial "troupes," which offered the closest adaptation of mass cultural forms. Paul Clérouc's troupe Chanteclair, for example, operated with the permission of the high command, and made five tours with more than 130 performances.[76] There was nothing small about this. Much was owed to Clérouc's own energy and success. He had headed another theater "Le Théâtre des Poilus" earlier in 1916 which had also used the slogan "By the poilus, for the poilus," and had performed one of his own revues for over twelve thousand *poilus* in a month's time.[77] The Theater of the 81st Territorials was also a long-running fixture. At one point in late 1915 and early 1916, they did forty-eight performances of just one revue, in which the audience reportedly included twenty-one generals.[78] By mid-1916, they were giving four regular shows a week as well as doing tours. When they had trouble making ends meet, they decided to get financial support from the business community of Nantes, the regiment's home town. One innovative method was to decorate their theater's curtain with advertisements from Nantes businesses. This relationship worked both ways; the soldiers got a sense of civilian support while seeing concrete reminders of home-town sites, and the civilians felt they were doing their share. One other important example was the Poilus-Park or Poilus Music Hall where two to three thousand soldiers crowded in for concerts, plays, revues, and singing, with "the military musicians leading the way."[79] According to Henry Bordeaux, part of its attraction was the warmth in the wintertime, as well as the camaraderie.

The cultural geography of zone B brought with it a different audience than in zone A. One found higher officers and civilians in a much more settled space and with a more formal system of invitations. As soldiers crowded into these makeshift theaters, officers often sat separately in nicer seats.[80] Some programs proudly announced having performed for officers such as General Roques, who headed the First Army at the time, or for a regiment's official day.[81] This reminds us of the difficulty at times in determining the line between official and unofficial. In the latter's case, the revue *Plaies et . . . boches* by a corporal André Bataille was played for the 251st Infantry regiment's fête on May 23 and 24, 1915, with the commander, Lieutenant-Colonel Guérin, presiding.[82]

Despite this obeisance, the first and most important audience was "les copains," and the main goal was still to distract "poilus" and to build a sense of community. An infantrymen's *Revue de détails* began with a speech describing the tough conditions under which they worked and begged the audience's indulgence—after all, it was all "between *poilus*."[83] Others sang of *poilus* bringing "gaiety" to other *poilus*. For instance, even a revue from late in the war ended with the full cast singing:

Et maintenant avant de nous quitter	And now before we leave
Chantons en choeur, chantons cette chanson,	Let us sing in chorus, let us sing this song,
Car à la guerre il est bon de chanter!	Because at war it's good to sing!
[Refrain]	[Refrain]

Pour couvrir la voix du canon.	To cover the voice of the cannon.
Pour engendrer la joie et la gaieté,	To bring joy and gaiety,
A nos poilus quand ils sont sur le front,	To our *poilus* when they are at the front,
Que faut-il	What do we need
Pour chasser le cafard?	To chase away le cafard?
Des chansons!	Songs!
Des chansons!	Songs!
Des chansons!	Songs![84]

The song "Faut pas s'en faire" (written in 1917 or 1918) also had soldiers dance and sing while on *repos,* proclaiming "Our gaiety, this is our strength."[85] Soldiers came perilously close to sounding like the home front here. But they were well aware of the issue of whether it was appropriate to sing or not and how it might be interpreted.[86] For them, if the performers came from the same community as the audience, expressing these sentiments was fine. It was a long way from the preaching of Parisian professionals to the camaraderie of amateur soldier-*revuistes.* Not surprisingly, however, they also made fun of orders to perform or sing.

Furthermore, soldiers sometimes took advantage of officers' attendance by putting them on the spot. In one scene from "Pourvu qu'on Rigole!!" the piano began with an aria from Tosca, but then the *compère* explained that the famous tenor "Caresso" had not yet arrived.[87] The director suggested singing something else in the meantime "in the true Montmartre style," but the *compère* complained that they had exhausted their repertoire. At this point the director was supposed to turn to an "important person in the audience," and ask "General, would you sing something for us? Well, could we have a song improvised?" Officers also frequently got an earful of complaints and parodies, as soldiers took advantage of the traditionally satirical revue form.

While we will examine content in the next section, we should consider the soldiers' performance forms here, especially in order to ask where zone B sat relative to the home front. Looking at how forms migrated underlines the tension between soldiers' creating their own cultural idioms and using familiar or current forms. Soldiers imitated home-front mass culture in choosing to perform revues, since the revue form represented the most important genre of the modern French music hall at the outbreak of the war. The soldiers themselves were aware of the Parisian model, including the use of *compères* and *commères,* and some revues were dedicated to such important Parisian writers as Jean Bastia, Dominique Bonnaud, and Léonce Paco. Lyrics sometimes lamented missing scenery and costumes or "l'esprit parisien."[88] Mostly shorter than Parisian productions, some, nevertheless, had an amazing number of tableaux: nineteen or twenty in some cases, and thirty for one that premiered in the middle of 1917. This seems to have been an insider's joke, as some touted "a considerable quantity of tableaux" or "2 acts and quite a few tableaux."[89]

As in Paris, new lyrics were usually put to well-known song melodies, sometimes with five or six different tunes in a single scene. Revues relied on musical memories and a broad repertoire. They demonstrated some of the very old tunes soldiers knew, such as "Cadet Rousselle," "Auprès de ma blonde," and "Le Roi d'Yvetot." But even more often, they incorporated Montmartre classics or recent *café-concert* hits. The works of big names such as Aristide Bruant, Xavier Privas, Maurice Mac-Nab, or Paul Delmet appeared over and over, with, for example, "Le Bal à l'Hôtel de Ville," "A Batignolles-Clichy," "Le Père la Victoire," or "En r'venant d' la R'vue" (the song made famous with Boulangism).[90] A "classic" was "traditional" in the sense that it was prewar and established, but it was not age-old. Less often, the soldiers rewrote the texts of old patriotic tunes; one finds Déroulède's "Le Clairon," for example. In the revue *En voulez-vous des Percos?* "All the *poilus*" welcomed their audience with the tune "Sambre et Meuse."[91] Just as often, composers used tunes such as "Je connais une blonde" and René de Buxeuil's "L'Ame des violons," which had appeared between 1900 and 1914, reflecting the widespread dissemination of the Parisian musical entertainment culture before the war.[92]

What soldiers do not appear to have known or chosen were many of the hits of the war period. In some sense, theirs was a frozen repertoire, a fact that may well have fed their propensity for nostalgia after the war. It was not Paris's latest that showed up, a process that would occur in World War II because of the radio. To take just one example, in the revue *A leur barbe!* which was performed in December 1915, the lyricist chose thirty-two older tunes and only one brand new one.[93] Somewhat typically, he included the 1890 "Le Pendu," the 1906 "Le Rêve passe," the 1913 "L'Ame des violons," and two patriotic tunes, the Belgian anthem "La Brabançonne" and "Le Clairon." Vincent Scotto's "Cri du poilu" (fig. 22) made some inroads in troop shows, as did "Quand Madelon," but remarkably little considering their popularity in Paris.[94] The prominence of Scotto's song may well have been due to its part in the erotic discourse.

If soldiers borrowed their melodies, they provided very different lyrics. The revue form actually encouraged this transformation, since its setting and purpose were based completely on *actualités*. So, while Paris revues centered on Parisian sites and therefore were urban, most of the soldiers' were set in the army zone, especially in *centres de repos* or small towns, as a recreation of those moments. Some took place at administrative headquarters where they poked fun at the army bureaucracy; others made a tour of the *cantonnement* by song. The *actualités* of life in the army zone were usually delivered with a comic or satiric slant. For example, the revue *Trois ans après* began with a chorus using the tune: "Cadet Roussel" and the performers were all "in gas masks."[95]

The generally less strict censorship in the army zone also allowed more freedom in language and in topics. Older forms of popular language—slang, insults, rude terms—could flourish, as well as sexual humor. Also in contrast to Paris, the lyricists took full advantage of the traditional songwriter's techniques of pauses in songs to stimulate an audience's imagination and reactions. This could foster erotic jokes, but was also used to ridicule civilians.[96] Sometimes the soldiers' productions were censored, but they then turned around and made fun of the censor.

One final important difference from Parisian revues was the lack of women—either as *commères* or in chorus lines. The soldiers, however, found many ways to make up for this, ways that again helped to define the community. Many songs complained that revues needed women, since, as one "spectator" said, he "sure hadn't come to see *poilus*!"[97] In another instance, soldiers sang of having lost the *commère*. More often than not, they had men in drag as *commères,* and even dancing "girls."[98] This was local popular culture, not Jelavich's modern body parts or refined music-hall "attractions."

The strain soldiers experienced between their subculture and their desire to remain a part of the national whole showed itself most pointedly in the issue of standards. Usually, soldiers praised performances for fellow soldiers, and in at least one instance, they severely condemned an opera star for having let his comrades down when he missed a performance.[99] Revues sometimes made fun of the civilian efforts to keep soldiers happy. And one revue's song joked about Joffre's deciding the soldiers needed distraction, with lyrics that sounded just like a government document:

Les acteurs les plus en renom,	The most famous actors,
Et les plus belles pensionnaires	And the most beautiful guests
Fur' volontaires pour le front;	Volunteered for the front;
C'est au cafard qu'ils font la guerre:	It's on *cafard* that they make war:
Après le Boche c'est vraiment	After the Boche, it's truly
Notre plus terrible adversaire,	Our most terrible adversary,
C'est l'opinion du Command'ment	This is the opinion of the High Command
Puisque Botrel à la Croix d' guerre.	Since Botrel got the *Croix de guerre*.[100]

Soldiers' own letters also described their performances as "worthy of a Montmartre *chansonnier*," or claimed that "Paris" would be jealous of such efforts.[101]

Figure 31. Program for the Théâtre Ambulant de la IVe Armée, no date given. Courtesy of the Bibliothèque Nationale de France, Paris.

But soldiers had also brought with them a hierarchy in which professionals were celebrated or at least deferred to. This presumption came across in the tentativeness surrounding their compositions, and through their dedication of revues to Parisian stars. They also tended to note in their diaries, letters, and even on some of the sketchiest programs, the credentials of performers they had the opportunity to hear. Musicians came from the "Paris Conservatory" or the "Paris Opéra" (fig. 31). This was an extra-trench status system.

Soldiers also wanted positive recognition or publicity for their efforts, outside of their own sphere. Some composers or writers wrote from the trenches to Parisian newspaper columnists or music editors with details of their performances. And in the fortuitous event that notices appeared, they asked that clippings be sent back to them.[102] In part, this reflected a particular problem with the nature of traditional popular culture, as well as the power of the home front. Much of what the combatants created was isolated and ephemeral. But the copies and descriptions that we still have in the archives are there because the soldiers wanted some of their culture remembered, and their acts recognized. It was the dominant culture that was to record history, or at least kept the archives. As one soldier put it, he was offering a "folklore en ballade" and "a bit of History."[103] But he also carefully noted that the document did not completely solve the problem, since two days after its third rendition, some of the performers (along with audience members) had been killed in an assault, and the revue could never be done again. Their culture was transitory, as were many of their lives, but saving a document meant somehow staying alive, or at least not being forgotten.

The Soldiers' Mentalité

It is a difficult task to analyze a broad pattern of thoughts across the entire military force, taking into account differences in types of units, ranks, and location. As the authors of *La Plume au fusil* (a collection of wartime correspondence from the Midi) discovered, "It was not just a matter of the famous 'Madelon.' The letters taught us that every regiment had its own repertoire, copious, varied in tone and in inspiration."[104] Yet it is possible to talk about wider patterns illustrating the most popular themes and indicating a broad chronological shift. While the soldiers had been happy to sing the compelling nationalist songs in 1914, these lyrics became less popular with the soldiers as the war continued. By late 1915, soldiers began to change drastically how they represented the war, driven by their needs and their belief in the importance of their voices. And by 1917, they had moved to open dissent and had resurrected older subversive repertoires.

Some historians have made distinctions between the bellicose nationalism of the home front and the national sentiment or patriotism of the soldiers.[105] Audoin-Rouzeau, for example, found patriotism to be an important topic in trench newspapers, but chose to use the phrase "national sentiment" for it.[106] This was, in fact, a distinction the soldiers themselves wanted to project. But singing shows some examples of strong, obvious nationalism, although within several different strands. Some lyrics expressed a rousing patriotism modeled after older regimental songs; others were politically detailed; and many were anti-German. Soldiers brought standards with them, so one finds Déroulède's tunes used, and some revues ended with the "Marseillaise." But this does not seem to have been the rule, contrary to Parisian beliefs. Moreover, songs show the subtlety of the soldiers' *mentalité* at times, a subtlety seen especially in their humor and in their mixture of more realistic descriptions of trench warfare with their attestations of patriotism.

Renditions of animated patriotism could follow a much older tradition and overlapped most closely with home-front examples. With its rituals, the army enforced the use of older tunes making them readily available for the soldiers themselves.[107] The revue *Quand-même,* written in May 1915 by Sergeant-Major Edouard Lenoir, used the ultrapatriotic tune "Sambre-et-Meuse" for a regimental song, calling it "the tune that led our forefathers to 'Glory.'"[108] And in the same revue, one finds Herman Lebovic's model of regional integration into nationalism. The performers identified themselves regionally, proudly singing, "We are the boys from Brittany," but then also sang of themselves as "the immortal *poilus*" "meriting the name" of France. In the old-fashioned stirring style, the lyrics used the first person plural imperative "Let us go kill this vermin," as well as the military order of "Forward, this is for our France." Finally, the audience was sent forth with these words:

Ce qu'il faut c'est la baïonnette	What we need is the bayonet
Rentrant dans les ventres gonflés	Driven into their swollen bellies
Tapons dans ces sales binettes,	Let us strike in the dirty mugs,
De choucroute toujours enflés.	Of always pompous sauerkraut.[109]

We can only imagine the effect this had following the performance, but we know that with the use of well-known tunes, comrades were encouraged to sing along. And many of these songs referred to going back up the line. The group singing reassured or reconfirmed the collectivity. This sort of patriotism was not necessarily separate or different from fighting for buddies.[110]

The *Bulletin* represented the official army, but songs submitted to it still illustrate some soldiers' desire to express their own patriotism with many sincere tunes sent to support the "valliant defenders of *la Patrie.*" Again, soldiers took older national tunes and adapted them. One song based on the eighteenth-century "Auprès de ma blonde" began its first verse with firm, almost gay, patriotism:

Dans le beau ciel de France	In the beautiful French sky
Un soleil radieux	A radiant sun
De gloire, d'espérance	Of glory, of hope
Resplendit à nos yeux	Shines in our eyes
Oubliant nos souffrances	Forgetting our suffering
Nous fredonnons joyeux:	We hum joyously:

This then led to the original, well-known refrain.[111] The adaptation was written after the start of Verdun, or in middle to late 1916, by a second lieutenant. Along with the "beautiful French sky," he did not hesitate to mention how "we" the soldiers had endured misery in "holes" with the rats and lice. But "we" had also held off the Germans and the kaiser (the *carogne* [*sic*], or bastard), and in the end the French would dictate the peace.

In one other revue, the soldiers chose Déroulède's "Le Clairon" for their last number. This was the nineteenth-century song that celebrated the heroic death of the bugler. In this instance, they optimistically modified the idea of the clarion's mortality with *poilus* overcoming death:

Pour la prochaine offensive	For the next offensive
La lutte sera plus vive	The battle will be brisker
Mais vous serez les plus forts.	But you will be the strongest.
Lorsqu'aura passé l'orage	When the storm has passed
Dans les horreurs du carnage	In the horrors of the carnage
Vous aurez vaincu la mort!	You will have conquered death![112]

In this song and others, soldiers mixed their own expressions with broader ideas of patriotism.

Although one can certainly find examples of serious patriotism that used language of glory and valor even late in the war, soldiers also modulated their patriotism with humor.[113] This was not joking that avoided nationalist identity. In fact, the many appearances of Napoleon, Vauban, Joan of Arc, or La Victoire (fig. 32) as characters in their revues show the soldiers' appreciation for French history.[114] Tellingly, the musical patriotism encompassed older symbols like the flag and previous armies, but not the current government or its leaders. But soldiers diverged from the home front in having a far wider spectrum of patriotic expressions. For instance, they were much less reverential toward patriotic symbols, and it was this familiarity that showed how the nationalism was their own. A revue given near the front in late 1915 was infused with patriotism and regimental pride. But the *commère*, called *la Gloire*, was a woman played by a man with great potential for humorous readings. When the trope of the 1914 send-off with kisses came up, the soldiers must have been laughing hard.[115] In another 1915 revue, *Toul'es Boches On les aura*, they used Joan of Arc as their *commère*, but she remained tantalizingly invisible throughout.[116] Eroticism could be comfortably combined with patriotism.

One of the soldiers' favorite musical targets was the enemy, which was almost always the Germans, and very rarely the Turks or Austrians.[117] Many of their songs reveal that soldiers were better informed than one

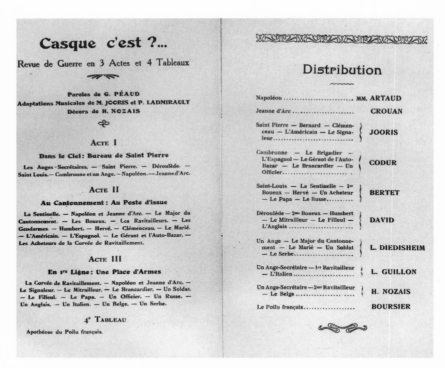

Figure 32. Program for the soldier's revue *Casque c'est?* by G. Péaud, for the Théâtre du 81e Territorial, July 6, 1916. Collection of the author.

might think—especially if one examines revue lyrics for zone B, which display less isolation than those from the trenches. Not necessarily written by an educated person, one song recorded the British leader as Lyold Georgs, but also referred to Germany's violation of Belgian neutrality and Woodrow Wilson's peace proposals.[118] Lyrics ranged from relatively light to brutal joking, even within a single song. Calling the Germans "dirty boches" or "bastards," and the kaiser "craven" abounded. One set of lyrics had the singer representing a German who said ridiculous things; in the second verse the Germans coveted "only" Belgium, France, Algeria, the Arctic pole, and the Moulin Rouge, and the fourth described their "grand victories," such as Verdun, "where we lost 400,000 men."[119]

Not all of the patriotism was humorous, however, and *revuistes* or *chansonniers* also sang sadly, but proudly, of worthy deaths.[120] It may be easier to conceive of rousing songs for musical revues with an audience, and especially officers, in attendance. But the revue *Trois ans après* contained a song written in 1917 to the prewar tune of "Le Dernier Tango," which combined frank descriptions of the war with soldiers' resolve:

Une fois partis, on court, sous la
    mitraille,
Les obus tombent éclatant de partout,
Le coeur se serre, mais comme c'est la
    bataille,
Chacun s'efforce et combat jusqu'au
    bout.
	Once departed, we run, under the
	    machine gun,
	Bombs fall exploding everywhere,
	One's heart tightens, but as this is
	    battle,
	Each forces himself and fights to the
	    end.[121]

The tone and details set it apart from the traditional model, even though the soldiers still sang as they gripped their guns and went into an assault. Adjutant B. Moneuquet's 1916 "La Marche du 95e" referred to the rain, mud, heavy loads and "suffering," but still professed to a shiver of patriotism. Other lyrics had troops—and thus audience members—finishing *repos* and resolutely going back up the line. In the revue number "Départ aux tranchées," probably from December 1915, they went to replace their "brave comrades" and to stop the invasion of "our country by the Prussians!"[122] Some patriotic sentiments could be performed by soldiers for soldiers. But the same sentiments would have aggravated a combatant, if sung by a civilian to a soldier. Overall, although these songs were certainly different from anything one would have heard on a Paris stage, they were still prescriptive and served to define the soldiers' purpose. They also allowed soldiers to hear praise for their own feats.

At the same time, some songs and revues showed a continuing devotion to individual regions, reaching out to comrades from certain regions. One particular author requested the *Bulletin* print his song, since "it would give pleasure to many of my comrades from the North who are like me in the trenches or in the army. I have no pretentions of marching in the footsteps of Victor Hugoo [*sic*] . . . but for the Lillois [those from Lille] everything written in *patois* is worthwhile."[123] The composer still referred to the French national culture, while identifying with a region. A corporal with a company of five hundred Creoles also consecrated "several of his hours of free time" to songwriting to satisfy his fellow Creoles.[124] In this case, it was French patriotism coming from colonial troops.

These sorts of songs worked in more than one way. They could feed homesickness and reinforce a prewar, or extrawar, identity, or they could help bridge regional divides through the sharing of repertoires with fellow soldiers. Vaillant-Couturier's example of the *chanteur ambulant* from Toulouse illustrates how men learned each others' melodies and lyrics.[125] Songs sometimes sounded like Third Republic geography lessons with verses devoted to different regions. In one example, the first three lines of numerous verses described characteristics of provinces, including Normand,

Auvergnat, Limousin, Flamand, Champenois, Parisien, Montagnard, and Provençal. Then lines four and five proffered all sorts of ways to fight well and to make one's province proud, for instance, by risking one's skin, never turning tail, fearing neither the cold or heat, or taking on three enemy soldiers at once.[126] This was once again an open-ended form, in which other soldiers could have added in their own origins and methods of fighting. In a letter to his parents, Louis Mairet described the mixture of "races" in his regiment with men from the "Nord" and from the "Midi." But he then also talked about how fortunate it was that "France is eternal." Despite all the damage, the "survivors," this same mixture, "linked by the idea of an eternal France, would rebuild the ruins."[127]

Gradually, though, the earlier identities blended with the soldiers' current lives, and the subculture expanded in importance. Soldiers developed extensive systems of slang, nicknames, occupational hierarchies, and subversive devices. In their catalogue and valuation of jobs, for example, they loved and hated "les cuistots" (the cooks), deemed "le vaguemestre" (the mailman) a sacred angel, and viewed cyclists as haughty because of their close contact with the high command. Those not in danger were often disdained as evaders. These constructions self-consciously separated the soldiers' existence and the representations of that experience from the home front, as well as from portions of zone B.

Songs incorporated trench slang quickly, especially since prewar lyrics had always used popular words molded to fit the rhythm and rhymes. Terms such as "bidasse" (soldier), "boyau" (trench), "flingue" or "flingot" (gun), and "pinard" (wine) were rampant and celebrated. As soldiers constructed their semblance of the war, an early and critical shift in song content also began portraying trench conditions in realistic terms, while not explicitly condemning the conflict, the government, or a ruling elite. This represented a sharp deviation from traditional war songs. A sense of disgust and almost panic at being filthy appeared in a song like "L'Attaque de nuit," for example, which reported the capture of a German trench with excruciating details of artillery salvos, knives, bayonets, and grenades creating "a true carnage" and too many deaths.[128] The "Garde de nuit à l'Yser" desperately sang about night duty in the trenches, when the ditch became a tomb and fear grasped soldiers: "This dark hour / When under our armor / creeps, steadily, / the hand of fear."[129] The songwriters were willing to cast the war in a more realistic light, disregarding any precept of composing songs for distraction. This genre was to emerge in Paris much later in the war and never enjoyed great success.

Other songs, however, did use a humorous, silly, or possibly sarcastic tone to describe the front. The satirical or comedic manner allowed individuals the opportunity to express frustration and even to feel themselves in a position of power. The song "Brise du soir" concentrated on the terrible smells of the trenches:

Choux pourris, tronçons de barbaque,	Putrid cabbage, slices of meat,
Épluchures, rats morts, vieux os,	Scraps, dead rats, old bones,
Souvent forment un grand cloaque	Often form a large cesspool
Où fourmillent les asticots.	Where maggots swarm.

And then its refrain said:

Et puis je me mets à chanter:	And then I begin to sing:
Ah! Ah! . . . Ah! Ah! . . .	Ah! Ah! . . . Ah! Ah! . . .
Brise du soir, brise si pure,	Evening breeze, breeze so pure,
Où monte aux cieux l'âme des fleurs,	Where the soul of the flowers rises to the heavens,
J'aime à respirer tes senteurs	I love to breathe in your scents
Quand tu t'épands sur la nature!	When you suffuse them in nature![130]

The song, subtitled "a Romance," parodied the prewar genre with constant references to the purity and gentleness of nature with a brutal juxtaposition. Forced to live with the elements of nature but in otherwise unrecognizable circumstances, soldiers were an audience that might laugh in the worst situations.[131]

Soldiers also adjusted by parodying their officers, their environment, government officials, and civilians, a tactic used also in the trench newspapers.[132] Some parodies decried the lack of leave, soldiers' low salaries and greedy civilians who raised prices on dear commodities such as wine.[133] They complained about doctors who sent soldiers to the front lines to improve their health, and made fun of the postal censors, for instance, by making them obnoxious characters in their revues. The commanders' strategy did not escape their commentary, either, for example with observations about the stupid misuse of artillery, when the French were not attacking.[134]

A more political genre complained about the government. The song "Leur idéal" bitingly pointed out that government officials ran the conscription process, while they lived comfortably in Paris and participated in war profits.[135] The trench newspaper *Le Gafouilleur*'s "Une inspection" employed a well-worn Parisian tune and described how a Parisian politician had inspected the troops' rations and returned to give civilians a glowing report. Since food was a serious complaint among infantrymen, the humor of the song had a bitter edge.[136] One of the more ingenious and possibly satisfying tactics composers used was to create revue characters who could be teased or denigrated on stage. In his *A leur barbe,* a certain E. Lajoue had members of the Chamber of Deputies visiting the "front" as part of the 333rd parliamentary commission. These characters were then forced to hear a whole musical litany of complaints including the lack of *pinard* and the problem of *embusqués* (shirkers), as well as having to hear the truth about the soldiers' valor.[137]

This form of satire was part of the soldiers' most complicated and volatile subject: their relationship to the home front and Paris. We have seen how soldiers relied on help from civilians in Paris and dedicated works to famous performers.[138] Some troop journals, such as *L'Echo des marmites* and *Le Poilu du 6-9,* also placed songs by famous Parisian composers on their front page.[139] In addition, the trench newspapers contained advertisements for theaters in Paris as well as for shops like Félix Potin on Boulevard de Sébastopol.[140] Some of the representations created by civilian composers clearly still held their interest, and they certainly kept track of behavior at the home front.

Combatants felt a need to respond to home-front representations, including the image of infantrymen singing gaily as they went to die. In a poem from 1917, a soldier told of being asked by his friends to sing a Montmartrois song to demonstrate how they knew "how to sing and die in Argonne." But he explained that his memories of all the blood prevented him from singing. He would still fight for the country, but as for those who had gone before: "They all knew how to die, but they didn't sing!"[141]

The most caustic antiwar songs expressed the distance the soldiers felt from civilians. These expressions proliferated most freely in the front lines and in soldiers' cultural products created for each other. As the soldiers moved in and out of the trenches, they found themselves unable to fit the civilians' images of an aggressive, cheerful fighter—the *poilu* of Rip's *1915.* Soldiers found it difficult, in particular, to compare their experiences to civilians' so-called hardships and benefits.

Parodies were most effective with well-known idioms, where familiar words were modified in an incongruous setting. The song "Quand Madelon," which idealized the war with drinking, very friendly waitresses, and no trenches, presents a particularly good example. "Quand Madelon" had a much more important career on the home front than among soldiers.[142] But the figure of Madelon was well enough established by late in the war that it was ripe for parody. The veteran André Ducasse, for example, remembered having heard it sung by Senegalese with a "delicious deformation."[143] It also made soldiers very unhappy that real "Madelons" did not exist for the *poilus*. The refrain of "La Véritable Madelon" cleared up any illusions:

Chez un bistrot, lorsque je voulais boire,	At a bistro, where I wanted a drink,
Je demandais un litre de pinard,	I asked for a liter of *pinard* [wine],
Un' vieill' femm' sans dent sur la mâchoire	An old lady without teeth in her jaw
M'disait: "Avez-vous vot' quart?"	Said to me "Will you have your quart?"
En ronchonnant, pour quatre francs cinquante,	While grumbling, for four francs fifty,
Ell' me versait un infâme poison,	She poured me the infamous poison,
Je n' sais pas si c'est ça la charmante	I don't know if this is the charming
Madelon, Madelon, Madelon!	Madelon, Madelon, Madelon![144]

The future film director Jean Renoir also recorded seeing an opera star sing "Quand Madelon" for troops. He claimed that despite its "immense popularity [behind the lines], this patriotic song did not suit the troops," and that when the troops laughed at the singer, the performer mistook their reaction for enthusiasm.[145]

One civilian slogan, which became popular in 1914 and 1915, was "pourvu que les civils tiennent," meaning that the war would end quickly, if the civilians held on. This idea soon wore thin with the soldiers, who then parodied it.[146] One early caricature sang of a soldier's time on leave, and his subsequent reaction to returning to the front:

Le civil boit ce qu'il veut	The civilian drinks what he wants
Le poilu boit ce qu'il peut;	The *poilu* drinks what he can;
. . . .	. . . .
Les uns disent: "Nous tiendrons!"	The former says "We will hold!"
Et c'est vrai qu'ils tiennent bon	And it's true that they hold well
Ils tiennent tous à leur peau,	They all hold their skin,
Et leur p'tit derrière au chaud.	And their rear end in the warmth.[147]

As expressed in the song, the soldier's reaction to the home front was often to want to return to the front:

Adieu, je vais prendr' mon train,	So long, I will take my train,
Mes amitiés aux copains,	My regards to my buddies,
N'tue pas tous les boch's sans moi,	Don't kill all the *boches* without me,
Laiss' m'en au moins deux ou trois.	Leave me at least two or three.

Indeed, when soldiers went on leave and were faced with the home-front culture, they found the reentry disorienting.[148] Civilians did not understand what the soldiers had seen and experienced, and the soldiers could not adjust to what used to be familiar surroundings.

Soldiers may have had trouble expressing themselves in person on the home front, but not back in their own sphere. As soldiers kept abreast of events in Paris, they could easily satirize the civilians' patriotic practices in their musical revues. P. Borel's *Voyez terrasse!* began with a character named "le Pessimiste," who represented a civilian moaning about the lack of movement on the front and complaining about having done so much to "hold."[149] "We have accepted the disruption of our lives, the lack of buses, the closing of cafés at 10 P.M. . . . . We have all cried: 'To Berlin!,' sent picture postcards making fun of the Boches, saluted the regimental flags, and put up the portrait of General Joffre in a nice spot in our dining rooms." Similarly, the song "Leur idéal," which had attacked lazy politicians, also specifically mocked President Poincaré's famous formula of "Jusqu'au bout," meaning the French would fight to the bitter end. The lyrics asked what exactly *Parisians* were fighting to the end of, and concluded that it was possibly just to the end of their tramway line.[150]

Paris also held accessible, well-known stereotypes, and was seen as the base of production for news, government regulations, and songs. Appearing in the trench journal *Face aux Boches* in June 1916, the lyrics to "Journaux à deux sous" offered a powerfully sarcastic critique. The song first noted the nice newspapers with sensational stories, which civilians used "to distract" themselves. Then it pitied the civilians who were having to do without pernod, sugar, or ice cream—a "sad" turn of events.[151]

More specifically, soldiers held certain powerful cultural figures responsible. An article called "Les Grands Etonnements du poilu" in *L'Echo des marmites* offered a general impression of Paris and then pointed a finger of guilt at the operators of the *cafés-concerts*.[152] The article was composed of a long set of questions, some of which asked:

> Why do the *cafés-concerts* directors insist on having the "Marseillaise" and the "Chant du départ" sung by semi-nude women who can't sing?
> Why do theater-set designers portray the trenches in a fashion with so little truthfulness? . . .
> Why does the patriotism of certain *embusqués* not go any farther than applauding the revue: "Jusqu'au bout" [to the bitter end] at the Folies-Bergère?

The soldiers were well aware that the older concepts of an offensive, glorious war had remained strong among civilians, promoted by the entertainment industry, and that the home front felt it had its own reasons to gripe.

This was a far cry from the unified singing of the "Marseillaise" and the "Chant du départ" of August 1914.

Paul Clérouc also wrote disparaging lyrics which told of those at the home front who loved to sing "On les aura" to show "false patriotism" and instructed those *embusqués* who might have been listening to be "less proud," since it was the infantrymen and gunners who would beat the Germans. His song "Ceux qui les auront" advised the "pessimists" on the café terraces who second-guessed the military strategists to leave matters to the authorities.[153]

Over and over again, the soldiers' songs and musical revues attacked *embusqués*. This was a figure which made Parisian censors very nervous, but here soldiers had the opportunity to criticize shirkers and even managed to convert some into fighters.[154] These characters were also a part of a larger effort to define themselves. René Des Touches recorded a moment in his diary when he was preparing to go on leave and was getting cleaned up. The other soldiers teased that if he went too far, he would look too much like an *embusqué*. They also debated the need to remain "hairy" which coincided with one meaning of the word *poilu*.[155] The soldiers found themselves negotiating a web of representations, attempting to determine their identities.

The same was true for the image of the *poilu*.[156] While the trench newspapers and many memoirs used the word "poilu" repeatedly and usually unself-consciously, the French soldiers also talked about their extreme distaste for the Parisian representation—the glorious *poilu*, happily facing death, seen on stage in Rip's revue *1915*.[157] In July 1915, a trench newspaper printed a Parisian composer's "Deux poilus," which showcased two heroic and comedic *poilus,* vermin-like Germans, and dancing cannons. But some notable changes were made to the text. In the verse in which one *poilu* declared they were both willing to die, for example, the word "delighted" was removed.[158]

But try as they might, the soldiers had great difficulty making much headway among civilians, a problem we will examine in the next chapter. The soldiers' patience for any home-front views had withered by April 1917, when *Le Crapouillot* wrote scathingly of the Paris products, "How many ultra-heroic, silly, stupid, sentimental, or simply sickening vulgar compositions. . . . It is to these jokers that we owe the idiotic caricature of the bearded, disheveled, ridiculous 'Poilu' who makes war a sport . . . singing and dying satisfied, a smile on his lips."[159] Unfortunately, April was to prove a particularly deadly month for soldiers, and would set off even more serious critiques.

Songs expressing soldiers' despair or disillusionment did not appear in great numbers until 1916 and 1917, and the deterioration of morale was not a straight decline. Soldiers' feelings toward the war rose and fell, often tied to certain victories and defeats, changes in commanders, and their occupation of different sectors.[160] But from January 1917 into May, morale slid precipitously. Serious dissent appeared with calls for a discussion of France's war aims and the possibilities of an early peace. In mid-April, General Nivelle received approval to launch a huge offensive at Chemin des Dames, even though other military leaders advised against it. During the campaign, the French suffered 271,000 casualties and within two weeks mutinies began.[161] One soldier recalled leaning against a wooden post toward the beginning of the debacle reciting to himself Déroulède's lyrics: "Forward! Too bad for those who fall."[162]

Despite all of the army's efforts to use music to promote *esprit de corps,* collective singing was also an important part of the rebellion among the troops. In the massive mutinies during May and June, soldiers refused to march or fight, but did not try to fraternize with or inform the enemy.[163] Most of the actions took place in zone B, or behind the lines, away from the trenches. Here, the soldiers found an "audience" comprised of both common infantrymen and the higher ranks. Thirty to forty thousand soldiers took part in the "collective acts of disobedience," when specific songs expressed soldiers' bitterness with unforeseen intensity and helped instigate further dissent.

At this moment, a prewar repertoire of subversive vocabulary and symbols resurfaced, as the mutinous troops now sang the "Internationale" and waved red flags.[164] Contemporaries reported the repeated singing of the workers' anthem as a tactic to show the mutineers' dissatisfaction, anger, and even loathing of the high command. Its lyrics called for joint action by workers and peasants, and even encouraged the shooting of generals.[165] Pétain's memo, outlining the insurrections for Paris officials, described one incident on May 20 where a unit "ran through the streets singing the 'Internationale,' ransacked the house of the camp's commander, and sent out three delegates charged with bearing their demands." On May 29, the general reported, "the regiments which are supposed to begin marching, are demonstrating, [they] form a procession and sing the 'Internationale,' while shouting 'We won't go up [the line]! "We won't go up!'"[166] Repeatedly, soldiers held demonstrations, shouted their complaints, shot in the air, and challenged officials. Some officers also sang the worker's anthem with their men, as the group "hurled calls to revolt and to strike."[167] Guy Pedroncini, in his comprehensive study, showed how the singing of the "Internationale" appeared in diverse units, used by mutineers who came from all backgrounds and parts of France. The French revolutionary song tradition was not strictly a Parisian tradition, and the mixing of troops encouraged its spread.[168] The past history of the "Internationale" had to have increased the authorities' fears—for the song had been a centerpiece of the antimilitarist campaign against the army throughout the fin-de-siècle period. Thus, the sound of the song signaled disaffection and insult. It also mobilized other soldiers to join the mutinies, and a high number of participants was vital for safety and success in the face of military authorities. Troops communicated with gestures, signs, and tunes. One memo, for example, described how mutinous troops being transported, "continued their excitement and tried to influence troops whom they met in passing: they made obscene gestures . . . they whistled, sang the 'Internationale,' waved pieces of red material, threw scraps on which they had written down their refusal to attack. And they incite their comrades to do likewise."[169] Others sang seditious songs from trains as they returned from leave in early June.

The soldiers' most critical grievance focused on the high command's offensive strategy, where thousands of men were sent over the top without the necessary artillery preparation or reinforcements. Highlighting this discontent, the mutinous troops involved were those that had had to participate in the disastrous battles of April and now refused to remount the line into the trenches. However, the soldiers also had numerous other complaints about their material condition, their lack of leave, and their pay compared to that of factory workers. Singing expressed these dissatisfactions.

Lyrics from 1917 show the bitter side of the soldiers' feelings toward all of the highest military leaders:

Jean de Nivelle nous a nivelés	Jean de Nivelle has leveled us
Et Joffre nous a offerts à la guerre!	And Joffre gave us to the war!
Et Foch nous a fauchés . . .	And Foch has flattened us . . .
Et Pétain nous a pétris . . .	And Pétain has kneaded us . . .
Et Marchand ne nous a pas marchandés	And Marchand has not bargained with us
Et Mangin nous a mangés!	And Mangin has eaten us.[170]

A government committee discovered only later how aggravated troops were with commanders such as Mangin.

Few new songs, however, were written openly, since when authors could be identified they were severely punished. The music historian, Robert Brécy, has uncovered the arrest of an itinerant singer in June for peddling hundreds of different songs at the front.[171] In the *colporteur*'s inventory was the disheartening song "Tragique ballade des tranchées," which strikingly illustrates the desperate feeling in May as well as the shifts in the soldiers' feelings from 1914 to 1917. The song began by nostalgically describing elements of prewar life: romance, affection, hope, desire, and "amoureux." Before the war, "Our hearts were full of pleasure / Our eyes were mad with desires." Then the 1914 mobilization occurred and good fortune granted a victory on the Marne, but "the cunning Boche dug into the earth." The bard could only counsel patience, while one suffered in silence.

By the third refrain, though, the real war intruded, with cannons, killing, and propaganda that "inebriated" the participants and convinced them of the appropriateness of their violence:

Pas de pitié pour les victimes.	No pity for victims.
Tuer des boches n'est pas un crime,	To kill boches isn't a crime,
On va ivre de poudre et de sang	One goes out intoxicated by gunpowder and blood
C'est la ballade des combattants.	This is the ballad of the combatants.

By the final verse, the soldiers were trapped, confronted by the enemy's artillery and left to bury endlessly their "copains" (buddies). The song ended with "la ballade des massacrés," emphasizing the savage and indiscriminate killing of all soldiers. The war had become both brutal and senseless, and the romance of the first refrain was now warped. This text, along with others, shows the soldiers' awareness of the propaganda campaigns, lending a vague political cast to its message. But the composer also implicated the soldiers themselves, a relatively rare indictment.

The most famous song written during the mutinies was "La Chanson de Craonne," which was sung especially by the infantry with the words modified according to a particular unit's location[172] (Craonne was at the heart of the April fighting and the subsequent mutinies). Front-line infantry soldiers had borne the brunt over the course of the war and had the most serious gripes. "La Chanson de Craonne" represented the starkest possible contrast to any song in the Paris repertoire because of its desperate and bitter tone, its sense of division, and its sentiment against peace by victory, at any cost. The "Chanson de Craonne" ironically employed a melody from a café-concert romance song "Bonsoir m'amour"; the lilting tune in 3/4 time created a counterpoint to its sharp lyrics. Its bleak refrain intoned:

Adieu la vie, adieu l'amour,	Farewell life, farewell love,
Adieu toutes les femmes.	Farewell to all women.

. . . .

C'est à Craonne sur le plateau,   It's at Craonne on the plain,

Qu'on doit laisser sa peau;   Where one must leave his skin;

Car nous sommes tous condamnés,   Because we are all condemned,

Nous sommes les sacrifiés.   We are the sacrificed.[173]

The war was no longer glorious or heroic but "infamous" and sordid; the soldiers were being sent to their deaths as sacrifices of the civilians within the government. The idea of the sacrificed painted the image of a religious war or machine in which random numbers of men were given up.

The third verse also delineated very clear grievances about Paris, with references to "the grand boulevards," "fat cats," "those men," and "property owners":

C'est malheureux d' voir sur les grands   It's miserable to see on the grands
   boul'vards   boulevards

Tous ces gros qui font leur foire;   All the fat cats who are living it up;

Si, pour eux, la vie est rose,   If, for them, life is a bed of roses,

Pour nous, c'est pas la mêm' chose.   For us, it's not the same thing.

Au lieu de s'cacher, tous ces embusqués   Instead of hiding, all those shirkers

F'raient mieux d'monter aux tranchées   Would do better to go up to the trenches

Pour défendr' leurs biens, car nous   To defend their goods, for we have
   n'avons rien,   nothing,

Nous autr's, les pauvr's purotins.   We others, the poor destitute.

Tous les camarades sont enterrés là,   All the comrades are buried there,

Pour défendre les biens de ces   To defend the property of those men.
   messieurs-là.

Anti-*embusqué* sentiments again appeared, reflecting wartime divisions. But the reference to defending property echoed prewar accusations from the worker and antimilitarist movements. This was especially true since the song included lines about how the soldiers were being forced to die for "Those who are rolling in dough." Here also, with a threatening tone, the "privates" pointed to an enemy within France.[174]

Mais c'est fini, car les trouffions   But it's done, because the privates

Vont tous se mettre en grève.   All begin to strike.

Ce s'ra votre tour, messieurs les gros,   It will be your turn, mister big shot,

De monter sur l' plateau,   To go up to the plain,

Car si vous voulez la guerre,   Because if you want the war,

Payez-la de votre peau!   Pay for it with your hide!

These clear class references and the song's call for a strike paralleled the situation in many French cities, where close to three hundred thousand men and women participated in strikes in 1917.[175] The text, however, remained abstract enough that most infantrymen could use it.

Unable to identify the lyricist, the government offered a reward for information about the song's origins and threatened to punish anyone caught singing it. One account described its being taught and sung in a café.[176] First one soldier requested it, and then everyone joined in on the first refrain. The singing began quietly as the soldiers sang about experiences through which each one had lived. When the last verse arrived with accusations against "messieurs les gros," the chorus became more aggressive, with the soldiers articulating their anger and frustration. The use of this piece during the mutinies highlights the subversive nature of the soldiers' performances and texts. Even with the government interdiction, the song was easily passed along within the spreading insurrections.

One compelling aspect of the mutinous soldiers' complaints clearly targeted the "scandalous" behavior of Parisians. Some of the units wished to march on Paris to clean it up and to join with other dissenting groups. As Pétain noted, the soldiers "no longer wanted to have to kill, when shirkers in the interior earned money, drove around in cars with women, took all the jobs, [and] when so many profiteers got rich."[177] Another lieutenant colonel went so far as to argue that "the principle cause of the rebellions, the one which, in my opinion, triggered the revolt, was the scandalous conduct of the rear." He also claimed that civilians had "forgotten their saviors and had let a life of pleasure go on whose echoes reached the front, greatly exaggerated. But soldiers on leave verified them with their own eyes when they had the chance to benefit from the short and rare leaves."[178] Indeed, one combatant had recorded in his notebook, after returning from a leave in 1917, his fear that since civilians could enjoy themselves despite the war, it might continue without end: "civilians weren't worried. The war could last, the rear would hold; the cinemas and *cafés-concerts* all operated. The boutiques overflowed with merchandise."[179]

Faced with the mutinies, the government took serious actions to restore confidence and discipline. Pétain reestablished morale with the help of the United States Army's arrival, but he also used "a repression that was at times paternal, at times merciless."[180] The repression included 3,427 convictions, with 554 mutineers given the death sentences, and 49 executed.[181] The deputies in parliamentary secret sessions tried to sort out what had happened and whether the punishments had been fair; one case centered on two soldiers who were prosecuted "for incitement to disobedience by way of songs." One officer had claimed that the lyrics sung had been

"perfectly innocent," and "could not have provoked the disobedience"—
and the soldiers were acquitted. The commanding general of the 37th
Corps argued just the opposite, however, believing that those involved
should have been condemned to death. Unfortunately, the titles of the
songs were not recorded in the parliamentary debate and the final result
was not clear. What is unmistakable is that gestures and lyrics of protest
presented a serious, potentially deadly issue, since these actions helped define disobedience and treason.[182]

Notwithstanding the penalties, the vocalized complaints did realize some
positive wide-ranging results. Pétain, having come to power in mid-May,
instituted strategic, material, and ideological changes. The high command's
tactics shifted away from its costly offensives, which had relied heavily on
manpower, toward a greater use of heavy artillery, and Pétain assured the
combatants that lives would not be wasted. He also set about improving the
soldiers' material lives with better food and more consistent leaves.

Many members of the general staff and, most especially, Pétain also
blamed the mutinies on a revolutionary contagion from the interior. In the
5th Division, for example, the high command argued that a seditious con-
spiracy had to have caused the insurrections, since troop morale had been
supported by professional performances and sports. As one memo explained, "this division [the 5th] has been the object of many considerations:
it has had access on *repos* to theatrical performances by professional
troupes, to real food supplements, [and] to the creation of sports teams, especially for football."[183] According to the military's longstanding philosophy, this should have been enough. As a result, army officials insisted that
Parisian authorities take greater repressive actions against any signs of pacifism. Pétain himself required better surveillance of mail between combatants and civilians, tighter regulations for soldiers going to Paris, and additional information on Parisian newspapers and their subversive
activities.[184] In the army zone, tougher measures were also instigated. Pétain ordered the confiscation of suspicious songs, and found examples that
castigated the ruling powers and incited troops to revolt.[185] In the eyes of
military leaders, a culture of resistance now linked Paris to the trenches—
fulfilling their worst nightmare.

One final remedy changed the conduct of troop rest periods. Pétain
made it clear that soldiers were to be given complete rest to begin with after
they came out of the trenches, followed by exposure to carefully supervised
amusements. He placed the commander in chief (of the rest camps) in
charge of providing "sports practices and the organization of assorted entertainment, such as the 'théâtre aux armées,' in order to contribute to the
physical rest of the men and to their moral relaxation *[détente morale]*."[186]

Authorities had not given up on professional entertainment, as evidenced by a flurry of army memos. Improvements for rest periods required a refurbishment of the French system of canteens and train stations, and the expansion of the Théâtres du Front.[187] If good morale demanded a healthier environment and more amusements, the army had decided to take the necessary steps.

A large part of the historiographic debate surrounding World War I has focused on the question of how men could live under such terrible circumstances and not give up. In the French case, one should not underestimate army discipline and the system of punishment.[188] Soldiers themselves recognized its power, sometimes resorting to the metaphor of a "theater of war" with cynicism. An article entitled "Un concert sur le front" appeared in *Le Gafouilleur* to mark Bastille Day in 1917. A soldier described being trapped between Wagner and Saint-Saëns, while providing "receipts" for the "management" in the form of German prisoners.[189] The war effort, however, also depended on patterns of living or surviving, and one must recognize the soldiers' own mechanisms within such a large army. What sort of cultural sphere the soldiers occupied or created was complicated. Combatants developed a subculture opposite the home front that was to offer purer, virtuous nationalism, and authentic voices. Although the popular culture was nourished by the segmented minute-by-minute contact among soldiers, it was not completely isolated. And this arrangement fed and undermined the subculture. It was most prevalent in the front trenches, but soldiers spent only a portion of their time there. They also moved across geographic spheres, inhabiting different parts of the army zone where their homogeneity was diluted by the higher ranks and by civilians. The whole of the army zone was also a recognized bureaucratic unit and soldiers referred to themselves as being in the army. But army command often resembled the home front more than the soldiers. Combatants also went on leave, which encouraged their sensitivity to home-front regions.

Moreover, while the subculture became identified with a limited and spatially confined population, which helped create local idioms, the soldiers' popular culture was also made up of elements of the larger, broader culture. Combatants were still imbricated in older practices and forms, and aware of the home front's power to set standards and create new representations. Soldiers found themselves caught between focusing on their immediate environment and face-to-face relationships while trying to remain a part of larger communities, either of fellow *poilus* in other sectors, or of the larger national community. Thus, the subculture was not impermeable nor did the dominant culture dominate—until the soldiers sought a voice in Paris.

CHAPTER EIGHT

The Reinternationalization of Mass Culture and the Turn to Nostalgia

By 1918, France had lost close to one million men, Russia had dropped out of the war, and the Americans had joined the allies. The French decision to stay the course held, however, as did the popularity of musical entertainment. And police censors still patrolled the borders of appropriate expression. But the war years of 1914–1918 should not be viewed as a single cultural period in Paris. Where the earlier years of 1914–1916 had seen an aggressively stringent nationalism, 1917–1918 saw an apparent return to the internationalism of the prewar years. A conspicuous influx of foreigners, especially Americans, reinternationalized Paris's population, and many music establishments responded to the new audiences. In many ways, the *années folles,* usually associated with the 1920s, began in 1917, well before the war ended. These developments led to nationalist anxieties and the roots of a defensive nostalgia for the Belle Époque.

In this period, the capital also faced a worsening standard of living and serious grievances, voiced by both soldiers and civilians. But the Parisian cultural matrix proved to be accommodating and well protected, which put it in a powerful position to determine representations. Musical entertainment contributed to Paris's ability to absorb criticisms by offering an arena in which complaints could be expressed and negotiated. When the sharpest dissenting voices burst forth in May 1917, they appeared in the less restrained public streets, not in *cafés-concerts* or music halls. But with the arrival of the Americans in June 1917, the French government found new ways to reinforce the prowar ethos of 1914. This final chapter investigates the ways in which the capital city dealt with dissent or unhappiness, first from civilians and then from soldiers, and how, in the process, it wrote the recipe for postwar culture well before the Armistice.

The Voicing of Grievances

The Parisian entertainment world proved to be both dynamic and exceptionally adaptable in the face of difficult and unexpected conditions. Patriotism led performers to new audiences, such as convalescing soldiers, and new stars rose to the occasion. When attendance fell in Paris, due to restrictions on coal for example, troupes transported sets and costumes from "room" to "room" to find an audience. In 1917, Henri Fursy reportedly traveled from his Parisian Boîte à Fursy across France and then back to the Parisian suburbs. For one performance in the *quartier* des Batignolles, fifteen hundred people, described as workers, *petits bourgeois,* soldiers on leave, and mothers with children, crowded in.[1]

Songwriters and their audiences chose to persevere by condemning or laughing about the restrictions and inconveniences in Paris. These songwriters had always excelled at such satire, and no subject was too sacred or removed from possible ridicule, except when censors' rules intervened. They made fun of the crowded metro, the lack of taxis at night, the loan drives, and military officers' "tough assignments" to attend galas. Even the Spanish influenza, which began to kill hundreds of people a week in the summer of 1918, received its own song, "La Grippe Espagnole," as well as a character in a musical revue. The song "Les Horreurs de la guerre," a very popular piece in mid-1917, complained about every tax imaginable that contributed to the high cost of living. This included men suffering when their "girlfriends" "raised their prices" or "took away credit." These were the "horrors of the war!"[2]

The public obviously wanted to hear the complaints and the jokes. A performer asked the audience at one of the performances of the Boîte à Fursy troupe for a subject with which to improvise. "Hundreds" called out "coal," the problem of the day, and the result was "furiously applauded." At the cabaret La Lune Rousse in 1918, after entreating the crowd not to volunteer a political figure, Fursy also asked for a topic, and they gave him "the tobacco crisis." According to the police informant, the improvised song drew loud hoots of laughter from the crowd.[3] A newspaper columnist astutely noted this process of shrugging off a day's aggravations with a night's entertainment. "The brave young woman who, in the morning, exhausts herself standing in line at the coal merchant's door, in the evening laughs at the time's austerity. Is this not one of the best ways to console oneself? It is our practice."[4] With a paternalist tone, the observer went on to propound the healthy aspects of humor and camaraderie.

These songs held the Paris community together by letting people share mutual problems. Complaining made them feel better, especially when the songs described people even worse off or kidded those caught whining about the wrong thing. Lyrics also complimented civilians on their toughness, and described Paris as "still smiling." These sentiments represented a continuation of the "normality" created in 1914–1915, and were part of a slew of songs and revues which celebrated how wonderful Paris was.[5] The earlier intensely nationalist phase helped make these much more chauvinist. They were still about Paris civilians' forbearance, and the censors' continuing cuts kept any social politics from appearing. Complaints could not be by one class against another.

Musical *artistes* offered laughs and encouragement, but they also negotiated the difference between good and bad civilian behavior. Ridicule of armchair warriors appeared over and over, and composers warned against gossip, too much self-importance, and even against war profiteers.[6] "Si j'étais un riche de la guerre" by the cabaret singer Mauricet was approved in February 1918, for example, and contained a critique of those owning munitions plants who could afford to think only of themselves. Unlike the "true French," they could go to all the chic restaurants and revues at the Folies-Bergère "like Americans."[7] One song even suggested that civilians should take a "leave" at the front to see the "real war."[8]

By early 1918 many theater owners were astonished with their success, only to face one final trauma—the German bombing of Paris during their spring offensive. Some theaters closed and then reopened, and bigger theaters suffered from the bourgeois flight from Paris and the cancellation of soldiers' leaves. But music halls and *cafés-concerts* now symbolized wartime normality, and the show had to go on. Thus, when in the spring and summer of 1918 bombs were falling at unpredictable intervals, people attended performances even with nightly alerts, and theaters were not necessarily evacuated. On March 11, for instance, an air alert sounded at 9:10 P.M., after all the programs had started. Mistinguett and Maurice Chevalier continued their revue at the Casino de Paris without interruption, and other theaters simply informed their audiences that the establishments had excellent "caves" (shelters). At the Comédie-Française, the actor Silvain delivered an aside in the middle of his monologue, saying "They tell me there's an alert. We continue, naturally."[9]

Even with cannon fire clearly audible in June and July, one police informant remarked on the crowded theaters and restaurants. Another reported that Paris had "no special countenance . . . ordinary life has recommenced or there about. We traverse one of those moments when it seems that the population has 'settled into the war' and awaits the end with confidence."[10] The original decision to continue "a normal life," established back in October and November 1914, had been both crucial and long-lasting. Parisians had learned to create at least the appearances of normal life, which included attending performances.

The Soldiers' Criticism in Paris

Stronger voices of dissent, both military and civilian, did exist, however. And civilians could not define their role by themselves in Paris. Soldiers had strong, distinct views, including bitter feelings of betrayal.[11] But before 1919 they did not have an easy time getting unrestricted voices heard in Paris. And when they did, their expressions had to mix with a wartime culture of civilian pride and complicity. This is a very important consideration in determining the power of specific representations. Some soldiers sent songs back to Paris to have them published in local papers. Maurice Doublier, for example, who had been in the workers' singing group La Muse Rouge, sent songs back to *Le Bonnet rouge*. But to get a hearing, they still had to deal with the Parisian censors, who guarded visas for performances closely. Since not all combatants' songs intended for Paris were negative, some were welcomed. "Ça! C'est la Perme!" by Paul Gonnet ("Brigadier au 105e d'Artillerie") and Ed. Brunswick ("Caporal au 138e d'Infanterie Territoriale") offered a very positive portrait of soldiers' time on *repos* and especially on leave, when they got to make up for lost time and make a "small new Frenchman." It received a visa in 1918.[12] There is no indication, however, that combatants received especially positive treatment. F. L. Bénech, a well-established Parisian composer who was mobilized as a *médecin aide major*, asked for a special review by the prefect for four of his songs.[13] The prefect reviewed all four but gave only two visas.

Some of the soldiers' specific complaints were picked up for Paris consumption. "L'Odyssée du permissionaire" presented the disappointing itinerary of one *poilu* who could not get a meal at a restaurant before five o'clock and had to settle for a nonalcoholic drink while he watched a woman have "three vermouth grenadines."[14] P. F. Stello's "Impressions de permission" also described an infantryman's frustrations when his sweetheart complained about his beard, and neighbors wondered why the army could not advance against the Germans. The *poilu* simply encouraged them "de t'nir" (to hold), since the soldiers needed their support.[15]

Marcel Dambrine's "Huit heures du soir" provides an excellent example, however, of the confrontation between a mobilized songwriter's biting critique of civilians and the censor's power. Throughout the fourteen verses, the song alternated between three different scenes all beginning at eight o'clock one evening. The first setting was in Paris, where a crowd headed for the Olympia and the Folies-Bergère. In the second, a widow sat with her son in a cold room praying for her dead husband, while in the third a *poilu* stood watch somewhere in the trenches. The figure attending the music hall was a *monsieur* who smoked a cigar, laughed, and sang; when the theater let out at eleven o'clock, the civilians complained about the cafés not being open—but said simply, "C'est la guerre!" The widow, meanwhile, held her son close while contemplating her husband's agonizing death. At eleven o'clock, the *poilu*, having spent the evening in freezing mud, was shot, and died a martyr. And, at the same time, in the very last verse, the bourgeois gentleman got into a warm bed and wondered when his hard life in Paris would end. Despite the fact that Dambrine had credentials in the Parisian musical entertainment community, once the song reached the city's censors it went no further. The prefect rejected it in March 1917.[16] The song illustrated the soldiers' intense feelings of betrayal, but the strongest of these sentiments could not permeate Parisian culture.

One of the only ways soldiers did get a "voice" was when certain soldier-songwriters returned from the front to initiate a critique from the stage. Augustin Martini was one of the best known of those who returned. After having been wounded at Verdun in 1916, Martini came back to Paris and became a regular *chansonnier* at several of the Montmartre *cafés-concerts*. In his song "Le Gai chanteur," he attacked "armchair warriors" and, more pointedly, Théodore Botrel for encouraging troops to march off to war, while he stayed at the "back":

Le bon chanteur a dit à ceux d'partout:	The good singer has said to those everywhere:
—Je suis d'tout' mon âme avec vous	—I am with you with all my spirit
Jusqu'au bout!	Until the end!
. . . .	. . . .
Mais l'choeur des poilus	But the choir of *poilus*
C'coup-ci a répondu:	Has retorted to him:
—Prends ton fusil Grégoire,	—Take your gun Gregoire,
Nous ne sommes pas des poires,	We are not suckers,
Prend ton fusil pour voir-e,	Take your gun to show us,
Tu chanteras après.	You will sing after.[17]

This represented a very sharp attack coming from a performer who had fought. Martini reinforced his criticism by using the tune of "La Paimpolaise," one of Botrel's prewar hits. The song was performed at Le Perchoir in December 1916, and as Martini toured Parisian cabarets, enthusiastic crowds welcomed him. He was soon getting top billing, and because of his military record, Parisians seemed willing to hear the criticisms. One theater reviewer remarked:

It's Martini they wait for. There is a small shudder in the audience, then silence. We know few examples of equal authority. . . . This wounded [soldier] of Verdun has new courage to plant himself before them while meting out justice to his colleagues. . . . They cheer him, they detain him. But go hear him. This is a new man.[18]

The censor chose to allow his criticism, finding some level of redress helpful.

All of this reveals a certain nervousness surrounding rebukes of Parisians. Did soldiers have the authority to judge civilians? Or did civilians have the right to evaluate the *poilus*? Neither could afford to ignore the other. Parisians kept themselves informed, collecting details about the soldiers' subculture. One source of news came from columns on the "theater in the trenches" in several major papers.[19] The critic Guillot de Saix regularly reviewed soldiers' musical revues or reported on specific performances. He commented on the combatants' ingenuity and patriotism, and related some of their criticism of Paris. In some cases, however, Saix seemed anxious about the soldiers' satire, observing that they faced far less censorship than civilians, and that at times patriotic content was lacking. But he also reassured Parisian readers that none of the revues went too far.[20]

These columns provided some of the recognition that soldiers sought. But they applied Parisian standards or values. One newspaper noted the prominent role of both amateurs and professionals, but was most interested in those who had been part of the Parisian theater world before the war.[21] Paris also set standards and broke down the separateness of the soldiers' community by holding a contest to judge the best songs, poems, and trench newspapers by combatants. The winning pieces were then performed in Paris.[22] The program illustrates the civilian effort to "understand" the trenches. It began with a piece called "Méditations dans la tranchée" and included others entitled "L'Arrière et l'avant" (The rear and the front) and "Je préfére le front" (I prefer the front). Trench culture was transposed into Paris, transformed in particular by the fact that most of the performers were women. This reinforced the image of the home front as feminine.

Taking pride in the Théâtre aux Armées, civilians also continued their own mission to entertain the troops. *Le Journal* organized a fundraiser for the Théâtre aux Armées at the Opéra in December 1916. The list of contributors in the program made up a virtual who's who of Paris, beginning with the president of the Republic. Reflecting the continuing prowar ethos of 1914, the program (fig. 33) was decorated with the handwritten melodies and words for the "Marseillaise," "Sambre et Meuse," and the "Chant du départ."[23] More generally, there was a certain self-congratulatory tone.

Figure 33. Back cover of program for Théâtre aux Armées, in Paris, December 1916. Courtesy of the Bibliothèque Nationale de France, Paris.

Newspapers describing the effort often began with the idea of the Théâtre aux Armées helping out the *poilus,* and ended with applause and accolades for the organization.[24] But there was also a tension surrounding the project, which sparked defensiveness. One particular article noted that the initiative had not been "unanimously praised. Some people [had] judged it untimely and somewhat futile."[25] In response, two performers, Cécile Sorel and Beatrix Dussane, tried to set the record straight, describing the hard work and poor conditions. It was not, Dussane pointed out, a party or a "picturesque excursion." What really mattered was "to make a connection, agreeable and affectionate, between this disparaged *[décrié]* 'rear' and the mysterious 'front.'"

Let us look at just one specific example of the tug of war between cultures, and how the home front took up soldiers' ideas, and forced them to respond. In chapter 7, we saw how argot helped define the soldiers' community, and early in the war one of the popular nicknames for their wine was *le pinard*. An army engineers' 1915 revue had soldiers complaining to members of Parliament about a lack of *pinard*, and, early on, Paul Clérouc had great success with his "Valse du pinard."[26] Further, a letter to the *Bulletin* in 1916 explained how a song about *pinard* represented a sign of the true trench culture, since "true soldiers" had a predilection for it.[27] Paris had also taken notice by 1916, and the concept began to appear at *cafés-concerts* in songs such as "Le Vrai pinard" (the Real Pinard) and "Le Père pinard" (the Father Pinard) and as a character in revues.[28]

For soldiers, the term and concept then lost its original value, and they turned away from it. An article in the trench newspaper *Marmita* from October, 1917 explained that true soldier-performers did not "exalt *le pinard* which is celebrated *back there* by composers who, with feet by the fire and sheltered from the bombs, have never drunk it."[29] Their parodies complained not just about ugly "Madelons," but also about expensive, diluted *pinard*. But Paris persisted. The rejection by the soldiers did not change the musical representation Parisian entertainers wanted to promote. The enormously popular revue *Laisse les tomber* of December 1917 included "Le Roi du pinard" (the king of the pinard) and the revue *Phi-Phi* which opened in November 1918 at the Bouffes-Parisiennes included a scene toasting *pinard*.[30] This operetta would run uninterrupted in Paris until November 1921.

May 1917 and the Return of the Repressed

If the sharpest dissenting voices could not be heard in the *cafés-concerts* or music halls, in contrast to the prewar period, where could they be heard? In May 1917, widespread demonstrations and labor strikes broke out in the streets of Paris, threatening the government's stability. This was the one place that saw a temporary return to the prewar's oppositional repertoire and practices.

In the Parisian streets of 1914, crowds had expressed the *union sacrée* with hallowed national anthems and fitting revanchist tunes. The atmosphere of August 1914 had called for a laying aside of working-class rhetoric, symbols, and practices, which were deemed divisive and thus harmful during wartime. The socialist anthem the "Internationale" disappeared. In 1915 and 1916, no May Day ceremonies or big marches took place.[31] May 1917 marked a sharp disjunction, and a link between prewar practices and the street demonstrations of the interwar years. By early 1917, the accumulated weight of the war was straining national morale. The battle of Verdun had resulted in horrendous losses, while consumer prices, whose climb had previously been softened by wage increases, exploded in the spring of 1917.[32] Just as frustration grew and then spilled over into flagrant disobedience in the trenches, workers expressed their grievances in Paris by turning to their radical musical repertoire.

The demonstration began on May 1 with a call to construction workers to stay away from work.[33] Attendance at trade meetings swelled, and according to one police report, "As they [the workers] left the hall, cries of: 'Long live peace! Down with war! Down with the Republic!' mingled with the chanting of the 'Internationale.'"[34] The workers then started for the Place de la République, while "a crowd intoned revolutionary songs . . . in great excitement. Once again there were cries of 'Down with war! Long live peace!' and even 'Long live Germany!'" This reappearance of powerful working-class symbols like the "Internationale" combined with antiwar slogans shocked officials and illustrated the gravity of the situation. These cultural signs reintroduced visible class divisions forbidden by the *union sacrée*. Like Pétain and his officers, Parisian officials knew the history of these expressions. The singing reformulated a community that could reject the war effort. The customary use of protest songs offered an alternative repertoire — a culture of resistance.

Throughout May and into early June, the demonstrations escalated.[35] One of the most visible groups on strike, two thousand *midinettes* (clothing workers) demanded the English week (of five and a half days) and fair wages. Carrying English flags, the seamstresses took to the streets, boisterously singing:

Et on s'en fout	We don't give a damn
On veut la s'maine anglaise	We want the English week
Et on s'en fout	We don't give a damn
On aura nos vingt sous.	We will have our twenty "sous."[36]

Their banners pointedly demanded "Return our husbands to us," and they did not hesitate to threaten violence against the bosses or replacement workers. These workers were willing to take the serious step of putting their needs above the requirements of the war, and like their predecessors in the nineteenth century, they chose to protest by creating a musical spectacle.[37] Faced with the strict censorship of printed material and police interference with public meetings, these women knew that their street demonstrations gave them the most effective way to gain support and to pressure the government to meet their demands.[38] By early June, the demonstrations clogged the thoroughfares of Paris, and compelled the prefect to send out special troops.

Meanwhile, despite all the excitement, the music-hall and *café-concert* programs for May and June 1917 were remarkably unaffected, a notable change from the prewar situation. At the large *cafés-concerts,* there were few or no references to the growing turbulence in the streets, as massive strikes spread.[39] These indoor performances—in which police could more effectively manage the choice of lyrics and threaten troublemakers—remained shielded from politics, as performers sang the patriotic "Le Père la victoire" and "Verdun on ne passe pas" (app. figs. 7, 11, and 12).

The strikers' spectacle forced the government to act decisively to prevent further danger. Authorities suppressed news and photographs of street activities, and put pressure on employers to negotiate with their workers.[40] Military authorities, meanwhile, posted signs telling soldiers on leave to avoid "mixing in any public demonstrations." All of this pushed the radical repertoire out of earshot and off the front page.

The government leaders also found more positive steps to divert attention from the labor crisis. Most especially, they arranged a warm welcome for the American troops on July 4, 1917, and Parisians turned out with flags and patriotic songs. Some tunes were American, reflecting an internationalization of the streets. The success of this demonstration was not lost on officials. Georges Clemenceau, who became prime minister and minister of war in November 1917, understood the benefits of public spectacles and participatory patriotism. And as part of his reintensification of the war effort, he worked to manage urban space and crowds, especially in the last months of the war and early 1919. In the meantime, the music halls followed the cue and began catering to the new audience.

Les Années Folles? 1917–1918

In 1917, the Americans' arrival offered new spectators and new enthusiasm, foreshadowing the tourism of the 1920s. By early 1918, some *cafés-concerts* were turning people away, and by October 1918, anticipating the Armistice a bit, the Folies-Bergère had both matinees and nightly shows every day.[41] Many historians have pointed to the boost in military power that the American troops gave the weary French, but the nurturing of civilian morale may have been just as important, especially since American soldiers did not see active duty for quite a while.

By this point in the war, music halls were showing less dependence or insistence on purely French things, and the last two years saw a reinternationalization of both content and form.[42] The spread of American themes, characters, drinks, dances, and performers occurred all over, but was most prevalent in the large halls. The bigger establishments hired "jazz-bands," which specialized in John Philip Sousa marches, cakewalks, and ragtime.[43] And some places returned to the prewar practice of printing programs in both French and English. In the revue *Kiss me, ma Poule!*, Madame Satan and Don Juan introduced audiences to American dances such as "Le Rag de Californie," "Le Goly-wog," "La Danse des prairies," and "La Valse de New-York." In another revue, a tableau called "A Boudoir Vision" included the characters the *Harvard Girl*, the *Columbia Girl*, the *Priceton* [*sic*] *Girl*, the *Cornelle* [*sic*] *Girl*, and so on.[44]

This shift was not just to American forms. It also marked a return to the British model of luxurious revues. Most featured variety acts, sumptuous costumes, and big dance numbers with chorus lines of "les girls." The revue *C'est Paris! Gay Paris!*, for example, offered thirty-five tableaux, six hundred costumes, and two hundred performers. Many places advertised the high number of extravagant costumes, but they also included some nudity. The columnist Guillot de Saix described a revue at the Théâtre Femina in January 1918, with effusive detail: "The new revue . . . is an explosion of sumptuous extravagance with plumes, silks, brocades, beaded tulles, gold fringe, crepe, appliqués."[45] Revues had moved a very long way from the purposeful austerity of *Paris quand même* in December 1914.

Some newspaper reviews were positive, but others expressed growing anxiety over this "invasion," as it was called at that time. In October 1918, a British revue, *Zig zag*, was transported from London with its American stars, English musical director, and "precision" chorus line, or as one newspaper column insisted on explaining:

The managers of the Folies-Bergère have just imported a revue, called Zig-Zag. It has come from London. The artists and dancers come from London. The props come from London. The music comes from London, and the author, although he is named Albert de Courville, is English. Only a few dresses are from Paris—and these are obvious.[46]

One critic called the revue "a brilliant show, in the British formula"; another hoped that going to such a show would allow him to "see more clearly the soul of the English soldier." But others were much more ambivalent. These revues were clearly different and not necessarily better. Compared to the "improvements" that had come with the nationalization process of 1914–1915, these revues lacked a narrative, one reviewer bemoaned; random scenes were just meant to show off costumes and legs.[47] Critics also disliked having to go look up the word "producer," only to find there was no French word for it, and they celebrated the fact that the Little Palace reopened in early November 1918 with a "perfectly French name," L'Arlequin.[48]

Finally, in September 1918 the Folies Marigny presented a revue by Edward Perkins, in what was billed as the "First and Only American Theater in Europe." It offered tableaux of well-known Parisian streets, such as the "Rue de la Paix" and "Outside Maxim's," as well as offering "A Spelling Lesson" with the song "M-i-s-s-i-s-s-i-p-p-i."[49] The critics were clearly frustrated with not understanding the English, and suspected the worst. They argued that although the United States was helping to win the war, Americans still had much to learn.[50]

The reviewers treated this internationalism as if it were a new problem. Few seemed to remember the prewar period's common use of other languages on programs or the international variety acts. Wartime Paris again represented a border of France, but this time it was the British and Americans invading. Critics admitted that Paris was being packaged or "represented," and recognized that this had been true earlier as well. What they deplored was that the picture was wrong. The earlier 1914–1915 promotion of "Paris" for Parisians, and of Paris as quintessentially French was at risk. As one put it, referring to a revue called *C'est Paris,* "It is Paris, obviously. But Paris, this is *something else* again." Moreover, even if an American producer thought he could imagine prewar Paris, the revues had that wrong, too. The French were clearly worried about losing control of the representations of themselves. And their response was more negative, since they believed that in the early war they had gotten it right.

One other important phenomenon appeared in 1917 and 1918 that contributed to imagining Paris and the transition to the 1920s: the invention of "le couple." With so many young men having died, the model of a glamorous, happy couple fed amorous fantasies. The first was the celebrated pair Maurice Chevalier and Mistinguett, followed by Gaby Deslys and Harry Pilcer. Each pair had elaborate revues built around their partnership and drew attention both on and off the stage. This phenomenon stood out against previous wartime conditions. For most of the war, performances relied heavily on female performers, and men on stage were often suspected of being shirkers. This only got worse after Georges Clemenceau launched his campaign against *embusqués* in early 1918. Chevalier, after having been wounded in 1914 and enduring two years in a prisoner-of-war camp, had returned to Paris in 1916.[51] For his first performances, the billboard carefully disclosed: "Wounded in the war, Returned prisoner of war."[52] He was a perfect follow-up to Augustin Martini, although he was to make his mark in the very biggest music halls. With all the right credentials—a veteran who had served in a camp, a young male, and someone who knew enough English—he stimulated great interest, as he began his climb to international fame. At the beginning of 1917, he became partners with Mistinguett, and they toured numerous music halls including the Bataclan, the Casino de Paris and the Folies-Bergère as "le couple."

The relationship furthered prewar developments, since Chevalier and Mistinguett had been paired together earlier. But it was only in 1917–1918 that they became the model couple. In many ways, they represented the transition the music entertainment industry itself made during the war. They had both come from relatively modest or poor backgrounds and had begun in the less respectable *cafés-concerts,* and the war gave them a new purpose. They did not just represent *les gamins,* or colorful lower-class Parisians, they personified French "popular culture" in a mass cultural form and on an international level. And this popular culture was now much more nationalist than socially political. Chevalier of 1918 had very little in common with Aristide Bruant, Gaston Montéhus, or Théodore Botrel of 1913.[53]

Emulating Chevalier and Mistinguett's huge success, the extremely successful wartime director Léon Volterra opened the extravagant revue *Laisse les tomber* on December 11, 1917, with fifty tableaux at the refurbished Casino de Paris. It starred Harry Pilcer and Gaby Deslys, who was fresh from a tour in the United States. Deslys set about popularizing the jazz band, ostrich plumes, the boys, and the grand staircase.[54] American officers recommended the show to their colleagues, and large crowds of soldiers and officers waited patiently to get in.[55] Receipts for the Casino de Paris rose astronomically from 247,147 francs in 1916 to 1,054,753 francs in 1917, finally reaching 4,085,164 in 1918.[56] The formula was so successful that by late January 1918, other performers were playing "Gaby Deslys" and "Chevalier," with the celebrities themselves in the audience.

The shift toward an encyclopedic, cosmopolitan program was less noticeable in the small cabarets, partly because of their reliance on language, verbal jokes, and a small, mostly French, audience. La Chaumière even advertised on its poster (in French) "Revue, shadow play, songs. N.B.: we don't speak English."[57] These places had established a strong following with their wartime attention to French popular culture. In 1918, one commentator argued for their importance, "Laughter disarms. That's why la Butte continues to give its war cry . . . The songsters dash off songs, while the Boches want to hogtie the World!"[58] This critic also made a pointed reference to the "truly French spirit" of the performers, who continued to defend "Frenchness." The internationalization of the big halls was condemned, as were the changes in the revue genre. The British form lacked imagination, critics complained, especially with the tendency to recycle tableaux. Although they now differentiated themselves from the larger music halls, until 1917 *cafés-concerts* and cabarets had had much in common with music halls. All of them had been transformed by the war and its nationalism, and had faced the censors' efforts to depoliticize musical entertainment. Though the *cafés-concerts* and cabarets claimed to be maintaining the "popular culture" of the Belle Époque, those claims were just as problematic. Anxieties over representations of Paris and the invasion of foreigners haunted both arenas, and both helped create a nostalgia for prewar Paris.

Even with the internationalization and the new audiences, the revues of 1917 and 1918 in the larger music halls still had patriotic pieces, although less often. Few tunes dealt specifically with soldiers in the trenches, although the characters of the *marraine* and *poilu* remained popular. By 1918, Paris had apparently learned enough about "combat." But revues and songs were still very interested in Paris in wartime, which now involved a much larger cast of international characters. But because this was still wartime, militarism and nationalism remained tightly intertwined.

The Last Moments of War

Nationalist militarism had been an important part of the prowar ethos from its start in August 1914, and the government had worked to keep it healthy. This was true not just in enclosed entertainment spaces, but also in the streets of Paris. The early war years had seen a host of special events honoring weaponry (the 75 mm guns) and specific military classes, using patriotic songs and symbols. The problems of May 1917 only made them redouble their efforts. Then in November 1917, Georges Clemenceau became prime minister, and he brought with him a renewed promotion of the war. He began a new attack on any form of pacifism, expanded searches for shirkers, and supported the public trials of traitors. He also paid greater attention to the possible powers of propaganda and spectacle.

The best example of Clemenceau's efforts came in October and November 1918, and illustrated the magnetism and maturity of the martial culture. As the end of the war approached, the government worked to keep the population going and hoped for a smooth transition to peace. Although Parisians had many reasons to be happy, France's victory was potentially Pyrrhic, with 1.3 million deaths and 130 billion francs consumed.[59] In addition, the country was in the throes of the deadly flu epidemic with reports of seven hundred new cases per day. Clemenceau's October and November festivities helped maintain stability at the end of a debilitating war.[60]

In late October, officials decided to take advantage of the fervor surrounding the liberation of the towns in the east, and launched the fourth loan drive of the war by redecorating the center of Paris with an immense display of captured enemy military equipment and multicolored flags and posters. Crowds had already been decorating the statues of Strasbourg and

Lille in the Place de la Concorde and reaffirming their patriotism with re-vanchist lyrics. A carefully arranged parade, accompanied by military bands positioned along the route, moved from the Invalides to the Hôtel de Ville, passing machine guns, tanks, and planes. A massive crowd (seven-to-eight-people deep) thronged the parade route despite a steady rain.[61] With collection booths set up at cannons and in airplanes along the Champs-Elysées, the public was encouraged to transform their cheering into concrete financial support for the war and the political regime.[62]

By Armistice day, the patriotic rituals had gained a strong following, as people massed in front of government buildings or at the central market, making optimistic declarations, and singing patriotic music. November 11 dawned with fair weather, and symbolic demands dictated that the war should end at the eleventh hour of the eleventh day of the eleventh month. At that moment, the bells rang out and cannons were fired at the Invalides. The fêtes occurred at multiple locations. Workers, including *midinettes,* and soldiers willingly sang the patriotic anthems the "Chant du départ" and the "Marseillaise" as well as the wartime *café-concert* favorites "Quand Madelon," and "Le Père la victoire"—an older belle époque tune that had become a salute to Clemenceau. The general public was now very well versed in such songs. New songs appropriately entitled "Le Retour" and "La Délivrance" also had big sales. This differed sharply from May 1917, when both combatants and workers had sung the "Internationale." Instead, these groups were reintegrated into the national culture, at least for the moment. The festivities also had an international side as British, American, and French soldiers helped improvise parades. Revelry continued long into the night as the boulevards were illuminated for the first time since August 1914.

Both the French government and the Parisian population chose the public repertoire of symbols and music over the course of war. But there was a continual tension between government management, the musical establishments' negotiated patriotic role, and civilians' own spontaneity. While the government needed to encourage the participation of the general public, the malleability of cultural forms such as song texts opened up subversive possibilities. But in this war, few times and places for dissent existed, as the state increased its coercive powers. During the most serious challenge to the government's prowar position, workers had found creative ways to voice their demands, throwing into question their attachment to the cause and reestablishing an identity outside of the *union sacrée.* In response, however, the government had strengthened its own active propagation of French nationalist, military rituals, while the censors continued their tight control over legitimate language and actions.

In November 1918, it was impossible to occupy an alternative cultural position. Parisians' improvisations were shaped in part by learned rituals, as a carefully promoted, wartime culture prevailed, a culture that made most societal divisions invisible and temporarily masked the horrendous price of the triumph. The celebration focused on the victory and the regime's leaders, especially Clemenceau, Foch, and Pétain, and the spontaneity of November 11 even included a mixture of soldiers and civilians, covering over the deep resentments that had grown up between these two groups. The notion of unity and sense of accomplishment, however, would be short-lived, and the possibilities for dissent would reappear after the joy dissipated. In fact, May 1917 had foreshadowed the street battles of the interwar years, while representing a unique moment in the context of wartime culture.

Conclusion

⤎

Questions regarding how to define soldiers and civilians as well as how they each should be judged are not particular to World War I; they plagued the entire twentieth century. When and how should one honor soldiers for risking their lives for a greater good, and when should soldiers be held responsible for their acts of violence? Were civilians helpful, patriotic, or defeatist? These issues shaped the representations and debates between 1914 and 1918 in France, and the documents I have relied upon are full of judgments. Parisians were accused of forgetfulness or of ignorance with regard to the trenches, while mutineers and strikers faced serious court proceedings. People found ways to understand and cope, but in the process they judged each other. And throughout the war, a struggle ensued over representations—of individual's identities (as soldiers or civilians), of their communities, and of the nation. All sorts of people expressed their ideas and feelings musically with varying volume and tone.

Part of what has come down to us in the memory of this war is the sharp polarity between civilians and soldiers, but we have seen other divisions as well. Parisians saw their portion of the home front as unique, and common soldiers never confused their trench with military headquarters. Some people stressed a front and rear split. But when civilian performers, for instance, claimed they had been to the "front," the soldiers corrected them, distinguishing between the front trenches and an area behind the lines. But soldiers also underlined their sense of distance from civilians. They developed their own popular culture, within which they could define themselves as "true *poilus*." The development of two separate cultures, however, one on the home front and one in the trenches, never reached a point where the two were mutually exclusive, and if one looks at participants, audiences, or rules, more than two cultural zones broke down the simple dichotomy. The trenches were not akin to the entire army zone; Paris did not embody the entire home front—even though some representations purposefully presented it this way. People also had overlapping identities between their prewar lives and roles as combatants or civilians. A classically trained musician took up both the cymbals and stretchers, or a trumpet and a gun.

French officials confronted a particularly delicate situation, since soldiers were often close by or in Paris. They carefully divided French territory into the army zone and the rear with checkpoints between, and they tried to control where soldiers could go on leave. In the representational sphere, though, an image such as the *poilu* was created and shaped by both Paris and combatants with some interaction between the two. And this book has been most interested in that communication—the support, frustration, or criticism voiced by individuals as part of larger discussions.

In their sharpest critiques, however, soldiers could affect the power of such a representation as the *poilu* only tangentially while the war continued. In the end, it was Parisian culture that dominated, with important implications for the period of the war and for postwar France. This power came, in part, from the strength and adaptability of its mass cultural industries, where *cafés-concerts,* music halls, and newspapers held center stage. But it was also because Parisians had their own "war experience," which involved an intricate martial culture and their own sense of sacrifice. The bombing of Paris in the spring of 1918, which made Parisians a military target, only strengthened these sentiments. The Parisian representations were so compelling that criticisms arising from some civilians, and more especially the soldiers, could be absorbed or deflected. Even after the war, when soldiers returned, their images, memories, and judgments mixed into a larger cultural blend affected by the home front's prowar ethos.

An important part of this ethos was the process of strident nationalization that began immediately to reshape cultural content in 1914. Older "popular" forms and practices such as the *cafés-concerts* and singing— which had previously been attacked by some as sordid and unworthy of France—were now deemed quintessentially French and necessary, national attributes. The music industry's influence and popularity stemmed from its maturity and its drive for respectability based on a patriotic stance. The war occurred with perfect timing, given the industry's powerful means of dissemination, the experience of the directors and managers, the celebrity status of many performers, and their older average age, which kept many from conscription. As the war continued, Paris also claimed a larger and more important audience than the fragmented front, with attendance fueled by rising wages, a high level of employment, and the presence of soldiers, both French and allied, on leave or in transit.

This nationalization also saw the mixing of elite, popular, and mass cultures with possible long-term effects. By popular mandate, the classical music repertoire had to respond to the demands of war, for example by excluding German music. One result was that as elite culture became nationalized and politicized, there was an increased fluidity of the borders between "classical" music, performers, and theater pieces and more "popular" stars and songs. Particular conditions of the war shaped the interplay, including the need to be, or at least appear to be, patriotic, the intensity of Germany's image as the enemy, and a suspicion of individual commercial motives. Moreover, although some of this fluidity was occurring before the war, it was the extreme nationalism of the war that encouraged officials to embrace as truly French a sanitized version of the *cafés-concerts* repertoires. This mixing also occurred in the army zone, but there it was because of the sociological makeup of the military as well as the propensity of soldiers to share their music.

The purifying nationalization predominated in Paris in 1914–1916. By 1917–1918, musical entertainment shifted back toward an internationalism that resembled prewar forms and practices. It responded to an international audience (albeit mainly of soldiers) with a return to grand revues. But the entertainment industry's passage through the earlier war period had done two things. First, it had taken some of the "popular" out of the "popular culture," because of the censors' project to clean up the *cafés-concerts*. Thus the projections of Paris culture and the "little guy," which became a part of Maurice Chevalier's international reputation in the interwar years, were significantly different from what had existed before 1914. And, second, the intense nationalism made Parisians suspicious of the return to internationalism—some critics even refused to recognize the fact that it was a return. Commentators regretted the loss of what they saw as French characteristics—a talent with language and a willingness to satirize the system—or in a word, French *esprit*. They recognized that, as the writer E.-G. Gluck put it in May 1918, "the public has changed! . . . One must please, not only Parisians, but also the allies."[1] Here, the elements of a nostalgia for the Belle Époque took form in 1917 and 1918, well before the Armistice. The "invasion" of tourists and of things American or British was not just about exciting *nouveautés*. Something else in the national identity was at stake. Interestingly, this nostalgia for "another time which already seems fabulous to us," in Gluck's words, came to be shared by the soldiers, who, in rejecting Parisian wartime representations and values, had created their own more traditional and conservative idea of what they were fighting for—their families, *foyers*, and a deeply rooted France. Thus members of both groups, soldiers and civilians, had reasons to find nostalgia appealing.

Towards the end of the war, Georges Clemenceau acted as a bridge between soldiers and civilians, answering combatants' concerns with his hunt for *embusqués*, for instance. And his acts reflect some of the lessons learned by the government over the four years. He championed the martial culture, encouraging traditional leftist patriotism and organizing the celebrations of weaponry. The viability of the Parisian wartime culture—with its well-established institutions of communication and sociability (all reshaped by the government's censors) and its portion of optimistic, amusing, and even bellicose representations—helps us to understand the continuing political and cultural status of Clemenceau, Ferdinand Foch, and Philippe Pétain. Despite the wartime criticism aimed at profiteers and "les gros" (big shots), elders such as Clemenceau were not denigrated. This stands in contrast to the severe attacks on the British generals Haig and French, or the German distaste for their civilian leaders.

During and after the war, performers and songwriters also held tight to the idea that entertainment had done its share to win the war, and other contemporaries agreed. While the French government may have lagged behind in its support, French society and certain individuals had argued that entertainment was indispensable, and the paying public had supported that position. It is extraordinarily difficult to evaluate individuals' motives for attending concerts or to comprehend how the music was experienced, but one can analyze the attendance and the content. Wartime productions were not simply a product of a tight-knit industry forcing a certain repertoire on its audiences, nor was it just an industry reflecting its audiences' ideas. During the war, Parisians chose entertainment that temporarily helped to suspend problems—the amusements were participatory, positive, and creative. Furthermore, a crucial emphasis was placed on the reformulation of the Parisian community at a time when the capital became a busy transit spot for thousands of people, and audiences were reassured and encouraged. However, censorship also warped the contours of what could be expressed, and a prowar mentality aided the hunt for *embusqués* and demanded civilian participation and devotion.

By 1918, the most prominent figures in the music industry, along with the government, believed they had found a formula to assure wartime morale, and when the next war broke out in 1939, professional troupes went to entertain the boys. Marc Bloch, in his classic text *Strange Defeat,* spoke of the French fighting the last war over; he talked of military strategy and class cultures. Along the same lines, in the fall of 1939, the military handed out songbooks and revived the Théatres du Front. In June 1940, however, the Germans succeeded in capturing Paris, and Hitler ordered the reopening of the music halls. Under dire but very different circumstances, the biggest stars, including Maurice Chevalier, performed for the sake of Parisian morale, following in their own footsteps.

APPENDIX A

Examples of Sheet Music

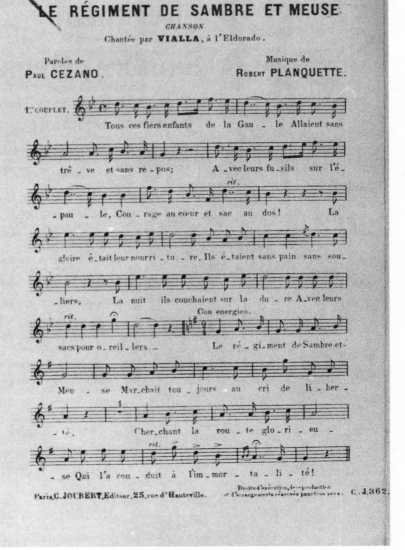

2

Pour nous battre ils étaient cent mille,
A leur tête, ils avaient des rois!
Le général, vieillard débile
Faiblit pour la première fois.
Voyant certaine, la défaite,
Il réunit tous ses soldats,
Puis il fit battre la retraite,
Mais eux, ne l'écoutèrent pas!

Le régiment de Sambre-et-Meuse *etc*.

3

Le choc fut semblable à la foudre,
Ce fut un combat de géants,
Ivres de gloire, ivres de poudre,
Pour mourir ils serraient les rangs!
Le régiment par la mitraille
Etait assailli de partout;
Pourtant la vivante muraille
Impassible, restait debout.

Le régiment de Sambre-et-Meuse *etc*.

4

Le nombre eut raison du courage,
Un soldat restait; — le dernier!
Il se défendit avec rage,
Mais bientôt fut fait prisonnier.
En voyant ce héros farouche
L'ennemi pleura sur son sort;
Le héros prit une cartouche,
Jura — puis se donna la mort!

Le régiment de Sambre-et-Meuse
Reçut la mort au cri de liberté;
Mais son histoire glorieuse
Lui donne droit à l'immortalité!

Paris, CAVEL Frès grav. imp. Fg St Denis, 1e.

Nouvelle adaptation *en DUO* ou *à une voix* (ad libitum)
(Créée par Mr et Mme DUPENEY de Chantloup,
dans tous les Concerts)
Sur les *motifs complets* du défilé national.
Piano et Chant, net 3f; petit format 0,50c

2.

Figure App. 2. Songsheet, "Français, toujours debout!" Courtesy of the Préfecture de Police. All rights reserved.

_bout! Ce n'est pas as_sez de l'Al _ sa _ce. C'est

quand le Rhin se _ra Fran _ çais, Que nous fe_

_rons si_gner la paix!__

2
Qu'un froid rictus trousse ta lèvre,
Apprête la griffe et la dent;
Que, dans tes yeux, brûle la fièvre
De l'ardent combat qui t'attend!
Tu sais qu'a ton foyer demeure
Celle qui jamais ne faillit...
Elle a compris qu'il faut qu'on meure,
La Française, pour son pays!
au Refrain

3
Le képi campe sur l'oreille,
Le sac te paraîtra léger;
Ton cœur contient cette merveille:
Le mépris complet du danger.!
Partout on sifflerons les balles,
Tu te dresseras sous les cieux,
Et tu nargueras les rafales,
D. un gai refrain de tes aïeux!
au Refrain

4
Fier de ton droit et de ta force,
Par la tourmente et dans le vent,
Face à l'Allemand qui s'efforce,
Clame ton terrible : "En avant."
Puis te lançant dans la fournaise,
Sous les plis flottants du drapeau,
Tout en hurlant la "Marseillaise"
Tu te feras crever la peau!
au Refrain

Imp. LEDOYEN
J. BRESSON Suc!
39 Rue St Antoine
·PARIS·

THIBAULT Sœurs

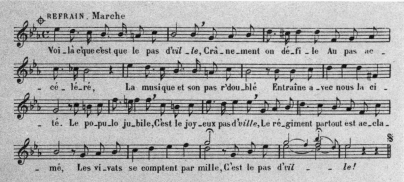

REFRAIN. Marche

Voi_là c'que c'est que le pas d'vil _le, Crà_ne_ment on dé_fi_le Au pas ac_cé_lé_ré, La musique et son pas r'dou_blé Entraîne a_vec nous la ci_té. Le po_pu_lo ju_bile, C'est le joy_eux pas d'ville, Le ré_giment partout est ac_cla_mé, Les vi_vats se comptent par mille, C'est le pas d'vil _ _ le!

2

Un fois dans les champs, si la route est belle,
Aprés un moment d'pas accéléré,
Le colon nous fait mettr' l'arme à la bretelle,
Puis vient le pas d'*route* qui met en gaîté.
Afin d'rigoler viv'ment on s'dégrouille
A s'interpeller par des noms d'oiseaux :
_Dis donc, l'abruti ?_Qu'est-c'que t'as, andouille?
_Râclur' de pied d'singe!_Ta gueule, eh! fourneau!
    Avanc' donc, boul' de son,
    Ne train'pas la savate
    Ou bien j'te casse un'patte,
    Espèc' de cornichon !
    La musique on ne l'entend plus,
    Alors, pour s'entraîner on chante :
    Les sapeurs sont des homm's poilus!
    La cantinière est épatante !
—(Pour la musique des 4 vers qui suivent,
    voir au Grand Format le N° 2 .)—
    C'est l'brosseur du capiston
    Qui vient d'lâcher un'perle,
    C'est l'brosseur du capiston
    Qui vient d'tirer l'canon !
        REFRAIN
Voilà c'que c'est que le pas d'*route*,
    Gaîment on casse un'croûte
    En arpentant l'chemin .
On blague, on s'chine entre copains,
En braillant en chœur un refrain .
    C'est l'grivois que l'on goûte
    En étant au pas d'*route*,
Ça fait rougir les filles du pat'lin ;
On march' quand mêm' coûte que coûte,
    C'est le pas d'*route!*

3

C'est surtout au feu que nous sommes à l'aise
Là nous retrouvons le plus beau des pas ,
L'étranger l'appelle la *furia* française ,
C'est l'chant national guidant les combats .
C'est en lettres d'or, nous apprend l'histoire ,
Que nos pères l'ont gravé autrefois
Dans le grand sentier que l'on nomm'«la Gloire»,
C'est l'pas d'charg' qui fit trembler tous les rois
    Quand, au feu, sacrebleu,
    On sent l'odeur de poudre
    On part comme la foudre
    Dans un élan furieux !
    La baïonnette est un jouet
    Dans les mains du pioupiou de France
    Mais si quelqu'un nous attaquait
    Avec elle il f'rait connaissance .
—(Pour la musique des 4 vers qui suivent,
    voir au Grand Format le N°3 .)—
    L'enn'mi s'trouv'sur l'plateau, là-haut ,
    Il guette, il nous attend ,
    C'est sa position qu'il nous faut ,
    Hardi! serrons les rangs!
        REFRAIN
Voilà c'que c'est que le pas d'*charge*,
    Qu'importe la décharge
    Des fusils, des canons ?
Quand s'élancent nos bataillons
Dans la plaine ou sur les mam'lons ,
    L'ennemi fuit au large
    Devant le pas de *charge*
Qui fait enl'ver les fortes positions .
Tout est fini , la route est large !
    C'est le pas d'*charge!*

Mᵉʳ Roy.Grav.17 rue des Panoyaux,Paris .

Paris. CAVEL ᵉᵗᵉˢ, grav. imp. fg St Denis 14.

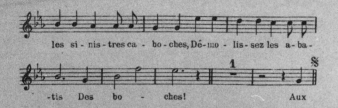

les si - nis - tres ca - bo - ches, Dé - mo - lis - sez les a - ba - tis Des bo - ches! Aux

2

Aux accents du Chant du Départ,
A ceux de notre Marseillaise,
Vous prenez une large part
En préludant...à la Française!
Et quand se mêlant au concert,
La voix du "soixant' quinze" monte,
Tous les "Pruscos" crèvent de honte,
Car c'est plus fort que du Wagner!

au REFRAIN

3

Pour la France et pour ses Alliés,
Pour la Liberté, pour la Gloire,
Tournez donc, moulins à café
Pour la Paix...après la Victoire!
Jetez au charnier, au tombeau,
Ces barbares, semeurs de haines,
Pour qu'au jour des moissons prochaines
Nos blés soient plus forts et plus beaux!

au REFRAIN

Grav. Imp. CAVEL, F^{res}, 18, F^g St Denis, Paris.

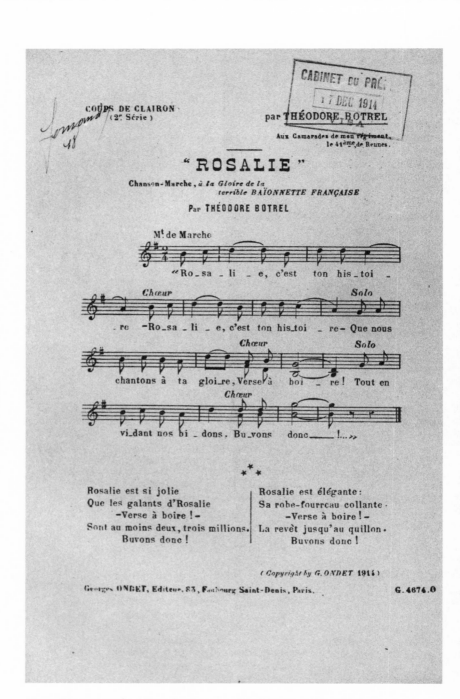

Mais elle est irrésistible
Quand elle surgit, terrible,
  –Verse à boire !–
Toute nue : baïonnette..en ! [1]
   Buvons donc !

Sous le ciel léger de France,
Du bon soleil d'Espérance.
  –Verse à boire !–
On dirait le gai rayon.
   Buvons donc !

Elle adore entrer en danse
Quand, pour donner la cadence,
  –Verse à boire !–
A préludé le canon.
   Buvons donc !

La polka dont ell' se charge
S'exécute au pas de charge,
  –Verse à boire !–
Avec tambours et clairons.
   Buvons donc !

Au mitan de la bataille
Elle perce, et pique, et taille,
  –Verse à boire !–
Pare en tête, et pointe à fond.
   Buvons donc !

Et faut voir la débandade
Des mecs de Lembourg et d'Bade,
  –Verse à boire !–
Des Bavarois, des Saxons.
   Buvons donc !

Rosalie les cloue en plaine :
Ils l'ont eue, déjà, dans l'aine....
  –Verse à boire !–
Dans l'rein bientôt ils l'auront.
   Buvons donc !

Toute blanche elle est partie,
Mais, à la fin d'la partie,
  –Verse à boire !–
Elle est couleur vermillon,
   Buvons donc !

Si vermeille et si rosée
Que nous l'avons baptisée :
  –Verse à boire !–
« Rosalie » à l'unisson.
   Buvons donc !

***

Rosalie ! sœur glorieuse
De Durandal et Joyeuse,
  –Verse à boire !–
Soutiens notre bon renom.
   Buvons donc !

Sois sans peur et sans reproches,
Et, du sang impur des Boches,
  –Verse à boire !–
Abreuve encor nos sillons !
   Buvons donc !

Nous avons soif de vengeance.
Rosalie ! verse à la France
  –Verse à boire !–
De la Gloire à pleins bidons !...
   Buvons donc ! »

[1] *Formule militaire du Commandement de* "BAÏONNETTE AU CANON !"

Figure App. 6. Songsheet, "Le Rêve passe." Courtesy of the Préfecture de Police. All rights reserved.

_rons! E_cou_tez! Re-gar-

-dez Les vo_yez-vous ___ Les hus-sards, les dra-gons la gar_de, Ils

saluent tous L'empe_reur qui les re_gar_de. Et dans un

2

Et dans un pays clair, où la moisson se dore
L'âme du petit bleu revoit un vieux clocher..
Voici la maisonnette où celle qu'il adore,
Attendant le retour, tient son regard penché..
Mais tout à coup douleur!..il la voit plus lointaine
Un voile de terreur a couvert ses yeux bleus!
Encor' les casques noirs! l'incendie..et la haine!
　　　Les voilà!. Ce sont eux!..

　　　　Les voyez-vous
　　Leurs hussards, leurs dragons, leur Garde
　　　　　Sombres hiboux
　　Entraînant la vierge hagarde!
　　　　　Le vieux Strasbourg
　　Frémit sous ses cheveux de neige!
　　　　　Mourez tambours
　　Voici le sanglant cortège!

　　　　　Bientôt le jour vermeil
　　　　　A l'horizon se lève,
　　　　　On sonne le réveil
　　　　　Et c'est encor le Rêve!
　　　　　Les Géants de l'an deux,
　　　　　Sont remplacés par d'autres
　　　　　Et ces soldats joyeux,
　　　　　France..ce sont les nôtres.

　　Blondes aimées, il faut sécher vos yeux!

　　　　　　Ecoutez!
　　　　　　Regardez!
　　　　　　Vos amis
　　　　　　Les voici!
　　　　　Les voyez-vous
　　Les hussards, les dragons, l'Armée?
　　　　　Ils mourront tous
　　　　Pour la nouvelle Epopée! (al Coda ⊕)

⊕ CODA

Epo_pé_e. Fiers enfants De la ra_ce

Maestoso rall.

Sonnez aux champs! ___ Le Rê_ve pas_se!

VERDUN! ON NE PASSE PAS

Paroles de
Jules CAZOL et Eug. JOULLOT

Musique de
René MERCIER

T° di Marcia

1er Couplet

Un ai - gle noir a pla - né sur la vil - le, Il a ju - ré d'ê-tre vic-to-ri-eux. De tous cô - tés les cor-beaux se fau-fi - lent Dans les sil-lons et dans les che-mins creux. Mais tout à coup le coq gau-lois clai-ron - ne: Co-co - ri - co, de-bout pe-tits sol-dats; Le so - leil luit par-tout le ca-non ton - ne, Jeu-nes hé-ros voi-ci le grand com-bat

plus lié

allarg.

a T° REFRAIN

Et Ver-dun, la' vic-to-ri - eu - se, Pousse un cri que portent là-bas Les é - chos des bords de la Meu-se, Hal-te là! on ne pas-se

EDITION UNIVERSELLE
52 Faub.g S.t Martin, Paris.

E. 991.i.

Figure App. 7. Songsheet, "Verdun, on ne passe pas." Courtesy of the Préfecture de Police. All rights reserved.

pas...Plus de mor-gue plus d'ar-ro-gan-ce Fuy-ez bar-ba-res et la-

allarg.

-quais, C'est i - ci la por-te de Fran-ce Et vous ne pas-se-

-rez_____ ja - mais. Les en-ne-

2

Les ennemis s'avancent avec rage,
Enorme flot d'un vivant océan
Semant la mort partout sur son passage
Ivres de bruit, de carnage et de sang;
Ils vont passer... quand relevant la tête
Un officier dans un suprême effort,
Quoique mourant crie: à la baïonnette
Hardi les gars, debout, debout les morts.
au Refrain

3

Mais nos enfants dans un élan sublime
Se sont dressés; et bientot l'aigle noir
La rage au cœur impuissant en son crime,
Vit disparaître son suprême espoir
Les vils corbeaux devant l'âme française
Tombent sanglants, c'est le dernier combat
Pendant que nous chantons la Marseillaise
Les assassins fuient devant les soldats.
au Refrain

Imp.GHIDONNE,23,F⁵ S! Denis,Pa.

Figure App. 8. Songsheet, "Ce que chantent les flots de la Marne." Courtesy of the Préfecture de Police. All rights reserved.

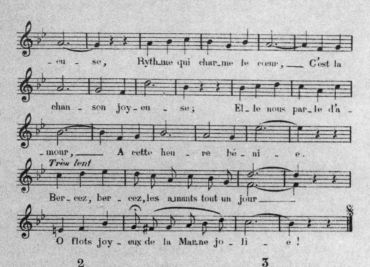

__ eu _ se, Rythme qui char_me le cœur, __ C'est la

chan _ son joy-eu _ se; El_le nous par_le d'a _

mour, __ A cette heu _ re bé_ni _ e.

Très lent

Ber_ cez, ber _ cez, les amants tout un jour _____

O flots joy_ eux de la Marne jo_ li _ e!

2

Mais certain jour, de la Marne attristée
On vit s'assombrir les jolis flots d'or,
Car l'ennemi dans un' folle poussée
Jusque chez nous osa venir encor;
Chacun connaît la célèbre bataille,
L'échec complet de leur sinistre plan,
Pourtant chez eux canons, obus, mitraille,
Se fabriquaient depuis quarant'-quatre ans.

....

Aussi quand le combat fut fini
On disait en écoutant ce bruit.

REFRAIN

C'est le chant des flots berceurs
  De la Marne rougie,
Rythme qui brise le cœur,
C'est la chanson meurtrie;
  Elle parle de combats
  A cette heure émouvante,
Pleurez, pleurez nos chers petits soldats
O flots rougis, de la Marne sanglante!

3

Puis la rivière a repris sa lumière,
Et sa splendeur, et sa gaîté d'antan
Près des parents et des bons vieux grands-pères
Les enfants jouent: c'est un tableau charmant.
Sur les genoux ils écoutent l'Histoire
De la Marne, de ses fiers défenseurs
Emerveillé par ce récit de gloire
Bébé s'écrie: Honneur à nos vainqueurs!

....

Maintenant sous l'étoile qui luit
Un murmur' monte dans l'infini

REFRAIN

C'est le chant des flots berceurs
  De la Marne rêveuse,
Rythme qui grise le cœur,
C'est la chanson glorieuse.
  Elle parle des succès
  De la France si belle,
Chantez, chantez la Liberté, la Paix;
O flots sacrés de la Marne immortelle!

Kiéfer, Grav.   Imp. Carel

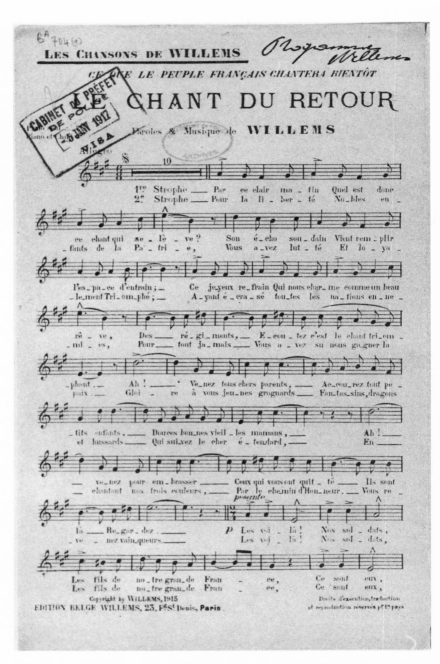

pas! On les au_ra, Ils n'pass'ront pas! Le suc_

_cès Est for_cé Pour nos ar_mes, Français! ou_bli_ons

PARLÉ (avec force)

nos a_lar_mes On les au_ra, Ils n'pass'ront pas!!

2

Depuis bientot vingt mois

L'ennemi aux abois

N'ayant pu jusqu'alors, jamais rompre nos lignes,

Dans un nouveau sursaut

Voulait, tentant l'assaut

Massacrer nos soldats par des moyens indignes.

Mais cuirassés d'airain

Nos poilus plein d'entrain

Courant sùs aux bandits, sous l'ouragan des balles,

Purent dompter le flot

Grâce à leur bon flingot

Montrant aux Allemands, qu'la France est leur rivale...

Au Refrain.

3

Ainsi que sur l'Yser

Les hordes du Kaiser

Fauché's par nos canons s'ammoncèlent sur place

Grâce à nos artilleurs

Valeureux et sans peur

Qui les prenant de flanc, les détruisent en masse

Du général *Pétain*

La France de demain

Saura se souvenir en dédicacant l'offre

De son admiration

En assemblant les noms

De *Castelnau, Maud'huy, de Maunoury, de Joffre*!

Au Refrain.

Ed. Andrieu, Grav.

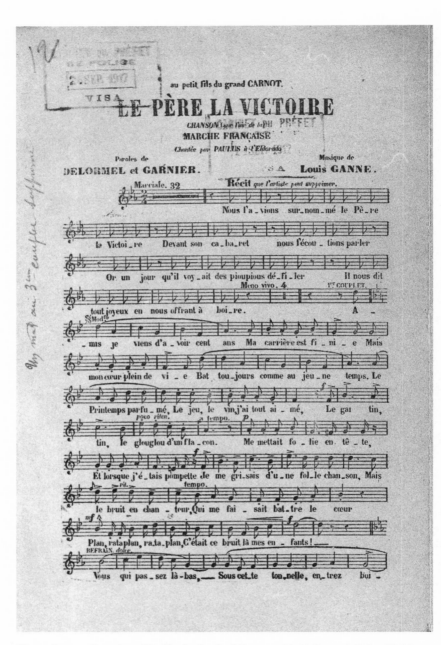

Figure App. 11. Songsheet, "Le Père la victoire." Courtesy of the Préfecture de Police.

_re, Ah!___ Bu_vez jeu_nes sol_dats Le vin du Pe_re___
poco rit. *tempo.*
la Vic_toi_re, Brillant ver_meil, Nec tar sans pareil___ Il remplit
le cœur de Vail_lan_ce,___ Vin___ de l'Es pé_ran
rit. *Marciale, 14*
_ce, Buvez en_fants Le vin de mes cent ans.___ J'ai

2

J'ai soupiré pour Madelon
Jeannette et Marguerite
Mon regard flambait vite
Dès que je voyais un jupon,
Un corsage fripon
Ou bien un mollet ferme et rond
Ma lèvre aimait fort à se reposer
Sur un joli menton rose,
C'est une bien douce chose
Que le son clair que produit un baiser
Pourtant, malgré cela
Le seul bruit qui me pinçait là,
Plan, rataplan, rataplan,
C'était ce bruit là, mes enfants.
REFRAIN.
Certes je fus aimé
Bichonné par plus d'une belle
Ah!
Corsage parfumé,
Cœur frissonnant sous la dentelle,
On m'adorait,
Rien ne me résistait
Maintenant : adieu la conquête!
C'est pour vous la fête,
Buvez, enfants
Le vin de mes cent ans.

3

J'ai vu la guerre au bon vieux temps
Quand nous faisions campagne
Là-bas en Allemagne,
A peine si j'avais vingt ans
Et ce petit ruban
J'ai dû le payer de mon sang
Pour mériter ce signe vénéré
Il fallait à la Patrie
Trente fois offrir sa vie
Oui, c'est ainsi qu'on était décoré
Alors un Soldat
N'eut pas vendu la croix d'honneur
Plan, rataplan, rataplan,
L'étoile était au plus vaillant.
REFRAIN.
Quand je vois nos soldats
Passer joyeux musique en tête
Ah!
Je dis marquant le pas
Comme jadis la France est prête
Comme autrefois
Soldats, je revois
Carnot décrétant la victoire
Marchez à la gloire
Mes chers enfants,
Revenez triomphants!

Bon

1

Ouvriers en métallurgie
Faites un colossal effort !...
Vous pouvez sauver la patrie...
C'est de vous que dépend son sort !(bis)
Allez travailler sans relâche,
En soulevant les lourds marteaux
Vos mains creuseront les tombeaux
De l'Allemand cruel et lâche !...

REFRAIN

Aux armes!citoyens!faites des munitions!
Forgeons!Forgeons!
Pour la victoire, Forgez-nous des canons!

2

Le jour, la nuit, dans les usines,
Sans trêve, sans repos, sans peur,
Faites manœuvrer les machines,
Créez l'engin libérateur !(bis)
Et pour activer vos courages,
Pensez à ceux qui sont là-bas...
Le sang de nos vaillants soldats
Vaut la sueur de vos visages !...

REFRAIN

Aux armes!citoyens!faites des munitions!
Forgeons!Forgeons!
Pour la victoire, Forgez-nous des canons!

3

Soixante-Quinze ! arme terrible !
Bijou d'acier! notre trésor!
Pour que nous soyons invincible,
N'arrête pas ! vomis la Mort !(bis)
Que le fer de nos baïonnettes
Ne se brise pas dans les mains
De nos valeureux fantassins,
A l'assaut des monts et des crêtes...

REFRAIN

Aux armes ! citoyens ! faites des munitions !
Forgeons!Forgeons!
Pour la victoire, Forgez-nous des canons !

4

Amour sacré de la Patrie
Soutiens le bras du travailleur...
C'est pour notre France chérie!
C'est pour chasser l'envahisseur(bis)
Que les cadavres s'amoncellent
Que sous des ouragans d'acier
Les bandits puissent expier
L'injustice de leurs querelles !...

REFRAIN

Aux armes!citoyens!faites des munitions!
Forgeons!Forgeons!
Pour la victoire, Forgez-nous des canons!

D'après le dessin de Lucien Métivel (Aux armes, citoyens) paru dans le Journal
du 23 Juin 1915.

Mlle Lambert grav.

Imp. L. Ghidone, 23, Fg St Denis, Paris.

Musical Establishments Open during the War

This chart provides the following information: (1) a reopening date according to the files in the Archives de la Préfecture de Police (Ba 1614); (2) the years for which receipts are given in the *Annuaire statistique de la ville de Paris, 1915–1918* (ASVP); and (3) the years for which files exist in the Rondel collection (from its *Inventoire* and files Ro 18.332 to Ro 18.490). This includes establishments from many categories listed in the *Annuaire statistique,* including theaters, *cafés-concerts,* music halls, cinemas, and *concerts d'artistes,* as long as they had either song turns or musical revues. In some cases, I have been able to indicate the *arrondissement* the theater was in.

In compiling this list, I have also relied on Parisian newspapers, André Sallée and Philippe Chauveau's *Music-hall et café-concert* and Elisabeth Hausser's *Paris au jour le jour: les événements vus par la presse, 1900–1919.* In some instances the sources do not coincide. For example, police censorship memos exist for some places for which the *Annuaire statistique* does not list any receipts. There is also some confusion caused by establishments having changed names or entertainment forms during the war. Wherever possible, I have indicated these.

	Reopening	ASVP	Rondel
L'Abri	5/1918		1918–19
Albert Ier	11/28/14	1916–18 (Th.)	1915, 1917
Alcazar Montparnasse, 14e			
Alcazar Saint-Georges, 9e			
Alhambra, 11e	4/2/15	1915–18 (M-h.)	1914
Ambassadeurs, 8e	1915	1915–17 (C-c.)	1914–17, 1919
Théâtre de l'Ambigu	3/20/15	1915–18 (Th.)	1917

	Reopening	ASVP	Rondel
Théâtre Antoine-Gemier	12/24/14	1915–18 (Th.)	1915–16, 1918
Apollo	11/25/15	1915–18 (Th.)	
Arlequin	10/18		1918
(This had been the Little Palace)			
Artistic, 11e	10/15	1918 (C-c.)	
(There was also a cinema with this name)			
Théâtre des Arts	11/4/15	1915–18 (Th.)	1917
Théâtre Athénée	11/30/15	1915–18 (Th.)	1915–16
Bataclan, 11e	12/18/14	1915–18 (C-c.)	1914–19
Bateaux-Parisiens		1918 (C-c.)	
(This became the Théâtre Lyrique du XVIe)			
Théâtre Belge			
Belleville	12/12/14	1915–18 (Th.)	
Bobino, 14e		1915–18 (C-c.)	1916
Boîte à Fursy			1917–19
Bosquet, 7e		1918 (Cin.)	
Bouffes du Nord		1918 (C-c.)	1917–19
Bouffes-Parisiens	4/6/15	1915–18 (Th.)	1918
Bruant		1918 (C-c.)	
Brunin, 12e		1918 (C-c.)	
Cadet Rousselle		1916–17 (C-c.)	1916–19
Cagibi			1915–16
(This had been the Comédie Royale, and later became the Caumartin)			
Théâtre des Capucines	10/19/15	1915–18 (Th.)	1914–19
Casino de Montmartre, 9e		1915–18 (C-c.)	
Casino Montparnasse, 14e		1915–18 (C-c.)	
Casino de Paris, 9e	3/13/15	1915–18(M-h.)	1914; 1916–19
Casino des Tourelles, 20e			
Casino Saint-Martin, 10e		1915–18 (C-c.)	1919
Caumartin			1916–19
(This had been the Comédie Royale and Cagibi)			
Le Caveau de la République		1918 (C-c.)	
(Police files have many censorship memos)			
Champs-Elysées	12/5/15	1916 (Th.)	1914
Chansonnia		1915–18 (C-c.)	
Château-d'Eau, 10e	11/14	1915–18 (Th.)	1917
(Called Concert Victoria in 1918)			
Théâtre du Châtelet	12/24/14	1915–18 (Th.)	1916

	Reopening	ASVP	Rondel
Chat-Noir		1918 (C-c.)	
La Chaumière		1915, 1918 (C-c.)	1915–19
La Cigale, 18e	2/16/15	1915–18 (C-c.)	1914–19
Cirque d'Hiver	12/19/14	1915–18 (Cin.)	
(A cinema with symphonic concerts)			
Cluny	10/20/15	1915–18 (Th.)	
(There was also a cinema with this name)			
Coliseum, 9e			
Concerts Colonne		1915, 1917 (as Concert d'Artistes)	
Comédie-Mondaine	10/15/15	1915–18 (Th.)	
Comédie-Royale		1915–18 (Th.)	1913–15
(This became the Cagibi and then Caumartin)			
Concert de Commerce, 11e			
(Police files have many censorship memos)			
Concerts du Conservatoire		1918 (as Concert d'Artistes)	
Concert Damia			
Concordia, 10e		1917–18 (C-c.)	
(Previously the Galerie Saint-Martin)			
Théâtre Dauphine			1916
Théâtre Déjazet	10/16/15	1915–18 (Th.)	1916
Théâtre des Deux Masques		1918 (C-c.)	1916
(This may have become Concert Damia)			
Théâtre Doré			1914
(This became La Lune Rousse)			
Eden, 11e (Eden-Concert)		1915, 1918 (C-c.)	
Éden-Lyrique, 20e		1918 (Th.)	
Théâtre Edouard VII	11/2/15	1917–18 (Th.)	1916
(This had been a cinema before the war, it reopened with a revue by Rip)			
Eldorado, 10e	12/4/14	1915–18 (C-c.)	1915–19
(Newspapers listed this opening as 12/18/14)			
Empire, 17e		1915–18 (C-c./Th.)	
(Previously the Étoile-Palace)			

	Reopening	ASVP	Rondel
Européen, 17e	12/18/14	1915–18 (Th/C-c.)	1916
Excelsior		1915–16, 1918 (C-c)	
(Police files have programs, 1914–17)			
Familia, 20e		1918 (Cin.)	
Fantasio, 18e		1915–18 (C-c.)	
Fauvette, 13e		1915–18 (C-c.)	
(Police files have programs, 1914–17)			
Féerique-Cinéma, 20e		1916–18 (Cin.)	
(Police files have programs with songs)			
Théâtre Fémina		1916–18 (Th.)	1914, 1917–19
Folies-Belleville, 20e	12/12/14	1918 (C-c.)	
Folies-Bergère, 9e	12/23/14	1915–18(M-h.)	1914–19
Folies-Dramatiques	12/23/14	1915–18 (Th./Cin.)	1914–15
Folies-Parisiennes, 19e		1915–18 (C-c.)	1914
(Police files have programs)			
Folies Montmartroises, 18e			
La Fourmi, 18e		1918 (C-c.)	
(Police files have many censorship memos)			
Gaîté	12/13/14	1915–18 (Th.)	
Gaîté-Montparnasse, 14e		1915–18 (C-c.)	
Gaîté-Parisienne	1914	1918 (Cin.)	
(Police files have programs, 1914–17)			
Gaîté-Rochechouart, 9e	12/18/14	1915–18 (C-c.)	1914–19
Gaîté Saint-Antoine, 11e			
Concerts Gaveau		1916 (as Concert d'Artistes)	
George V			
Gobelins	5/26/15	1915–18 (Th.)	
Le Grand Guignol	2/20/15	1915–18 (Th.)	
Concert Grande-Roue		1915–18(C-c.)	
Grenelle	12/19/14	1915–18 (Th.)	
Grévin		1915 (Th.)	
Théâtre du Gymnase	4/20/15	1915–18 (Th.)	1915–16
Théâtre Impérial		1916–18 (Th.)	1914, 1916–19
Kursaal, 17e		1915–18 (C-c.)	
Concerts Lamoureux		1915, 1918 (as Concert d'Artistes)	
Concert Le Peletier, 9e			1915
Libre-Échange, 17e (See Marjal)			
Little Palace		1915–18 (Th.)	1914–18
(This became the Arlequin)			

	Reopening	ASVP	Rondel
Luna Park			
Lune Cinema	10/3/14		
(Police files have programs)			
La Lune Rousse		1916–18 (C-c.)	1917–19
Concerts du Luxembourg		1915 (C-c.)	
Cinéma Magic-Théâtre			
Théâtre Marigny	5/8/15	1915–18 (M-h.)	1914–18
(There was also a cinema by			
this name)			
Marjal (see Libre-Échange)		1916–18 (C-c.)	
(Police files have programs,			
1915–17)			
Concert Mayol, 10e	11/28/14	1915–18 (C-c.)	1914–18
Mésange, 5e		1918 (Cin.)	
(Previously the Concert d'Arras)			
Métro, 17e			
Théâtre Michel	7/12/15	1915–18 (Th.)	1914–18
Théâtre Moderne		1915–18 (Th.)	1914–19
Théâtre Moncey	12/18/14	1915–18 (Th.)	
Montmartre		1915 (Th.)	
Montparnasse	12/5/14	1915–18 (Th.)	
Moulin de la Chanson		1915–18 (C-c.)	1914–19
Moulin Rouge, 18e	11/28/14	1915 (M-h.)	1914–15
(burned in February 1915)			
Concert des Mousquetarres			
(Police files have programs,			
1916–17)			
Noctambules		1918 (C-c.)	1917–19
Nouveau-Cirque	12/10/14	1915–18 (Cir.)	1915
(Newspapers listed this			
opening as 12/18/14)			
Nouveau Théâtre	11/28/14		1914
Théâtre Nouveau		1915–18 (Th.)	
Odéon	3/4/15	1915–18 (Th.)	
Olympia	12/4/14	1915–18 (M-h.)	1914–15, 1919
(Newspapers listed this			
opening as 12/18/14)			
Ciné-Olympic			
(Police files have programs,			
1914–18)			
Opéra	12/15	1915–18 (Th.)	
Opéra-Comique	12/6/14	1915–18 (Th.)	
Palais de Glace		1915–18 (Cir./C-c.)	
Palais du Travail	11/28/14	1918 (C-c.)	
(Police files have programs,			
1914–17)			

	Reopening	ASVP	Rondel
Théâtre du Palais Royal	4/22/15	1915–18 (Th.)	1915
Parisiana-Cinéma (and Concert), 20e			
(Police files have programs,			
1914–18)			
Cinéma-Parodi, 10e			
(Police have programs,			
1915–18)			
Perchoir, 9e		1918 (C-c.)	1916–19
Persan (Café), 4e			
(Police files have programs,			
1914–18)			
Le Petit Casino, 9e		1915–18 (C-c.)	
Petit-Palais des Champs-Elysées			
La Pie Qui Chante		1915–18 (C-c.)	1915–19
Populaire		1915–17 (Th.)	
Porte Saint-Martin	2/18/15	1915–18 (Th.)	
Poste, 7e			
(Police have programs,			
1915–18)			
Presse, 2e		1915–18 (C-c.)	
(Became Palmirium)			
Théâtre des Princes			1916
Programme Enthoven			
Quat'z' Arts		1917–18 (C-c.)	1916, 1918–19
Théâtre Réjane	1/30/15	1915–18 (Th.)	1917
Renaissance, 19e	2/20/15	1915–18 (Th.)	
(Police files have programs,			
1914–17)			
Renaissance Lyrique		1916–18 (C-c.)	
Concerts Rouge		1915–18 (C-c.)	
Comédie Royal			1914–15
Théâtre Royal		1918 (C-c.)	1914
Sarah-Bernhardt	4/1/15	1915–18 (Th.)	
La Scala, 10e	9/21/15	1915–18 (Th.)	1914–16
Senga, 9e		1916–18 (C-c.)	
La Sirène		1916–18 (C-c.)	1915
Splendid-Palace		1918 (Cin.)	
Terminus			
Tivoli du Gros-Caillou, 7e			
Touche		1915–18 (C-c.)	
Trianon	12/20/14	1915–18 (Th.)	
Tuileries		1915–17 (C-c.)	
Univers, 17e	10/23/14	1915–18 (C-c.)	
Variétés	11/22/15	1915–18 (Th.)	
Variétés-Parisiennes, 15e		1915–18 (C-c.)	
Variétés Saint-Charles, 15e			

	Reopening	ASVP	Rondel
Théâtre du Vaudeville	4/3/15	1915, 1917–18 (Th.)	1915–19
Théâtre du Vieux-Colombier		1918 (Th.)	
XXe Siècle		1916–18 (C-c.)	
(Police files have programs, 1914–17)			
Visions de Guerre		1916 (C-c.)	
Zénith, 20e		1915–18 (Cin./C-c.)	

Notes

❧

Introduction (Pages 1–14)

1. See Arthur Marwick, *The Deluge: British Society and the First World War* (New York, 1965), 11; Raymond Aron, *The Century of Total War* (Garden City, N.Y., 1954); Henri Bernard, *Guerre totale et guerre révolutionnaire*, 3 vols (Brussels, 1965).

2. Pierre Miquel, *La Grande Guerre* (Paris, 1983), 232–252, 244.

3. Note, also, the memoir by Léon Daudet entitled *La Guerre totale,* published in 1918. Soldiers used the term "la paix totale" in their musical revues to refer to the only suitable peace.

4. Jürgen Kocka, *Facing Total War: German Society 1914–1918*, trans. Barbara Weinberger (Cambridge, Mass., 1984); K. Burk, ed., *War and the State: The Transformation of British Government* (London, 1982); Volker R. Berghahn and Martin Kitchen, *Germany in the Age of Total War* (London, 1981).

5. Eric J. Leed, *No Man's Land: Combat and Identity in World War I* (Cambridge, 1979), x.

6. Elizabeth Kahn, *The Neglected Majority: "Les Camoufleurs," Art History, and World War I* (New York, 1984), 3–4.

7. Cf. Louis Léon-Martin, *Le Music-hall et ses figures* (Paris, 1928); Louis Roubaud, *Music-hall* (Paris, 1929); Romi [Robert Miguel], *Petite histoire des cafés-concerts parisiens* (Paris, 1950); and Edouard Beaudu, et al., *Histoire du music-hall* (Paris, 1954). Charles Rearick's recent book is an exception: *The French in Love and War: Popular Culture in the Era of the World Wars* (New Haven, 1997).

8. Paul Fussell, *The Great War and Modern Memory* (New York, 1975), ix. John Keegan also rigorously dissected the linguistic traditions of military history to show how language represented the "experience" of war. *The Face of Battle: A Study of Agincourt, Waterloo and the Somme* (New York, 1976).

9. Kahn, *The Neglected Majority*, 9.

10. Samuel Hynes, *A War Imagined: The First World War and English Culture* (London, 1990). The few texts that have looked at art and war have also dealt specifically with avant-garde painters. Theda Shapiro, *Painters and Politics* (New York, 1976); Kenneth Silver, *Esprit de Corps: The Art of the Parisian Avant-Garde and the First World War, 1914–1925* (Princeton, 1989).

11. Approximately seventy million men went into military service. J. M. Winter, *The Experience of World War I* (New York, 1989), 7.

12. In twentieth-century history, fascism often represents the irrational and exceptional political culture. But newer work has begun to examine cross-currents in fascist culture that were common to other Western democracies, such

as consumerism or internationalization. See the work of Victoria de Grazia, for example, in *The Sex of Things: Gender and Consumption in Historical Perspective*, Victoria de Grazia and Ellen Furlough, eds. (Berkeley, 1996).

13. See Claude Bellanger, et al., eds., *Histoire générale de la presse française*, vol. 3: *1871 à 1940* (Paris, 1972); René de Livois, *Histoire de la presse française* (Paris, 1965), vol. 2; Michael B. Palmer, *Des petits journaux aux grandes agences: Naissance du journalisme moderne, 1863–1914* (Paris, 1983).

14. Jacques Lethève, *La Caricature sous la IIIe République* (Paris, 1986), 5–6.

15. James Smith Allen, *In the Public Eye: A History of Reading in Modern France, 1800–1940* (Princeton, 1991), 42–43 and table A.3; Theodore Zeldin, *France 1848–1945: Taste and Corruption* (Oxford, 1980), 192, 178–199. By the turn of the century there were fifty dailies in Paris alone. Provincial political papers had four million subscribers by 1914.

16. The publication of books also increased after the turn of the century, as prices fell and popular literature benefited from mass production. See especially Allen's *In the Public Eye* and François Furet and Jacques Ozouf, *Reading and Writing: Literacy in France from Calvin to Jules Ferry* (Cambridge, 1982).

17. One must remember, however, that the number of "active readers" was considerably lower, and ability and exposure varied widely by region and class. See Allen, *In the Public Eye*, esp. ch. 2, and Harvey J. Graff, *The Legacies of Literacy: Continuities and Contradictions in Western Society and Culture* (Blomington, Ind., 1987).

18. Marjorie Anne Beale, "Advertising and the Politics of Public Persuasion in France, 1900–1939" (Ph.D. diss., University of California, Berkeley, 1991), 6.

19. On technological and substantive changes in popular imagery, see Beatrice Farwell, *The Cult of Images: Baudelaire and the Nineteenth-Century Media Explosion* (Santa Barbara, 1977), and Frances Carey and Antony Griffiths, eds., *From Manet to Toulouse-Lautrec: French Lithographs 1860–1900* (London, 1978).

20. See Ado Kyrou, *L'Age d'or de la carte postale* (Paris, 1966); and Claude Dohet, *Les Spectacles à la Belle Epoque: album de cartes postales illustrées* (Bruxelles, 1976).

21. Cf. Zeldin, *Taste and Corruption*, 41; Leo Charney and Vanessa R. Schwartz, eds., *Cinema and the Invention of Modern Life* (Berkeley, 1995); René Jeanne and Charles Ford, *Le Cinéma et la presse, 1895–1960* (Paris, 1961); Richard Abel, *The Ciné Goes to Town* (Berkeley, 1994).

22. See Vanessa R. Schwartz, *Spectacular Realities: Early Mass Culture in Fin-de-Siècle Paris* (Berkeley, 1998).

23. For this discussion, I have relied heavily on studies of oral traditions and those that juxtapose orality and literacy. Cf. Walter Ong's review of developments in this field in *Orality and Literacy: The Technologizing of the Word* (New York, 1982), as well as Jack Goody, *The Interface between the Written and the Oral* (New York, 1987) and *The Domestication of the Savage Mind* (New York, 1977).

24. Most of the current historiography on music halls and singing in France has either concentrated somewhat nostalgically on individual performers' lives and new forms of entertainment, or has studied the protest songs of the revolutionary or republican tradition. See, for example, Pierre Brochon, *La Chanson sociale de Béranger à Brassens* (Paris, 1961); Serge Dillaz, *La Chanson française de contestation de la Commune à mai 1968* (Paris, 1973); André Gauthier, *Les Chansons de notre histoire* (Paris, 1967).

25. This contrasts sharply to the "sparse linearity" associated with writing composition. See Ong, *Orality and Literacy*, 34 and 39–41. Also, see my chapter 1 for a more in-depth discussion of musical skills in the prewar period.

26. Ong. *Orality and Literacy*, 67.

27. Chandra Mukerji and Michael Schudson, introduction to *Rethinking Popular Culture: Contemporary Perspectives in Cultural Studies,* ed. Mukerji and Schudson (Berkeley, 1991), 3. The idea of "popular culture" as specifically workers' culture adds to the puzzle.

28. Ibid.

29. One finds this, for example, in Lawrence Levine's work, in which he draws a line between a broader, popular mass culture and an older, less widespread folk culture. Levine, "The Folklore of Industrial Society: Popular Culture and its Audiences," *American Historical Review* 97, no. 5 (December 1992): 1369–1399. This definition is taken up by Charles Rearick in *The French in Love and War.*

30. Ong, *Orality and Literacy.* Ong does allow for the possibility for "massive residual orality," which he argues is characteristic of Ireland, for example.

31. See T. J. Clark's discussion of the nebulous construction of the "popular" and bourgeois reactions in early Third Republic France, *The Painting of Modern Life: Paris in the Art of Manet and His Followers* (New York, 1985), 205–238, esp. 227–230 and 234–238. Also, Lawrence W. Levine, *Highbrow/Lowbrow: The Emergence of Cultural Hierarchy in America* (Cambridge, Mass., 1988).

32. For the idea that popular culture forms itself in conflict with elite culture, see Jacques Revel, "Forms of Expertise: Intellectuals and 'Popular' Culture in France (1650–1800)," in *Understanding Popular Culture: Europe from the Middle Ages to the Nineteenth Century,* ed. Steven L. Kaplan (New York, 1984), 255–273; and Stuart Hall, "Notes on Deconstructing 'The Popular,'" in *People's History and Socialist Theory,* ed. Raphael Samuel (London, 1981), 227–240.

33. One finds sharply differing views in two recent books. Charles Rearick's *The French in Love and War,* which examines the mass culture of music halls and cinema, puts the war squarely in the twentieth century, with few hints of older practices or *mentalités.* Jay Winter's *Sites of Memory, Sites of Mourning: The Great War in European Cultural History* (Cambridge, 1995) has emphasized the war's reinvigoration of "traditional" mythologies and forms such as the *images d'épinal.*

34. Cf. André Rossel, *1870: La première "grande" guerre par l'affiche et l'image* (Paris, 1970); Michel Lhospice, *La Guerre de 70 et la Commune en 1000 images* (Paris, 1965), 158.

35. Stéphane Audoin-Rouzeau, *1870: la France dans la guerre* (Paris, 1989), 320.

36. Allen, *In the Public Eye,* table A.7.

37. Peter Paret, Beth Irwin Lewis, Paul Paret, eds., *Persuasive Images: Posters of War and Revolution from the Hoover Institution Archives* (Princeton, 1992); Wolfgang G. Natter, *Literature at War, 1914–1940: Representing the Time of Greatness in Germany* (New Haven, 1999).

38. Cf. J. G. Fuller, *Troop Morale and Popular Culture in the British and Dominion Armies, 1914–1918* (Oxford, 1991), 94–110, 118–130; Fussell, *The Great War and Modern Memory,* ch. 6 especially; and my chapter 7.

39. *Le Petit Parisien* sold 1,453,000 copies in 1914 and broke all international records in 1916 with 2,183,000. Zeldin, *Taste and Corruption,* 183–184.

40. See Marie-Monique Huss, "Pronatalism and the Popular Ideology of the Child in Wartime France: The Evidence of the Picture Postcard," in Richard Wall and Jay Winter, eds., *The Upheaval of War: Family, Work and Welfare in Europe, 1914–1918* (Cambridge, Eng., 1988), 329–368, specifically 333. Huss indicates that a single card often had an initial printing of 100,000 (359). See also Serge Zeyons, *Le Roman-photo de la grande guerre* (Paris, 1976).

41. Two-thirds of them died between 1920 and 1930. André Sallée and Philippe Chauveau, *Music-hall et café-concert* (Paris, 1985), 189. Any encroachment by the cinema before the war was heavily dependent on music, stars, and settings from the stage. The French film industry, however, struggled during the war.

42. According to Pierre Carles, under the Fourth Republic, music still existed in the military, but as simple distraction and not as propaganda. He surmised "that the soldier after World War II sang less than his ancestors, less even than his ancestor from before 1939." Carles, *Des millions de soldats inconnus, la vie de tous les jours dans les armées de la IVème République* (Paris, 1982), 198. Zeldin also concluded that in the later part of the twentieth century, "Music, more than ever, has become an individual experience." Zeldin, *Taste and Corruption*, 143.

43. See Herman Lebovics's book *True France: The Wars over Cultural Identity, 1900–1945* (Ithaca, N.Y., 1992.)

44. Stéphane Audoin-Rouzeau's work has challenged those who have presented soldiers as a race apart by revealing the links which kept them at least partially within a broader national culture. Audoin-Rouzeau, *Men at War, 1914–1918: National Sentiment and Trench Journalism in France during the First World War* (New York, 1992), 135–143.

45. Back in 1977, Patrick Fridenson and Jean-Jacques Becker called for more work on the home front to "focus the spotlight upon the hidden face of this war: life at the rear, in fact, the interior front." See Patrick Fridenson, ed., *1914–1918, L'Autre Front*, Cahiers du Mouvement Social, no. 2 (Paris, 1977), 12. This call has partly been answered by Becker's own work and by the ambitious comparative project of Jay Winter and Jean-Louis Robert, *Capital Cities at War: Paris, London, Berlin 1914–1919* (Cambridge, Eng., 1997). The study of gender and women's experiences in war has also shifted attention to the "home front."

46. Fussell, *The Great War and Modern Memory*, 64.

47. See William Bouwsma's argument that "the creative interpretation of experience also shapes experience, which is only in the abstract independent of the meaning imposed upon it." Bouwsma, "From History of Ideas to History of Meaning," *Journal of Interdisciplinary History* 12, no. 2 (Autumn 1981), 288.

48. I do have the work of Laura Mason and James Johnson as a guide. Mason, *Singing the French Revolution: Popular Culture and Politics 1787–1799* (Ithaca, N.Y., 1996); and Johnson, *Listening in Paris: A Cultural History* (Berkeley, 1995).

49. But see Robert Brécy's pithy chapter in *Florilège de la chanson révolutionnaire de 1789 au front populaire* (Paris, 1978), 217–241; and Pierre Barbier and France Vernillat, *L'Histoire de France par les chansons* (Paris, 1961), vol. 8, section 3.

50. Henry Poisot has maintained, curiously, that excitement over music in the 1920s was a reaction to the fear and suffering of the war when the *cafés-concerts* were silenced for four years "except for those at the rear and in the hospitals." Poisot, *L'Age d'or de la chanson française, 1932–1972* (Paris, 1972), 138. See also Charles Rearick, *Pleasures of the Belle Epoque* (New Haven, 1985), 214–215; there, he described how the war "eclipsed the France of laughter and gaiety." Rearick includes the war in his recent work, which covers the period 1914–1945, but his interest lies less with popular singing practices and politics than with the messages of mass culture.

Chapter 1 (pages 17–41)

1. *L'Autorité*, February 26, 1911. Jean-Denis Bredin identified similar lyrics as the "Marche antisémite" in his description of antisemitic riots in Algeria in 1898. Bredin, *The Affair: The Case of Alfred Dreyfus*, trans. Jeffrey Mehlman (New York, 1986), 287. On the origins of "Ça ira," see Laura Mason, *Singing the French Revolution: Popular Culture and Politics 1787–1799* (Ithaca, N.Y., 1996), 34–60 and the introduction.

2. Archives de la Préfecture de Police, Paris (hereafter APP), Ba 1642. See also newspaper accounts in *L'Autorité*, *La Libre Parole*, and *Le Temps*.

3. The historiography on French *cafés-concerts*, music halls, and songs remains splintered and underdeveloped. Theodore Zeldin, for example, wrote two distinct, unrelated sections on "music" and "music halls"; the discussion of music halls fell under the rubric of "humor." Zeldin, *France 1848–1945 Taste and Corruption* (Oxford, 1980), 134–143, 351–360.

4. Robert Isherwood, in *Farce and Fantasy: Popular Entertainment in Eighteenth-Century Paris* (New York, 1986), 2–21, shows the centrality of street singers in the Parisian popular culture of the eighteenth century.

5. In examining the forty cartons of songs submitted to censors between 1914 and 1918 at the police archives, I have compiled a list of approximately 190 publishers. There were also separate printers and retailers. APP, Ba 697–736. Artists such as Edouard Manet, Jules Chéret, and Toulouse-Lautrec all created designs for songsheets.

6. Charles Rearick, *Pleasures of the Belle Epoque* (New Haven, 1985), 75. Rearick's interpretation follows Theodor Adorno's "The Culture Industry: Enlightenment as Mass Deception," in Max Horkheimer and Theodor Adorno, *Dialectic of Enlightenment* (New York, 1972). This approach tends to underestimate the political potential of singing practices and the way lyrics and tunes were appropriated.

7. Although very difficult to define precisely, the *cafés-concerts* and cabarets offered free access, drinking at tables, and men and women could talk, smoke, and join in the program. The music halls, on the other hand, charged an entrance fee, often seated people on benches, and offered drinks at a separate bar. The *cafés-concerts* were the most numerous.

8. The Eldorado first opened in 1858 with many of the features of a music hall, including an entrance fee, fifteen hundred seats, and a luxurious interior, but was still called a *café-concert*. On the *goguettes*, see Pierre Brochon, *Béranger et son temps* (Paris, 1956), 7–28; and Marie-Véronique Gauthier, *Chanson, sociabilité et grivoiserie au XIXe siècle* (n.p., 1992).

9. Charles Rearick, "Song and Society in Turn-of-the-Century France," *Journal of Social History*, 22, no. 1 (Fall 1988), 45. Rearick has counted 260 businesses ranging from elaborate music halls to neighborhood haunts. *Le Figaro Illustré* counted 274 in 1896; T .J. Clark, *The Painting of Modern Life: Paris in the Art of Manet and His Followers* (New York, 1985), 305, n. 16. See also André Sallée and Philippe Chauveau, *Music-hall et café-concert* (Paris, 1985), 16. Clearly not enough archival work has been done to comprehend the complete network.

10. André Rossel provides reproductions of songsheets distributed during the Franco-Prussian War including "La Marseillaise," "La Badinguinette," and "Défense de Paris." Rossel, *1870, la première grande guerre par l'affiche et l'image* (Paris, 1970), 7, 13, and 74.

11. Cf. Clark, *The Painting of Modern Life*, 205–238, esp. 212–216; Rearick, "Song and Society," 49–50.

12. Cf. the work of Susanna Barrows, "'Parliaments of the People': The Political Culture of Cafés in the Early Third Republic," in *Drinking: Behavior and Belief in Modern History*, ed. Barrows and Robin Room (Berkeley, 1991), 87–97. On the growth of public sites of "popular pleasure" in late-nineteenth-century Paris, see Vanessa R. Schwartz, "Cinematic Spectatorship before the Apparatus: The Public Taste for Reality in *Fin-de-Siècle* Paris," in *Cinema and the Invention of Modern Life*, ed. Leo Charney and Vanessa R. Schwartz (Berkeley, 1995), 297–319.

13. Lenard Berlanstein, *The Working People of Paris, 1871–1914* (Baltimore, 1984), 128. Berlanstein's work challenges the views of bourgeois observers and painters who viewed the *café-concert* world as fundamentally bourgeois or petit

bourgeois and workers' leisure culture as "impoverished." See Berlanstein's chapter "Off-the-Job Life," 122–150.

14. Jeanne Bouvier, *Mes mémoires ou 59 années d'activité industrielle, sociale et intellectuelle d'une ouvrière 1876–1935* (Paris, 1983), 92.

15. On modernity in the late nineteenth century, see Charney and Schwartz's introduction to *Cinema and the Invention of Modern Life*, 1–12.

16. Their positions are often linked to their positive or negative views on mass culture. See, for example, Chantal Brunschwig, Louis-Jean Calvet, and Jean-Claude Klein, *100 ans de chanson française* (Paris, 1972), introduction; Jacques Charles, *Cent ans de music-hall* (Paris, 1956), 120; Serge Dillaz, *La Chanson française de contestation de la Commune à mai 1968* (Paris, 1973), 45; and Clark, *The Painting of Modern Life*, 224.

17. The tune of the American "Star-Spangled Banner," for example, came from a British drinking song.

18. The "Marseillaise" represents one of the best examples of this. At least twelve new renditions using the "Marseillaise" melody exist in the police song archives for 1914–1918. APP, Ba 716.

19. On an even more fluid system of "communal re-creation," see Lawrence Levine, *Black Culture and Black Consciousness: Afro-American Folk Thought from Slavery to Freedom* (New York, 1977), 3–80, esp. 29.

20. On the need for gestures, see Louis Calvet, *Chanson et société* (Paris, 1981), 68–70.

21. APP, Ba 735. Verses seven and eight were censored during the war. See chapter 3 for a discussion of the censorship system.

22. On genres, see Sallée and Chauveau, *Music-hall et café-concert*, 14–16; François Caradec and Alain Weill, *Le Café-concert* (Paris, 1980), 53–58, 129–180; Bettina L. Knapp, "The Golden Age of the Chanson," *Yale French Studies* 32 (May 1964), 82–98.

23. Serge Dillaz, in particular, has attacked Bruant, claiming that "to sing in the gutter has never been to sing of the people." *La Chanson française*, 48. See also Sallée and Chauveau, *Music-hall et café-concert*, 40.

24. Brunschwig, Calvet, and Klein, *100 ans de chanson française*, 119. Rearick has called the themes of flag, France, and army "large common-denominator themes," but this discounts the wrestling among political groups to attach themselves to cultural symbols. Rearick, "Song and Society," 51.

25. See Madeleine Schmidt, ed., *Chansons de la revanche et de la grande guerre* (Nancy, 1985), 12–129.

26. Dillaz, *La Chanson française*, 207.

27. Ibid., 27. This was not simply by chance; censorship officials encouraged composers and playwrights to forget the "Civil War" and remember Alsace-Lorraine. Josette Parrain, "Censure, théâtre, et commune (1871–1914)," *Le Mouvement social* 29 (April 1972), 329.

28. On how the song was originally written see Pierre Andrieu, ed., *Souvenirs des frères Isola: cinquante ans de vie Parisienne* (Paris, 1943), 61.

29. Alistair Horne, *The French Army and Politics, 1870–1970* (London, 1984), 18.

30. Michael Burns, *Rural Society and French Politics: Boulangism and the Dreyfus Affair, 1886–1900* (Princeton, 1984), 82.

31. Ibid., 89, 103.

32. Quoted in Rearick, "Song and Society," 51.

33. Gareth Stedman Jones, *Languages of Class: Studies in English Working Class History, 1832–1982* (Cambridge, 1983), 179–238, esp. 204 ff.

34. Botrel was born in Dinan in Britanny in 1868 and was sent to Paris at age eleven.

35. Herman Lebovics, *True France: The Wars over Cultural Identity, 1900–1945* (Ithaca, 1992), 143–144.

36. Botrel included bellicose and pro-army songs in his collection *Chansons des clochers-à-jour,* published in 1912.

37. Rearick, "Song and Society," 52.

38. Dillaz, *La Chanson française,* 206.

39. They followed in the footsteps of Pierre-Jean Béranger or the Christian socialist poets of 1848. See Pierre Brochon, *La Chanson sociale de Béranger à Brassens* (Paris, 1961); Edgar Leon Newman, "Sounds in the Desert: The Socialist Worker Poets of the Bourgeois Monarchy, 1830–1848," *Proceedings from the Third Meeting of the Western Society of French History* (Las Cruces, N.M., 1975), 269–301.

40. APP, Ba 697. According to a copy in the police archives this song had been approved for use before the war under the title "Guerre à la guerre."

41. On Montéhus, see Dillaz, *La Chanson française,* 65; Caradec and Weill, *Le Café-concert,* 98; and Guy Erismann, *Histoire de la chanson* (Paris, 1967), 146; Gaston Montéhus, *Recueil des chansons humanitaires* (Paris, 1910).

42. "Gloire au 17e" was also known as the "Hymne au 17e"; Maurice Agulhon, *The French Republic 1879–1992* (Cambridge, Mass., 1993), 130–131.

43. Dillaz, *La Chanson française,* 212–213.

44. Gaston Montéhus, *Chansons de Montéhus* (Paris, n.d.).

45. Berlanstein, *The Working People of Paris,* 130.

46. According to files from 1908, police were still tracking antimilitarist songs and performers, despite the fact that official song censorship had ended in 1906. The dossier on Montéhus reveals also that the police knew his repertoire quite well. APP, Ba 1495.

47. *La Guerre sociale,* March 1–7, 1911, 2.

48. Eugen Weber, *France: Fin de Siècle* (Cambridge, Mass., 1986), 175.

49. Caradec and Weill, *Le Café-concert,* 116; and Sallée and Chauveau, *Music-hall et café-concert,* 188.

50. This fractured view of singing as having both good and bad purposes reflects nineteenth-century ideas, in contrast to the Old Regime elite's views of song culture as vulgar and frivolous. See Mason, *Singing the French Revolution,* ch. 1.

51. Government tactics included censorship and surveillance. See Clark, *The Painting of Modern Life,* 227–234; Jacques Rancière, "Le Bon Temps ou la barrière des plaisirs," *Les Révoltes logiques,* Spring-Summer 1978.

52. Cf. Albert Dupaigne, *L'Enseignement du chant dans les écoles* (Paris, 1879); Amand Chevé, minister of public instruction, *Rapport sur l'enseignement du chant dans les écoles primaires* (Paris, 1881); Camille Saint-Saëns, et. al., *Rapports sur l'enseignement du chant dans les écoles primaires* (Paris, 1881); *Enseignement du chant: travaux de la commission, rapports et programmes* (Paris, 1884). The cause had already provoked some interest in the Second Empire; cf. *Etat de l'instruction primaire en 1864, d'après les rapports officiels des inspecteurs d'académie* (Paris, 1866).

53. Weber, "Who Sang the Marseillaise?" in *The Wolf and the Lamb: Popular Culture in France,* ed. Jacques Beauroy, Marc Bertrand, and Edward Gargan (Saratoga, Calif., 1976), 169. See also Dupaigne, *L'Enseignement du chant,* esp. 6.

54. Dupaigne, *L'Enseignement du chant,* 9–12. School textbooks also incorporated other rhyming materials, such as poetry, which could be memorized. Cf. Albert Bayet, *Morale et instruction civique: leçons élementaires* (Paris, 1904).

55. According to Weber, this comprised "seven and a half million out of the thirty million souls in France." Weber, "Who Sang the Marseillaise," 164. Scholars have criticized Weber for having relied too heavily on the least developed areas of France. Cf. Martyn Lyons, "What did the Peasants Read? Written and Printed Culture in Rural France, 1815–1914," *European History Quarterly* 27, no. 2 (1997): 165–197.

56. Weber, "Who Sang the Marseillaise," 167.

57. Archives Nationales (hereafter, AN), F21 3985.

58. Although Félix Pécaut argued that harmony would give a singer or listener "le sens de l'harmonie morale, de l'ordre, de l'accord" which would help form "la communauté de sentiments et de pensées" necessary for "la vie politique commune." Pécaut, *L'Education publique et la vie nationale* (Paris, 1897), 118–119.

59. Quoted in the 1920 report on "La Diffusion de l'Education Musicale" for the Chamber of Deputies, no. 2258, 71–80. AN, F21 3985.

60. See, for instance, the criticism of the bourgeois commentators Georges D'Avenel and Frédéric Passy discussed in Rearick, *Pleasures of the Belle Epoque*, 111.

61. Quoted in Clark, *The Painting of Modern Life*, 210.

62. Dupaigne, *L'Enseignement du chant*, 6, 9.

63. AN, F21 3985.

64. With regard to funding orchestras in small towns, one deputy in 1913 claimed, "C'est la meilleure des politiques que de les aider. Il n'y a pas de besogne plus utile pour l'Administration et pour nous que de travailler à la culture de ce pays." AN, F21 3985.

65. In the government reports or writings on school pedagogy, one does not find the term "classical music" often, but they sought to teach an appreciation of "des oeuvres magistrales des grands classiques" and "les chefs-d'oeuvre des maîtres." See, for example, AN, F21 3985.

66. Cf. Dupaigne, *L'Enseignement du chant*, 13, and Pécaut, *L'Education publique*, 121–122.

67. See chapters 2 and 6, in particular.

68. Cf. Michel Vovelle, "La Marseillaise, la guerre ou la paix," in *Les Lieux de mémoire: la République*, vol. 1, ed. Pierre Nora (Paris, 1984), 85–136. See also Calvet, *Chanson et société*, 123 ff.

69. Weber, "Who Sang the Marseillaise," 171, 172.

70. Maurice Bouchor, *Chants populaires pour les écoles* (Paris, 1895), 3–4. See Mason, *Singing the French Revolution*, 93–103 on the anthem's early years.

71. Weber, *France: Fin de Siècle*, 108.

72. Reported in *Le Temps*, March 4, 1911.

73. Quoted in Weber, "Who Sang the Marseillaise," 172.

74. Mona Ozouf, *L'École de la France: Essais sur la révolution, l'utopie et l'enseignement* (Paris, 1984), 199, 201. See also, Raoul Girardet, ed., *Le Nationalisme français, 1871–1914* (Paris, 1983), 70. A good example of this attempt to define legitimate wars appeared in the textbook by Jules Payot, *La Morale à l'école* (Paris, 1908), 220–224.

75. Cf. Peter M. Rutkoff, *Revanche and Revision: The Ligue des Patriotes and the Origins of the Radical Right in France, 1882–1900* (Athens, Ohio, 1981); Zeev Sternhell, "Paul Déroulède and the Origins of Modern French Nationalism," in *Contemporary France: Illusion, Conflict, and Regeneration*, ed. John C. Cairns (New York, 1978).

76. According to Serge Dillaz, Déroulède wrote his *Chants du soldat* while convalescing from a wound he received helping to suppress the Commune. Dillaz, *La Chanson française*, 27.

77. Dupaigne, *L'Enseignement du chant*, 12.

78. Girardet, *Le Nationalisme français*, 58–59, 131–132.

79. Quoted in Jean-Denis Bredin, *The Affair*, 19.

80. Sébastien Herscher, *Paul Déroulède: poète, patriote, chrétien* (Paris, 1915?), 10–11.

81. Eugen Weber, *Peasants into Frenchmen: The Modernization of Rural France, 1870–1914* (Stanford, Calif., 1976), 333, 440–442.

82. Ibid. See also Pécaut, *L'Education publique*, 115–125.

83. Bouchor, *Chants populaires*, 7. Notice the overlap with the "Marseillaise" in lines 3 and 6–9.

84. Michel Corday, *The Paris Front* (New York, 1934), 147. See also Jacques Ellul, *Histoire de la propagande* (Paris, 1967), 100.

85. Proposal to the Conseil Municipal de Paris on June 20, 1911, 1. Contained in AN, F21 3985. In the 1902–1903 Paris recruitment class, for example, one fifth of the clerks "from the Thirteenth and Eighteenth arrondissements claimed some accomplishment on musical instruments, especially the violin and flute." Berlanstein, *The Working People of Paris*, 149.

86. See, for example, Pierre-Jakez Hélias's autobiography, *The Horse of Pride: Life in a Breton Village*, trans. June Guicharnaud (New Haven, 1978). In the second half of the nineteenth century, music ethnographers swarmed over the countryside collecting "popular" melodies and lyrics. Cf. Julien Tiersot, *Histoire de la chanson populaire* (Paris, 1889); Tiersot, *Mélodies populaires des provinces de France* (Paris, 1928); Patrice Coirault, *Notre chanson folklorique* (Paris, 1941). See also Pierre Aubéry, "Poésies et chansons populaires de la Commune," in *Images of the Commune*, ed. James A. Leith (Montreal, 1978), 47–67, esp. 51–52.

87. Ozouf, *L'École de la France*, 21.

88. Weber, *France: Fin de Siècle*, 173. See also, Nathan A. Therien, "Popular Song as Social Experience in Nineteenth-Century France: From National Culture to Commodity" (Ph.D. diss., Harvard University, 1985). Other organizations that were not explicitly musical also wrote songs. A member of the Société de Tir, "La Revanche," of Cuvergnon (Oise) composed a "Chanson marche" in 1913, which described his comrades marching forth "without fear" for "la France, notre mère." Archives du service historique de l'Armée de terre, 5 N 566.

89. *Le Soleil*, July 6, 1914. See AN, F7 12881.

90. Gérard Boutet explains how the separation of Church and State had forced the creation of two opposing *orphéons* in his village of Josnes. Boutet, *Ils étaient de leur village: le temps des guerres, 1914–1939* (Paris, 1981), 79.

91. *L'Aquitaine*, February 6, 1914; *L'Univers*, June 15, 1913. Reports came from both large and small towns including Saumur in Maine-et-Loire, Montauban, Sainte Marthe near Marseille, Amiens, and Audencourt.

92. AN, F7 12881.

93. See Martha Hanna, "Iconology and Ideology: Images of Joan of Arc in the Idiom of the Action Française, 1908–1931," *French Historical Studies* 14, no. 2 (Fall 1985): 215–239; Gerd Krumeich, "Joan of Arc Between Right and Left" in *Nationhood and Nationalism in France: From Boulangism to the Great War 1889–1918*, ed. Robert Tombs (New York, 1991), 63–73.

94. On the rising nationalism, although focusing mainly on elites, see, for instance, Eugen Weber, *The Nationalist Revival in France 1905–1914* (Berkeley, 1959) and Philip Nord, "Social Defence and Conservative Regeneration: The National Revival, 1900–14" in Tombs, *Nationhood and Nationalism*, 210–228. On the reappearance of revanchism in teaching manuals, see Ozouf, *L'École de la France*, 226. On the emergence of an antimilitarist movement, see Michel Auvray, *Objecteurs, insoumis, déserteurs: histoire des réfractaires en France* (Paris, 1983), 124–145.

95. Cf. Dillaz, *La Chanson française*; Brochon, *La Chanson sociale*. Most works on the revolutionary tradition view the incipient commercialization of entertainment and singing in the early Third Republic as damaging to the political effectiveness of song culture.

96. Quoted in Weber, *France: Fin de Siècle*, 127. (This is his translation.)

97. Bouvier, *Mes mémoires*, 104.

98. The meetings were announced regularly in *La Guerre sociale*, the main socialist paper; see, for instance, February 15–21, 1911, and March 5, 1911. See also Robert Brécy, *Florilège de la chanson révolutionnaire de 1789 au front populaire* (Paris, 1978), and Robert Brécy, "Les Chansons du premier mai," *Revue d'histoire moderne et contemporaine* 28 (July 1981), 393–432.

99. Aubéry, "Poésies et chansons," 50.

100. *La Guerre sociale*, May 30, 1911.

101. Dillaz, *La Chanson française*, 203–205.

102. Dorrya Fahmy, *L'Histoire de France à travers la chanson* (Alexandria, Egypt, 1950), 321–323.

103. Michelle Perrot, *Les Ouvriers en grève*, vol. 2 (Paris, 1974), 529, 549, 562–563.

104. Bouvier, *Mes mémoires*, 103.

105. See John Horne, *Labour at War: France and Britain 1914–1918* (New York, 1991), 26–38, concerning the serious problems of disorientation and poor relations between the Socialist Party and the trade unions between 1911 and 1914.

106. Cf. APP, Ba 1642, and newspaper accounts in *Le Petit Parisien*, *Le Radical*, *L'Humanité*, and *l'Eclair*, all of which noted the sense of unity and the constant singing.

107. This was a response by the Union des syndicats de la Seine quoted in *Le Temps*, September 23, 1911.

108. The police report estimated the crowd was only between sixteen and nineteen thousand, whereas *La Guerre sociale* and the Socialist Party claimed there were at least sixty thousand despite the heavy rain. *La Guerre sociale*, September 27–October 4, 1911.

109. *L'Eclair*, September 25, 1911.

110. This musical, political script was also followed at subsequent gatherings. See APP, Ba 1642.

111. H. Pearl Adam, *Paris Sees It Through: A Diary 1914–1919* (New York, 1919), 1–2. Adam does not indicate when this occurred, but the confrontation may have been early in the summer of 1914.

112. APP, Ba 1642. See also newspaper accounts in *La Libre parole* (February 28, 1911), and *Le Temps* (February 25–March 5, 1911, and February 27, 1911, in particular).

113. As Jean-Denis Bredin has noted, by the 1890s "Numerous priests wrote and published anti-Jewish songs denouncing 'the Jews and Masons . . . who want to devour a priest every day.'" Bredin, *The Affair*, 289. See also Pierre Sorlin, *La Croix et les Juifs* (Paris, 1967).

114. Barbier and Vernillat, *Histoire de France*, 202–203.

115. The song is entitled "La France bouge." Barbier and Vernillat, *Histoire de France*, 198–199.

Chapter 2 *(pages 42–67)*

1. Cf. Jean-Jacques Becker, *Le Carnet B: les pouvoirs publics et l'antimilitarisme avant la guerre de 1914* (Paris, 1973). Regarding workers' reactions to the threat of war, see Jean-Jacques Becker and Annie Kriegel, *Juillet 1914: le mouvement ouvrier français et la guerre* (Paris, 1964).

2. See, for example, anthropologist David Parkin's explanation that "rituals, however they are defined, are not just expressive of abstract ideas but do things, have effects on the world, and are work that is carried out—that they are indeed performances." David Parkin, "Ritual as Spatial Direction and Bodily Division" in

Understanding Rituals, ed. Daniel de Coppet (New York, 1992), 14. For a useful definition of ritual, see Stanley Jeyaraja Tambiah, *Culture, Thought, and Social Action: An Anthropological Perspective* (Cambridge, Mass., 1985), 128.

3. I have chosen to use the term "cosmology" here because I am referring to the most deeply rooted assumptions concerning France's place in a larger world-view. These beliefs explain France's willingness to call on God for assistance in this conflict.

4. Eric Leed, *No Man's Land: Combat and Identity in World War I* (Cambridge, 1979), 69.

5. See Edward Berenson's *The Trial of Madame Caillaux* (Berkeley, 1992).

6. *Le Figaro*, July 26, 1914. The three-year law had extended the mandatory military service for young men from two years to three in 1913.

7. *La Guerre sociale*, July 29, 1914. Jaurès was assassinated just four days later.

8. *Le Figaro*, July 28, 1914.

9. *La Guerre sociale*, July 29 and 30, 1914. Voices urging the French to remain calm and dignified, in contrast to the "unruly" demonstrations being reported in Vienna and Berlin, foreshadowed the war years.

10. One such poster is reproduced in Gérard Boutet, *Ils étaient de leur village: le temps des guerres, 1914–1939* (Paris, 1981), 42–43.

11. The reports in *Le Figaro* for August 1 and 2, 1914, are full of references to songs, cheers, and "l'enthousiasme." See also André Ducasse, Jacques Meyer, and Gabriel Perreux, *Vie et mort des français, 1914–1918* (Paris, 1959), 25; Roland Dorgelès, *Le Château des Brouillards* (Paris, 1932), the chapter entitled "la dernière nuit"; Elisabeth Hausser, *Paris au jour le jour: les événements vus par la presse, 1900–1919* (Paris, 1968), 535.

12. *Le Figaro*, August 2, 1914.

13. Ibid.

14. Alistair Horne, *The French Army and Politics, 1870–1970* (London, 1984), 31. See also Ducasse, Meyer, and Perreux, *Vie et mort*, 24.

15. Gilbert Lewis has explained that, although participants may not know all the steps or meanings, they see it as "a ritual" that "is supposed to follow some time-hallowed precedent in order to be effective or simply to be a proper performance." See Parkin, "Ritual as Spatial Direction," 15.

16. Cf. René Des Touches, *Pages de gloire et de misère* (Paris, 1917), 9–10 or Pierre-Jakez Hélias's passage in which he tells of his mother and father working furiously at the harvest, only to stop short at the sound of the bell. Hélias, *The Horse of Pride: Life in a Breton Village*, trans. June Guicharnaud (New Haven, 1980), 30–31.

17. *Le Figaro*, August 2, 1914.

18. André Benoit, *Trois mois de guerre au jour le jour (1914)* (Paris, 1967), 9–11. Fernand Darde mentions that three cannon shots marked the declaration. Darde, *Vingt mois de guerre à bord du Croiseur "Jeanne d'Arc" 9 août 1914–12 avril 1916* (Paris, 1918), iii.

19. In his 1920 novel, Jean Bernier wrote, "La mobilisation qui, dans cet août au soleil virulent, vanna sur l'aire publique, les mairies et les gares, la pleine récolte de Français, les avait dédaignés." Bernier, *La Percée* (Paris, 1920), 9.

20. *Le Figaro*, August 2, 1914.

21. August 3, 1914, report. Archives Nationales (hereafter, AN), F7 12938.

22. Quoted in Boutet, *Ils étaient de leur village*, 56.

23. Prefect reports mentioned performances organized by civic organizations such as community bands or choruses. For departures, this role was often filled by the regimental bands. See, for instance, reports in AN, F7 12937.

24. Roger Boutefeu, *Les Camarades: soldats français et allemands au combat 1914–1918* (Paris, 1966), 39–42.

25. Gérard Baconnier, André Minet, and Louis Soler, *La Plume au fusil: les poilus du Midi à travers leur correspondance* (Toulouse, 1985), 129. In at least one instance, "les hommes mobilisés" just showed up at the prefecture and sang "chants patriotiques" for officials. AN, F7 12938.

26. August 6, 1914. AN, F7 12938.

27. AN, F7 12936–12939.

28. *Le Figaro*, August 1, 1914.

29. See Tambiah, *Culture, Thought, and Social Action*, 129. I disagree sharply here with those who see the accounts of singing as isolated or as trivial. Maurice Agulhon, for example, calls the "cries of 'To Berlin!'" and "endless singing of the 'Marseillaise'" "a superficial aspect of memory." Agulhon, *The French Republic 1879–1992* (Cambridge, Mass., 1993), 152.

30. Sally Moore and Barbara Myerhoff have described a "tradition-like effect," where "even if it [the ritual] is performed once . . . its internal repetitions of form or content" as well as its reliance on the shared cultural backgrounds of the participants allows it "to carry the same unreflective conviction as any traditional repetitive ritual." Moore and Myerhoff, introduction to *Secular Ritual,* ed. Moore and Myerhoff (Assen, 1977), 8–9.

31. Jean-Paul Bertaud, *La Vie quotidienne des soldats de la Révolution, 1789–1799* (Paris, 1985), 23–30, esp. 24, and Jean-Paul Bertaud, *The Army of the French Revolution: From Citizen-Soldiers to Instrument of Power* (Princeton, 1988).

32. See letter 3 by Gaston N in Charles Foley, *1914–1915: la vie de guerre contée par les soldats* (Paris, 1915), 6.

33. Yves Pourcher, *Les jours de guerre: la vie des Français au jour le jour entre 1914 et 1918* (Paris, 1994), 27. Pourcher provides a very detailed chapter on "Août 1914," 7–93.

34. Stéphane Audoin-Rouzeau, *1870: la France dans la guerre* (Paris, 1989), 87–88, 47.

35. Audoin-Rouzeau shows us the power of the historical example in quoting from a police report in July 1870: "D'après ce que je vois et ce que j'entends, je crois pouvoir affirmer qu'il faut se rapporter à 1792 et 1793 pour se faire une idée de l'élan national. L'enthousiasme de la France pour venger tant d'années d'humiliations est égal à celui qui existait, il y a quatre-vingt ans, pour défendre nos frontières." Audoin-Rouzeau, *1870: la France,* 51.

36. See, for example, Jeanne Bouvier, *Mes mémoires ou 59 années d'activité industrielle, sociale et intellectuelle d'une ouvrière 1876–1935* (Paris, 1983), 122, and Georges Ohnet, *Journal d'un bourgeois de Paris pendant la guerre de 1914* (Paris, 1914).

37. Jean Giraudoux, *Lectures pour une ombre* (Paris, 1918), 67.

38. Jean Bernier remarked on how the very public nature of the 1914 mobilization was the same as 1793, except for the lack of women to bandage wounds and very young drummers. Bernier, *La Percée,* 9.

39. On the myth of the bayonet, see Charles Roetter, *The Art of Psychological Warfare, 1914–1945* (New York, 1974), 44, and Robert Brécy, *Florilège de la chanson révolutionnaire de 1789 au front populaire* (Paris, 1978), 223.

40. The anthropologist Michael Cartry, for example, has wondered "whether the form resulting from the interdependence of the elements in a ritual is not analogous to the form that links the parts, or voices, of a musical score." Cartry, "From One Rite to Another: The Memory in Ritual and the Ethnologist's Recollection" in de Coppet, *Understanding Rituals,* 29.

41. Archives de la Préfecture de Police, Paris (hereafter APP), Ba 716.

42. APP, Ba 704. See also R. P. Jameson and A. E. Heacox, eds., *Chants de France* (Boston, 1922), 5–8.

43. The "Régiment de Sambre et Meuse" and the "Marseillaise" both called to the "children" (enfants) of the country in their very first lines.

44. Leed, *No Man's Land*, 39–72; Robert Wohl, *The Generation of 1914* (Cambridge, Mass., 1979), 5–27.

45. See Becker's article, "Voilà le glas de nos gars qui sonne" in *1914–1918: l'autre front*, Cahiers du Mouvement Social, no. 2, ed. Patrick Fridenson (Paris, 1977), 13–33 and especially his book, *1914: comment les Français sont entrés dans la guerre* (Paris, 1977).

46. Barbier and Vernillat also argue that the rural areas remained quieter. Pierre Barbier and France Vernillat, *Histoire de France par les chansons* (Paris, 1961), 217. De la Gorce has emphasized the concern for the harvest in Paul Marie De la Gorce, *The French Army* (London, 1963), 94. René Des Touches's personal account concentrates on the sad response of the peasants in his town. He calls his town's experience "less theatrical" (than the cities'), but his narrative shows that the inhabitants still followed the same steps. *Pages de gloire*, 9–28.

47. Becker, "Voilà le glas," 27.

48. Becker's work has been very influential. For example, Maurice Agulhon, in his work *The French Republic 1879–1992*, says that "chiefly, the general feeling in public opinion was one of resignation and of a duty accepted far more than of enthusiasm for war" (152). See also Charles Rearick's use of Becker in *The French in Love and War: Popular Culture in the Era of the World Wars* (New Haven, 1997), 2–5.

49. APP, Ba 1614.

50. Tambiah, *Culture, Thought, and Social Action*, 133.

51. Pierre B. Gheusi, *Guerre et théâtre, 1914–1918* (Paris, 1919), 14.

52. Ibid., 19.

53. *Le Figaro*, August 2, 1914.

54. Herbert Adams Gibbons, *Paris Reborn: A Study in Civic Psychology* (New York, 1916), 12.

55. On the creative process, see Victor Turner, *The Ritual Process: Structure and Anti-Structure* (Ithaca, N.Y., 1969), 42–43. See also, Tambiah, *Culture, Thought, and Social Action*, 130.

56. Tambiah, *Culture, Thought, and Social Action*, 145, 126.

57. Darde, *Vingt mois de guerre*, vii.

58. *Le Figaro*, August 2, 1914.

59. Gheusi, *Guerre et théâtre*, 19.

60. See Théodore Botrel, "Les Souvenirs d'un barde errant," *La Revue Belge* (January 1, 1923), 54–72, and Brécy, *Florilège de la chanson*, 224.

61. Pascal Sevran, *Le Music-hall français, de Mayol à Julien Clerc* (Paris, 1978), 15.

62. Théodore Botrel, *Les Chants du bivouac* (Paris, 1915); *Les Chansons de route* (Paris, 1915); *Chants de bataille et de victoire* (Paris, 1920).

63. Théodore Botrel, *Les Mémoires d'un barde Breton* (Paris, 1933), 13.

64. *Bulletin des armées*, supplementary edition, November 1914.

65. Cf. Jean-Jacques Becker, *The Great War and the French People* (Dover, N.H., 1985), 36–41.

66. Brécy, *Florilège de la chanson*, 218.

67. Montéhus used the tune from a song entitled "Pan! Pan! L'Arbi" or the "Marche des Zouaves," originally written by the Zouaves in 1855 during the Crimean War. See André Gauthier, *Les Chansons de notre histoire* (Paris, 1967), 161, and Brécy, *Florilège de la chanson*, 219.

68. Barbier and Vernillat, *Histoire de France*, 217–218, and Brécy, *Florilège de la chanson*, 219.

69. *La Guerre sociale*, August 6, 1914. There is no indication, however, that Montéhus ever reentered the army.

70. Brécy, *Florilège de la chanson*, 232. The song censors helped Montéhus eliminate unwelcome ideas.

71. Ibid., 221. In 1915, Léo Lelièvre, who had been an anarchist in his youth, dedicated "une chanson de guerre à 'La Révolution'" and described how this time the revolution would happen in Germany, bringing down their "horrifying kultur."

72. The postcard is reproduced in Brécy, *Florilège de la chanson*, 231.

73. The ground work for Déroulède's rehabilitation had been underway before the war began, and the municipal council had just renamed a street "L'Avenue Paul-Déroulède" on July 23.

74. A January 1915 ceremony at Notre Dame, marking the first anniversary of his death, paid tribute to his determination. Sébastien Herscher, *Paul Déroulède: poète, patriote, chrétien* (Paris, 1915), 13.

75. Reported in a prefect report, dated August 3, 1914. AN, F7 12937. In Montmartre, according to the historian Louis Chevalier, it was two well-known pimps who enforced proper serious behavior, compelling certain *cafés-concerts* to close. Louis Chevalier, *Montmartre du plaisir et du crime* (Paris, 1980), 301.

76. AN, F7 12937, report dated August 3, 1914. Gérard Boutet confirms this for his own town of Josnes. Boutet, *Ils étaient de leur village*, 79.

77. *Le Figaro*, August 2, 1914.

78. AN, F7 12938 and 12937. At least two of these sorts of incidents occurred in Clermont-Ferrand and Bellegarde.

79. *La Guerre sociale*, July 31, 1914.

80. *La Guerre sociale*, August 7, 1914.

81. Mona Ozouf, *L'École de la France: essais sur la révolution, l'utopie et l'enseignement* (Paris, 1984), 212–213.

82. Quoted in Jacques Suffel, *La Guerre de 1914–1918 par ceux qui l'ont faite* (Paris, 1968), 200.

83. Horne, *The French Army*, 35.

84. Before the war, these songs made up only one strand, opposite the antimilitarist repertoire and the genre of the *comique troupier*. Ouvrard, Polin, and Bach became famous dressed as conscripts in a caricature that bordered on ridicule.

85. Boutefeu, *Les Camarades*, 32.

86. Jacques Heugel, *Aveux et souvenirs* (Paris, 1968), 35–45.

87. Giraudoux, *Lectures pour une ombre*, 93, see also 95. The quote continued "Artaud found this new song superb. He came on a pause to ask me to copy it for him."

88. Boutefeu, *Les Camarades*, 83, 31.

89. Early on, some government reports referred simply to "hommes mobilisés." See also André Benoit, *Trois mois de guerre au jour le jour (1914)* (Paris, 1967), 13–24.

90. Giraudoux, *Lectures pour une ombre*, 83–84, 77–78.

91. Louis Mairet, *Carnet d'un combattant, 11 Février 1915–16 Avril 1917* (Paris, 1919), 31–32. Bernier, *La Percée*, 21. Emile-François Julia also talks about the "pacifists" overcoming their lack of knowledge and becoming "veterans." Julia, *La Fatalité de la guerre: scènes et propos du front* (Paris, 1917), 5–13. See also Georges Gaudy, *Les Trous d'obus de Verdun* (Paris, 1922), 31.

92. For a broader discussion of masculinity in fin-de-siècle France, see Robert Nye, *Masculinity and Male Codes of Honor in Modern France* (New York, 1993).

93. Jules Payot, *La Morale à l'école* (Paris, 1908), 68 (my emphasis).

94. Serge Dillaz, *La Chanson française de contestation de la Commune à mai 1968* (Paris, 1973), 194–195.

95. John A. Lynn, *The Bayonets of the Republic* (Chicago, 1984), 148, 174.

96. APP, Ba 724. Jameson and Heacox, *Chants de France,* 12–13.

97. See Lynn, *The Bayonets of the Republic,* 150, 192.

98. These lines are from "Sambre et Meuse," verse 3.

99. See Horne, *The French Army,* 33, on France's military theory as well as Liddell Hart, *Foch, The Man of Orleans* (London, 1931); and James Marshall-Cornwall, *Foch as Military Commander* (London, 1972). The strategy had partly countered criticisms of overly defensive tactics during the Franco-Prussian War.

100. See David G. Herrmann, *The Arming of Europe and the Making of the First World War* (Princeton, 1996), esp. 230; and Jack Snyder, *The Ideology of the Offensive: Military Decision Making and the Disasters of 1914* (Ithaca, N.Y., 1984), esp. ch. 5.

101. Quoted in Marshall-Cornwall, *Foch as Military Commander,* 55.

102. Général Andolenko, *Recueil d'historiques de l'infanterie française* (Paris, 1969).

103. Quoted in Ducasse, Meyer, and Perreux, *Vie et mort,* 38.

104. Andolenko, *Recueil d'historiques,* 34, 41, 161. The 144th employed, "Il faut resplendir pour partir, pour combattre et pour mourir" and the 45th, "Petits soldats de plomb, marchons à l'appel du canon" (172).

105. This formula carried from the prewar period well into the later stages of the war; see, for instance, "En avant les p'tits gars!" (c. 1913), APP, Ba 708; "Français, toujours debout!" (c. 1914), Ba 709; "la Chanson des mitrailleuses," Ba 703; "Ils vont vers la Gloire," Ba 712; "En Avant! les bleus," Ba 708; "En avant les gars à Pétain!" (c. 1916), Ba 708.

106. Botrel, *Les Chants du bivouac,* 5–6.

107. Quoted in Guy Breton, *Le Cabaret de l'histoire,* vol. 1 (Paris, 1973), 123–124. The third verse of the song "Cadences militaires" summed up the classic theory: "C'est surtout au feu que nous sommes à l'aise / Là nous retrouvons le plus beau des pas, / L'étranger l'appelle la *furia* française, / C'est l'chant national guidant les combats . . . Quand, au feu, sacrebleu, / On sent l'odeur de poudre / On part comme la foudre / Dans un élan furieux!" APP, Ba 701.

108. Julia, *La Fatalité de la guerre,* 16–17.

109. Heugel, *Aveux et souvenirs,* 49.

110. Chevalier, *Montmartre du plaisir,* 307.

111. Eugen Weber, *Action Française: Royalism and Reaction in Twentieth-Century France* (Stanford, 1962), 89–112.

112. Becker, *The Great War,* 83.

113. APP, Ba 708. Also quoted in René Josian, *La Muse des armées, 1914–1919* (Paris, n.d.), 38.

Chapter 3 (pages 71–97)

1. See carton Ba 697, Archives de la Préfecture de Police, Paris (hereafter, APP), for the letters and memos; Ba 724 for the song text.

2. Chamber of Deputies, January 25, 1916.

3. Concern for soldiers' morale had a much older history in military literature.

4. On rules forbidding the loud hawking of newspapers on public thoroughfares, for instance, see APP, Ba 1614.

5. For reports on the public's volatility, see Archives Nationales, F7 12937, 12938, and 12939. The government concerned itself with all forms of communication; for example, people were forbidden to use English on telephones until late 1917.

6. Some written correspondence between officials and music-hall participants still exists, but much of the negotiating was done verbally. Cf. APP, Ba 697.

7. See, for instance, Phillip Knightley, *The First Casualty: From the Crimea to Vietnam: The War Correspondent as Hero, Propagandist, and Myth Maker* (New York, 1975), 80–111; A. G. Marquis, "Words as Weapons: Propaganda in Britain and Germany during the First World War," *Journal of Contemporary History* 13 (July 1978): 467–498. Gary Stark's "All Quiet on the Home Front: Popular Entertainments, Censorship and Civilian Morale in Germany, 1914–1918," in *Authority, Identity and the Social History of the Great War*, ed. Frans Coetzee and Marilyn Shevin-Coetzee (Providence, R.I., 1995), 57–80, offers a new direction.

8. Jean-Jacques Becker, *The Great War and the French People*, trans. Arnold Pomerans (Dover, N.H., 1985), 2, 102; see also 29–63.

9. But on the censorship of books, see Geneviève Colin's essay in Becker, *The Great War*, 161–177.

10. See Stark, "All Quiet."

11. Becker points to the law of August 8, 1849 (state of siege), and the July 29, 1881, press law (updated in October 1913). Becker, *The Great War*, 48. See also Emile Mermet, et al., eds., *Annuaire de la presse* (Paris, 1915), 37.

12. The military governor of Paris acted on August 22, once he found that some entertainment places had managed to stay open. See APP, Ba 1614. Paris had four different prefects of police during the war: Hennion, Laurent, Hudelo, and Raux. In office from September 1914 to June 1917, Emile Laurent was the most influential. The process of censoring other media also evolved toward greater civilian participation.

13. Police also reviewed posters and postcards, but these industries were not accustomed to the same ritualized process, nor did police have to worry about the performative aspect. See Marie-Monique Huss's "Pronatalism and the Popular Ideology of the Child in Wartime France: The Evidence of the Picture Postcard," in *The Upheaval of War: Family, Work and Welfare in Europe, 1914–1918*, ed. Richard Wall and Jay Winter (Cambridge, 1988), 329–368; APP, Ba 1642; Archives du Service Historique de l'Armée de Terre (hereafter ASHAT), 5 N 342; 5 N 360.

14. Germany's censorship laws were also triggered by a declaration of a state of siege at the beginning of August, and authorities pursued an older agenda, which similarly linked public morality and morale. But, in contrast to France, Germany had a decentralized system run mainly by military officials, reflecting how the "German military enjoyed extraordinary power over civil life." Stark, "All Quiet," 60–62.

15. This legal arrangement remained in effect for the whole war, although military supervision was tightened under Georges Clemenceau's government in early 1918. See ASHAT, 6 N 145, and Odile Krakovitch, "La censure des théâtres durant la grande guerre" in *Théâtre et spectacles hier et aujourd'hui: actes du 115e congrès national des sociétés savantes* (Paris, 1991), 331–353.

16. The system had ended in June 1906 because of a lapse in funding, not because lawmakers had abrogated the laws or statutes. See Josette Parrain, "Censure, théâtre, et Commune (1871–1914)," *Le Mouvement social* 29 (April 1972): 339. These laws were not eliminated until October 1945. Philippe J. Maarek, *La Censure cinématographique* (Paris, [1982]), 10–11.

17. On censorship in the early Third Republic, see T. J. Clark, *The Painting of Modern Life: Paris in the Art of Manet and His Followers* (New York, 1985), 227–234; Jacques Rancière, "Le Bon Temps ou la barrière des plaisirs," *Les Révoltes logiques* (Spring-Summer 1978); Alberic Cahuet, *La Liberté du théâtre en France et à l'étranger: histoire, fonctionnement et discussion de la censure dramatique* (Paris, 1902), 244–304.

18. *Circulaires émanées du Préfet de Police, 1917–1918* (Paris, 1919), 25–28 of 1917.

19. The Archives de la Préfecture de Police in Paris houses the songs arranged al-

phabetically in thirty-four cartons: Ba 697–730. Cartons Ba 731–736 contain modified songs and duplicates. The Bibliothèque Nationale also has sheet music, but not all songs registered with them are now in their collection.

20. There had to have been a larger staff to examine all of the scripts for the musical revues and plays.

21. A song's approval for a newspaper was never grounds for its approval for live performances. See, for example, "Vous oubliez," by Robert Lanoff, which attacked the wealthy, factory owners, and government leaders. The text appeared in *La Bataille* in January 1916, but received no visa. APP, Ba 697.

22. APP, Ba 697.

23. According to a circular of May 1917, some unspecified theaters had permanent police surveyors, while others received only random visits. *Circulaires, 1917–1918*, 25–28 of 1917.

24. APP, Ba 697 and Ba 700. "Il jouait des castagnettes" also lost its visa after an officer visiting the Cinéma Magic heard a previously suppressed final verse performed. APP, Ba 711.

25. Paul Allard, *Images secrètes de la guerre: 200 photographies et documents censurés en France* (Paris, 1933), 27.

26. Parrain, "Censure, théâtre, et Commune," 327–342.

27. Allan Mitchell, "The German Influence on Subversion and Repression in France," *Francia* (1986), 409–433, esp. 415. Unfortunately, the history of popular censorship has not had any definitive treatment, but see also Annie Stora-Lamarre, *L'Enfer de la IIIe République: censeurs et pornographes, 1881–1914* (Paris, 1990); Yves Jamelot, *La Censure des spectacles: théâtre, cinéma* (Paris, 1937). And see the newspaper articles in Rt 900 and Rt 934(2), in the Fonds Rondel at la Bibliothèque de l'Arsenal.

28. According to a December 22, 1871, circular, quoted by Parrain, "Censure, théâtre, et Commune," 328, n. 3. See also the November 25, 1872, directive in *Recueil des lois, décrets, arrêtés, règlements, circulaires, se rapportant aux théâtres et aux établissements d'enseignement musical et dramatique* (Paris, 1888), 141.

29. *Recueil des lois*, 142–143.

30. The year 1881 is the best known date for the end of "censorship," even though some forms of censorship continued. Cf. Gonzalo J. Sanchez, "The Challenge of Right-Wing Caricature Journals: From the Commune Amnesty Campaign to the End of Censorship, 1878–1881," *French History* 10, no. 4 (1996): 451–489.

31. James Smith Allen, *In the Public Eye: A History of Reading in Modern France, 1800–1940* (Princeton, 1991), 89, 84–92, 102–103. See also F. W. J. Hemmings, *Theatre and State in France, 1760–1905* (Cambridge, 1995); and Neil Carruthers, "Theatrical Censorship in Paris from 1850 to 1905," *New Zealand Journal of French Studies* 3 (1982): 21–41.

32. Susanna Barrows, "Venus and Bacchus in an Era of Mechanical Reproduction" (unpublished manuscript), esp. 17, 25, 28. See also Barrows, " 'Parliaments of the People': The Political Culture of Cafés in the Early Third Republic," in *Drinking: Behavior and Belief in Modern History*, ed. Susanna Barrows and Robin Room (Berkeley, 1991), 87–97.

33. Marcel Berger and Paul Allard, *Les Secrets de la censure pendant la guerre* (Paris, 1932). Berger and Allard wrote cynically of the political role of newspaper and visual censorship in protecting those in power.

34. Ibid., 14.

35. Paris authorities reviewed songs to be performed for troops by civilian professionals. See chapter 6.

36. On the military censorship of songs, see ASHAT, 5 N 342, 5 N 346, 5 N 371–373, 7 N 951.

37. "Voyage officiel," APP, Ba 697. Its lyrics depicted a stereotypical government minister making inane speeches in the provinces—all normal grist for the prewar mill.

38. See, for example, "Sur le front," APP Ba 735. For more specific evidence of this political and social censorship, see my article "*La Pudique Anastasie*: Wartime Censorship and French Bourgeois Morality," in *World War I and the Cultures of Modernity*, ed. Douglas Mackamon and Michael Mays (Jackson, Miss., 2000).

39. See "On dit que," APP, Ba 734.

40. APP, Ba 697. See also "Tout en poussant les Anglais," and Lucien Boyer's prewar song "Sympathique"; both had to be modified. Ba 697 and Ba 735. Prewar songs with humorous escapades between German and British citizens could not be sung.

41. One example was "Le Beau Gosse," whose 1908 version was *non visée*. APP, Ba 700. These song rules overlapped with decisions on photographs. For instance, a photograph of American soldiers entertaining themselves by playing at surrendering was forbidden as a parody of war. Allard, *Images secrètes*, 7, 9, 12.

42. Stéphane Audoin-Rouzeau, *Men at War 1914–1918: National Sentiment and Trench Journalism in France during the First World War*, trans. Helen McPhail (Providence, R.I., 1992), 20–33, esp. 20.

43. *La Fusée*, 5 November 1916.

44. "La Question des corps nus," APP, Ba 735. See also "La Bonne à Lisa," Ba 697 and 701.

45. APP, Ba 735. See the even more caustic "Y a du vent dans les voiles" (Ba 736), which was banned.

46. It was also permissible to refer to Clemenceau as an object of enemy hatred. APP, Ba 711.

47. "Le Tigre," APP, Ba 736.

48. APP, Ba 697 and Ba 708; see also, "A votre santé," Ba 697 and Ba 700; "Ses affaires," Ba 697; and "Veuve du Rocambole," Ba 697 and Ba 729.

49. APP, Ba 697.

50. Quoted in Becker, *The Great War*, 45.

51. Ibid., 57–59.

52. APP, Ba 1614, November 1915 report.

53. Similar rules pertained to photographs and postcards. See Allard, *Images secrètes*, 16–17, and Huss, "Pronatalism and the Popular Ideology," 336.

54. "On dit que," APP, Ba 734.

55. See, for example, "Ma patrie," APP, Ba 697 and Ba 734; "Dieu," Ba 707; "Le Voeu d'Isaac," Ba 729 and Ba 697; and "L'Bon dieu embarrassé," Ba 701.

56. See also Montéhus's "Soldat devant le Christ," APP, Ba 735.

57. For a careful examination of popular religion in France during and after the war, see Annette Becker, *La Guerre et la foi: de la mort à la mémoire* (Paris, 1994).

58. This specific change was ordered in "Suivant le grade," APP, Ba 735.

59. "Les Hommes du jour," APP, Ba 711.

60. APP, Ba 734.

61. APP, Ba 712. Even after civilian leaders had recognized Joffre's weaknesses and had eased him out of power by early 1916, censors still monitored the representations of him.

62. See the remarkable newspaper quotes in Becker, *The Great War*, 29–42; and the letters in Charles Foley, *1914–1915: la vie de guerre contée par les soldats* (Paris, 1915).

63. See "Il court, il court, l'embusqué," APP, Ba 711, and "Quand l'amour part pour la guerre," Ba 735.

64. APP, Ba 701. See also the "dialogue militaire" by Bouchaud (known as Du-

fleuve), APP, Ba 700. Charles Rearick comments on the continuing popularity of this genre during the war, but does not indicate that these songs were being sung in a modified form. Rearick, "Madelon and the Men—in War and Memory," *French Historical Studies* 17 (Fall 1992), 1008.

65. APP, Ba 735. See also, "Faut d'l'imagination" where a reservist's complaint to his general about the shabby quality of bread was deleted. Ba 708.

66. This name comes from Allard, *Images secrètes*, 3. Anastasie was a sobriquet for the censor throughout the nineteenth century. Cf. Robert Justin Goldstein, *Censorship of Political Caricature in Nineteenth-Century France* (Kent, Ohio, 1989).

67. Pierre Bourdieu, "What Makes a Social Class? On the Theoretical and Practical Existence of Groups," *Berkeley Journal of Sociology* 32 (1987): 10–11.

68. Cf. the song "Bellevillois, prends ton fusil!" APP, Ba 700.

69. Obviously, the term "bourgeois" represents a broad category, and the censors were only a small portion of the government. But the use of the term is suggested first because the struggle had originated prior to the war and on the part of the dominant social groups, and, second because the language of the enterprise reveals a sense of social hierarchy in the need to "raise up" and improve, or to clean out lower, undesirable sites or habits. According to Charles Rearick, in late-nineteenth-century France, "the government," assisted by "prominent bourgeois residents and politicians," "gave force to bourgeois sensibilities by censoring songs and plays that were too politically threatening or too racy." *Pleasures of the Belle Epoque: Entertainment and Festivity in Turn-of-the-Century France* (New Haven, 1985), 113–114, 42–43.

70. Cf. the censored "La Mauvaise Graine," in which "l'proprio brutal'ment" threw "un bon travailleur" out into the cold. APP, Ba 716.

71. APP, Ba 697 and 725.

72. See chapter 1, and Robert Brécy, *Florilège de la chanson révolutionnaire de 1789 au front populaire* (Paris, 1978); Laurent Marty, *Chanter pour survivre: culture ouvrière, travail et techniques dans le textile, Roubaix 1850–1914* ([Lille?], [1982]).

73. See also "Y a qu'l Populo!" APP, Ba 736. Reflecting the prowar ethos, republican examiners were not bothered by countless references to monarchical heroes, and Joan of Arc's stature became sacrosanct.

74. "Soyez bons pour les ouvriers!" APP, Ba 735. The song received a visa in January 1918 with suppressions.

75. "L'Agent Peinard," APP, Ba 697. See also, "Réflexions du Garde," Ba 697 and Ba 724; "Quand on n'est pas riche," Ba 735; and "La Soupe à l'oignon," Ba 735.

76. Cf. "Vive la République," APP, Ba 729.

77. Cf. "L'Agent démocrate," APP, Ba 697.

78. APP, Ba 735.

79. Even Bruant's famous songs met a similarly harsh fate—for example, "A Mazas," "A Montrouge," "Amoureux," "A la Roquette," and "Ronde des marmites" were all *non visée*, and "A la Bastoche" had to be modified. APP, Ba 698 and Ba 725.

80. "Oh! Ce n'est rien" (© 1911), APP, Ba 734. In a later verse, the agent remarked on how innocent individuals were sometimes convicted at the Palais d'Justice. See also "Valse de minuit," Ba 729, and "Valse de nuit," Ba 736.

81. APP, Ba 736.

82. See "Les Tambours du régiment," APP, Ba 736.

83. See "Les Bienfaits de la République," APP, Ba 701.

84. Kenneth Silver has also noted the change in representations of the French Revolution in art forms. See Silver, *Esprit de Corps: The Art of the Parisian Avant-Garde and the First World War, 1914–1925* (Princeton, 1989), 196.

85. "La Baïonnette," APP, Ba 700. The modified song was approved in February and March 1918.

86. APP, Ba 736. In another typical case, an examiner allowed the two verses of "Un soir de Paris," which described the love and mystery of Paris, but not the last verse, which celebrated past Parisian uprisings with an exciting refrain: "Ecoutez! . . . c'est Paris / Coeur du monde / Battant avec fierté / Un cri de liberté / C'est le bruit / Qui grandit / D'un peuple qui surgit." Ba 735. It was submitted to the censor in 1917, when large labor strikes would have made the censors even more careful.

87. Parrain, "Censure, théâtre, et Commune," 30.

88. My discussion here is influenced by Pierre Bourdieu's work. See especially, "The Uses of the 'People' " in *In Other Words: Essays Towards a Reflexive Sociology*, trans. Matthew Adamson (Stanford, Calif., 1990), 150–155, and *Language and Symbolic Power* (Cambridge, 1991), chs. 1, 3, and 11. See also Richard Jenkins, *Pierre Bourdieu* (New York, 1992).

89. APP, Ba 697. This particular tune described a household where the bourgeois masters acted crudely and bizarrely. The performer offered to change the title to "Le Domestique sans place," while "toning down" (*édulcorer*) specific words, and the song did eventually get a visa.

90. APP, Ba 697 (emphasis in original).

91. The use of the word "language" would include the censors' attention to "body language" or gestures.

92. "Y a qu' l'amour," APP, Ba 736.

93. Cf. "Tâchez d'faire attention," APP, Ba 736.

94. Cf. "Oui! Mais voila!" APP, Ba 734. In the song "Le Train des conscrits," in which young men depart for the front, the third verse ends with "Ah! oui, l'émotion était vive, / Guillaum' était traité d'bourreau; / Y'm'semblait qu'la locomotive / Criait: l'salaud, l'salaud, l'salaud!" This last line could have evoked a fervent, noisy reaction from an audience, but was cut for the 1915 and 1916 performances. Ba 728.

95. Allard, *Images secrètes*, 27 (emphasis in original).

96. APP, Ba 735. He did finally get approval for the modified version. See, also, the changes made to "Affair de coeur," Ba 697.

97. See "Battez tambours!!" APP, Ba 700.

98. See APP, Ba 697 for the memo; Ba 716 and Ba 734 for the song texts.

99. APP, Ba 697 under "Zeppelinade," and Ba 736. The song was also known as "Nuit de Mars."

100. See "Absinthe et picolo," APP, Ba 697.

101. Cf. "Toutes jolies," APP, Ba 736, and "La Fille à ma concierge," Ba 709 and Ba 697.

102. Cf. "Ah! Ben Alors," APP, Ba 697. Even when songs had a moralistic reading, the censors would not allow the performances. See, for example, "L'Accident de Jeannette," Ba 697, and "La Taxe sur les célibataires," Ba 736.

103. "Ah! Claudia!" APP, Ba 697; see also "Aglaé," Ba 697.

104. "Quelques recettes pratiques," probably from mid-1917. APP, Ba 735.

105. This strategy meant that representations of soldiers' sense of betrayal and their misogynist narratives had a harder time spreading within the Parisian sphere during the war. Once it ended, the restraint was lifted. Cf. Mary Louise Roberts, *Civilization without Sexes: Reconstructing Gender in Postwar France, 1917–1927* (Chicago, 1994), 19–45.

106. APP, Ba 709. Domestic violence, like the slaying of mothers-in-law (another staple of French humor), was also no longer funny. See "Les Femmes sont nos victimes," Ba 709 and "Hitchy Kou," Ba 733.

107. See "Toutes jolies" and "The Beautiful Américan," APP, Ba 736. Paul Allard also noted this concern in *Images secrètes*, 25.

108. See "Il était un pioupiou," APP, Ba 711, and "Bon Républicain," Ba 701.

109. Bananas seem to have caused a consistent problem. See, also, "L'Agrément du Métro," APP, Ba 697, and "Si j'étais le Bon Dieu," Ba 735.

110. See "Bal de bienfaisance," APP, Ba 700; "Quand ils s'en vont," Ba 735; "Ah! C'qu'on se l'est tirbouchonné," Ba 697; and "Faut d'l'imagination," Ba 708.

111. Soldiers appear to have been regular seducers or objects of seduction in prewar songs. Cf. "Folle complainte," which was blocked "definitively" by the prefect. APP, Ba 709.

112. Allard, *Images secrètes*, 25–26.

113. Cf. "Types de femmes," APP, Ba 736; "Le Bec de gaz m'a dit," Ba 700; "La Femme à tout le monde," Ba 709.

114. "On ferme!!!" APP, Ba 734.

115. See for example, "Hello hello Tommy!" APP, Ba 711.

116. The cuts included some prewar tunes about garrison life in which examiners suppressed references to cheap sex during regimental service. Cf. "Vas-y mon pote!" APP, Ba 736; or "La Femme au régiment," Ba 709. But in the song "Ah! Je l'attends," a "soldier" talked about how "au régiment" one had as many women as one wanted; the censors allowed this song in December 1916 and November 1917. Ba 697.

117. In a much more serious, but related, vein, one sees this conflict in the debates over what to do about the *enfants du barbare*, as they were called, who had resulted from the German rapes in 1914. See Ruth Harris, "The 'Child of the Barbarian': Rape, Race, and Nationalism in France during the First World War," *Past and Present* 141 (November 1993): 170–206. It was, however, easy enough to prohibit songs which expressed an adversion to having children, which meant the song censors' efforts paralleled the government's confiscation of "neo-malthusian" pamphlets. See the 1909 "La Vertu de Madeleine," APP, Ba 736, and "La Mauvaise graine," Ba 716.

118. The aggressive pronatalist campaign in the prewar period had been dominated by a vocal elite making this an important part of the prewar conservative bourgeois ideology. As Marie-Monique Huss has explained, "Most pronatalist authors came from the professional classes: doctors, . . . lawyers, . . . politicians, . . . economists, . . . journalists and writers." Huss, "Pronatalism and the Popular Ideology," 330–331.

119. See "On cherre, on cherre," APP, Ba 734; "Les Quatre jours des poilus," Ba 735; "Bouscule pas le pot de fleurs!" Ba 701; "Qu'est-c' qu'on f'ra," Ba 735.

120. Cf. "La Bonne Épouse," in *Les Chansons de la guerre* (Paris, 1916), 16.

121. APP, Ba 708 (emphasis in original).

122. ASHAT, 16 N 1529.

123. See M. le capitaine Massy's *Moyens à employer pour maintenir et relever le moral des soldats en campagne*, quoted in René Thorel, *Un Cercle pour le soldat* (Paris, 1909), 269.

124. See cartons APP, Ba 737–740, which contain typewritten programs for the music establishments within city limits.

125. Intervention by other government ministries rarely occurred but could sway the prefect's ruling. See "Les Sales boîtes," for example. APP, Ba 697.

126. APP, Ba 697; see the letter concerning the song "Opérations Russes."

127. See, for instance, the correspondence surrounding the songs "La Plainte du fumeur," APP, Ba 697, "Mirabeau Mirabelle, and "Tête de pipe" in Ba 697.

128. See APP, Ba 697 and Ba 713. See also, "Elle est de Bruxelles," Ba 697 and Ba 707.

129. APP, Ba 697. See also, "L'Equitable justice."

130. APP, Ba 697.

131. Emile Laurent of the Folies-Parisiennes also claimed that a particular song ("Les Pan pan") "had nothing uncalled-for or obscene" in it. "Besides," he asserted, "I . . . do not have a habit of performing unwholesome songs." The song still suffered some modifications. APP, Ba 697.

132. Correspondence regarding "Chose et machin" by D. Pinel is in APP, Ba 697. Groups fighting against the government before the war had defended French *gauloiserie* against foreign puritanism. Rearick, *Pleasures of the Belle Epoque*, 43, 46.

133. APP, Ba 697. Jules Chapelle, the composer of "Les Vaches," also questioned why his song—which had always gotten visas under the "severe" previous regime—could not get one now. He claimed the lyrics were very popular with the public "dans un sens propre" and that not one word attacked "authority." Ba 697.

134. Cf. "Les Sacrifiés" and "Les Semailles de la raison," which both faced cuts in 1917. APP, Ba 735.

135. In November 1917, Clemenceau announced plans to suppress "la censure politique," and on December 29, 1917 he authorized new access to the army zone for newspapers. ASHAT, 6 N 145 contains government correspondence for 1917–1918.

136. ASHAT, 5 N 371. In the fall of 1917, Pétain also tightened up the review of trench newspapers. Audoin-Rouzeau, *Men at War*, 22.

137. Brécy, *Florilège de la chanson*, 237.

138. See chapter 7.

139. APP, Ba 1614, early 1916 report.

140. APP, Ba 1614.

141. Stark, "All Quiet," 62–63, 76.

Chapter 4 (pages 98–133)

1. Although postcards were an adaptive popular form, unlike songs they were created only at the home front and then appropriated in the trenches. Posters, on the other hand, represented one of the most official and centralized forms of communication. One soldier from the Midi claimed to have sent between one and five postcards per day to his wife. Gérard Baconnier, André Minet, and Louis Soler, *La Plume au fusil: les poilus du Midi à travers leur correspondance* (Toulouse, 1985), 109. The *franchise militaire* was routing more than four million pieces of mail a day in 1915.

2. Cf. Jay Winter's section on how the *images d'épinal* offered older images to this modern war. Winter, *Sites of Memory, Sites of Mourning: The Great War in European Cultural History* (Cambridge, 1995), 119–131; as well as George Mosse's chapter "The Process of Trivialization" in his *Fallen Soldiers: Reshaping the Memory of the World Wars* (New York, 1990), 126–156.

3. There are exceptions; see Hubertus Jahn, *Patriotic Culture in Russia during World War I* (Ithaca, N.Y., 1995); and Nicoletta Gullace, "Women and the Ideology of War: Recruitment, Propaganda, and the Mobilization of Public Opinion in Britain, 1914–1918" (Ph.D. diss., University of California at Berkeley, 1993). Jacques Ellul discusses the importance of private organizations, but stresses their coordination by the government. See his *Histoire de la propagande* (Paris, 1967).

4. See Annie Stora-Lamarre, *L'Enfer de la IIIe République: censeurs et pornographes (1881–1914)* (Paris, 1990), esp. 37, 57–58, 62; and Anne M. Wagner, "Rodin's Reputation," in *Eroticism and the Body Politic*, ed. Lynn Hunt (Baltimore, 1991), 227.

5. Ouriel Reshef, *Guerre, mythes et caricature* (Paris, 1984), 163.

6. Paul Hammond, *French Undressing: Naughty Postcards from 1900 to 1920* (London, 1988), 10.

7. This fascination contrasted sharply to Paul Fussell's portrait of the innocent, unsuspecting Edwardian British who failed to hear "obvious *double entendres*" and used words such as "intercourse, or erection, or ejaculation without any risk of evoking a smile or a leer." Fussell, *The Great War and Modern Memory* (Oxford, 1975), 23.

8. For many more examples, see Ba 700 at the Archives de la Préfecture de Police in Paris (hereafter APP). Note that this genre did not escape the censors' revisions, and not all kisses were sexual. For example, mothers also offered a love that gave courage.

9. "Filles d'Alsace," APP, Ba 709. See also, "Hardi les bleus," Ba 711.

10. Cards also existed that combined images and song lyrics. See Serge Zeyons, *Le Roman-photo de la grande guerre* (Paris, 1976), 11; see also 16, 21, and 28 for references to 1870.

11. Some postcard examples could be quite erotic, but generally did not feature nudity. See, for example, the card "Les Baisers," *Images de 1917* (Paris, 1987), 131.

12. The Germans also had a genre of postcards with romantic farewells in civilized surroundings. See Zeyons, *Le Roman-photo*, 104–106.

13. "Les Adieux de Tommy," APP, Ba 697.

14. APP, Ba 700.

15. The French also have a colloquialism, "sur le front," which means on the forehead or at the front; "baiser sur le front" became particularly suggestive once a distinct military front formed. On this phrase's use on several postcards, see Marie-Monique Huss, "Pronatalism and the Popular Ideology of the Child in Wartime France: The Evidence of the Picture Postcard," in *The Upheaval of War: Family, Work and Welfare in Europe, 1914–1918,* ed. Richard Wall and Jay Winter (Cambridge, 1988), n. 48, 362–363.

16. The fiancée was a prewar *café-concert* character, which had appeared in the revanchist repertoire. Cf. Madeleine Schmidt, ed., *Chansons de la revanche et de la grande guerre* (Nancy, 1985), 62–68.

17. See "Ils vont vers la Gloire," APP, Ba 712, and "L'Heure d'amour," Ba 733. See also the illustration of the phrase "La Victoire en chantant" with *la Victoire* as a showgirl in Charles Rearick, *The French in Love and War: Popular Culture in the Era of the World Wars* (New Haven, 1997), 31.

18. "Un baiser qui passe," APP, Ba 700. See also "A nos morts," Ba 699.

19. Général Andolenko, *Recueil d'historiques de l'infanterie française* (Paris, 1969), 86. In its May 20, 1915, edition, the newspaper *Le Journal* reported on a conversation between a combatant E. Helsey and a buddy. Helsey supposedly said, "You know, I'm not married, so I'm going to get engaged." And when asked, "To whom?" he replied with a remarkable echo of the nineteenth-century military refrain: "To victory [*la victoire*]." Quoted in Jean-Jacques Becker, *The Great War and the French People* (Dover, N.H., 1985), 39.

20. Cf. the 1915 song "Berceuse de la fiancée," APP, Ba 700; "Ca . . . ! C'est l'amour," Ba 701; and "Chansons et frissons," Ba 703.

21. The caption was in French, English, and Russian. See Elisabeth Hausser's *Paris au jour le jour: les événements vus par la presse, 1900–1919* (Paris, 1968), 578.

22. Cf. the song "Adieu mon petit gas," APP, Ba 697, and "Hardi les bleus," where "soldiers" announced that "Pour mériter ce petit coeur / Il faut la Croix d'Honneur," Ba 711.

23. See "Le Béguin de Tommy," APP, Ba 700.

24. APP, Ba 697.

25. APP, Ba 700. Madeleine Schmidt calls this song "Le P'tit pioupiou"; see *Chansons de la revanche*, 136–137.

26. "Le Beau Sergent" was composed by the famous revanchist songwriting

duo Villemer and Delormel, APP, Ba 700, and Schmidt, *Chansons de la revanche*, 21–22.

27. "Baiser de l'Alsacienne," APP, Ba 700. See also "Baiser du soleil," Ba 700.

28. See APP, Ba 738.

29. These included Gaby Montbreuse and Rose Amy.

30. See also Parisian *chansonnier* Lucien Boyer's "Le Retour" in the September 20, 1916, edition of *L'Echo des marmites*.

31. In the Fonds Rondel at la Bibliothèque de l'Arsenal (hereafter, BA), Rf 82355.

32. For an earlier example, see the 1915 revue in which "la Gloire" came looking for the wonderful French soldiers of the 211th. BA, Rf 82340.

33. For example, "Le Bon Permissionnaire," APP, Ba 701.

34. This song begins with the soldier in his tank, so it had to have come from late in the war. APP, Ba 707. See also "Que c'est donc(?) bon l'amour," Ba 735.

35. Huss, "Pronatalism and the Popular Ideology," 331. One might note that during the Vietnam War the saying went, "Girls say yes to boys who say no," this time in support of resisting the draft.

36. "Le Cafard," APP, Ba 701.

37. Cf. G. J. Barker-Benfield, "The Spermatic Economy: A Nineteenth-Century View of Sexuality," in *Feminist Studies* 1 (1972), 45–74.

38. Quoted in Geneviève Colin's essay in Becker, *The Great War*, 164. Note that Lavedan's remark was made in 1915, but Joffre's accolade was delivered thirty days into the battle of Verdun in the spring of 1916. In an interview recorded in 1917, Cécile Sorel described meeting troops at performances near the front, and of feeling their "virile energy" (*énergie virile*). See BA, Rf 82489, pièce 5.

39. See "Le Bon Soldat," APP, Ba 701 or "Il était un pioupiou," Ba 711.

40. Quoted in Françoise Thébaud, *La Femme au temps de la guerre de 14* (Paris, 1986), 137, 138–140.

41. Quoted in Thébaud, *La Femme*, 139.

42. Cf. Laurent Gervereau's essay in *Images de 1917*, 128. Some publications, such as *La Vie Parisienne*, had numerous illustrations with women admiring men in uniform.

43. Gervereau has also noted this imprecision in his essay. Ibid., 128.

44. See "Idylle de poilu," APP, Ba 711, copyright 1915, and "La Permission," Ba 721. The song received a visa in December 1916.

45. Reshef, *Guerre, mythes et caricature*, 163–167, esp. 166.

46. Wagner, "Rodin's Reputation," 235.

47. Lithographic pinups abounded in the nineteenth century with *grisettes*, *lorettes*, and nudes. Beatrice Farwell, *The Cult of Images: Baudelaire and the Nineteenth-Century Media Explosion* (Santa Barbara, 1977), 12–13, 91 ff. See also Hammond, *French Undressing*, 12.

48. Guy de Maupassant, *Boule de suif et autres contes normands* (Paris, 1971), 1–43, 385–397, esp. 396. I appreciate having received these references from Susanna Barrows.

49. Susanna Barrows, "Venus and Bacchus in an Era of Mechanical Reproduction" (unpublished manuscript), esp. 18, 17–21.

50. See also Pierre Sorlin, "Words and Images of Nationhood," in *Nationhood and Nationalism in France: From Boulangism to the Great War 1889–1918*, ed. Robert Tombs (New York, 1991), 85–86.

51. Zeyons presents some messages from the backs of specific cards in *Le Roman-photo*, as do Tonie and Valmai Holt in *Till the Boys Come Home. The Picture Postcards of the First World War* (London, 1977).

52. Baconnier, *La Plume au fusil*, 113.

53. Ibid., 114. According to the Holts, in Britain "public display of sensual or suggestive poses" on postcards was not allowed, and British soldiers avidly collected the French examples. But they put them up in the trenches rather than send them home. *Till the Boys Come Home*, 164–169.

54. Note the similarity between *marraine* and *Marianne*, the personification of France. Cf. Maurice Agulhon, *Marianne au pouvoir: l'imagerie et la symbolique républicaines de 1880 à 1914* (Paris, 1989); and Paul Ducatel, *Histoire de la IIIème République, vue à travers l'imagerie populaire et la presse satirique*, vol. 4 (Paris, 1978), 20–23, 33–35.

55. The various Parisian programs are discussed in Thébaud's *La Femme*, 141–143. Sue Grayzel's work also emphasizes the ambiguity of the *marraines*, as well as highlighting some of the anxieties surrounding women's roles. Susan R. Grayzel, "Mothers, Marraines, and Prostitutes: Morale and Morality in First World War France," *International History Review* 19, no. 1 (February 1997): 66–82.

56. See also the ads in *La Vie Parisienne*, quoted in Thébaud, *La Femme*, among the illustrations following 182; see also 141.

57. See for example "Le Cafard du poilu," APP, Ba 701; "Petite marraine," Ba 721; "La Marraine de la vie parisienne" (a medley of anecdotes about soldiers and *marraines*); and "La Marraine des poilus," Ba 716.

58. Cf. "Marraine d'amour," APP, Ba 716; and "Chère marraine," Ba 704.

59. *Voyez Terrasse!*, 1915. BA, Rf 82367.

60. In "En embuscade" by E. Genval, a *poilu* cunningly detailed the good life of the trenches to a shirker (*embusqué*). The malingerer was quite impressed with the concept of the *marraine*, which was described in a musical number replete with suggestive pauses about what the *marraines* had to offer soldiers. BA, Rf 82400.

61. Stéphane Audoin-Rouzeau, *Men at War 1914–1918: National Sentiment and Trench Journalism in France during the First World War*, trans. Helen McPhail (Providence, R.I., 1992), 128–131, esp. 133.

62. *Rigolboche*, July 20, 1915. See also James Daughton, "Sketches of *Poilu Mentalité*: French Trench Cartoons and the Great War" in *World War I and the Cultures of Modernity*, ed. Douglas Mackamon and Michael Mays (Jackson, Miss., 2000).

63. *81 me poil . . . et plume*, 1916(?). See also the February 29, 1916, edition of *Echo des marmites*.

64. "La Marraine du poilu," *Le Poilu du 6-9*, September 1, 1916. See also, the December 1, 1917, article in which soldiers demanded *marraines*.

65. *Le Plus-que-Torial*, January 15, 1916, 2. Lieutenant F. Bossuyt was the director of the paper.

66. Although the *marraine* system was new, a musical genre of romances that combined soldiering, eroticism, and fantasy was not. Old songs such as "Auprès de ma blonde" and "Le Départ du soldat" had expressed the pain of separation, and others had highlighted the "comforts" of garrison life between battles. See, for example, John A. Lynn, *The Bayonets of the Republic* (Chicago, 1984), 150; "Heureux soldats!" APP, Ba 733; and nineteenth-century infantry refrains in Andolenko, *Recueil d'historiques*, 148, 189.

67. Hammond, *French Undressing*, 100; see also, Zeyons, *Le Roman-photo*, 111.

68. "La Permission du poilu," APP, Ba 721. (The phrase "prouver sa flamme" appears repeatedly.)

69. Cf. *La Vie Parisienne*, January 1915.

70. Dorrya Fahmy, *L'Histoire de France à travers la chanson* (Alexandria, Egypt, 1950), 339.

71. Henri Meynard, *L'Anti-Cafard*, 31. BA, Rf 82448.

72. Michel Corday, *The Paris Front* (New York, 1934), 74.

73. Chapter 2 discusses the earliest phase.

74. Théodore Botrel, *Les Chants du bivouac* (Paris, 1915), 46–49.

75. Eve Sedgwick, *Between Men: English Literature and Male Homosocial Desire* (New York, 1985), esp. the introduction and 38, 162, and 19. For a different view, see J. Glenn Gray, *The Warriors: Reflections on Men in Battle* (New York, 1959), esp. 59–95.

76. He also published three volumes of songs for general consumption.

77. Eugénie Buffet, *Ma vie, mes amours, mes aventures* (Paris, 1930), 133.

78. For a reproduction of the front page, which included the music, see Robert Brécy, *Florilège de la chanson révolutionnaire de 1789 au front populaire* (Paris, 1978), 225.

79. See G. Hébert, *La Culture virile et les devoirs physiques de l'officier combattant* (Paris, 1918). Its chapter entitled "Des qualités viriles de l'officier" spoke of "virile qualities" such as *l'énergie, la volonté, le courage, le sang-froid, le coup d'oeil, la décision, la fermeté*, and *le goût de l'initiative* (58–59).

80. Older French colloquial phrases also connected virility and weapons; the phrase "to fire a shot" (*tirer un coup*), for instance, referred to men ejaculating. On pornographic art, literature, and violence, see Stora-Lamarre, *L'Enfer de la IIIe République*, 39.

81. Botrel even referred to the "Marseillaise" in verse fourteen of "Rosalie."

82. Lynn, *The Bayonets of the Republic*, 192.

83. See also Lynn, "En avant! The Origins of the Revolutionary Attack," in *Tools of War: Instruments, Ideas, and Institutions of Warfare, 1445–1871*, ed. John A. Lynn (Chicago, 1990), 154–176, esp. 171–172. Michel Lhospice provided two photographs of a large cannon that protected Paris in 1870 and earned the nickname Joséphine. Lhospice, *La Guerre de 70 et la Commune en 1000 images* (Paris, 1965), 152–153.

84. For instance, "Rondeau de Rosalie," "Rosalie, hommage à notre glorieuse baïonnette," and "Rosalie-Mazurka," APP, Ba 725 and Ba 735, as well as "Ma Baïonnette," written late in the war, Ba 715, and "On cherre, on cherre," Ba 734.

85. APP, Ba 703 and Ba 725. "C'est Rosalie" was sung repeatedly in 1915 and 1916; it was not censored.

86. "Ballade héro-ironique," APP, Ba 700, and "Le Cabot au front," Ba 701. Sometimes, as in the song "Tricoter" by Léon Durocher, other "weapons" were used, still reflecting the phallic shape and role of the preferred weaponry. Guy Breton, *Le Cabaret de l'histoire*, vol. 1 (Paris, 1973), 125–126.

87. APP, Ba 701. This song appears not to have been censored.

88. Cf. Maurice Donnay's praise in Botrel, *Les Chants du bivouac*, 203.

89. Cf. François Déchelette, *L'Argot des poilus* (Paris, 1918), 187–189, and L. Sainéan, *L'Argot des tranchées* (Paris, 1915), 110. One postcard read "The Greeting to the Bayonet: 'Hail to thee, Rosalie, thou fount of charms.'" Corday, *The Paris Front*, 74. See also Zeyons, *Le Roman-photo*, 74–75.

90. APP, Ba 725.

91. Audoin-Rouzeau, *Men at War*, 95.

92. Other soldiers' songs mentioned the bayonet as a weapon worthy of the French. See Henri Meynard, *L'Anti-Cafard*, 13, 5–7. BA, Rf 82448.

93. See, for instance, "De la tranchée," which said: "A part ça, tout va bien. Comme sur des roulettes / Ça barde et ça pète. / Nos baïonnettes font de la pénétration / Dans ces gros Teutons." Vincent Hyspa, "De la tranchée" in *Les Chansons de la guerre* (Paris, 1916), 87–89.

94. Louis Albin, "Les Honneurs du front" in *Les Chansons de la guerre*, 7–8.

95. Botrel, *Chants de bataille et de victoire* (Paris, 1920), 75–78. See also "La Chanson des mitrailleuses," APP, Ba 703, and "Le Canon '75," Ba 701.

96. The broadsheet entitled *La Victoire en chantant* can be found at the Hoover Library, Stanford, California.

97. See "Le Chansonnier," APP, Ba 703. This tune was performed in Paris in November 1915 and in June 1918 spanning two and a half years.

98. Lafond, *Ma mitrailleuse* (Paris, n.d.), 58–63, esp. 59.

99. Ibid., 52–53.

100. For other ambiguous images of women and weaponry, see *Images de 1917*, 122, 165.

101. Fussell, *The Great War and Modern Memory*, 270–309.

102. On prewar anxiety about sexual alternatives, see Annelise Maugue, *L'Identité masculine en crise au tournant du siècle* (Paris, 1987), 145–150, and chs. 1–3.

103. In his essay on propaganda, Gervereau remarked on the eroticism in some of the drawings of German atrocities. *Images de 1917*, 104–105. Reshef's research illustrates the deep roots of this derision. *Guerre, mythes et caricature*, 56, 65–67 ff.

104. APP, Ba 714. Cf. Zeyons, *Le Roman-photo*, 91–92.

105. APP, Ba 697. See also "La Fin de Guillaume II," Ba 709.

106. "C'est Rosalie," APP, Ba 703 and Ba 725.

107. Cf. "Kamarades," APP, Ba 714; "Ils ramass'nt les boch's!!" Ba 712. The jeers did not always call for using the bayonet—sometimes shooting sufficed. See Jean Parigot's "Chanson des poilus," Ba 703.

108. See, for example, "Le Père et le fils" by Maurice Hugnon. BA, Rf 82409.

109. These were reproduced on a postcard which appears in *Images de 1917*, 99. See also the cartoon in *L'Echo des marmites*, January 1917.

110. Quoted in Becker, *The Great War*, 31, 38. See also 30–32, 40–42.

111. Ibid., 163.

112. APP, Ba 700.

113. Madelon represented another wonderful example of ambiguity and patriotic behavior. At least in the Parisian wartime version she was not pronounced a prostitute, nor did she explicitly sleep with any soldier; when one soldier asked to marry her she replied, "Why would I take just one when I love [*aimer*] the whole regiment." On this particular song, see Charles Rearick, "Madelon and the Men—in War and Memory," *French Historical Studies* 17, no. 4 (Fall 1992): 1001–1034.

114. See, for instance, Archives du Service Historique de l'Armée de Terre, 5 N 346, and *Le Rire aux éclats*.

115. Cf. "Permission de Repeuplement," APP, Ba 734.

116. "Quand un soldat," which told soldiers what to say to women in Paris, ran into trouble with the censors because the orchestra had drowned out words leaving obscene possibilities. In this case, the censors finally agreed to changes, but let the basic premise stand. APP, Ba 735.

117. See, for example, "La Perme du poilu," APP, Ba 734. The line between what a censor would or would not accept appears here to have been rather difficult to see.

118. Hunt, *Eroticism and the Body Politic*, 12.

119. See Eric J. Leed, *No Man's Land: Combat and Identity in World War I* (Cambridge, 1979), 8, 101.

120. Louis Chevalier, *Montmartre du plaisir et du crime* (Paris, 1980), 314.

121. Mary Louise Roberts, *Civilization without Sexes: Reconstructing Gender in Postwar France, 1917–1927* (Chicago, 1994), ch. 1.

122. Breton, *Le Cabaret de l'histoire*, vol. 1, 130–131. The song "Nos petits doigts," published in the trench newspaper *La Fusée* in November 1916, also described how women's fingers (particularly those of Parisians) could write tender words or break his heart.

123. "Oui, Madame, c'est la mode," also called "Chanson pour les blessés," APP, Ba 720. This was performed in late 1917.

124. *La Victoire en chantant*.

125. Michelle Perrot, "The New Eve and the Old Adam: French Women's

Condition at the Turn of the Century," in *Behind the Lines: Gender and the Two World Wars*, ed. Margaret Randolph Higonnet, et al. (New Haven, 1987), 60.

126. On World War II and representations of women, see Susan Gubar's article, "'This Is My Rifle, This Is My Gun': World War II and the Blitz on Women," in Higonnet, *Behind the Lines*, 227–259. Aircraft pilots also watched pornography on American naval carriers prior to their bombing missions over Baghdad during the Persian Gulf war in 1991.

Chapter 5 (pages 137–167)

1. Archives de la Préfecture de Police, Paris (hereafter APP), Ba 1587.

2. Jean-Emile Bayard, *Montmartre Past and Present*, trans. Ralph Anningson and Tudor Davies (New York, n.d.), 88. See also Jean-Jacques Becker, *The Great War and the French People*, trans. Arnold Pomerans (Dover, N.H., 1985), 101.

3. In the case of Nazi Germany, for example, Detlev Peukert has described how Germans "craved" normality, even before World War II began, and their need for it made the Nazi utopia, or "Führer myth," attractive. Peukert, *Inside Nazi Germany: Conformity, Opposition, and Racism in Everyday Life*, trans. Richard Deveson (New Haven, 1987), 41–42, 76.

4. See Robert Eben Sackett, *Popular Entertainment, Class, and Politics in Munich, 1900–1923* (Cambridge, Mass., 1982), 77; Gary Stark, "All Quiet on the Home Front: Popular Entertainments, Censorship and Civilian Morale in Germany, 1914–1918," in *Authority, Identity and the Social History of the Great War*, ed. Frans Coetzee and Marilyn Shevin-Coetzee (Providence, R.I., 1995), 57–80, esp. 62 and 76.

5. See APP, Ba 1614.

6. Pierre B. Gheusi, *Guerre et théâtre, 1914–1918* (Paris, 1919), 88.

7. According to a Parisian newspaper on September 12, artists requested that the theaters be reopened, but they were told to wait. Louis Chevalier, *Montmartre du plaisir et du crime* (Paris, 1980), 309.

8. Becker also emphasizes this in *The Great War*, 102.

9. They gleaned information from the wounded coming into the capital, for example.

10. Cf. Gheusi, *Guerre et théâtre*, 95–96, 115–116.

11. APP, Ba 1614.

12. On police actions, see APP, Ba 1614.

13. Eugénie Buffet, *Ma vie, mes amours, mes aventures* (Paris, 1930), 138.

14. Michel Corday, *The Paris Front* (New York, 1934), 27.

15. APP, Ba 1614.

16. Chevalier, *Montmartre du plaisir*, 309; see also Gabriel Perreux, *La Vie quotidienne des civils en France pendant la grande guerre* (Paris, 1966), 273–274.

17. Gheusi, *Guerre et théâtre*, 2.

18. Ibid., 94.

19. On how private initiative also drove the military bureaucracy forward in art and propaganda, see Elizabeth Kahn, *The Neglected Majority: "Les Camoufleurs," Art History, and World War I* (New York, 1984), 4–5, 13.

20. By the end of 1915, six hundred thousand francs had gone to the Assistance Publique. APP, Ba 1614; *Annuaire statistique de la ville de Paris, 1915–1918* (Paris, 1921), 549–556. One source indicates that the original requirement was 15 percent for charities. See Perreux, *La Vie quotidienne*, 274.

21. AN, F21 4031; *Le Figaro*, January 10, 1915.

22. Quoted in Elisabeth Hausser, *Paris au jour le jour* (Paris, 1968), 550. See also APP, Ba 1614.

23. Gheusi, *Guerre et théâtre*, 115.

24. Ibid., 106.

25. Corday, *The Paris Front*, 39.

26. Hausser, *Paris au jour le jour*, 549.

27. The December openings included both smaller *cafés-concerts* and the largest music halls. APP, Ba 1614, the police memo for 1918.

28. This means roughly, "you take things as they come," but the phrase would have been particularly apropos since "guerre" means "war." The program and lyrics can be found in Ro 18340 at la Bibliothèque de l'Arsenal (hereafter BA).

29. Both contemporaries and histories have found it difficult to define the categories of *concert*, theater, *café-concert*, or music hall. American readers may associate theaters just with plays, but French theaters often included musical entertainment. A distinction between music halls and *cafés-concerts* had partially broken down by 1914, as many *cafés-concerts* enlarged their stages and installed benches. But in dealing with a wide range of sites here, I am keeping some of the French distinction between music halls as very large, few in number, and directed at tourists, and *cafés-concerts* as more numerous, smaller, and viewed as more indigenous.

30. Paris revues were already being staged in Marseille in February 1915.

31. APP, Ba 1614.

32. Theodore Felstead pointed to the older ages of members of the British music-hall industry as part of the reason for its decline after 1913. Sidney Theodore Felstead, *Stars Who Made the Halls: A Hundred Years of English Humor, Harmony and Hilarity* (London, [1946]), 11–12. See also David F. Cheshire, *Music Hall in Britain* (Rutherford, 1974), 52–59.

33. For example: Jean Bastia (1878); Dominique Bonnaud (1864); Théodore Botrel (1868); Henri Christiné (1867); Vincent Hyspa (1876); Paul Marinier (1866); Gaston Montéhus (1872).

34. Business went so well that the new team purchased the hall in 1916. In 1917, Léon Volterra left to run the Casino de Paris which also had great success. André Sallée and Philippe Chauveau, *Music-hall et café-concert* (Paris, 1985), 171.

35. Chantal Brunschwig, Louis-Jean Calvet, and Jean-Claude Klein, *100 ans de chanson française* (Paris, 1972), 255.

36. Louis Chevalier has described the "invasion" in his sketch of Montmartre in 1916. *Montmartre du plaisir*, 311.

37. Reports on the composition of audiences are scattered and sketchy, and few contemporary reports mention the difference in gender makeup. Some references can be found in the police archives, since the police evaluated audiences to judge morale. See especially APP, Ba 1614.

38. H. Pearl Adam, *Paris Sees It Through: A Diary 1914–1919* (New York, 1919), 37.

39. Jean Marnold, *Le Cas Wagner* (Paris, 1920), 128.

40. Ibid., 70.

41. See, for instance, the June 5, 1915, program at the Gaîté Parisienne arranged by a deputy from Paris, Charles Bernard. APP, Ba 738.

42. Beethoven was first played at the Salle Gaveau in October 1915, according to the *Mercure de France*; it was Beethoven's "Heroic Symphony," with soldiers in attendance.

43. The Olympia, for example, had been printing its programs in Spanish, French, and English, obviously in response to foreign tourism.

44. APP, Ba 740.

45. On the integration of mass cultural forms in the late nineteenth century, see *Cinema and the Invention of Modern Life*, ed. Leo Charney and Vanessa Schwartz (Berkeley, 1995).

46. My research suggests that the theory that people single-mindedly sought out the darkness of cinemas in wartime Paris does not hold up, at least through 1917. While cheap prices made them more appealing, film industries in Europe suffered from wartime problems.

47. Sallée and Chauveau, *Music-hall et café-concert*, 171.

48. BA, Ro 18373.

49. See, for instance, 1905 files in Archives Nationales, F18 1677.

50. The well-established songwriter Dominique Bonnaud, for example, had published individual songs called "Page de Guerre (Authentique)" by the fall of 1914 which cost only thirty centimes.

51. Jean-Pierre Auclert, *La Grande Guerre des crayons: les noirs dessins de la propagande en 1914–1918* (Paris, 1981), 62.

52. Cf. "C'est moi le Zeppelin," APP, Ba 703; "C'est la pip' que t'as pris," Ba 702.

53. These included La Pie Qui Chante, Le Moulin de la Chanson, Le Caveau de la République, La Chaumière, La Lune Rousse (from 1917 on), Les Noctambules (from 1916 on), Perchoir, Le Casino de Montmartre, and Le Boîte à Fursy. A new Chat Noir appeared in 1918.

54. On their roots, see Herbert, *Chanson à Montmartre*; Mariel Oberthur, *Cafés and Cabarets of Montmartre*, trans. Sheila Azoulai (Salt Lake City, 1984); Roger Shattuck, *The Banquet Years: The Arts in France, 1885–1918* (London, 1958); and Jerrold Seigel, *Bohemian Paris: Culture, Politics and the Boundaries of Bourgeois Life, 1830–1930* (New York, 1986).

55. BA, Ro 18470.

56. Ibid.

57. BA, Ro 18419.

58. Peter Jelavich, *Berlin Cabaret* (Cambridge, 1993).

59. On the popular roots of musical revues, see also Nancy Perloff, *Art and the Everyday: Popular Entertainment and the Circle of Erik Satie* (Oxford, 1986), ch. 1.

60. Not everyone had applauded the shift. See, for example, BA, Ro 18339.

61. Revues were rarely printed. One must rely on theater programs and especially on newspaper critics who passed on plots, jokes, and lyrics.

62. Soldiers also created their own revues; see chapter 7.

63. An individual tableau combined dialogue, lines sung in quick couplets and refrains, and one or two longer songs. Composers borrowed one old tune after another just as in the vaudevilles of the eighteenth century. See Robert M. Isherwood, *Farce and Fantasy: Popular Entertainment in Eighteenth-Century Paris* (New York, 1986), esp. 65.

64. BA, Ro 18387.

65. APP, Ba 1614, November 1915.

66. *La Journée du 75* referred to a special holiday held in 1915 to celebrate the French cannon (the 75) and to collect money.

67. Isherwood, *Farce and Fantasy*, 62.

68. For an excellent prewar example, see the reviews of "Très moutarde" in BA, Ro 18339.

69. BA, Ro 18383.

70. This was in a revue at the Pie Qui Chante in 1915. BA, Ro 18384.

71. In the nineteenth century an avalanche of books appeared on Paris with streets "lovingly" illustrated (such as *Paris chez soi* in 1855), and wood engravings and lithographs portrayed "urban types" like ragpickers, milliners, and *la Parisienne*. Cf. Beatrice Farwell, *The Cult of Images: Baudelaire and the Nineteenth-Century Media Explosion* (Santa Barbara, UCSB Art Museum, 1977), 12, 42, 57. See also Aristide Bruant's classic collections *Dans la rue: chansons et monologues*, 2 vols. (Paris, 1889 and 1895).

72. Just prior to the war, for example, Henri Bergson became a very popular character along with *la Bergsonnienne.*

73. APP, Ba 1614.

74. Rip, *1915* (Paris, 1915), preface. BA, Rf 70827. *1915* was also one of the first revues to be published.

75. Ibid., 2.

76. Wagner's opera *Parsifal* had had its Paris premiere in early 1914.

77. Silver's book discusses the war's repressive effects on the Paris art world. Kenneth Silver, *Esprit de Corps: The Art of the Parisian Avant-Garde and the First World War, 1914–1925* (Princeton, 1989), 10–13 esp. See also Theda Shapiro, *Painters and Politics: The European Avant-Garde and Society, 1900–1925* (New York, 1976).

78. Rip, *1915,* 6.

79. Ibid., 7–8.

80. For definitions of this decadence, see Eugen Weber, *France: Fin de Siècle* (Cambridge, Mass., 1986), 9–26.

81. APP, Ba 1614.

82. Rip, *1915,* 106.

83. Ibid., 113.

84. BA, Ro 18383.

85. Corday, *The Paris Front,* 68.

86. Guy Breton, *Le Cabaret de l'histoire,* vol. 1 (Paris, 1973), 124, 143. The music registries in the Archives Nationales, F18* VIII 142–149 illustrate this pattern, although the number of new patriotic songs fell off in 1918.

87. Adam, *Paris Sees It Through,* 42.

88. Ibid., 57.

89. Corday, *The Paris Front,* 78. He claimed that the newspapers did not report the huge crowds and thus condoned the "embarrassing" situation (225).

90. The *Annuaire statistique,* for example, reported that receipts doubled between 1915 and 1916. The police received 150 programs (with 2,000 songs) each week. APP, Ba 1614.

91. The local barracks in Paris usually had free tickets to theaters and to the Opéra for soldiers on leave. Wartime prices at the Opéra ranged from one to seven francs, whereas prewar prices had been sixteen to twenty francs. Weber, *France: Fin de Siècle,* 167. Elisabeth Hausser has claimed that soldiers on leave made up 40 percent of the audiences in the *salle de spectacles* by 1916. Hausser, *Paris au jour le jour,* 612.

92. Stark, "All Quiet," 63.

93. Sallée and Chauveau, *Music-hall et café-concert,* 161–162.

94. See Laurent Gervereau's essay "La Propagande par l'image en France 1914–1918," in *Images de 1917* (Paris, 1987), 98–185, on the various themes in visual materials, and the tenacity of anti-German ridicule.

95. APP, Ba 1614.

96. Brunschwig, Calvet, and Klein, *100 ans de chanson française,* 48.

97. APP, Ba 729.

98. Two other very popular songs from this period, both by Willems, were "Ce que chantent les flots de la Marne" and "Le Chant du retour," which expressed equally vivid patriotism.

99. BA, Ro 18409. In the popular song "Ils ne passeront pas," Pétain led resolute *poilus* against the "dirty boches." Its refrain called for a march in 2/4 time, then incorporated one melodic line from the "Marseillaise" and one from "On les aura," and then ended with a shout. APP, Ba 712.

100. APP, Ba 704.

101. It was sung, for instance, at the Folies Belleville, and at the Kursaal in January and March 1916. See also "Idylle de poilu." APP, Ba 711.

102. These included the Zenith, Théâtre Edouard VII, Brunin, and Casino de Paris.

103. Sallée and Chauveau's extensive list shows that no musical establishments closed in 1915, 1916, and 1917, and at least five new places opened. *Music-hall et café-concert*, 114–190. The police claimed that five new places opened in 1917 alone. The information on individual places during the war is quite fragmented and sometimes contradictory. See appendix B.

104. Stark, "All Quiet," 63.

105. Quoted in André Ducasse, Jacques Meyer, and Gabriel Perreux, *Vie et mort des français, 1914–1918* (Paris, 1959), 250, 261.

106. Cf. Ducasse, Meyer, and Perreux, *Vie et morts*, 261, and Corday, *The Paris Front*, 126, 209.

107. Corday, *The Paris Front*, 211. For a similar complaint in the provinces, see Becker, *The Great War*, 143–146.

108. Ducasse, Meyer, and Perreux, *Vie et mort*, 263.

109. Quoted in Corday, *The Paris Front*, 189.

110. *Le Crapouillot*, 1915(?).

111. APP, Ba 702.

112. Robert Brécy, *Florilège de la chanson révolutionnaire de 1789 au front populaire* (Paris, 1978), 228.

113. Cf. "Ce qu'ils font pendant la guerre," APP, Ba 702.

114. APP, Ba 738, and Pierre Barbier et France Vernillat, *Histoire de France par les chansons*, vol. 8 (Paris, 1961), 227–229.

115. *Journal Officiel de la République Française. Annexes.* Documents Parlementaires, Chambre, 1916. (Annexe no. 1866, 336).

116. After negotiations, cinemas chose Tuesdays, *concerts* Wednesdays, and theaters Fridays. At the same time, all outside illumination was suppressed and inside lights lowered for cinemas and theaters.

117. Jean Bernard Passerieu, *La Vie de Paris, 1917* (Paris, 1918), 152.

118. Ibid., 75–79.

119. BA, Ro 18434.

120. APP, Ba 1614, and *Annuaire statistique*.

Chapter 6 (pages 168–198)

1. Paul Marie De la Gorce, *The French Army*, trans. Kenneth Douglas (London, 1963), 103.

2. For more detailed descriptions of life in the trenches, see also André Ducasse, Jacques Meyer, and Gabriel Perreux, *Vie et mort des français, 1914–1918* (Paris, 1959); Jacques Meyer, *La Vie quotidienne des soldats pendant la grande guerre* (Paris, 1966); Paul Fussell, *The Great War and Modern Memory* (New York, 1975), esp. ch. 2; and Eric Leed, *No Man's Land: Combat and Identity in World War I* (Cambridge, 1979).

3. Leed, *No Man's Land*, 101.

4. Henry Malherbe used the term "personnalité abrégée," quoted in Ducasse, Meyer, and Perreux, *Vie et mort*, 88.

5. Leed, *No Man's Land*.

6. Cf. Fussell, *The Great War*; Stéphane Audoin-Rouzeau, *Men at War, 1914–1918: National Sentiment and Trench Journalism in France during the First World War* (New York, 1992). John Fuller's study goes the furthest in asserting that Brit-

ish soldiers remained citizens in uniform, having brought all of their own popular culture with them. J. G. Fuller, *Troop Morale and Popular Culture in the British and Dominion Armies* (Oxford, 1990).

7. Kenneth Silver, for example, has argued that the "front itself was rather free of ideology," compared to Paris. As long as they kept performing their duties, the army was not overly concerned with soldiers' cultural expressions. Silver, *Esprit de Corps: The Art of the Parisian Avant-Garde and the First World War, 1914–1925* (Princeton, 1989), 81–84. See also Elizabeth Kahn, *The Neglected Majority: "Les Camoufleurs," Art History, and World War I* (New York, 1984), 100.

8. Besides Audoin-Rouzeau's and Kahn's work, see James Daughton, "Sketches of the Poilu World: Trench Cartoons from the Great War" in *World War I and the Cultures of Modernity,* ed. Douglas Mackaman and Michael Mays (Jackson, Miss., 2000).

9. Ducasse, Meyer, and Perreux, *Vie et mort,* 90.

10. On the British use of rituals, see Paul Fussell, *The Great War,* 131.

11. Emile-François Julia, *La Fatalité de la guerre, scènes et propos du front* (Paris, 1917), 21; and Meyer, *La Vie quotidienne,* 265–266.

12. See Jean Bernier's chapter entitled "Chanson du tir de barrage" in *La Percée* (Paris, 1920), 198–200.

13. See, for example, Georges Gaudy, *Les Trous d'obus de Verdun* (Paris, 1922), 167; Julia, *La Fatalité de la guerre,* 222, 16–17; and Rf 82488, pièce 14, in the Fonds Rondel at la Bibliothèque de l'Arsenal (hereafter BA).

14. André Bridoux, *Souvenirs du temps des morts* (Paris, 1930), 140–141.

15. Louis Mairet gave a complicated, depressing explanation in one of his diary entries from late 1916: "N'y manque-t-il pas, avant tout, la voix formidable des batteries, la musique impérieuse des obus dans leurs trajectoires, le fracas de leurs éclatements, . . . —effrayant orchestre qu'aucune plume ne saurait imiter, accompagnement nécessaire de tout ce qui se passe là-bas, . . . ébranlement de la terre et des airs qui bourdonne dans les oreilles longtemps encore après qu'on ne l'entend plus." Mairet, *Carnet d'un combattant, 11 Février 1915–16 Avril 1917* (Paris, 1919), 247.

16. On naval ritual, see Fernand Darde, *Vingt mois de guerre à bord du Croiseur "Jeanne d'Arc" 9 août 1914–12 avril 1916* (Paris, 1918), 228, 166–167.

17. Jacques Heugel, *Aveux et souvenirs* (Paris, 1968), 35, 56.

18. See Archives du Service Historique de l'Armée de Terre (hereafter ASHAT), 7 N 403; and Heugel, *Aveux et souvenirs,* 62.

19. Regimental musicians represented themselves as soldiers first, then musicians; artists in the *camoufleur* unit did the reverse. Kahn, *The Neglected Majority,* 18, 44.

20. Heugel, *Aveux et souvenirs,* 48.

21. Ibid., 7–8, 23–24, 108–109.

22. *L'Homme libre* in 1917 and in *L'Illustration*; quoted in Georges Lafond, *Covered with Mud and Glory: A Machine Gun Company in Action,* trans. Edwin File Rich (Boston, 1918), xiv-xv.

23. Général (Gabriel Sainte Marie) Bon, *Causeries et souvenirs, 1914–1915* (Paris, 1916), 18.

24. From *Le Journal,* April 17, 1918. Cited in Elisabeth Hausser, *Paris au jour le jour: les événements vus par la presse, 1900–1919* (Paris, 1968), 676. See also René Des Touches, *Pages de gloire et de misère* (Paris, 1917), 156–164.

25. Maurice Barrès, in *Scènes et doctrines du nationalisme* (Paris, 1902), 137; quoted in Jean-Denis Bredin, *The Affair: The Case of Alfred Dreyfus,* trans. Jeffrey Mehlman (New York, 1986), 6–7.

26. Quoted in Gérard Boutet, *Ils étaient de leur village: le temps des guerres, 1914–1939* (Paris, 1981), 182–183.

27. BA, Rf 82485 (4).

28. Mairet, *Carnet d'un combattant*, 269.

29. Bernier, *La Percée*, 56–65, esp. 64–65; see also Julia, *La Fatalité de la guerre*, 26.

30. Mairet, *Carnet d'un combattant*, 59.

31. BA, Rf 82371; see also Roland Dorgelès, *Le Cabaret de la belle femme* (Paris, 1928), 162–163, 188.

32. Mairet, *Carnet d'un combattant*, 186, 291.

33. See Maurice Genevoix, *Ceux de 14* (Paris, 1950), 14; Ducasse, Meyer, and Perreux, *Vie et mort*, 82; Gaudy, *Les Trous d'obus*, 94–96.

34. Charles Foley, *1914–1915: la vie de guerre contée par les soldats* (Paris, 1915), 170–171.

35. Captain Massy, *Moyens à employer pour maintenir et relever le moral des soldats en campagne*, quoted in René Thorel, *Un Cercle pour le soldat* (Paris, 1909), 269.

36. We can only imagine the specific lyrics as a part of the erotic genre discussed in chapter 4. Lafond, *Ma mitrailleuse* (Paris, n.d.), 75. See also, Bon, *Causeries et souvenirs*, 17–18.

37. BA, Rf 82350 and Rf 82485/5, pièce 34. The 106th Infantry regiment's marching song was, not surprisingly, in 2/4 time, and began and ended *fortissimo*. See BA, Rf 82322.

38. Emile-François Julia specifically used the example of popular songs. Julia, *La Fatalité de la guerre*, 119–120, 123–124.

39. Mairet, *Carnet d'un combattant*, 59, 69, 160–161.

40. Pierre-Maurice Masson, *Lettres de guerre, août 1914–avril 1916* (Paris, 1917), 118.

41. Heugel, *Aveux et souvenirs*, 58.

42. BA, Rf 82349.

43. Lafond, *Ma mitrailleuse*, 58.

44. Ibid., 59.

45. Ibid., 90.

46. John Brophy describes British marching songs, but says that songs were not sung in battle. John Brophy and Eric Partridge, *The Long Trail: What the British Soldier Sang and Said in the Great War of 1914–1918* (London, 1965), 23.

47. *La Jeune France*, August 13, 1916; quoted in Boutet, *Ils étaient de leur village*, 132.

48. Lafond, *Ma mitrailleuse*, 175–177. See also André Gauthier, *Les Chansons de notre histoire* (Paris, 1967), 189; Guy Breton, *Le Cabaret de l'histoire*, vol. 1 (Paris, 1973), 127; Foley, *1914–1915: la vie de guerre*, 38 and 257; as well as Charles Rearick's newspaper examples in "Madelon and the Men—in War and Memory," *French Historical Studies* 17, no. 4 (Fall 1992): 1007, n. 8.

49. Julia, *La Fatalité de la guerre*, 228–229.

50. Michel Corday, *The Paris Front* (New York, 1934), 199.

51. Roger Boutefeu, *Les Camarades: soldats français et allemands au combat 1914–1918* (Paris, 1966), 44.

52. Pierre Chaine, *Les Mémoires d'un rat* (Paris, [1917?]), 78–79. As a second lieutenant, Charles de Gaulle also experienced the traditional cues used under futile circumstances. See Ducasse, Meyer, and Perreux, *Vie et mort*, 39.

53. Ducasse, Meyer, and Perreux, *Vie et mort*, 122–123.

54. On the elision of war and ritual, see Leed, *No Man's Land*, 32, 38, 122; and Tony Ashworth, *Trench Warfare 1914–1918: The Live and Let Live System* (London, 1980), 90.

55. Raymond Lefebvre and Paul Vaillant-Couturier, *La Guerre des soldats* (Paris, 1919), 49–62.

56. Ibid., 53, 55.

57. On "irony-assisted recall," see Fussell, *The Great War*, 30.

58. Lefebvre and Vaillant-Couturier, *La Guerre des soldats*, 57–58.

59. Ibid., 62.

60. ASHAT, 6 N 110; BA, Rf 82489, pièce 27.

61. See BA, Rf 82485 (4), pièce 30; Rf 82485 (5), pièce 5; Rf 82485, pièce 23; Rf 82487, pièces 2 and 18. The other common example referred to the Zouaves' theater during the siege of Sebastopol. See BA, Rf 82485 (4), pièce 40; Rf 82491, pièce 26.

62. BA, Rf 82489, pièce 5.

63. BA, Rf 82485 (1–4), esp. 3 and 4.

64. Thorel, *Un Cercle pour le soldat*, 129 and part 2, section H; see also the newspaper clippings in BA, Rf 82485 (4).

65. Thorel, *Un Cercle pour le soldat*, 135. He also targetted tuberculosis, alcoholism, and antimilitarism (11–16).

66. A Captain Deverin, who wrote in support of the campaign, maintained that officers' participation would strengthen (*resserrer*) "les liens de camaraderie et d'amitié qui . . . surtout, au jour du danger, si vous aviez à marcher contre les ennemis du dehors, augmenteraient votre force et votre courage!" Ibid., 269.

67. Ibid., 275. Thorel paid special attention to the necessary infrastructure, explaining how to raise money and providing several blueprints for the *salles de récréation*. At the 113th Infantry's Théâtre Maurice de Saxe (at Blois), soldiers came every Thursday for "projections lumineuses, une comédie, des chansonnettes et un orchestre avec piano, violons, violoncelles, etc." (277).

68. ASHAT, 6 N 110.

69. *Bulletin des Armées* and ASHAT, 5 N 566. The army did not seem as comfortable with the soldiers' own creations (and subculture) as with the Parisian professional composers. Then in late 1917 the paper changed its content and format to resemble trench newspapers more closely.

70. ASHAT, 5 N 566.

71. See Lafond, *Ma mitrailleuse*, 94; Foley, *1914–1915: la vie de guerre*, 91–92, 134, 225. This combination of official army and religion would have made republicans more nervous before 1914.

72. In one case in 1918, a committee headed by Camille Saint-Saëns of the Institut de France requested fifty men to form a military symphony; here, the army's concern for manpower overrode the propaganda value for civilians. ASHAT, 6 N 110.

73. Lafond, *Ma mitrailleuse*, 165.

74. Heugel, *Aveux et souvenirs*, 51. See also BA, Rf 82362.

75. Louis Huot and Paul Voivenel, *La Psychologie du soldat* (Paris, 1918).

76. Théodore Botrel, *Les Mémoires d'un barde Breton* (Paris, 1933), 13.

77. Eugénie Buffet, *Ma vie, mes amours, mes aventures* (Paris, 1930), 128–132.

78. Ibid., 136.

79. Like Botrel and Buffet, de Buxeuil had been active in the Ligue des Patriotes and a supporter of the radical right. In Buffet's words, "l'héroïsme de nos grands soldats était exalté en de magnifiques et sonores couplets." Ibid., 132.

80. Ibid., 128–156, esp. 138–140.

81. Ibid., 135–136.

82. Botrel, "Les Souvenirs d'un barde errant," *La Revue Belge*, January 1, 1923. See BA, Ro 14524.

83. A photograph of Botrel on the cover of the magazine *Paris Qui Chante* in February 1916 shows him with an armband that reads "Ministre de la Guerre."

84. Kahn, *The Neglected Majority*, 6.

85. Maurice Barrès, who attended a concert, declared: "In what a noble milieu, I find myself! This is truly a ready foyer, from which the enthusiasm of the battle, the

acceptance of sacrifice, the great shiver of heroism will leave." Quoted in Théodore Botrel, *Les Chants du bivouac* (Paris, 1915), x.

86. For various newspaper articles on Botrel, including his obituaries, see BA, Ro 14527 and Ro 14528, especially the April 26, 1922, article from *Le Devoir.*

87. ASHAT, 5 N 567.

88. Archives de la Préfecture de Police, Paris (hereafter APP), Ba 711.

89. BA, Ro 14527.

90. See ASHAT, 16 N 2404.

91. ASHAT, 6 N 110.

92. See BA, Rf 82486, pièce 21; Rf 82481, pièce 15. As Buffet described it, "Nous chantions n'importe où, n'importe comment, . . . dans la boue et dans le sang." *Ma vie, mes amours,* 138.

93. Beatrix Dussane, *Reines de théâtre, 1633–1941* (Lyon, 1944), 197.

94. Suze Rueff, *I Knew Sarah Bernhardt* (London, 1951), 225; Dussane, *Reines de théâtre,* 197–200.

95. G. G. Geller, *Sarah Bernhardt,* trans. E. S. G. Potter (London, 1933), 259.

96. Cf. BA, Rf 82486, pièces 24 and 25, and Rf 82489, pièce 5, which has photographs.

97. ASHAT, 16 N 2404; 6 N 110.

98. BA, Rf 82488, pièce 18.

99. BA, Rf 82491, pièce 15.

100. BA, Rf 82489, pièce 5.

101. BA, Rf 82486, pièce 4; Rf 82491, pièce 15.

102. ASHAT, 16 N 2404.

103. See, for example, Nelly Martyl dramatically displayed on the cover of *Je sais tout.* BA, Rf 82488, pièce 4; Rf 82487, pièce 2.

104. BA, Rf 82489, pièce 5.

105. This remark referred to Beatrix Dussane. Ducasse, Meyer, and Perreux, *Vie et mort,* 230. See also BA, Rf 82491, pièce 15.

106. BA, Rf 82486, pièces 7 and 26.

107. BA, Rf 82485 (4); see also BA, Rf 82486, pièce 20.

108. BA, Rf 82486, pièce 28 bis. A postwar memo credited military leaders such as Commander Poulet, and Generals Bonnier, Nivelle, and Pétain.

109. Cf. September 13, 1917, memo; ASHAT, 18 N 386 and March 9, 1918, memo; ASHAT, 16 N 2404.

110. BA, Rf 82485 (5), pièce 13.

111. ASHAT, 6 N 110.

112. See BA, Rf 82486 pièce 28 bis and *L'Illustration;* photographs appear in Hausser, *Paris au jour le jour,* 603, and Rf 82486, pièce 22.

113. See ASHAT, 18 N 386, for a copy of the blueprints.

114. See memos in ASHAT, 16 N 2404 and 18 N 386. See also BA, Rf 82491, pièces 5 and 19.

115. BA, Rf 82485 (5), pièce 13.

116. This program may have taken place at a military hospital in St. Dié in the Vosges. BA, Rf 82491, pièce 21, as well as pièces 19, 20, and 22.

117. BA, Rf 82485/5, pièce 31.

118. APP, Ba 702.

119. See, for example, the program for the "Théâtre du Front / 54e R.I. / Matinée récréative." BA, Rf 82491, pièce 13.

120. The decorators worked out a set of six motifs to decorate each theater, once they had the larger orders. These included celebrating the patriotic "coq gaulois" singing, sets of musical instruments, illustrations of popular songs, images of *le pinard,* or soldiers' wine, depictions of the most picturesque corners of Paris, and

the symbols of reconquered Alsace. These all fit within the formula of promoting "popular" culture, patriotism, and Parisian culture. BA, Rf 82485 (5), pièce 13.

121. ASHAT, 16 N 2404, and BA, Rf 82485/5, pièce 13.

122. See memo 181/G, dated March 8, 1918, in ASHAT, 16 N 2404, as well as the November 22, 1918, memo in 18 N 386.

123. With regard to Sarah Bernhardt's performances, see Cornelia Otis Skinner, *Madame Sarah* (Boston, 1967), 322, and Phillippe Jullian, *Sarah Bernhardt* (Paris, 1977), 254. Some of the response was prearranged; officers chose "jeunes soldats" "capables de prononcer quelques mots de compliment," who were to present a bouquet to the female artist. BA, Rf 82491, pièce 26.

124. BA, Rf 82486, pièce 13; Rf 82488, pièce 3.

125. Boutefeu, *Les Camarades*, 141–145.

Chapter 7 *(pages 199–236)*

1. On Renoir's techniques and goals, see Jean Renoir, *My Life and My Films*, trans. Norman Denny (New York, 1974); and Christopher Faulkner, *Jean Renoir: A Guide to References and Resources* (Boston, 1979). Concerning one actual prison camp, a report described the French having organized a 140-member chorus which sang "chants patriotiques" composed by fellow prisoners, accompanied by home-made instruments including violins and cellos. Archives du Service Historique de l'Armée de Terre (hereafter ASHAT), 6 N 23. See also ASHAT, 7 N 955 and the revues *Cafard, revue prisonnière et libre* and *L'Ange en Salza* in the Fonds Rondel.

2. Quoted in Paul Fussell, *The Great War and Modern Memory* (New York, 1975), 115.

3. Stéphane Audoin-Rouzeau, *Men at War, 1914–1918: National Sentiment and Trench Journalism in France during the First World War* (New York, 1992), 28. He also pointed out, however, that only a minority of the soldiers had the opportunity or ability to read the papers (25). Jacques Lethève also called trench newspapers "organes de circonstance." *La Caricature sous la IIIe République* (Paris, 1986), 141.

4. As one ethnographer explained "Une des caractéristiques de la vieille chanson, c'est le mystère qui entoure son origine. . . . [E]lle est l'oeuvre non pas d'un seul auteur, mais de générations de chanteurs." Gaston Sévrette, *Les Vieilles chansons des pays de France* (Paris, 1922), 9–10.

5. Letters by Eugène Gaschy(?), 242nd Infantry, and by B. Moneuquet(?), 95th Territorial. ASHAT, 5 N 566.

6. Letter by Humbert, Téléphoniste, 104th Territorial. ASHAT, 5 N 566.

7. Not all of the letters, however, were completely self-effacing. See, for example, André Laphin's letter regarding "l'Armée Pétain" which claimed that thousands of copies of his song had already been distributed. ASHAT, 5 N 566.

8. Rf 82448 in the Fonds Rondel at la Bibliothèque de l'Arsenal (hereafter BA). Pierre-Jakez Hélias described his father creating a book of Breton and French songs during his military service, helped by a noncommissioned officer. *The Horse of Pride: Life in a Breton Village*, trans. June Guicharnaud (New Haven, 1980), 16.

9. Cf. *Rigolboche, Le Poilu du 6–9* or *L'Etoupilles* compared to *La Fusée* or *Jusqu'au Bout!* Audoin-Rouzeau, however, does caution against relying solely on appearances.

10. See the letters from an E. Robert and G. Michaux and from a captain Lapelle. ASHAT, 5 N 566.

11. Ozzin(?) Hyacinthe's song, "Courage Boche," had been written "en première ligne" in late 1916. ASHAT, 5 N 566.

12. See BA, Rf 82340; Jacques Heugel, *Aveux et souvenirs* (Paris, 1968), 78, 100–101, and BA, Rf 82436.

13. See the letter from a sub-lieutenant Couture. ASHAT, 5 N 566; and BA, Rf 82416.

14. Ibid. (emphasis in the original). See also, the letters from A. Jodry and Corporal L. Hirou. Officers' memoirs sometimes noted having songs dedicated to them by one of their soldiers. In André Benoît's case, it was a song about tobacco. *Trois mois de guerre au jour le jour (1914)* (Paris, 1967), 66.

15. Here, the writer carefully noted he sought "no profit from his offer." ASHAT, 5 N 566.

16. Meyer, *La Vie quotidienne des soldats*, 28–29, 357. Annick Cochet, "Les Paysans sur le front en 1916," *Bulletin du Centre d'Histoire de la France Contemporaine* 3 (1982): 38; David Englander, "The French Soldier, 1914–18" *French History* 1, no. 1 (March 1987): 67.

17. Gérard Baconnier, André Minet, and Louis Soler, *La Plume au fusil: les poilus du Midi à travers leur correspondance* (Toulouse, 1985), 91.

18. See the letter from F. Serrie (9th Regiment), or from Bernard(?) (141st Territorial). ASHAT, 5 N 566.

19. BA, Rf 82448.

20. The May 1916 edition of *81 me poil . . . et plume* also contained a "Pot-pourri destructeur des Boches" by "X," who simply advised it should be sung: "in chorus on the well-known older tunes." See also Catriens and Levy, *Pourvu qu'on Rigole!!*, 1915, 9. BA, Rf 82373.

21. See adjudant B. Moneuquet's "Verdun 'on n'passe pas'" set to the music "Sur les bords de la Riviera" (by L. Daniderff and Bertal-Maubon, c. 1913). ASHAT 5 N 566.

22. Excerpts of "Revues de détails: scènes d'actualité de la campagne 1914–1915" appeared in *Fantasio*. BA, Rf 82436.

23. These professionals included Maurice Hamel and Marcel Dambrine, as well as Pierre Chagnon, Robert Casa, and Henri Le Point from the magazine *Paris qui chante*.

24. Before the war, he had given music lessons in Paris and played organ in his church. Georges Lafond, *Ma mitrailleuse* (Paris, n.d.), 171.

25. Jacques Heugel, the regimental musician, provides another good example of this transformation.

26. Not all of the professionals came from Paris; Clérouc's troupe, for instance, included professionals from the Kursaal in Reims, the Théâtre in Namur, and the Conservatoire of Tourcoing.

27. This tension can be seen particularly well in the letter from Adrien Raynal to the *Bulletin*, which he ended with two separate closings: "Soldat Adrien Raynal / au Commandement d'Etapes / de Brienne-le-Chateaux (Aube)" and then below "Adrien Raynal / Compositeur de musique / Lauréat de l'Institut / 30 Rue le Prince(?) / Paris." ASHAT, 5 N 566.

28. See the article in the trench newspaper *Marmita*, October 1, 1917. It is reproduced in BA, Rf 82485/5, pièce 32.

29. See, for instance, the letters by E. Bertaud and André Fiquet. ASHAT, 5 N 566.

30. As part of the popular culture, trench newspapers were also distributed for free or for a very low fee. But they were much more expensive to produce, so that even when editors did not want to charge, they were often forced to or they took subsidies from civilians. Audoin-Rouzeau, *Men at War*, 25–27.

31. From *Marmita*, May 30, 1915, quoted in Audoin-Rouzeau, *Men at War*, 7.

32. *Ma mitrailleuse*, 28. Roland Dorgelès's novel *Le Cabaret de la belle femme*

(Paris, 1928), also included the character Belin, "ce petit Parigot" who returned from leave "having learned the latest hits by heart," 295; see also 248, in which a song taught by Belin reminded the main character of his "cher Paris, un coin de rue mouillée, le joueur de guitare, deux têtes de trottin sur la même chanson."

33. Raymond Lefebvre and Paul Vaillant-Couturier, *La Guerre des soldats* (Paris, 1919), 33–35.

34. Pézard incorporated both Chopin (repeatedly) and an adaptation of music-hall tunes. André Pézard, *Nous autres à Vauquois 1915–1916* (Paris, 1918), 13, 33, 38, 49.

35. Lafond, *Ma mitrailleuse*, 28, 31, 32, 67, 74. This manner of expression seems analogous to John Fuller's British examples of music-hall lyrics entwined with regular communication. J. G. Fuller, *Troop Morale and Popular Culture in the British and Dominion Armies* (Oxford, 1990), 121–122.

36. Lafond, *Ma mitrailleuse*, 32. Lafond also recalled Burette singing at least thirty verses of "A Montparnasse," one of Aristide Bruant's well-known pieces about Paris (133).

37. Quoted in Lafond, *Ma mitrailleuse*, 123–125.

38. Ibid., 125.

39. Ibid., 127. For another example of a nighttime raid described as "a premiere at the Grand-Guignol," see ibid., 229.

40. This was reportedly true for Americans and British also. Cf. John J. Niles, Douglas Moore, and A. A. Wallgren, *The Songs My Mother Never Taught Me* (New York, 1929), 9, and John Brophy and Eric Partridge, *The Long Trail: What the British Soldier Sang and Said in the Great War of 1914–1918* (London, 1965), 23.

41. Quoted in Baconnier, *La Plume au fusil*, 92.

42. Even some small villages had theaters, and churches were quite numerous. This moves the French experience away from Eric Leed's description. Leed, *No Man's Land: Combat and Identity in World War I* (Cambridge, 1979).

43. Jean Giraudoux, *Lectures pour une ombre* (Paris, 1918), 158. Guillot de Saix even mentioned "Montmartre cabarets" having been set up in the bombed out cellars of Reims. See BA, Rf 82487, pièce 18.

44. Heugel, *Aveux et souvenirs*, 49. In one case, a classical pianist played "overtures" and "symphonies" by heart and gave a lesson in music analysis; another sang famous arias including parts of Georges Bizet's "Carmen."

45. Louis Mairet, *Carnet d'un combattant: 11 Février 1915–16 Avril 1917* (Paris, 1919), 62.

46. Phonographs traveled on naval ships where lugging them around was not an issue. See Fernand Darde, *Vingt mois de guerre à bord du Croiseur "Jeanne d'Arc" 9 août 1914–12 avril 1916* (Paris, 1918).

47. BA, Rf 82486, pièce 5. The correspondent praised their choice of pieces as "toujours de belle tenue," and listed Glück, Chopin, Massenet, Widor, and Saint-Saëns.

48. Tony Ashworth, *Trench Warfare 1914–1918: The Live and Let Live System* (London, 1980), 139.

49. Lefebvre and Vaillant-Couturier, *La Guerre des soldats,* 83–90.

50. Ibid., 89.

51. Some impromptu, informal singing, cited repeatedly in memoirs, occurred the night before battles, often accompanied by drinking. The entertainment seemed to act as a release from the pressure or as an escape from foreboding thoughts. See Lafond, *Ma mitrailleuse*, 211–225, esp. 213–215; Mairet, *Carnet d'un combattant*, 204, and 81.

52. André Bridoux, *Souvenirs du temps des morts* (Paris, 1930), 68–69.

53. Ibid., 39–59.

54. The distance across No Man's Land varied from an average of two to three hundred yards to as little as having only sandbags between the two sides.

55. Although Tony Ashworth's argument, that these truces were very widespread, has been challenged, anecdotal evidence certainly exists. See, for example, Roger Boutefeu, *Les Camarades: soldats français et allemands au combat 1914–1918* (Paris, 1966), 86, 115, 209–210; Heugel, *Aveux et souvenirs*, 62; and Michel Corday, *The Paris Front* (New York, 1934), 47 (no translator named).

56. Roland Dorgelès's chapter on Christmas Eve described the soldiers singing the "Marseillaise," with "échos qui jaillissaient du ventre des tranchées, comme si la terre même eût chanté." Other songs included "Minuit, Chrétiens," "les Montagnards," a music-hall tune, and some Schumann by the Germans. *Le Cabaret*, 246. See also Charles Foley, *1914–1915: la vie de guerre contée par les soldats* (Paris, 1915), 227–230.

57. Ashworth points to regular exchanges of musical entertainment in different sectors. Ashworth, *Trench Warfare*, 139–140.

58. Boutefeu, *Les Camarades*, 115.

59. Paul Allard provides another such photograph taken in Champagne in 1915. Allard, *Images secrètes de la guerre; 200 photographies et documents censurés en France* (Paris, 1933), 40.

60. See, for example, the letters sent to the *Mercure de France* by soldiers weighing in on the debate over playing German music in Paris. Jean Marnold, *Le Cas Wagner* (Paris, 1920), appendix. See also, Georges Etienne Bonnet, *L'Ame du soldat* (Paris, 1917), 57–58, 66.

61. See chapter 1.

62. See Edouard Audy's letter with his trench revue *Paris-C. 17*. BA, Rf 82359 and Rf 82486, pièce 24. C. 17 was an aviation squadron.

63. For hospital performances see, for instance, "Cyrano chez la Croix-Rouge," BA Rf 82357, as well as Rf 82412; Rf 82418; Rf 82445; Rf 82446; Rf 82447; Rf 82455 (the last was called a "revue chirurgico-militaire").

64. BA, Rf 82486, pièce 18. Other theater locales included St. Dié, Ville-en-Woëvre, Toul (near Nancy), Châtel-sur-Moselle, and Beaumetz-les-Loges.

65. This was at the Dépôt des Eclopés. BA, Rf 82486, pièce 6. Teulet also did at least one trip with the Théâtre aux Armées in February 1917.

66. There appear to have been no women. This program was for September 9, 1917, from 2 P.M. to 6 P.M. The price was twenty-five centimes. Someone handwrote on the artifact: "Présents 1000 poilus et officiers." BA, Rf 82491, pièce 29.

67. Quoted in Gérard Boutet, *Ils étaient de leur village: le temps des guerres, 1914–1939* (Paris, 1981), 72–74.

68. BA, Rf 82436. See also Rf 82486, pièce 13, which mentions that the Poilu-Park was "no more" than eight kilometers from the Germans. And Maurice Hugnon's letter to Guillot de Saix, in BA, Rf 82409.

69. BA, Rf 82341. This revue took place in January 1918. See also "Saint-Brieuc . . . Chine!," BA, Rf 82455 bis.

70. At one point Le Civil interrupted the *commère*, saying "je m'étonne que vous, notre bonne ville de Vendôme, vous autorisiez cette bande de jeunes fous, à venir ainsi trouble le calme de nos demeures!"

71. As noted in chapter 6, the production of theatrical amusements and revues was not new in World War I; the practice extended back into the eighteenth century.

72. He mentioned only one that was rehearsed but never performed. BA, Rf 82487, pièce 18. Although assembled quickly, some revues were typed, while others were printed. Fortunately, some were transmitted to the archives; the Arsenal, which contains over fifty revues for World War I, actually has more printed versions of revues from the troops than for wartime Paris. See BA, Rf 82311 ff.

73. Of these, the biggest group represented noncommissioned officers and subalterns.

74. ASHAT, 5 N 566.

75. See, for example, BA, Rf 82487, pièce 9, and Rf 82359.

76. BA, Rf 82485/5, pièce 32.

77. BA, Rf 82486, pièces 24 and 25; see also Rf 82485/6, pièce 1, which has wonderful photographs of the performers.

78. According to a Nantes newspaper; see BA, Rf 82486, pièce 16, and Rf 82450. A letter attached to the revue explains how the composer was urged to write it by a commanding officer, and that he had never written one before.

79. BA, Rf 82486, pièce 13.

80. The officers also seem to have sometimes come from farther afield. A mimeographed copy of a revue given at Tilly for the 211th carefully explained which officers, companies, and artillery units came to each performance, as well as thanking the mayor and some civilians for coming. See BA, Rf 82340.

81. See BA, Rf 82354; this revue was printed by the Imprimerie Typographique de l'Armée.

82. BA, Rf 82362.

83. BA, Rf 82436.

84. BA, Rf 82355, p. 46. See also the finale of Act I of *Ques Aco? Berlin Gott!* from December 1915. BA, Rf 82366.

85. This song was sent into the *Bulletin* without any information on the composer. ASHAT, 5 N 566.

86. A few revues indicated that it was good to sing while on *repos,* but not in the trenches. See, for example, *Quand-Même,* BA, Rf 82433.

87. BA, Rf 82373.

88. The revue *Pourvu qu'on Rigole!* even began with a song that defined a revue for the audience. BA, Rf 82373.

89. BA, Rf 82466; Rf 82429.

90. Many used the same tunes that were being used all the time in Paris, such as "Je connais une blonde," "Tout le long du Missouri," and "A la Martinique."

91. BA, Rf 82371.

92. Soldiers also sang the big music-hall hits themselves as well as borrowing the tunes. René Des Touches, for example, mentioned "La Petite Tonkinoise" (1906) and "Le Long du Missouri" (1912), both by Henri Christiné. *Pages de gloire et de misère* (Paris, 1917), 180–183.

93. This revue was put together by a *sapeur* with the help of two sergeants, a sergeant-major, and a corporal. BA, Rf 82421.

94. For example, "Quand Madelon" did not appear on the four-hour program at the Théâtre du Parc in September 1917. See also, *Crache pas dans l'masque!* by the Third Colonial Division, or *Trois ans après* by the 65th D.I. BA, Rf 82345; Rf 82355.

95. BA, Rf 82355.

96. See the strategically placed ellipses in BA, Rf 82340, or Rf 82367, 24–25.

97. BA, Rf 82387.

98. BA, Rf 82366.

99. See the letter in BA, Rf 82340.

100. See the 1918 revue *Après le soupe . . . Bouilly gros sel!* BA, Rf 82441.

101. BA, Rf 82485/5, pièce 32.

102. See BA, Rf 82363 and Rf 82409.

103. See the letter written to *Fantasio* in 1915, and BA, Rf 82436.

104. The letters show the private transmission of songs from front to home and vice versa. That they expected to find "Quand Madelon" and not so much variety reflects a postwar perspective. Baconnier, *La Plume au fusil,* 92. For a very similar

description of this transmission process, see Gaston Sévrette, *Les Vieilles chansons du pays de France* (Paris, 1922), 109.

105. See, for example, L. L. Farrer's questioning of the common definitions in his "Nationalism in Wartime: Critiquing the Conventional Wisdom," in *Authority, Identity, and the Social History of the Great War*, ed. Frans Coetzee and Marilyn Shevin-Coetzee (Providence, R.I., 1995), 133–151.

106. Audoin-Rouzeau, *Men at War*, 155–184.

107. See also BA, Rf 82387, which shows remarkable divisional pride.

108. This was probably written for the 73rd Infantry regiment. BA, Rf 82433.

109. Ibid.

110. See "Chanson d'assaut," ASHAT, 5 N 566. A song praising military musicians for having led an assault at Verdun appeared as late as March 1918 in the trench newspaper *Cingoli-Gazette*.

111. The refrain was "Auprès de ma blonde / Qu'il fait bon, fait bon, fait bon, / Auprès de ma blonde, / Qu'il fait bon dormir." ASHAT, 5 N 566.

112. BA, Rf 82421. See also the song "Les poilus," which was dedicated to Déroulède. ASHAT, 5 N 566.

113. See, for example, the song "Clair de lune de Verdun," and "L'Armée Pétain" where the songwriter changed the romantic, drinking song "Quand Madelon" to a patriotic piece. Pétain replaced the waitress, and the line "Madelon. Madelon. Madelon" became "En avant! En avant! En avant!" ASHAT, 5 N 566.

114. Vauban was a military engineer under Louis XIV.

115. BA, Rf 82340.

116. BA, Rf 82354.

117. This attention to the enemy has been noted by both veterans and historians, but it has often been couched in terms of a seriousness that made the French less flexible and more prone to mutiny. Songtexts illustrate how often the French used humor in describing the enemy. Cf., Fuller, *Troop Morale and Popular Culture*, esp. ch. 3.

118. "La Paix . . . 'Guillaume.'" ASHAT, 5 N 566. See also, the song "1914."

119. "Le Boniment d'Hollweg (bêtman)" was by a soldier in the 68th Territorial. ASHAT, 5 N 566. See also "les Cerveaux pointus."

120. See, for instance, the song "Fais dodo." ASHAT, 5 N 566.

121. BA, Rf 82355. See also, the song "Eh! dis donc, Poilu," in the trench newspaper *Le Plus-que-torial*, January 15, 1916. The refrain reassured everyone that "les Poilus vont bien / Et la France est forte; / Dormez, citoyens, / Les Poilus vont bien."

122. *Ques Aco? Berlin Gott!!* BA, Rf 82366.

123. See the letter from a Maurice Deschodt de Lille, ASHAT, 5 N 566.

124. See the letter accompanying the song "Debout Créoles," ASHAT, 5 N 566. Others composed for Alsatians and Bretons.

125. Lefebvre and Vaillant-Couturier, *La Guerre des soldats*, 89. Lafond's chapter called "Chants du pays" described a chorus of men from Languedoc, Nîmes, Montpellier, and Toulouse. *Ma mitrailleuse*, 211–225.

126. The composer is identified only as a certain Pierre Le Floch(?). ASHAT, 5 N 566.

127. Mairet, *Carnet d'un combattant*, 62–65, 67.

128. Written by Marcel Dambrine, a soldier-songwriter. Archives de la Préfecture de Police, Paris (hereafter APP), Ba 699.

129. Robert Brécy, *Florilège de la chanson révolutionnaire de 1789 au front populaire* (Paris, 1978), 234.

130. Anonymous, "Brise du Soir," *Les Chansons de la guerre* (Paris, 1916), 21–22. This song may have appeared in the trench newspaper *L'Écho des tranchées*, in October 1915.

131. See also "La R'lève," APP, Ba 735.

132. Since parodies were usually situational and ephemeral, they are harder to locate for the historian. They were less likely to be written down, especially because they were often improvised parodies of existing songs.

133. Most French soldiers were not granted any leave until July 1915; after that it tended to be given irregularly. Pay for an infantryman averaged approximately twenty-five centimes compared to ten to fifteen francs per day for workers. De la Gorce, *The French Army*, 124.

134. BA, Rf 82421. See also *Pourvu qu'on Rigole!!*, BA, Rf 82373; and *A leur barbe!*, Rf 82421.

135. Brécy, *Florilège de la chanson*, 222. See also "Les Auxiliaires," which was written anonymously. *Les Chansons de la guerre*, 18–20.

136. *Le Gafouilleur*, July 14, 1917, 3.

137. BA, Rf 82421.

138. In his analysis of trench newspapers, Stéphane Audoin-Rouzeau has identified other links that remained between soldiers and civilians, such as mail and leave. Audoin-Rouzeau, *Men at War*, 135–143.

139. Dominique Bonnaud, Lucien Boyer, and Jean Bastia were all represented. See also the tribute to Bastia in the March 25, 1916, edition of *L'Echo des marmites*.

140. Cf. *La Fusée*.

141. The poem was called "Chantez!" ASHAT, 5 N 566.

142. On the career of "Quand Madelon" see Charles Rearick's "Madelon and the Men—in War and Memory," *French Historical Studies* 17, no. 4 (Fall 1992): 1001–1034. Rearick has asked the question of why "Madelon" became such a powerful icon, and it is telling that most of the article deals with post-1918.

143. André Ducasse, Jacques Meyer, and Gabriel Perreux, *Vie et mort des français, 1914–1918* (Paris, 1959), 299.

144. Guy Breton, *Le Cabaret de l'histoire* (Paris, 1973), 128–129.

145. Renoir, *My Life*, 146. See also Boutet, *Ils étaient de leur village*, 110–111.

146. In one example, the newspaper *La Fusée* gave its prices as follows: "10 centimes; 3 fr 50 [per year] pour militaires; Pour les Civils: 100 fr. 'ceux qui tiennent'; 500 fr. pour 'les autres.'" *La Fusée*, November 5, 1916.

147. Pierre Barbier and France Vernillat, *L'Histoire de France par les chansons* (Paris, 1961), 223–224. A scene from Henri Barbusse's famous, best-selling novel *Le Feu*, first published in 1916 and based on Barbusse's own experience, corroborated these sentiments of bitterness and incomprehension. Barbusse, *Under Fire* (New York, 1933), 298–299.

148. See also an expression of the frustration of being "disoriented" "au milieu des 'civils'" by Georges Pineau, one of the editors of *Le Poilu de France*, a veterans' newspaper. September 20, 1919.

149. BA, Rf 82367.

150. The phrase "Jusqu'au bout" was used from the beginning of the war, for example on Gallieni's famous poster before the battle of the Marne.

151. "Ça distrait un peu / Les gens près du feu / Car ces pauvres victimes / S'ennuyant beaucoup, / Estim'nt qu'après tout / Ça vaut bien dix centimes."

152. *L'Echo des marmites*, no. 11 (May 25, 1916), 5.

153. APP, Ba 703. There is no indication whether this received a visa, or whether it was ever performed in Paris.

154. In *Paris-C. 17* by Edouard Audy, the first act took place in Paris with *les civils, marraines, le flirt*, and *l'embusqué*. BA, Rf 82359. See also, BA, Rf 82367.

155. Des Touches, *Pages de gloire*, 167–168.

156. Some veterans claimed that "poilu" was not liked until relatively late in the war and was never very popular, especially compared to the home front. See, for

instance, Ducasse, Meyer, and Perreux, *Vie et mort*, 87, and Meyer, *La Vie quoti-dienne des soldats*, 16.

157. See chapter 5 on this particular revue. In some cases, the term was used self-consciously or uneasily. In Pierre-Maurice Masson's letters, he did not start using it until early 1916 and then began by placing it in quotation marks. Pierre Masson, *Lettres de guerre: août 1914–avril 1916* (Paris, 1917).

158. The song was by Dominique Bonnaud and appeared in *Rigolboche* (July 20, 1915). For the Paris version, see APP, Ba 707.

159. *Le Crapouillot*, April, 7, 1917. Quoted in Kahn, *The Neglected Majority*, 64.

160. On troop morale, see Leonard V. Smith, *Between Mutiny and Obedience: The Case of the Fifth Infantry Division during World War I* (Princeton, 1994).

161. Pierre Miquel, *La Grande Guerre* (Paris, 1983), 406. The figure covers the dates April 1 to May 9.

162. Boutefeu, *Les Camarades*, 328.

163. For a thorough work on the mutinies, see Guy Pedroncini, *Les Mutineries de 1917* (Paris, 1967). See also, Smith, *Between Mutiny and Obedience*, 175–214.

164. See Pedroncini, *Les Mutineries de 1917*, 113–179, and Henri Philippe Pétain, *Une Crise morale de la nation française en guerre, 16 avril–23 octobre 1917* (Paris, 1966), 66–67, 76, 78, 80.

165. See chapter 1.

166. Quoted in Paul Allard, *Les Dessous de la guerre révélés par les comités secrets* (Paris, 1932), 174–176.

167. From a report written by a Colonel Dussange, commander of the 310th Infantry. Quoted in Allard, *Les Dessous de la guerre*, 198.

168. British troops, on the other hand, did not have the same prewar, revolutionary repertoire to turn to.

169. Pétain, *Une Crise morale*, 76. This appears to refer to the 129th Infantry.

170. Quoted in Brécy, *Florilège de la chanson*, 234. Notice that much of the word play here is lost in the English translation.

171. Brécy, *Florilège de la chanson*, 237.

172. Ibid., 235. Florent Fels, in *Voilà*, also mentioned many units singing it. Quoted in Ducasse, *Vie et mort*, 90.

173. Barbier and Vernillat, *Histoire de France par les chansons*, 233–235.

174. This contrasts with Eric Leed's opinion that soldiers did not have a target for their disillusionment or a clear author for the war. *No Man's Land*, 35.

175. Bernard and Dubief give the figures: 696 strikes, with at least 293,810 participants in 1917. Philippe Bernard and Henri Dubief, *The Decline of the Third Republic, 1914–1938*, trans. Anthony Forster (Cambridge, 1985), 54.

176. Lefebvre and Vaillant-Couturier, *La Guerre des soldats*, 143–150. In this instance the song was called "La Chanson de Lorette."

177. Pétain, *Une Crise morale*, 72.

178. Boutefeu, *Les Camarades*, 340.

179. Ibid., 320.

180. Allard, *Les Dessous de la guerre*, 212.

181. Bernard and Dubief, *The Decline of the Third Republic*, 49.

182. Allard, *Les Dessous de la guerre*, 204–207.

183. Quoted in Pedroncini, *Les Mutineries*, 122–3.

184. While Pedroncini's careful work has shown that no revolutionary influence really existed, the belief had repercussions at the time. On Pétain's strong fears, see Pétain's *Une Crise morale*, 70–71 and 106–110.

185. For instance, "La Terre nationale," "Révolution," and "Révoltez-vous, parias des usines." ASHAT, 5 N 371.

186. Pétain, *Une Crise morale*, 128.

187. Military archives, cartons 18 N 386; 19 N 37; 16 N 1529; 16 N 2404; 16 N 271. Blueprints of a model canteen were drawn up showing "salles de distractions" and theaters.

188. The army sent men to worse sectors, took away valuable equipment or shot soldiers, sometimes with a minimum of legal safeguards. Michel Auvray, *Objecteurs, insoumis, deserteurs: histoire des refractaires en France* (Paris, 1983), 156. As many as three thousand court martials were handed out in just 1914 alone, and the number rose to as many as twenty-six thousand in the first four months of 1917. De la Gorce, *The French Army*, 127.

189. The article is remarkable in its knowledge of music, pacing, and tone. *Le Gafouilleur*, July 14, 1917.

Chapter 8 (pages 237–252)

1. Ro 18434 at la Bibliothèque de l'Arsenal (hereafter BA).
2. Archives de la Préfecture de Police, Paris (hereafter APP), Ba 711.
3. APP, Ba 1587.
4. BA, Ro 18434.
5. Charles Rearick discusses the importance of this genre after the war, but does not link it to this period. Rearick, *The French in Love and War: Popular Culture in the Era of the World Wars* (New Haven, 1997), esp. ch. 4.
6. See, for example, Jean Péheu's "C'était un Patriote," APP, Ba 703.
7. APP, Ba 735. This contrasted with German rules which forbid jokes about profiteers or other problems like food shortages. Gary Stark, "All Quiet on the Home Front: Popular Entertainments, Censorship and Civilian Morale in Germany, 1914–1918," in *Authority, Identity and the Social History of the Great War*, ed. Frans Coetzee and Marilyn Shevin-Coetzee (Providence, R.I., 1995), 72.
8. "La Perme des civils," APP, Ba 721.
9. Quoted in Elisabeth Hausser, *Paris au jour le jour: les événements vus par la presse, 1900–1919* (Paris, 1968), 670.
10. APP, Ba 1614
11. See Mary Louise Roberts, *Civilization without Sexes: Reconstructing Gender in Postwar France, 1917–1927* (Chicago, 1994), ch. 1.
12. APP, Ba 701.
13. See APP, Ba 697 and Ba 709.
14. "L'Odyssée du permissionaire," APP, Ba 734.
15. APP, Ba 712.
16. APP, Ba 711.
17. Robert Brécy, *Florilège de la chanson révolutionnaire de 1789 au front populaire* (Paris, 1978), 229. Martini's "Les Bouffeurs de Boches en chambre" also criticized Gaston Montéhus and explained how soldiers hated "ces sacrés bourreurs de crâne." APP, Ba 701.
18. See the newspaper clippings in BA, Ro 18470. The columnist Guillot de Saix also described Martini's "singular authority" which allowed him to "chastise" pacifists.
19. See, for example, BA, Rf 82487, pièces 3, 11, 16, and 18. See also the article in *Le Gaulois*, August 21, 1916, entitled "Ce que chantent nos soldats."
20. BA, Rf 82486, pièce 24; Rf 82487, pièce 10.
21. BA, Rf 82486, pièces 19 bis and 24.
22. BA, Rf 82485/5, pièces 24, 28–30.
23. BA, Rf 82488, pièce 18.
24. See, for example, BA, Rf 82489, pièce 27.

25. BA, Rf 82489, pièce 5.

26. BA, Rf 82421; Rf 82485 (5), pièce 32.

27. At the Archives du Service Historique de l'Armée de Terre (hereafter, ASHAT), 5 N 566.

28. "Le Vrai pinard" was sung in July 1916 and October 1917; "Le Père pinard" in August 1916; "C'est le pinard" in October 1916. APP, Ba 738.

29. BA, Rf 82485/5, pièce 32 (my emphasis).

30. Jean Bastia wrote *La Revue du Pinard* for his cabaret in March 1917.

31. The Labor truce was also evident in the small number of strikes in 1915—only 98 compared to 1,073 in 1913. Philippe Bernard and Henri Dubief, *The Decline of the Third Republic, 1914–1938*, trans. Anthony Forster (Cambridge, 1985), 23.

32. On early 1917 and the price increases, see Jean-Jacques Becker, *The Great War and the French People*, trans. Arnold Pomerans (Dover, N.H., 1985), 205–206.

33. Although as early as early April 1917, at a small meeting of leftist intellectuals, the whistling of the supremely patriotic "Marseillaise" had been drowned out by the "Internationale," intermingled with cries of "A bas la guerre" and "Vive la paix!" Archives Nationales (hereafter AN), F7 13372.

34. Quoted in Becker, *The Great War*, 209. See also the prefect reports in AN, F7 13372.

35. Ultimately, the strikes affected seventy-one industries and involved more than one hundred thousand workers in the Paris region. Becker, *The Great War*, 210.

36. Hausser, *Paris au jour le jour*, 636.

37. The strikers got a sympathetic reception from some observers, while other commentators expressed shock at their unladylike behavior. For instance, Abel Hermant, a well-known columnist, wrote somewhat nervously: "Alas! These strikers are charming. . . . [B]ut, when they sing, . . . it is not at all flowers that fall from their lips, nor pearls." Hermant, *La Vie à Paris* (Paris, 1918), 111, and Michel Corday, *The Paris Front* (New York, 1934), 253.

38. When negotiations slowed, the vocal marchs picked up again and bargaining went forward. *Le Petit Parisien*, May 22, 1917.

39. See, APP, Ba 737–740.

40. Paul Allard, *Images secrètes de la guerre: 200 photographies et documents censurés en France* (Paris, 1933), 31; Marcel Berger and Paul Allard, *Les Secrets de la censure pendant la guerre* (Paris, 1932), 174.

41. On the growing crowds, see Louis Chevalier, *Montmartre du plaisir et du crime* (Paris, 1980), 317.

42. One can see a parallel in film where by 1918 the only French films being shown were views of the war from the Armée Cinématographique. The United States had the rest of the field. See APP, Ba 1614. One must also note, however, that internationalization also saw French celebrities like Sarah Bernhardt and Eugénie Buffet make tours to neutral or allied countries from 1916 on.

43. *Le Journal*, September 14, 1918. The bands included "The Tickle Toe Jazz Band" and the "American Jazz Band."

44. BA, Ro 18479. The shift was also true in theater, where, for instance, the American comedy "*La Vérité toute nue*" had 170 performances at the Gymnase beginning in September 1918.

45. BA, Ro 18473.

46. BA, Ro 18747.

47. BA, Ro 18474.

48. BA, Ro 18462.

49. BA, Ro 18479.

50. The critic Balsan de la Rouvière maintained that: "Si nous avons beaucoup à

apprendre de ces derniers quant à l'industrie, au confortable et à l'hygiène, il semble bien que nous ayons encore bien des leçons à leur donner quant aux lettres, aux arts et au théâtre. Pour précieuse qu'elle nous soit, notre alliance avec eux ne réprime pas 'a priorri(?)' toute critique de notre part." BA, Ro 18479.

51. Cf. Michael Freedland, *Maurice Chevalier* (New York, 1981), 63–64.

52. Frédérique Deghelt, *Mistinguett: la valse renversante* (Monaco, 1995), 234. A small note on the program for La Cigale in January 1918, said "La Direction de 'La Cigale' informe le public que tous les artistes hommes figurant au programme ont tous répondu à leurs obligations militaires." BA, Ro 18471.

53. I would argue that there was therefore nothing populist about this. For a different view, see Rearick, *The French in Love and War*, 94–125.

54. Pascal Sevran, *Le Music-hall français, de Mayol à Julien Clerc* (Paris, 1978), 15–16. Deslys had gone off to New York in 1911 and returned with English and "Americanisms." David Bret, *The Mistinguett Legend* (New York, 1990), 74–77.

55. See APP, Ba 1587, and Hausser, *Paris au jour le jour*, 659.

56. *Annuaire statistique de la ville de Paris*, 554.

57. Quoted in Chevalier, *Montmartre du plaisir*, 313.

58. BA, Ro 18478.

59. Pierre Miquel, *La Grande Guerre* (Paris, 1983), 606.

60. APP, Ba 1587.

61. Clemenceau himself wrote the instructions for the displays of German weapons, and he encouraged Parisians to take souvenirs. ASHAT, 6 N 145; see also ASHAT, 7 N 2015 and 7 N 175 for the government plans for parades in Paris, and *Le Temps*, October 20, 1918.

62. Officials still tried to "manage" the Parisians' excitement, warning newspapers not to "amplify the enthusiasm." Berger and Allard, *Les Secrets de la censure*, 358–362.

Conclusion (pages 253–256)

1. Bibliothèque de l'Arsenal, Ro 18471.

Selected Bibliography

Archival Sources

Archives Nationales, Paris (AN): Series F7: 12881; 12936–12939; 13372. Series F18 1677; Series F18* VIII 142–149. Series F21: 3985.

Archives de la Préfecture de Police de Paris (APP): Series Ba 697–730; 731–736; 737–740; 741–743; 770–773; 831–863; 1495; 1587; 1614; 1642.

Bibliothèque de l'Arsenal, Paris (BA): Fonds Rondel: Series Rf 70827; Rf 82311–82477. Series Ro 14524; 14427; 14528; 18339; 18340; 18373; 18383; 18419; 18434; 18470. Series Rt 900 and Rt 934(2).

Archives du Service Historique de l'Armée de terre (ASHAT): 5 N 269; 5 N 342; 5 N 360; 5 N 371; 5 N 566; 6 N 23; 6 N 110; 6 N 145; 7 N 175; 7 N 403; 7 N 955; 7 N 2015; 16 N 270; 16 N 271; 16 N 1529; 18 N 386.

Bibliothèque de Documentation Internationale Contemporaine (Nanterre and Hôtel des Invalides): Trench journals and a superb collection of sixty thousand postcards, posters, and lithographs.

Newspapers and Periodicals

L'Action française
L'Autorité
La Baïonnette
Bulletin des armées de la République
Le Carnet de la semaine
La Croix
L'Echo de Paris
Le Figaro
Le Gaulois
La Guerre sociale
L'Humanité
Le Journal
La Libre Parole
Le Matin
Paris qui chante
Le Petit Journal
Le Petit Parisien
La Presse
Le Temps
La Vie Parisienne

Trench Newspapers

81me poil . . . et plume
L'Echo des marmites
L'Eclat
L'Etoupilles
Face aux Boches
La Fusée
Jusqu'au Bout
Mar-Gaz (previously called *Marmoutier-Gazette*)
Le Plus-que-Torrial
Le Poilu du 6–9
Le Rigolboche
Le Rire aux Eclats
Le Tord-Boyau

Selected Primary Sources

Adam, H. Pearl. *Paris Sees It Through: A Diary 1914–1919*. New York: Hodder and Stoughton, 1919.

L'Ame de Paris: tableaux de la guerre de 1914. Paris: G. Crès et Cie, 1915.

Annuaire statistique de la ville de Paris, 1915–1918. Paris: Imprimerie Nouvelle, 1921.

Barbusse, Henri. *Le Feu*. Paris: Flammarion, 1916. English edition: *Under Fire*. New York: E. P. Dutton & Co., Inc., 1933.

Barnard, Charles Inman. *Paris War Days: Diary of an American*. London: T. Werner Laurie, 1915.

Benoit, André. *Trois mois de guerre au jour le jour (1914)*. Paris: Librairie Vuibert, 1967.

Bernier, Jean. *La Percée*. Paris: Albin Michel, 1920.

Bon, Général [Gabriel Sainte Marie]. *Causeries et souvenirs, 1914–1915*. Paris: H. Floury, 1916.

Bonnaud, Dominique. *Chansons de guerre*. Nancy: Berger-Levrault, s.d.

Botrel, Théodore. *Les Chansons de route*. Paris: Librairie Payot et Cie, 1915.

———. *Chants de bataille et de victoire*. Paris: Payot et Cie, 1920.

———. *Les Chants du bivouac*. Paris: Payot et Cie, 1915.

———. *Les Mémoires d'un barde Breton*. Paris: P. Lethielleux, 1933.

———. "Les Souvenirs d'un barde errant." *La Revue Belge*, January 1, 1923, 54–72.

Boyer, Lucien. *La Chanson des poilus (1914–1918)*. Paris: F. Salabert, 1918.

Brancour, René. *La Marseillaise et le chant du départ*. Paris: H. Laurens, 1916.

Bridoux, André. *Souvenirs du temps des morts*. Paris: Albin Michel, 1930.

Buffet, Eugénie. *Ma vie, mes amours, mes aventures*. Paris: E. Figuière, 1930.

Cahuet, Alberic. *La Liberté du théâtre en France et à l'étranger: histoire, fonctionnement et discussion de la censure dramatique*. Paris: Dujarric, 1902.

Les Chansons de la guerre. Paris: Librairie Militaire Berger-Levrault, 1916.

Chenu, Charles. *De l'arrière à l'avant: chronique de la guerre*. Paris: Plon, 1916.

Chevé, Amand (Ministère de l'instruction publique). *Rapport sur l'enseignement du chant dans les écoles primaires*. Paris: Imprimerie Nationale, 1881.

Circulaires émanées du Préfet de Police, 1917–1918. Paris: Imprimerie Chaix, 1919.

Le Coeur de Paris en 1915. Paris: Georges Crès et Cie, 1916.

Constant, Eugène. *Chansons satiriques d'Action française*. Lille: Ligue d'Action Française, 1913.

Corday, Michel. *The Paris Front*. New York: E. P. Dutton & Co., Inc., 1934.

Darde, Fernand. *Vingt mois de guerre à bord du Croiseur "Jeanne d'Arc" 9 août 1914–12 avril 1916*. Paris: Perrin et Cie, 1918.

Dauzat, Albert. *L'Argot de la guerre*. Paris: Armand Colin, 1918.

Déchelette, Français. *L'Argot des poilus*. Paris: Jouve & Cie, 1918.

Déroulède, Paul. *Chants du soldat: marches et sonneries*. Paris: Calmann Lévy, 1884.

———. *De l'éducation militaire*. 1881.

Des Touches, René. *Pages de gloire et de misère*. Paris: de Boccard, 1917.

Dorgelès, Roland. *Le Cabaret de la belle femme*. Paris: Albin Michel, 1928.

Dupaigne, Albert. *L'Enseignement du chant dans les écoles*. Paris: Hachette, 1879.

Enseignement du chant. Travaux de la commission. Rapports et programmes. Paris: Imprimerie Nationale, 1884.

Foley, Charles. *1914–1915: la vie de guerre contée par les soldats*. Paris: Berger-Levrault, 1915.

Gaudy, Georges. *Les Trous d'obus de Verdun*. Paris: Plon-Nourrit et Cie, 1922.

Gay, Ernest. *Paris, héroïque: la grande guerre*. Paris: Charles-Lavauzelle & Cie, 1920–1923.

Gheusi, Pierre B. *Guerre et théâtre 1914–1918*. Paris: Berger-Levrault, 1919.

Gibbons, Herbert Adams. *Paris Reborn: A Study in Civic Psychology*. New York: The Century Co., 1915.

Giraudoux, Jean. *Lectures pour une ombre*. Paris: Emile-Paul Frères, 1918. English edition: *Campaigns and Intervals*. Trans. Elizabeth S. Sergeant. Boston: Houghton Mifflin Co., 1918.

Hermant, Abel. *La Vie à Paris: 1917*. Paris: E. Flammarion, 1918.

———. *La Vie à Paris: dernière année de la guerre*. Paris: E. Flammarion, 1919.

Heugel, Jacques. *Aveux et souvenirs*. Paris: Hors Commerce, 1968.

Julia, Emile-François. *La Fatalité de la guerre: scènes et propos du front*. Paris: Perrin, 1917.

Lafond, Georges. *Ma mitrailleuse*. Paris: Arthème-Fayard et Cie, n.d. English edition: *Covered with Mud and Glory: A Machine Gun Company in Action*. Trans. Edwin Gile Rich. Boston: Small, Maynard & Company, 1918.

Laudet, Fernand. *Paris pendant la guerre: impressions*. Paris: Perrin, 1915.

Lefebvre, Raymond, and Paul Vaillant-Couturier. *La Guerre des soldats*. Paris: Ernest Flammarion, 1919.

Mairet, Louis. *Carnet d'un combattant: 11 Fèvrier 1915–16 Avril 1917*. Paris: Crès, 1919.

Marnold, Jean. *Le Cas Wagner*. Paris: Georges Crès et Cie, 1920.

Masson, Pierre-Maurice. *Lettres de guerre: août 1914–avril 1916*. Paris: Hachette, 1917.

Mayol, Félix. *Mémoires*. Paris: Louis Querelle, 1929.

Millandy, Georges. *Lorsque tout est fini . . . souvenirs d'un chansonnier du Quartier Latin*. Paris: A. Messein, 1933.

Ohnet, Georges. *Journal d'un bourgeois de Paris pendant la guerre de 1914*. Paris: P. Ollendorff, 1914.

Passerieu, Jean Bernard. *La Vie de Paris, 1917*. Paris: Librairie Alphonse Lemerre, 1918.

Pécaut, Félix. *L'Education publique et la vie nationale*. Paris: Hachette, 1897.

Pétain, Henri Philippe. *Une Crise morale de la nation française en guerre, 16 avril–23 octobre 1917*. Paris: Nouvelles Editions Latines, 1966.

Pézard, André. *Nous autres à Vauquois 1915–1916*. Paris: La Renaissance du Livre, 1918.

Rip [Georges-Gabriel Thenon]. *1915*. Paris: Paul Ollendorff, 1915.

Robert, Frederic. *Lettres à propos de la Marseillaise*. Paris: Presses Universitaires de France, 1980.

Sévrette, Gaston. *Les Vieilles chansons du pays de France.* Paris: Armand Colin, 1922.
Suffel, Jacques. *La Guerre de 1914–1918 par ceux qui l'ont faite.* Paris: Plon, 1968.
Tiersot, Julien. *Histoire de la chanson populaire.* Paris: E. Plon, Nourrit et Cie, 1889.
Tiersot, Julien. *Mélodies populaires des provinces de France.* Paris: Heugel, [1928].
Weiss, René; André Kling, and Daniel Florentin. *La Croix de guerre de la ville de Paris: Paris pendant la guerre.* Paris: Imprimerie Nationale, 1921.

Selected Secondary Sources

Abel, Richard. *French Cinema: The First Wave, 1915–1929.* Princeton: Princeton University Press, 1984.
Agulhon, Maurice. *Marianne au pouvoir: l'imagerie et la symbolique républicaines de 1880 à 1914.* Paris: Flammarion, 1989.
Allard, Paul. *Les Dessous de la guerre révélés par les comités secrets.* Paris: Les Editions de France, 1932.
——. *Images secrètes de la guerre: 200 photographies et documents censurés en France.* Paris: La Société Anonyme les Illustrés Français, 1933.
Allen, James Smith. *In the Public Eye: A History of Reading in Modern France, 1800–1940.* Princeton: Princeton University Press, 1991.
Andolenko, Général. *Recueil d'historiques de l'infanterie française.* Paris: Eurimprim, 1969.
Andrieu, Pierre, ed. *Souvenirs des frères Isola: cinquante ans de vie parisienne.* Paris: Flammarion, 1943.
Ashworth, Tony. *Trench Warfare 1914–1918: The Live and Let Live System.* London: The Macmillan Press, 1980.
Aubéry, Pierre. "Poésies et chansons populaires de la Commune." In *Images of the Commune,* ed. James A. Leith, 47–67. Montreal: McGill-Queen's University Press, 1978.
Audoin-Rouzeau, Stéphane. *1870: la France dans la guerre.* Paris: Armand Colin, 1989.
——. *Men at War, 1914–1918: National Sentiment and Trench Journalism in France during the First World War.* New York: Berg, 1992.
Baconnier, Gérard; André Minet, and Louis Soler. *La Plume au fusil: les poilus du Midi à travers leur correspondance.* Toulouse: Editions Privat, 1985.
Barbier, Pierre, and France Vernillat. *L'Histoire de France par les chansons.* Vols. 5–8. Paris: Librairie Gallimard, 1961.
Barrows, Susanna. "'Parliaments of the People': The Political Culture of Cafés in the Early Third Republic." In *Drinking: Behavior and Belief in Modern History,* ed. Susanna Barrows and Robin Room. Berkeley: University of California Press, 1991.
Becker, Annette. *La Guerre et la foi: de la mort à la mémoire.* Paris: Armand Colin, 1994.
Becker, Jean-Jacques. *Les Français dans la grande guerre.* Paris: R. Laffont, 1980.
——. *The Great War and the French People.* Trans. Arnold Pomerans. Dover, N.H.: Berg Publishers Ltd., 1985.
——. *1914: comment les Français sont entrés dans la guerre.* Paris: Presses de la Fondation Nationale des Sciences Politiques, 1977.
Becker, Jean-Jacques, Annette Becker, and Stéphane Audoin-Rouzeau, eds. *Guerre et cultures: vers une histoire culturelle comparée de la première guerre mondiale.* Paris: Armand Colin, 1994.
Berger, Marcel, and Paul Allard. *Les Secrets de la censure pendant la guerre.* Paris: Editions des Portiques, 1932.

Selected Bibliography / 342

Berlanstein, Lenard. *The Working People of Paris, 1871–1914*. Baltimore: Johns Hopkins, 1984.

Bernard, Philippe, and Henri Dubief. *The Decline of the Third Republic, 1914–1938*. Trans. Anthony Forster. Cambridge: Cambridge University Press, 1985.

Booth, Mark W. *The Experience of Songs*. New Haven: Yale University Press, 1981.

Bourdieu, Pierre. *La Distinction: critique sociale du jugement*. Paris: Les Editions de Minuit, 1979.

———. *In Other Words: Essays Towards a Reflexive Sociology*. Trans. Matthew Adamson. Stanford: Stanford University Press, 1990.

Boutefeu, Roger. *Les Camarades: soldats français et allemands au combat 1914–1918*. Paris: Fayard, 1966.

Boutet, Gérard. *Ils étaient de leur village: le temps des guerres, 1914–1939*. Paris: Editions Denoël, 1981.

Bouwsma, William J. "From History of Ideas to History of Meaning." *Journal of Interdisciplinary History* XII, no. 2 (Autumn, 1981).

Brécy, Robert. *Florilège de la chanson révolutionnaire de 1789 au front populaire*. Paris: Editions Hier et Demain, 1978.

Bret, David. *The Mistinguett Legend*. New York: St. Martin's Press, 1990.

Breton, Guy. *Le Cabaret de l'histoire*, vol. 1. Paris: Presses de la Cité, 1973.

Brochon, Pierre. *Béranger et son temps*. Paris: Editions Sociales, 1956.

———. *La Chanson Sociale de Béranger à Brassens*. Paris: Les Editions Ouvrières, 1961.

Brophy, John, and Eric Partridge. *The Long Trail: What the British Soldier Sang and Said in the Great War of 1914–1918*. London: Andre Deutsch, Ltd., 1965.

Brunschwig, Chantal, Louis-Jean Calvet, and Jean-Claude Klein. *100 ans de chanson française*. Paris: Editions du Seuil, 1972.

Burns, Michael. *Rural Society and French Politics: Boulangism and the Dreyfus Affair, 1886–1900*. Princeton: Princeton University Press, 1984.

Calvet, Louis-Jean. *Chanson et Société*. Paris: Payot, 1981.

Canini, Gérard. *Mémoire de la Grande Guerre: témoins et témoignages*. Nancy: Presse Universitaire de Nancy, 1989.

Caradec, François, and Alain Weill. *Le Café-concert*. Paris: Hachette-Massin, 1980.

Carruthers, Neil. "Theatrical Censorship in Paris from 1850 to 1905." *New Zealand Journal of French Studies* 3 (1982).

Charles, Jacques. *Cent ans de music-hall*. Paris: Editions Jeheber, 1956.

Charney, Leo, and Vanessa R. Schwartz, eds. *Cinema and the Invention of Modern Life*. Berkeley: University of California Press, 1995.

Charpentreau, Simone, and Jacques Charpentreau. *La Chanson française*. Paris: Les Editions Ouvrières, 1960.

Chartier, Roger, ed. *The Culture of Print*. Trans. Lydia G. Cochrane. Princeton: Princeton University Press, 1989.

Chevalier, Louis. *Montmartre du plaisir et du crime*. Paris: Edition Robert Laffont, 1980.

Cochet, Annick. "Les Paysans sur le front en 1916." *Bulletin du Centre d'histoire de la France contemporaine* 3 (1982): 37–48.

Coetzee, Frans, and Marilyn Shevin-Coetzee, eds. *Authority, Identity and the Social History of the Great War*. Providence, R.I.: Berghahn Books, 1995.

Daniel, Joseph. *Guerre et cinéma: grandes illusions et petits soldats 1895–1971*. Paris: Armand Colin, 1972.

De Certeau, Michel. *The Practice of Everyday Life*. Trans. Steven Rendall. Berkeley: University of California Press, 1984.

De la Gorce, Paul Marie. *The French Army*. Trans. Kenneth Douglas. London: Weidenfeld and Nicolson, 1963.

De Coppet, Daniel, ed. *Understanding Rituals.* New York: Routledge, 1992.

Deghelt, Frédérique. *Mistinguett, la valse renversante.* Monaco: Editions Sauret, 1995.

Dillaz, Serge. *La Chanson française de contestation de la Commune à mai 1968.* Paris: Editions Seghers, 1973.

Ducasse, André, Jacques Meyer, and Gabriel Perreux. *Vie et mort des français, 1914–1918.* Paris: Librairie Hachette, 1959.

Ellul, Jacques. *Histoire de la propagande.* Paris: Presses Universitaires de France, 1967.

Englander, David. "The French Soldier, 1914–18." *French History* 1, no. 1 (March 1987): 49–67.

Erismann, Guy. *Histoire de la chanson.* Paris: Editions Hermes, 1967.

Fahmy, Dorrya. *L'Histoire de France à travers la chanson.* Alexandrie: Université Farouk, 1950.

Fridenson, Patrick, ed. *1914–1918, L'Autre Front,* Cahiers du Mouvement Social, no. 2. Paris: Les Editions Ouvrières, 1977.

Fuller, J.G. *Troop Morale and Popular Culture in the British and Dominion Armies, 1914–1918.* Oxford: Clarendon Press, 1991.

Furet, François, and Jacques Ozouf. *Reading and Writing: Literacy in France from Calvin to Jules Ferry.* Cambridge: Cambridge University Press/Editions de la Maison des Sciences de l'Homme, 1982.

Fussell, Paul. *The Great War and Modern Memory.* New York: Oxford University Press, 1975.

Gauthier, André. *Les Chansons de notre histoire.* Paris: Pierre Waleffe, 1967.

Girardet, Raoul, ed. *Le Nationalisme français, 1871–1914.* Paris: Editions du Seuil, 1983.

Goody, Jack. *The Interface between the Written and the Oral.* New York: Cambridge University Press, 1987.

———. *The Domestication of the Savage Mind.* New York: Cambridge University Press, 1977.

Hall, Stuart. "Notes on Deconstructing 'The Popular.'" In *People's History and Socialist Theory,* ed. Raphael Samuel, 227–240. London: Routledge & Kegan Paul, 1981.

Haste, Cate. *Keep the Home Fire Burning: Propaganda in the First World War.* London: Allen Lane, 1977.

Hausser, Elisabeth. *Paris au jour le jour: les événements vus par la presse, 1900–1919.* Paris: Les Éditions de Minuit, 1968.

Hemmings, F. W. J. *Theatre and State in France, 1760–1905.* Cambridge: Cambridge University Press, 1995.

Herbert, Michel. *La Chanson à Montmartre.* Paris: La Table Ronde, 1962.

Herrmann, David G. *The Arming of Europe and the Making of the First World War.* Princeton: Princeton University Press, 1996.

Higonnet, Margaret Randolph, Jane Jenson, Sonya Michel, and Margaret Collins Weitz, eds. *Behind the Lines: Gender and the Two World Wars.* New Haven: Yale University Press, 1987.

Horne, Alistair. *The French Army and Politics, 1870–1970.* London: Macmillan Press, 1984.

Hunt, Lynn, ed. *Eroticism and the Body Politic.* Baltimore: Johns Hopkins University Press, 1991.

Images de 1917. Musée d'Histoire Contemporaine, BDIC, Universités de Paris, 1987.

Isherwood, Robert. *Farce and Fantasy: Popular Entertainment in Eighteenth-Century Paris.* New York: Oxford University Press, 1986.

Jamelot, Yves. *La Censure des spectacles: théâtre, cinéma.* Paris: Jel, 1937.

Jameson, R. P., and A. E. Heacox, eds. *Chants de France*. Boston: D. C. Heath & Co., 1922.

Jelavich, Peter. *Berlin Cabaret*. Cambridge: Harvard University Press, 1993.

Johnson, James H. *Listening in Paris: A Cultural History*. Berkeley: University of California, 1995.

Kahn, Elizabeth Louise. *The Neglected Majority: "Les Camoufleurs," Art History, and World War I*. New York: University Press of America, 1984.

Keegan, John. *The Face of Battle: A Study of Agincourt, Waterloo and the Somme*. New York: The Viking Press, 1976.

Krakovitch, Odile. "La censure des théâtres durant la grande guerre." *Théâtre et spectacles hier et aujourd'hui: actes du 115e congrès national des sociétés savantes,* 331–353. Paris: Editions du Comité des travaux historiques et scientifiques, 1991.

Kyrou, Ado. *L'Age d'or de la carte postale*. Paris: Balland, 1966.

Lebovics, Herman. *True France: The Wars Over Cultural Identity, 1900–1945*. Ithaca: Cornell University Press, 1992.

Leed, Eric J. *No Man's Land: Combat and Identity in World War I*. Cambridge: Cambridge University Press, 1979.

Levine, Lawrence W. *Black Culture and Black Consciousness: Afro-American Folk Thought from Slavery to Freedom*. New York: Oxford University Press, 1977.

———. "The Folklore of Industrial Society: Popular Culture and its Audiences." *American Historical Review* 97, no. 5 (December 1992): 1369–1399.

Lhospice, Michel. *La Guerre de 70 et la Commune en 1000 images*. Paris: Editions Robert Laffont, 1965.

Livio, Robin. *La Grande Guerre, 1914–1918 en 1.000 images*. Paris: Cercle Européen du Livre, 1963.

Lynn, John A. *The Bayonets of the Republic*. Chicago: University of Illinois Press, 1984.

Lyons, Martyn. "What Did the Peasants Read? Written and Printed Culture in Rural France, 1815–1914." *European History Quarterly* 27, no. 2 (1997): 165–197.

MacAloon, John J., ed. *Rite, Drama, Festival, Spectacle: Rehearsals toward a Theory of Cultural Performance*. Philadelphia: Institute for the Study of Human Issues, 1984.

Mackaman, Douglas, and Michael Mays, eds. *World War I and the Cultures of Modernity*. Jackson: University Press of Mississippi, 2000.

Marquis, A. G. "Words as Weapons: Propaganda in Britain and Germany during the First World War." *Journal of Contemporary History* 13 (1978).

Marty, Laurent. *Chanter pour survivre: culture ouvrière, travail et techniques dans le textile, Roubaix 1850–1914*. [Lille?]: Atelier Ethno-histoire et Culture Ouvrière, Fédération Leo Lagrange, [1982].

Mason, Laura. *Singing the French Revolution: Popular Culture and Politics 1787–1799*. Ithaca: Cornell University Press, 1996.

Maugue, Annelise. *L'Identité masculine en crise au tournant du siècle*. Paris: Editions Rivages, 1987.

Meyer, Jacques. *La Vie quotidienne des soldats pendant la grande guerre*. Paris: Librairie Hachette, 1966.

Miquel, Pierre. *La Grande Guerre*. Paris: Fayard, 1983.

Moore, Sally F., and Barbara G. Myerhoff, eds. *Secular Ritual*. Assen: Van Gorcum, 1977.

Mosse, George. *Fallen Soldiers: Reshaping the Memory of the World Wars*. New York: Oxford University Press, 1990.

Mukerji, Chandra, and Michael Schudson, eds. *Rethinking Popular Culture: Contemporary Perspectives in Cultural Studies*. Berkeley: University of California Press, 1991.

Niles, John J. *Singing Soldiers*. New York: Charles Scribner's Sons, 1927.

Niles, John J., Douglas Moore, and A. A. Wallgren. *The Songs My Mother Never Taught Me*. New York: The Macaulay Company, 1929.

Oberthur, Mariel. *Cafes and Cabarets of Montmartre*. Trans. Sheila Azoulai. Salt Lake City: Gibbs M. Smith, Inc., 1984.

Ong, Walter. *Orality and Literacy: The Technologizing of the Word*. New York: Routledge, 1982.

Ozouf, Mona. *L'École de la France: essais sur la révolution, l'utopie et l'enseignement*. Paris: Gallimard, 1984.

Paret, Peter, Beth Irwin Lewis, and Paul Paret, eds. *Persuasive Images: Posters of War and Revolution from the Hoover Institution Archives*. Princeton: Princeton University Press, 1992.

Parrain, Josette. "Censure, théâtre et Commune (1871–1914)." *Le Mouvement social* 79 (April 1972): 327–342.

Pedroncini, Guy. *Les Mutineries de 1917*. Paris: Presses Universitaires de France, 1967.

Perloff, Nancy Lynn. *Art and the Everyday: Popular Entertainment and the Circle of Erik Satie*. Oxford: Clarendon Press, 1986.

Perreux, Gabriel. *La Vie quotidienne des civils en France pendant la grande guerre*. Paris: Librairie Hachette, 1966.

Porch, D. *The March to the Marne: The French Army 1871–1914*. Cambridge: Cambridge University Press, 1981.

Rancière, Jacques. "Le Bon Temps ou la barrière des plaisirs." *Les Révoltes logiques* (Spring–Summer 1978): 29–48.

Rearick, Charles. *The French in Love and War: Popular Culture in the Era of the World Wars*. New Haven: Yale University Press, 1997.

———. "Madelon and the Men—in War and Memory." *French Historical Studies* 17, no. 4 (Fall 1992): 1001–1034.

———. *Pleasures of the Belle Epoque*. New Haven: Yale University Press, 1985.

———. "Song and Society in Turn-of-the-Century France." *Journal of Social History* 22, no. 1 (Fall 1988): 45–63.

Rebérioux, Madeleine. "Roman, théâtre et chanson: quelle Commune?" *Le Mouvement social* 79 (April 1972): 273–292.

Reshef, Ouriel. *Guerre, mythes et caricature*. Paris: Presses de la Fondation nationale des sciences politiques, 1984.

Revel, Jacques. "Forms of Expertise: Intellectuals and 'Popular' Culture in France (1650–1800)." In *Understanding Popular Culture: Europe from the Middle Ages to the Nineteenth Century*, ed. Steven L. Kaplan, 255–273. New York: Mouton Publishers, 1984.

Roberts, Mary Louise. *Civilization without Sexes: Reconstructing Gender in Postwar France, 1917–1927*. Chicago: University of Chicago Press, 1994.

Rutkoff, Peter. *Revanche and Revision: The "Ligue des Patriotes" and the Origins of the Radical Right in France, 1882–1900*. Athens: Ohio University Press, 1981.

Sackett, Robert Eben. *Popular Entertainment, Class, and Politics in Munich, 1900–1923*. Cambridge: Harvard University Press, 1982.

Sallée, André, and Philippe Chauveau. *Music-hall et café-concert*. Paris: Bordas, 1985.

Schmidt, Madeleine, ed. *Chansons de la revanche et de la grande guerre*. Nancy: Presses Universitaires de Nancy, 1985.

Schwartz, Vanessa R. *Spectacular Realities: Early Mass Culture in Fin-de-Siècle Paris*. Berkeley: University of California, 1998.

Segel, Harold B. *Turn-of-the-Century Cabaret: Paris, Barcelona, Berlin, Munich, Vienna, Cracow, Moscow, St. Petersburg, Zurich*. New York: Columbia University Press, 1987.

Sellier, Henri, A. Bruggeman, and Marcel Poëte. *Paris pendant la guerre*. Paris: Presses Universitaires de France, 1926.

Sedgwick, Eve. *Between Men: English Literature and Male Homosocial Desire*. New York: Columbia University Press, 1985.

Seigel, Jerrold. *Bohemian Paris: Culture, Politics and the Boundaries of Bourgeois Life, 1830–1930*. New York: Penguin Books, 1986.

Shattuck, Roger. *The Banquet Years: The Arts in France, 1885–1918*. London: Faber and Faber, 1958.

Silver, Kenneth E. *Esprit de Corps: The Art of the Parisian Avant-Garde and the First World War, 1914–1925*. Princeton: Princeton University Press, 1989.

Smith, Leonard V. *Between Mutiny and Obedience: The Case of the Fifth Infantry Division during World War I*. Princeton: Princeton University Press, 1994.

Stedman Jones, Gareth. *Languages of Class: Studies in English Working Class History, 1832–1982*. Cambridge: Cambridge University Press, 1983.

Stora-Lamarre, Annie. *L'Enfer de la IIIe République: censeurs et pornographes, 1881–1914*. Paris: Editions Imago, 1990.

Tambiah, Stanley Jeyaraja. *Culture, Thought, and Social Action: An Anthropological Perspective*. Cambridge: Harvard University Press, 1985.

Thébaud, Françoise. *La Femme au temps de la guerre de 14*. Paris: Stock, 1986.

Tombs, Robert, ed. *Nationhood and Nationalism in France: From Boulangism to the Great War 1889–1918*. New York: HarperCollins, 1991.

Vernillat, France, and Jacques Charpentreau. *Dictionnaire de la chanson française*. Paris: Librairie Larousse, 1968.

Vovelle, Michel. "La Marseillaise, la guerre ou la paix." In *Les Lieux de mémoire: la République*, vol. 1, ed. Pierre Nora, 85–136. Paris: Gallimard, 1984.

Weber, Eugen. *Action Française, Royalism and Reaction in Twentieth-Century France*. Stanford: Stanford University Press, 1962.

———. *France: Fin de Siècle*. Cambridge, Mass.: Belknap Press, 1986.

———. *Peasants into Frenchmen: The Modernization of Rural France, 1870–1914*. Stanford: Stanford University Press, 1976.

Weber, William. "Mass Culture and the Reshaping of European Musical Taste, 1770–1870." *International Review of Aesthetics & Sociology of Music* 8, no. 1 (June 1977): 5–21.

Williams, John. *The Home Fronts: Britain, France and Germany, 1914–1918*. London: Constable, 1972.

Winter, Jay, and Jean-Louis Robert. *Capital Cities at War: Paris, London, Berlin 1914–1919*. Cambridge: Cambridge University Press, 1997.

Winter, Jay. *Sites of Memory, Sites of Mourning: The Great War in European Cultural History*. Cambridge: Cambridge University Press, 1995.

Winter, J. M., and R. M. Wall, eds. *The Upheaval of War: Family, Work and Welfare in Europe 1914–1918*. Cambridge: Cambridge University Press, 1988.

Wohl, Robert. *The Generation of 1914*. Cambridge: Harvard University Press, 1979.

Zeldin, Theodore. *France 1848–1945: Taste and Corruption*. Oxford: Oxford University Press, 1980.

Zeyons, Serge. *Le Roman-photo de la grande guerre*. Paris: Editions Hier et Demain, 1976.

Index

Bouffes-Parisiennes, 244

Boulangism, 22, 26, 216; and General Boulanger, 26, 82

Bourdieu, Pierre, 84

Bousquet, Louis, 27. *See also* "Quand Madelon"

Bouvier, Jeanne, 20, 38, 39

Boyer, Lucien, 186

Brécy, Robert, 231

Breton, Guy, 157

Briand, Aristide, 41, 72

Bridoux, André, 209

Bruant, Aristide, 23, 38–39, 86, 216, 249, 329n36

Buffet, Eugénie, 27, 30, 122, 141, 186–87

Bulletin des armées, 57, 65, 123, 220, 244, 325n69; and song culture, 182, 201–3, 205, 213, 223; versus trench culture, 182, 197–98

Burns, Michael, 26

de Buxeuil, René, 27, 187, 216, 325n79. *See also* "La Chanson des mitrailleuses"

"Ça ira," 17, 38, 47

Cabarets: and the Belle Époque, 6, 19, 22–23, 295n7; and censorship, 80, 84; criticism of, 76, 94, 181; and popular culture, 149–51, 250; and war, 141, 165, 190–91, 238, 241, 249

"Cadences militaires," **262–63,** 305n107

cafés-concerts, 6–7, 18–19, 295n7; and audiences, 19–20, 38, 146, 158–59, 163, 238–39, 295n13; and Belle Époque, 6, 100, 107, 119, 151, 206, 216; and censorship, 75, 79, 84, 88, 90–91; and criticism, 31, 76, 84, 94–95, 181, 228–29; and performers, 145, 241, 248; and politics, 42, 58, 63, 246; and war, 4, 138, 142, 147, 181, 193, 209–10, 215–16, 249. *See also* singing and politics

Caillaux Affair, 43, 44

Camelots du Roi, 41

Les Capucines, 190

"La Carmagnole," 10, 17, 32, 36, 37, 38, 40, 47

Casino de Paris, 239, 248–49

Le Caveau de la République, 84

Cavell, Edith, 148

Cazol, Jack, 80

Cazol, Jules, 270–71. *See also* "Verdun on ne passe pas"

censorship, 4, 11, 67; and civilian behavior, 138, 155, 200, 240–42; and class, 84–90, 239, 245, 255, 309n69; cultural censorship, 72, 74, 95–96; history and procedures, 74–77, 93–96, 130, 186, 237, 307n30; and police surveillance, 17, 20, 29–30, 37, 73 137–40, 142, 158, 167, 237–39, 245; and political satire, 152–53, 165, 238, 249; and views of soldiers, 156. *See also* army and censorship

"Ce que c'est qu'un drapeau," 158, 193

"Ce que chantent les flots de la Marne," 272–73, 319n98. *See also* Willems

"C'est Rosalie," 128, 130, 212, 316n85

Cezano, Paul, 1, 258–59. *See also* "Le Régiment de Sambre et Meuse"

Chaine, Pierre, 179

"La Chanson de Craonne," 232–34

"La Chanson des mitrailleuses," 264–65, 305n105. *See also* Parigot, Jean; Buxeuil, René de

"Le Chant du départ": and August 1914 mobilization, 43–55, 61; and criticism of Paris, 228–29; lyrics **50–51,** 52–53; and national identity, 14, 33, 147; and soldiers, 62, 175; and wartime nationalism, 60, 87, 148, 242, **243,** 251

"Le Chant du retour," 274–75, 319n98. *See also* Willems

Charles, Jacques, 139, 145

La Chaumière, 249

Chenal, Marthe, 164

Chevalier, Louis, 66, 131

Chevalier, Maurice, 139, 239, 248–49

La Cigale, 193

Ciné-Olympic, 147

Civil War (American), 64

"Le Clairon," 34, 39, 58–59, 148, 216, 221; lyrics, 63

Classical music, 32, 35, 298n65; and army zone, 173, 181, 183–84, 191, 193, 204, 206, 210, 329nn44 and 47; and musical metaphor, 171; and nationalization, 54, 146–47

Clemenceau, Georges: and songs, 79, 82, 251, 256; and 1917–1918 prowar ethos, 95–96, 173, 246, 248, 250, 252, 255, 337n61

Clérouc, Paul, 205, 213, 229, 242

Clovys, 59

Comédie-Française, 17, 40, 143, 163, 188–89, 191, 193, 195–96, 239

comique-troupier, 83, 186, 193, 304n84, 308–9n64

Commune (Paris), 19, 22–23, 38, 56; and fears, 31, 76, 81, 87, 142

Concert Mayol, 193

ABOUT THE AUTHOR

Regina Sweeney is the author of a number of articles on French history and music, including a recent one on song censorship and bourgeois morality, which appeared in the volume *World War I and the Cultures of Modernity* (2000).